Rome's Enemies Within

Rome's Enemies Within

Rome's Enemies Within

Imperial Conspiracies and Assassinations in the
Roman Empire during the First Century AD

John S. McHugh

Pen & Sword
MILITARY

First published in Great Britain in 2024 by
Pen & Sword History
An imprint of Pen & Sword Books Limited
Yorkshire – Philadelphia

ISBN 978 1 39906 155 1

A CIP catalogue record for this book is
available from the British Library

Typeset by Mac Style
Printed in the UK by CPI Group (UK) Ltd, Croydon, CR0 4YY.

MIX
Paper | Supporting
responsible forestry
FSC
www.fsc.org   FSC® C013604

Pen & Sword Books Limited incorporates the imprints of After
the Battle, Atlas, Archaeology, Aviation, Discovery, Family History,
Fiction, History, Maritime, Military, Military Classics, Politics,
Select, Transport, True Crime, Air World, Frontline Publishing, Leo
Cooper, Remember When, Seaforth Publishing, The Praetorian Press,
Wharncliffe Local History, Wharncliffe Transport, Wharncliffe True
Crime and White Owl.

For a complete list of Pen & Sword titles please contact

PEN & SWORD BOOKS LIMITED
47 Church Street, Barnsley, South Yorkshire, S70 2AS, England
E-mail: enquiries@pen-and-sword.co.uk
Website: www.pen-and-sword.co.uk
or
PEN AND SWORD BOOKS
1950 Lawrence Rd, Havertown, PA 19083, USA
E-mail: uspen-and-sword@casematepublishers.com
Website: www.penandswordbooks.com

In praise of family. For my parents, Thomas and my late mother, June, whom I am now aware was a frustrated academic like myself.

Also to Mary, Joseph and Patrick, and Emily, without whose help this book would not have been possible.

To nobility of soul regardless of class, race, sex, gender or religion.

Contents

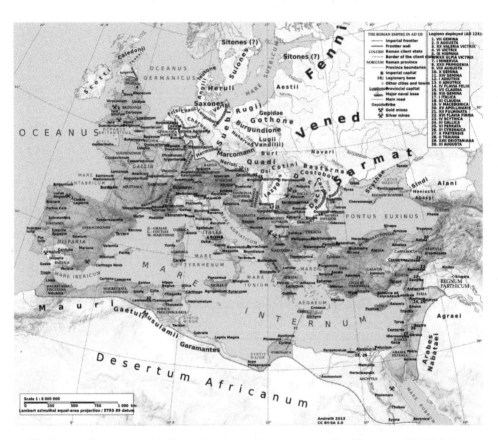

The Roman Empire, AD 125. (*User: Andrein, with the assistance of EraNavigator, CC BY-SA 3.0 <https://creativecommons.org/licenses/by-sa/3.0>, via Wikimedia Commons*)

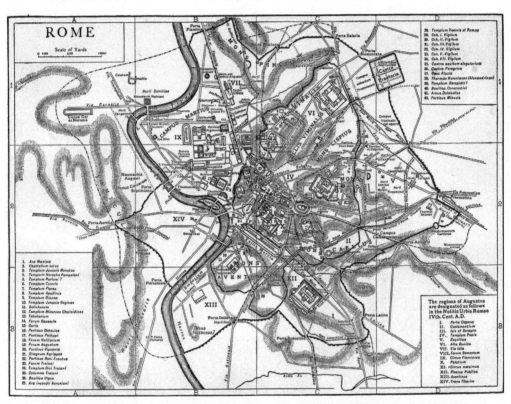

Ancient Rome. (*Based on Plan in Heinrich Kiepert's Formae Orbis Antiqui, by permission of Dietrich Reimer, Berlin; engraved by Emery Walker, Public domain, via Wikimedia Commons*)

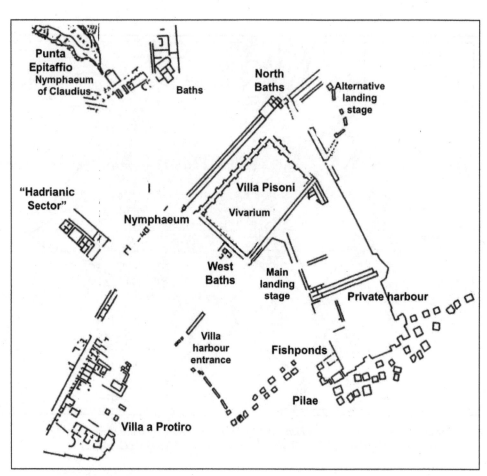

Villa of Calpurnius Piso at Baiae, where it was initially planned to murder Emperor Nero. (*Rjdeadly, CC BY-SA 4.0 <https://creativecommons.org/licenses/by-sa/4.0>, via Wikimedia Commons*)

Dates of the Emperors

JULIUS CAESAR (dictator) 49–44 BC

JULIO-CLAUDIAN DYNASTY

AUGUSTUS (assumed name in 27 BC) 31 BC–AD 14
TIBERIUS AD 14–37
GAIUS (CALIGULA) 37–41
CLAUDIUS 41–54
NERO 54–68

CIVIL WAR

GALBA 68–69
OTHO 69
VITELLIUS 69

FLAVIAN DYNASTY

VESPASIAN 69–79
TITUS 79–81
DOMITIAN 81–96

ADOPTIVE EMPERORS of the ANTONINE DYNASTY

NERVA 96–98
TRAJAN 98–117
HADRIAN 117–138
ANTONINUS PIUS 138–161
MARCUS AURELIUS and LUCIUS VERUS 161–169
MARCUS AURELIUS (sole rule) 169–180
COMMODUS (son of Marcus Aurelius) 180–192

Family Tree of Annius Vinicianus

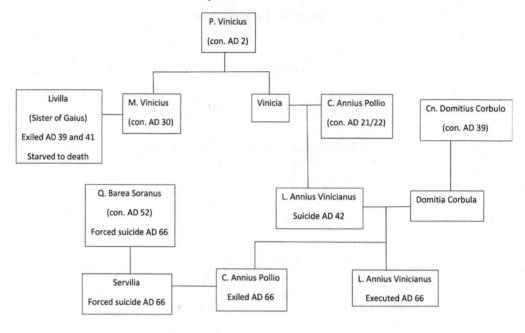

Family tree of Gaius Calpurnius Piso (conjectured)

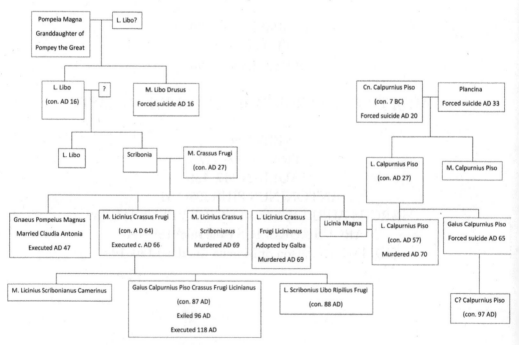

Julio-Clavdian Family Tree

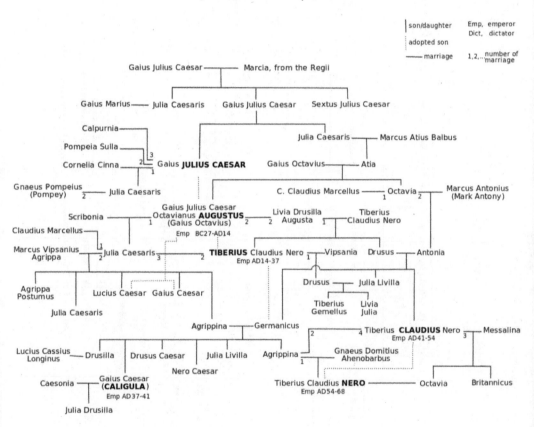

Flavian Family Tree

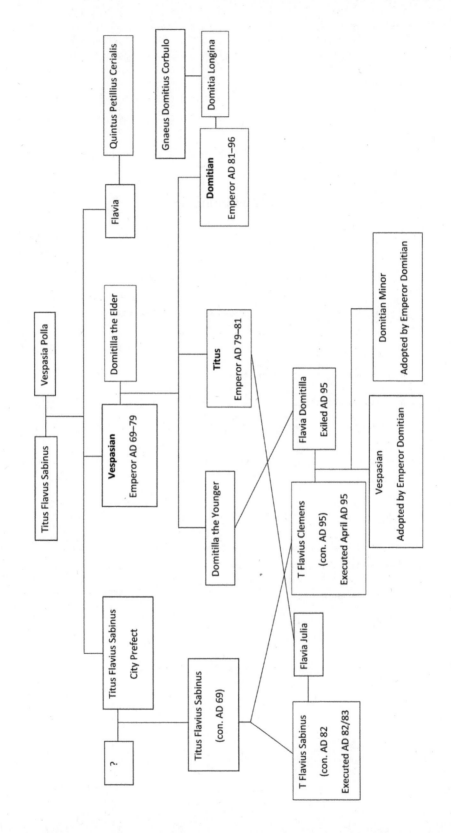

The Family of L. Arruntius Camillus Scribonianus

M. Furius Camillus
(con. AD 8)

Livia
Scriboniana

M. Furius Camillus

Livia Medullina
Died c. AD 9 on wedding day
to Claudius

? Aemilia

L. Arruntius
(con. AD 6)

Adopted

L. Arruntius Camillus Scribonianus
(con. AD 32)
Executed AD 42

? Vinicia/Vibia
Exiled AD 52

L. Arruntius Camillus Scribonianus
Exiled AD 52

The Relatives of M. Junius Brutus

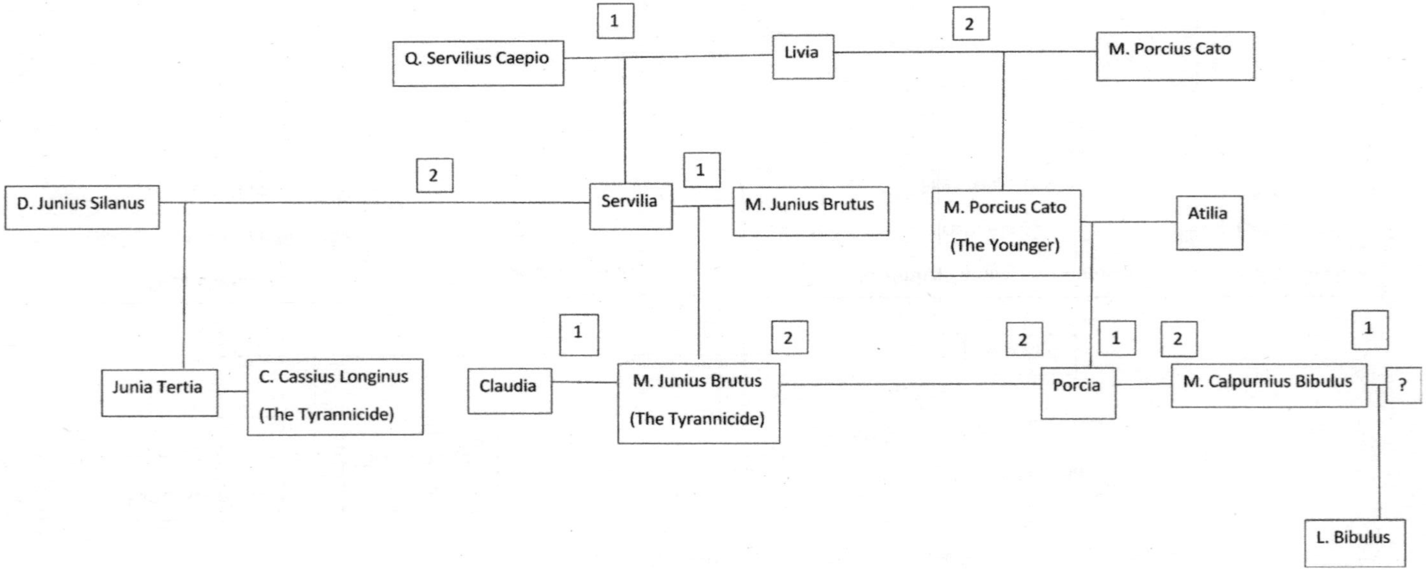

Timeline

82 BC: Lucius Cornelius Sulla becomes dictator after defeating the forces of Gaius Marius in a civil war.

80 BC: Sulla resigns his dictatorship and retires to private life.

59 BC: Caesar joins with Marcus Licinius Crassus and Pompey the Great in the First Triumvirate.

53 BC: Crassus defeated and killed by the Parthians at the Battle of Carrhae in Syria. End of the First Triumvirate.

49 BC: Julius Caesar crosses the River Rubicon with his army after conquering Gaul to invade Italy and attack senatorial forces led by Pompey the Great.

48 BC: Caesar decisively defeats Pompey the Great at the Battle of Pharsalus in Greece. Pompey is killed in Egypt a month later.

46 BC: Caesar defeats Cato the Younger at the Battle of Thapsus in Africa. Cato chooses to commit suicide. Caesar is appointed dictator for ten years by the Senate in Rome.

45 BC (March): Caesar defeats the last of the Pompeian forces led by the sons of Pompey at the Battle of Munda in Spain.

45 BC (September): Caesar returns to Rome.

44 BC (January): Caesar dismisses his Spanish bodyguard. Rumours start to circulate that he wants to be acclaimed king.

44 BC (before 15 February): Caesar made dictator in perpetuity by the Senate.

44 BC (15 February): at the festival of *Lupercalia*, Mark Antony offers a crown to Caesar, and he publicly rejects it.

44 BC (mid-February): Cassius Longinus recruits Marcus Junius Brutus into his conspiracy.

44 BC (15 March): on the Ides of March, Caesar is murdered in the Curia attached to the Theatre of Pompey.

44 BC (17 March): the Senate authorizes Caesar's will at the suggestion of Mark Antony and ratifies all his previous acts as well as granting him a public funeral.

44 BC (18 March): the date Caesar planned to leave Rome to campaign for three years on the Danube and then against Parthia.

44 BC (20 March): Mark Antony leads the public funeral for Julius Caesar, leading to riots, whilst the tyrannicides escape the capital.

43 BC: Second Triumvirate formed by Mark Antony, Octavian and M. Aemilius Lepidus to avenge Caesar's murder.

42 BC: senatorial forces led by Brutus and Cassius defeated at the Battle of Philippi in Greece. Both Brutus and Cassius commit suicide.

31 BC: the naval forces of Octavian, commanded by M. Vipsanius Agrippa, defeat those of Mark Antony and his Egyptian ally, Cleopatra, at the Battle of Actium. Octavian effectively becomes the ruler of the Roman Empire.

30 BC: suicide of Antony and Cleopatra in Alexandria.

29 BC: L. Licinius Crassus, the governor of Macedonia, defeats the Bastarnae and kills their king in single combat.

27 BC (January): the Senate votes Octavian the name Augustus.

27 BC: the First Constitutional Settlement: Augustus rules the Roman world through possession of the office of consul with chosen colleagues, and retains command of the army through control of the imperial provinces, where most of the armed forces are stationed. The Principate is established, cloaking supreme authority in the powers and offices of the old Republic.

25 BC: Augustus marries his daughter, Julia the Elder, to his nephew, Claudius Marcellus.

23 BC (early): Augustus falls seriously ill and nearly dies.

23 BC (July): the Second Constitutional Settlement: Augustus is granted powers greater than a consul through the awarding of *imperium maius* and those of a tribune of the plebs through *tribunicia potestas*. He relinquishes the office of consul but retains control of the army through control of the imperial provinces.

23 BC (early autumn): Claudius Marcellus dies.

23 BC (autumn): trial of M. Primus, who is defended by Varro Murena.

23 BC (late autumn): plot of Caepio and Varro Murena.

22 BC (early): capture and execution of Caepio and Varro Murena.

22 BC (mid): Augustus leaves Rome for Sicily and then Syria.

21 BC: Julia the Elder married to Augustus' new heir, Vipsanius Agrippa.

19 BC: plot of Egnatius.

18 BC: *lex Julia de adulteriis coercendis* made adultery a public crime, prosecuted in the state courts.

17 BC: Augustus adopts Gaius and Lucius Caesar, the children of Julia the Elder and Vipsanius Agrippa.

12 BC (February): death of Vipsanius Agrippa.

11 BC: Tiberius is married to Julia the Elder, having been forced to divorce his wife, Vipsania, the daughter of Vipsanius Agrippa. Tiberius is Augustus' heir.

9 BC: the death of Tiberius' brother, Nero Drusus, whilst campaigning in Germany.

6 BC: Tiberius chooses to go into voluntary exile in Rhodes.

5 BC: the sons of Julia the Elder, Gaius and Lucius Caesar, raised to adulthood. They replace Tiberius as Augustus' chosen successors.

2 BC: the Senate honours Augustus with the title *Pater Patriae* (Father of his Country).

2 BC (autumn): Julia the Elder exiled for adultery and treason. Augustus annuls her marriage to Tiberius. Office of Praetorian Prefect created by Augustus.

AD 2: death of Lucius Caesar. Tiberius returns to Rome.

AD 4: death of Gaius Caesar. Augustus adopts Tiberius, who in turn must adopt Germanicus despite having a son of his own, Drusus. Augustus also adopts Agrippa Postumus.

AD 6: Agrippa Postumus exiled to Surrentum on the Bay of Naples.

AD 7: Junius Novatus arrested for distributing leaflets attacking Augustus in the name of Agrippa Postumus. Agrippa Postumus moved to the island of Planasia near Corsica.

AD 7?: conspiracy and exile of Lucius Aemilius Paullus, husband of Julia the Younger.

AD 8: Julia the Younger accused of adultery with Decimus Junius Silanus and exiled.

AD 12: Tiberius effectively co-ruler with Augustus.

AD 14 (19 August): Augustus dies and Tiberius ascends the throne.

AD 14 AD (soon after 19 Augustus): execution of Agrippa Postumus, Lucius Aemilius Paullus and exiled conspirators allied with Julia the Elder.

AD 14 (September): mutiny of the legions on the Rhine and in Pannonia suppressed by Germanicus and Tiberius' son, Drusus.

AD 15: Sejanus made sole Praetorian Prefect.

AD 16: Clemens, the former slave and impersonator of Agrippa Postumus, captured after attempting to raise a revolt against Tiberius.

AD 16 (September): Marcus Scribonius Libo Drusus charged with treason and use of magic, and forced to commit suicide.

AD 19: death of Germanicus in Syria.

AD 26: Tiberius withdraws to the island of Capri, never to return to Rome.

AD 29: death of Livia, former wife of Augustus and mother of Tiberius.

AD 29 (before October): death of Nero, brother of Germanicus, in prison.

AD 29 (after 31 August): Gaius summoned to Capri by Tiberius.

AD 31 (October): Sejanus accused of treason and executed in Rome. Macro becomes Praetorian Prefect.

AD 33: deaths of Gaius' mother, Agrippina the Elder, and his brother, Drusus, whilst imprisoned.

AD 37 (March): death of Tiberius and accession of Gaius (Caligula).

AD 37 (after 21 September): Gaius falls seriously ill but recovers.

AD 37 (near end of the year): Tiberius' grandson, Tiberius Gemellus, put to death by Gaius.

AD 38 (early): Praetorian Prefect Macro and his wife executed by Gaius.

AD 39 (February): discovery of conspiracy against Gaius led by former consuls.

AD 39 (10 June): death of Drusilla, Gaius' sister.

AD 39 (September–October): Plot of the Three Daggers involving Gaius' sisters, M. Aemilius Lepidus and Cornelius Gaetulicus in Upper Germany. Lepidus executed with Gaetulicus, and his sisters exiled.

AD 40 (end of May): Gaius returns to Italy but remains in Campania.

AD 40 (August): Gaius enters Rome.

AD 40 (late): conspiracy of Betilinius Bassus against Gaius.

AD 41 (early January): consular senator Pomponius accused of conspiracy by Timidius, who named the senator's freedwoman and mistress, Quintilia, as a witness.

AD 41 (24 January): assassination of Gaius.

AD 41 (25 January): date Gaius planned to leave Rome for Alexandria.

AD 42: execution of Appius Silanus. Conspiracy of Annius Vinicianus and revolt of L. Arruntius Camillus Scribonianus.

AD 43: invasion of Britain.

AD 47: trial and death of D. Valerius Asiaticus.

AD 48: Messalina, the wife of Claudius, accused of adultery and treason with Gaius Silius. Both are executed.

AD 49: Agrippina the Younger marries Claudius.

AD 50: Claudius adopts Agrippina the Younger's son, Nero.

AD 51: Burrus appointed Praetorian Prefect.

AD 54 (13 October): Claudius dies, possibly poisoned by Agrippina the Younger. He is succeeded by Nero, who is guided by his mother, the Praetorian Prefect Burrus and Seneca.

AD 54 (late October): Narcissus killed on the orders of Agrippina the Younger.

AD 55: Britannicus poisoned at a banquet.

AD 58: Suillius Rufus lays charges against Seneca, but Rufus is convicted and exiled by Nero after a successful counter-prosecution.

AD 59: Agrippina murdered by her son, Nero.

AD 62: Burrus dies, leaving Seneca isolated. The philosopher retires to his estates.

AD 62: Seneca and Gaius Calpurnius Piso face 'secret charges' laid by the *delator* Romanus, but they are dismissed.

AD 64: Great Fire of Rome.

AD 65: conspiracy of Piso.

AD 66: trail of Barea Soranus and his daughter, Servilia.

AD 66: conspiracy of Annius Vinicianus in Beneventum (Vinician Conspiracy).

AD 66 (autumn): Nero travels to Greece.

AD 67: execution of the commander of the eastern armies, Domitius Corbulo, and the governors of the German provinces, Publius Sulpicius Scribonius Rufus and Publius Sulpicius Scribonius Proculus, in Greece by Nero.

AD 68 (March): revolt of Vindex in Gaul and Sulpicius Galba in Spain.

AD 68 (June): suicide of Nero and acclamation of Galba.

AD 69: civil war after the murder of Galba by Praetorians bribed by Otho. Otho defeated by Vitellius, who in turn is defeated by the forces of Vespasian.

AD 79 (June): death of Vespasian and accession of Titus.

AD 81 (September): death of Titus and accession of Domitian.

AD 82: conspiracy led by T. Flavius Sabinus and leading senators, including Dio of Prusa.

AD 87: plot against Domitian indicated from inscription by the Arval Brethren.

AD 89: revolt of Saturninus on the Rhine.

AD 91: death of Julia Flavia.

AD 95 (April/May): T. Flavius Clemens and his wife, Domitilla, accused of atheism. Clemens is executed and Domitilla exiled. Glabrio and possibly Epaphroditus associated with their fall.

AD 96: murder of Domitian and accession of Nerva.

AD 96: conspiracy of C Calpurnius Crassus Frugi Licianus discovered.

AD 97 (summer): Praetorians mutiny and murder Parthenius and Petronius Secundus.

AD 97 (September): Nerva adopts Trajan as his son and names him his heir.

AD 98 (January): death of Nerva. Trajan becomes sole emperor.

AD 117 (August): death of Trajan and accession of Hadrian.

1

A Death Foretold

The Murder of Julius Caesar (15 March 44 BC)

'It is better, he said, to die once than always be in fear of death.'

(Caesar's response on being advised by his friends to restore
his bodyguard. Plutarch, *Caesar*, 57)

Julius Caesar had many enemies, and he knew he was hated by many. In war, he could easily differentiate friend from foe. However, on the political battlefield of Rome, enemies wore smiles and greeted him with a kiss. He had returned to the capital in September of 45 BC, having completed the final destruction of the Republican cause on the plains of Munda in southern Spain. The battle had been close and brutal. Many of those soldiers who stood facing Caesar had previously received his pardon for taking up arms against him, but had returned to the Pompeian cause and knew there would be no second reprieve. Caesar's legions had wavered and nearly broke, only to be steadied by their general's personal intervention. He joined the ranks and stood firm. His bravery restored morale, and by the close of the day, 30,000 enemy dead littered the field. According to Plutarch: 'As he was leaving the battlefield, he said to his friends that he had often before struggled for victory, but this was the first time that he had to fight for his life.'[1] A year later, almost to the day, he would again be desperately fighting for survival, surrounded by enemies disguised as friends, their daggers drawn and covered in his blood.

Despite the slaughter of Roman lives across three continents in four years of civil war, Caesar decided to celebrate his victory at Munda with a triumphal procession through the capital. These were magnificent affairs, voted by the Senate to honour a general's victory over the enemies of Rome. He had also been granted the honorific title of 'Liberator' and 'Imperator' (general) permanently.[2] His victorious soldiers marched through the streets behind the spoils of his victories in Spain. Then came Caesar, drawn in a four-horsed chariot, his face painted red in imitation of Capitoline Jupiter, wearing the regalia of Rome's legendary kings; a purple and gold toga, red boots, with his head crowned with laurel. The crowds chanted his name, his soldiers sang songs and the air was filled with incense and music, with flowers thrown in front. To many of the elite, especially those who had lost sons, fathers and brothers in fighting Caesar, this was an affront to their memory and the Republic.

The procession was slow; as it entered the Forum, Caesar's chariot passed the seats of Rome's magistrates. All bar one stood to offer their respect to the *triumphator*. As he rode past the benches reserved for the tribunes, he noticed one of the ten had failed to stand 'and shouted in fury at a certain Pontius Aquila, who had kept his seat: "Hey, there, Aquila the tribune! Do you want me to restore the Republic?" For several days after this incident, he added to every undertaking he gave: "With the kind consent of Pontius Aquila."'[3] Aquila was a former supporter of Pompey the Great, but despite being pardoned by Caesar, some of his estates had been confiscated. [4] The tribune's Republican zeal was fired by personal resentment. On the Ides of March, he would have his revenge and plunge his dagger into Caesar.

He was not the only one angered by the triumph. Many of the aristocracy who had fought with Pompey the Great but been pardoned after his defeat at the Battle of Pharsalus, stood at Caesar's entrance into the Forum. They may have lacked the courage of Aquila, but they still burned with resentment as he passed. Pompey had been murdered in Egypt, whilst his eldest son had soon been captured at the Battle of Munda, executed and his head sent for Caesar to inspect. Other leading nobles had lost their lives in the civil war. Numbered among the many were Cato the Younger, who chose suicide rather than receive Caesar's pardon, and the son of Rome's last dictator, Cornelius Sulla, who was executed to satisfy the demands of Caesar's troops.[5]

The historian Plutarch considers the October triumph a political disaster all of Caesar's making,

> 'for it displeased the Romans more than anything else he had done. For this was not the case of his having conquered foreign generals or kings of native tribes; on this occasion what he had done was to annihilate the children and the family of one who had been the greatest of Romans, and who had met with misfortune. It did not seem right for Caesar to celebrate a triumph for the calamities of his country and to pride himself upon actions for which the only possible excuse that could be made in the eyes of both gods and men was that they had been forced upon him.'[6]

The shedding of Roman blood was not to be celebrated, especially that of Rome's noblest character, Pompey the Great, and his eldest son.

In Caesar's absence in Spain, the defeated Pompeians could reassure themselves that once the civil war was over, Caesar would restore the constitution. In the past, dictatorship had always been temporary. After his victory in a civil war in 82 BC, the Senate had made Lucius Cornelius Sulla dictator, with no time limit set on his tenure of the supreme office of state. However, after initiating a series of reforms, Sulla disbanded his legions and in 80 BC retired into private life to write his memoirs. Caesar, they hoped, would be no different. They were to be greatly disappointed.[7]

Gaius Cassius Longinus, one of the first conspirators, had accepted Caesar's pardon after the crushing defeat at Pharsalus. A noble, philosopher and military man of great renown, he had commanded Pompey's fleet but had been captured attempting to reach Pharnaces II, the king of Pontus, with the aim of continuing the resistance in Asia Minor. Caesar welcomed him with open arms,[8] and, with wicked humour, tasked him with defeating the king to whom he had initially tried to escape. Cicero later tried to excuse Cassius's accommodation with Caesar by claiming that he planned to murder Caesar in 47 BC at the mouth of the River Cnidus in Cilicia, but he was frustrated when Caesar moored his ships on the opposite bank to where Cassius was waiting. This tall tale has been discounted by historians. Cassius was content simply to be alive, to see his wife and son again, and he soon retired to Italy and a quiet life of philosophical contemplation.[9]

Cassius discarded Stoicism, which he had studied in Rhodes as a young man,[10] for Epicureanism. Cicero, in a letter to him written whilst Caesar was fighting in Spain, jokes that he had abandoned the school and Virtue for the kitchen and the 'charms of Pleasure'.[11] Epicurus advocated a withdrawal from active politics, as it was a distraction from the search for peace and tranquillity. Cassius took the jesting in good heart, but significantly his interpretation of this philosophy was more nuanced than the traditional Epicurean ideas on withdrawal from public life. This thinking probably helped to reinforce his decision to retire to his estates, but he clearly hoped the new regime would return to constitutional government. In his reply to Cicero, he corrects his friend by asserting that 'to live pleasantly is impossible without living well and justly'. In the same letter, he asks for an update on the events in Spain and recognizes that Caesar was the better man when compared to Pompey's son, for

'upon my life I feel anxious, and prefer to have our old and merciful master rather than a new and bloodthirsty one. You know what a fool Gnaeus is: you know how he thinks cruelty is courage: you know how he always thinks that we laugh at him. I am afraid he will want to retort the joke in rustic fashion with a blow of the sword.'[12]

Cassius's judgement is surprising and remarkable. He preferred a Caesarian victory in Spain over his former ally, recognizing the leniency with which he had been treated after his capture whilst judging Gnaeus Pompey as both cruel and vindictive. Caesar's return, however, only brought disillusionment and anger. He may have dismissed Caesar's Spanish triumph as a matter of poor judgement, but soon many extravagant, unprecedented honours and powers were gifted to the dictator by a sycophantic Senate.

Caesar was made dictator for ten years, making all other magistrates subordinate to him. The hopes were dashed that, like Sulla, he might withdraw from his position as the supreme arbiter of offices, governorships, commands and honours. The state was to be run by Caesar and his closest friends, his *amici*, in private meetings of his *concilium* (council). Caesar even publicly announced that Sulla had been a fool for laying down his powers. He controlled Rome's armies and the state treasury, and as *Pontifex Maximus* had oversight over religion. When he was at meetings in the Forum or Senate, he was permitted to sit on a golden chair between the consuls. An ivory statue of him stood on the Capitol amongst those of the gods, and it was carried in a ceremonial litter before the games. Towards the end of 45 BC, the Senate announced he was to be honoured as *divus Julius* (the divine Julius).[13]

Senators wishing to gain Caesar's favour made ever more extravagant proposals which were readily approved by the majority. This was because Caesar had appointed many new senators after their ranks had been seriously depleted in the civil war and to reward supporters for loyal service to him. The elevation of these 'foreigners' antagonized the Italian-born aristocracy, but they kept their opposition to anonymous posters and chants from the crowd. Opposition was hidden in the shadows, for anyone brave or foolish enough to openly vote against such proposals risked the sudden ending of their careers and limited access to future gifts for themselves or their *amici* and clients. Some of Caesar's enemies proposed ever greater honours to increase hostility towards the dictator. Amongst those alienated were those aristocrats with more conservative and traditional opinions. According to Plutarch: 'His enemies are thought to have joined with his flatterers in getting these measures passed. They wanted to have every possible pretext to act against him and to appear to have good reasons on their side when they came to make an attempt upon his life.'[15]

Roman society was based on reciprocity, where gifts and favours were exchanged to create bonds of friendship and obligation. Status was also of paramount importance to every Roman. Social equals used the language of friendship in forming these social and political relationships to create networks of *amicitiae* (friendships). Relationships that formed between individuals of different social status were framed by the traditions and customs of the patron and client. Caesar's political dominance and control over all the offices of the state and its finances made him the supreme patron. The aristocracy, his former equals in status, were no longer in any political, economic or social position to return any gifts or favours that they received from him. Essentially, they had all become his clients, in a position of social inferiority, so 'the fact that they benefitted at his hands, both by gifts of property and by appointments to offices, was a special source of grievance, since he alone was able to bestow such benefits, and everyone else was ignored as of no importance'.[16] Their only way to repay Caesar's *beneficia* – his gifts of offices, estates, governorships, money and so on – was through loyalty (*fides*). This is what Caesar expected from those he pardoned, like Cassius. He also recalled many who had been exiled and appointed former enemies to governorships and offices of state, considering them to be obligated and indebted. He believed that 'to surround himself with peoples' goodwill was … the best and truest security'.[17]

However, many of the conspirators did not feel they were under compulsion. Firstly, Caesar's control of the state's wealth and magistracies placed them in the humiliating position of clients rather than his social and political equals. Secondly, *amicitiae* had to be based on virtue, especially *fides* not *utilitas* (usefulness). However, for *fides* to be binding, it had to be based upon common goals and aims.[18] Caesar's assumption of supreme power, at first for ten years, and then in February 44 BC forever, negated the personal debts owed by a loyal citizen, who now owed a greater duty to the constitution and the state. Dictatorship 'meant an undisguised tyranny: his power was now not only absolute but perpetual'.[19]

Cassius claimed descent from a legendary tyrannicide. In 485 BC, soon after the expulsion of the kings from Rome and the founding of the Republic, Spurius Cassius Vecellinus was accused by his father of plotting to become a king himself and killed. The Roman nobility extolled their famous ancestors to enhance their status and prestige. Every morning, their *amici* and clients would gather in the *atrium* of their mansion, surrounded by statues, busts and portraits of the famous members of their family. The *atrium* opened through the *tablinum* into a courtyard garden. The *tablinum*, a sort of study, was where the owner stood when greeting his guests and heard their petitions and requests. Within it stood a large wooden cupboard containing the *imagines*, often death masks, of his family stretching back to the founding of their *gens*. The rooms and corridors of their houses were resplendent with the statues of illustrious ancestors, their faces carved in likeness to these preserved images. At the funerals of these great men, hundreds of actors wore these masks as they walked in public procession before the bier. This glorified his lineage and nobility. Some saw themselves as the descendants of gods;[20] Julius Caesar claimed descent from the Trojan hero Aeneas and, through him, the goddess Venus.

After the murder of Caesar, Cicero extolled the pedigree of the leaders of the plot, including Cassius, 'who too, belongs to a clan [*gens*] incapable of tolerating not only autocracy but even excessive power in any single individual'.[21] Cassius interpreted Epicureanism as an active search for peace and freedom rather than pursuing a disinterest in political affairs. Epicurus advocated any form of governance based on consent, but tyranny threatened the value of 'truthful speaking' and so was incompatible with attaining the reward of pleasure which was achieved through freedom from pain and anxiety.[22] His philosophical views may not have been his primary motive for plotting to kill Caesar, but rather a cloak to justify his more personal reasons.

Cassius burned with a passionate hatred, whose origins lay in what he interpreted as slights to his status and prestige. His motivations are questioned; his character is denigrated and flawed. He was 'a hater of Caesar on his own private account', initially as some lions he had bought, probably for games he hoped to provide as *aedile*, were confiscated when Megara fell to Caesar after the Battle of Pharsalus. Significantly, no source refers to Cassius serving as an *aedile*, implying he was denied this office.[23]

Subsequently, his letter to Cicero in January 45 BC suggests he had come to recognize he had been treated reasonably in receiving a pardon from the dictator. However, Caesar made a bid to alienate Cassius from his brother-in-law, M. Junius Brutus.

Brutus had lost his father at a young age, murdered by Pompey the Great. In 77 BC, the Sullan general Pompey had promised to spare his father and namesake in battle, but upon his surrender executed him. The 7-year-old boy went to live with his uncle, Cato the Younger, surrounded by philosophical debate on morality and personal freedom. His mother, Servilia, the half-sister of Cato the Younger, subsequently married D. Junius Silanus, with whom she had three daughters. The youngest married Cassius. Cato became the father figure he had lost, whom he admired both for his Stoicism and devotion to the Republic. It was Cato who had persuaded Brutus to fight alongside Pompey despite the treacherous death of his father at his hands.[24] Once committed, Brutus became a fervent and dedicated disciple to the cause, fighting with distinction at Pharsalus. As Caesar observed: 'It's a great question what he wants, but whatever it is he wants he really does want it.'[25] Yet Caesar was so concerned about his safety that after the battle he ordered his soldiers to find Brutus and bring him back unharmed. Brutus was rapidly pardoned and made governor of the strategically important province of Cisalpine Gaul.[26] This spared Brutus the pain of joining Caesar in the African war against his uncle, Cato.

The remnants of the Pompeian resistance were cleared in Africa and Cato turned himself into a Stoic saint by refusing to submit to his victor. In imitation of Socrates, he dined with his *amici* and discussed whether a man who was truly free could ever become a slave. He decided to choose the ultimate freedom in ending his own life. Cato then withdrew, stabbed himself in the abdomen and passed out. His servants and doctor then attempted to save him by stitching up his wound. However, upon recovering consciousness, he tore open the wound again and died.

Brutus must have felt the pangs of guilt, especially as he was a Stoic himself. However, he followed the views of Plato, who considered it wrong to commit suicide.[27] To the Greeks it was a cowardly act, but to Stoics it became an expression of ultimate freedom. Brutus had, though, readily accepted the friendship of the dictator, being admitted into Caesar's advisory council, his *Concilium*. The governorship of a province that straddled the key communication routes between Italy and the Caesarian legions in Gaul was a public declaration of trust in both his abilities and loyalty. His star was on the rise: 'Brutus himself; who honoured Caesar in person, and whose company also Caesar greatly esteemed.'[28]

The summer of 45 BC saw Brutus a greatly troubled man. The brave, symbolic death of his surrogate father stood in opposition to his accommodation with Caesar. He had written a eulogy to Cato extolling his life, to which Caesar responded with his polemic 'AntiCato'. Brutus embraced Cato's surviving family. He surprised all by divorcing his wife and marrying Porcia, his own cousin and Cato's daughter, as well as becoming the guardian of her son, Bibulus. The decision was one that probably disappointed his mother, who regularly quarrelled with his new wife. The marriage was a public repudiation of Caesar; his wife's relatives were all anti-Caesarian and there was no political advantage to be gained in the union.[29]

Brutus had also expected a restoration of the Republic upon Caesar's return from Spain, but like his brother-in-law, Cassius, he was disappointed.[30] Caesar, clearly worried by Brutus's behaviour, acted to divide the two and retain the loyalty of Brutus. He had been given the power to appoint his nominees to magistracies for the three years he intended to be absent from Rome campaigning on the Danube and against Parthia. Both men felt entitled to the offices that carried the greatest prestige. Brutus had a great name, claiming descent from L. Junius Brutus, who had expelled the last of the kings from Rome and was one of the first two consuls of the new Republic in 509 BC. His bronze statue stood on the Capitol near that of Julius Caesar. Through his mother, he claimed descent from another legendary tyrannicide in Servilius Ahala, who stabbed Spurius Maelius to death in the Forum as he was trying to usurp absolute power.[31] Furthermore, even at a young age, Cicero had identified Brutus as a future leader: he was 'first among the younger generation and soon, I hope, to be first man in the state'.[32] Brutus believed in his destiny.

Caesar played both Brutus and Cassius, knowing the fiery-tempered Cassius could be baited. Both men were appointed to praetorships for 44 BC, but Brutus was allotted the prestigious office of city praetor. This added oxygen to the fire. Caesar made it known he had debated the merits of each with *amici* and recognized the greater merit of Cassius, but felt he could not deprive Brutus. The message to Brutus was clear: his prospects were assured if he remained a friend of Caesar, to whom he owed everything. A future consulship was guaranteed, and he was held in such favour that it was rumoured he was Caesar's son, the result of an affair with Servilia. There was no mention of consulship for his brother-in-law. Cassius was incandescent, being 'not so grateful for what he got as he was angry over what he had lost'.[33] The cares of the world engulfed him and he may have regretted abandoning the more traditional doctrines of Epicurean philosophy.

His anger was directed at Caesar, but also at Brutus, their relationship becoming cold, distant and hostile. Cassius did have precedence, being the older man with as noble a lineage as Brutus and also having a distinguished military record. After the massacre of a Roman army under Crassus at Carrhae in 53 BC, Cassius had held Syria against the Parthian onslaught that followed and, with his depleted forces, even defeated the invaders. During the civil war, Pompey had given him command of his fleet, which he used to burn Caesar's naval forces off the coast of Sicily. Brutus had fought with personal distinction at Pharsalus, but his military record was insignificant.[34] The flame of Cassius's hatred of Caesar thus burned bright.

Caesar's appointments to the various offices of state were meant to secure Rome and its provinces in his planned absence, as well as reward loyal service. However, it had the opposite effect. Many were overlooked, their hopes for the future going unsatisfied. Some, like Cassius, felt their reward lacked the prestige that their experience, lineage or loyalty deserved. All knew where they stood in the Caesarian regime. The dictator had to placate his former enemies, as well as those who had served him. This antagonized the latter, for 'his friends were incensed at being rated as equal to those whom they themselves had taken prisoners, and indeed they were even outranked by some of them'. L. Minucius Basilus, who had served Caesar in Gaul, had been made a praetor in 45 BC. He expected a governorship after his year in office came to an end, but there were only a limited number of such posts available, with many former supporters of Pompey being allotted them. To compensate Basilus, he was gifted a considerable sum of money. However, he was not grateful, and instead felt so grievously insulted he made his anger public and joined the conspiracy against his benefactor.[35]

Another praetor of 45 BC, L. Tillius Cimber, was awarded a province for the following year. He was a close confidant of Caesar, a bold yet violent man who had a reputation for hard drinking. A province, though, was not his greatest desire; he wanted Caesar to recall his brother from exile. For unknown reasons, his petitions were consistently rejected. Frustrated, he plotted Caesar's murder and helped to restrain his friend as the blades rained down on him.[36]

Another former legate of the Gallic War with a personal axe to grind was the aristocratic Servius Sulpicius Galba. He had stood for a consulship in 49 BC with Caesar's backing, but lost the election. For this, he blamed his former general rather than himself. He was probably vocal in his anger, like Basilus and Cimber, which would explain why Caesar 'passed him over for the consulship' in subsequent years. Furthermore, he had been in financial difficulty: having guaranteed a large loan Pompey had made, he was held responsible for it after the defeated general's estate was confiscated by the state. Caesar ultimately paid the loan himself. Despite the personal gift of the dictator, Galba joined the assassins, motivated by a sense of humiliation, his *dignitas* sullied.[37]

Another *amicus* of Caesar who appears to have faced financial problems was P. Servilius Casca. Casca stood for the office of *aedile* in 44 BC, but he struggled to raise the funds for both his campaign and probably for the games he would be responsible for should he have been elected. Cicero, however, asserted that Casca and his brother had higher motives for murdering Caesar: love of the Republic. This was made in a speech attacking Antony, a loyal friend of Caesar, whilst suggesting Antony himself had discussed murdering his commander with another conspirator, C. Trebonius, when at Narbo returning from the war in Spain. Cicero's testimony is not to be trusted.[38]

The main motivating factors in driving the conspiracy were personal grievances and not ideological principles. Cicero's attempts to sanitize the plotters are exemplified by Trebonius himself. He had fought with distinction in Gaul and helped capture Massilia from Pompey's forces. His service was rewarded, and he was made a consul from October 45 BC until the end of the year. He was the first of his family to attain this office, which ennobled him and all his descendants. It was a great honour, as was his nomination to the prestigious governorship of Asia for the following year.

On the last day of the year, his fellow consul died and Caesar, wishing to reward as many of his supporters as possible, granted the request of Gaius Caninius Rebilus to be made consul for the one remaining day of the year. Trebonius had also served as a legionary commander in Gaul, and during the civil war he campaigned in Africa and fought at Munda. The aristocracy was horrified by the perceived insult to the dignity of the Senate and the prestige of the office itself. Cicero, who presented himself as the guardian of the constitution, raged that 'in the consulship of Caninius, nobody lunched. Still, nothing untoward occurred while he was consul; for so wonderfully wide awake was he, that during his whole consulship he saw no sleep. All very funny, you think; if you were an eyewitness, you could not keep back your tears.'[39]

This was perceived to be a 'violation of precedent' that went against ancestral custom but also sullied the office of the consul.[40] It is significant that Trebonius, a man promoted and honoured by Caesar, would within a few weeks of this event plot to murder his benefactor. He felt his consulship had been debased by the appointment of Caninius to the same office for a day.

The aggrieved and discontented coalesced into several small groups, but each was restricted to only two or three people. Their activities were limited to spreading false rumours or derogatory verses and proposing extravagant honours in the Senate, and then distributing critical pamphlets. Caesar was aware of them, but his preferred method to counter them was 'to discourage rather than punish such plots', and when he 'became aware of secret nocturnal meetings' he would 'announce openly that he knew about them.'[41] Such gatherings probably took place under the guise of dinner invitations to carefully selected *amici* who were known to share their host's views. Such discussions would have to be private rather than in a public space such as the Forum in case they were overheard, and there would need to be a social connection between the participants to disguise the reason for the gathering. Consequently, several plots centred on different friendship groups might exist at one time, each unaware of the others.

One of the first groups to form, and the most important, was centred on the *amici* of Cassius. Plutarch's account of Cassius in his *Life of Brutus* draws heavily on two primary sources: an account written by Emphylos, a confidant of Brutus, and the biography written by Calpurnius Bibulus, Brutus's stepson. Although Brutus is portrayed as the kingpin in the plot, it is evident that he only joined the conspiracy in the final few weeks before the assassination.[42] Plutarch refers to the *hetairia* of Cassius throughout his account, and this description is mirrored in Appian's work. A *hetairia* is a Greek term used for a party of aristocrats who formed a political grouping. There is no doubt in the minds of both writers that Cassius was the real author of the plot and that it was his group that formed the core of the conspiracy throughout. These would have initially been his closest *amici*, whose views were canvassed over a series of banquets where 'Cassius felt his friends, and did stir them up against Caesar: they all agreed, and promised to take part with him'.[43] Appian repeatedly refers to the 'party of Cassius' and 'Cassius and his friends' when describing the development of the plot, from its formation to the assassination.[44]

Cassius, however, made little progress in expanding this group, as it was seen as merely consisting of aggrieved Pompeians who had failed to come to terms with the new regime. Furthermore, relations with Brutus remained cold, and Cassius's well-known personal hostility to Caesar would have made a commitment too risky. Caesar was also guarded by 2,000 Spanish horsemen who travelled with him. Cicero, who banqueted with him at the villa of their friend, Philippus, near Puteoli in December 45 BC, described how 'the house was so thronged by the soldiers that there was hardly a spare room for Caesar himself to dine in'. Sentries were posted and a military camp was made on the grounds.[45] The problem for those planning his murder was not the act itself, but surviving its aftermath. Caesar would be easy to approach because, like all members of the aristocracy, he personally heard requests and accepted petitions. However, his guard would immediately strike down any attacker, and the conspirators wanted to live and gain the rewards they felt their act of tyrannicide deserved.

A solution was found. In January 44 BC, an unknown senator proposed that Caesar disband his bodyguard and instead rely on an honour guard of senators and equestrians. This was extremely difficult to turn down without insulting the Senate. All members had taken an oath before the gods to protect him. The Spanish troops were dismissed and Caesar accepted the decree, but he employed his own *amici*, freedmen and clients as an escort. He believed that his distribution of gifts, honours and offices engendered enough loyalty to guarantee his safety, taking false hope in the inevitable consequence of his murder, a renewal of the civil war. He knew there existed several plots against his life, but he 'often said: "It is more important for Rome than for myself that I should survive. I have long been sated with power and glory; but should anything happen to me, Rome will enjoy no peace. A new civil war will break out under far worse conditions than the last."'[46] These were prophetic words.

At around the same time, the Senate offered Caesar the dictatorship for life. As he had no intention of relinquishing his powers, he accepted. He was now king in all but name, but this was a title he had no intention of accepting. After all, he did not need to. His opponents, however, were now able to unite opposition to him by spreading insidious rumours that he intended to restore the monarchy. This was an extremely powerful vehicle, as the nobility considered monarchy synonymous with tyranny and a threat to their social and political ascendancy. In the opinion of many, it was only a small step from a dictator in perpetuity to a king. Furthermore, Caesar had been voted a golden chair and on formal occasions he wore regal red boots, as his family claimed descent from the legendary kings of Alba Longa. He thus outwardly appeared to already have the trappings of kingship.[47]

A concerted campaign began in early 44 BC to cause alarm amongst Rome's aristocracy. Cassius and his *amici* worked in the shadows to spread the rumour that Caesar aimed to be king. Pretending to be seeking Caesar's favour, some in the Senate proposed that he be given the title 'king', but he rapidly turned this down and ordered any who did so in the future be arrested. On 26 January,

Caesar was returning from the Alban Mount after officiating at the Latin Festival as Pontifex Maximus. As the procession returned to the Forum, it was seen that a prominent golden statue of Caesar on the Rostra had been crowned with regal laurel. Two tribunes of the people, Epidius Marullus and Caesetius Flavus, pretending to be enforcing Caesar's decree, ordered the crown removed and the offender imprisoned. Their actions were meant to add credence to the rumours, especially as Caesar had not had the opportunity to have it removed himself. They were acclaimed by ringleaders in the crowd as Brutuses. This was both to undermine Caesar and to make a direct appeal to Marcus Brutus.[48]

Soon after, Caesar was returning to the city and, as was the custom at an *adventus*, he was greeted at the gates by magistrates, senators and his clients and *amici*. A hidden voice in the crowd acclaimed him as 'Rex' (king). Responding quickly, Caesar joked, "I am not King, I am Caesar," as though they had mistaken his name.' His cousin, who had been consul in 68 BC, was called Quintus Marcius Rex. The tribune, Epidius Marullus, had his attendants supposedly hunt down the offender, who was arrested and brought before his tribunal in the Forum. A public trial followed and he was found guilty. Both incidents had been carefully staged. Caesar was furious and criticized the actions of the tribunes. The same tribunes then issued a proclamation stating they were unable to speak their minds freely on behalf of the people. They provoked the reaction they had hoped for; Caesar declared he could 'put up with it no longer and accused the faction of Marullus before the Senate of artfully conspiring to cast upon him the odium of royalty. He added that they were deserving of death, but that it would be sufficient if they were deprived of their office and expelled from the Senate.' Clearly, Caesar was well aware that they were members of a conspiracy against him, for 'he continued that their action was one which indicated a more serious resolution and plot: if somehow they might slander him to the people as a seeker after unconstitutional power, and thus (themselves stirring up an insurrection) to slay him.'[49]

Although the constitution protected the tribunes, as they were sacrosanct whilst in office, Caesar overreacted and ordered their arrest, deposition and exile. He soon realized his mistake, but the damage had been done. At the elections, voters were organized to support the tribunes' recall. Caesar was said to have used his dictatorial power to undermine the laws of the Republic, which increased anger amongst the nobility. He told his *amici* to protect him, but when they suggested he recall his Spanish bodyguard, he said: 'There is nothing more unlucky than perpetual watching; that is the part of one who is always afraid.'[50]

Rumours dressed as facts gathered pace into February: Caesar supposedly planned to move the capital to Troy or Alexandria, a lie playing on his claim to be descended from Aeneas and his liaison with Cleopatra. Furthermore, it was said he was going to leave Rome under the supervision of his closest *amici*, and was going to introduce conscription for all eligible men for his forthcoming campaigns.[51] The most persistent rumour was that he was aiming to restore the monarchy. Information and misinformation could be communicated by pamphlets, but these were limited to the wealthy who had received an education. The most effective method was therefore the use of the morning *salutatio*. *Amici*, clients and freedmen would gather in the *atrium* of Rome's elite to receive the latest 'news'. This they would pass on to their friends and associates, as they tended to live in poorer areas not frequented by the rich. Rumours thus spread from the mansions of the elite to the tenements and inns of the poor. The lower classes had no interest in preserving the primacy of the Senate, but they feared being forced to fight in wars in distant lands.[52]

Caesar decided to use his own staged performance to counter the most destructive falsehood that he wished to be king. The ancient festival of the *Lupercalia* on 15 February was an ancient and popular event that was supervised by Caesar as *Pontifex Maximus*. The magistrates, led by the consul Antony, ran around the streets of the capitol dressed in loincloths striking spectators with whips to purify the city. Antony entered the Forum and was given a crown. He then ran to the tribunal Caesar was sat upon and raised up the crown. He already wore a purple toga and golden wreath; honours voted him by the Senate. The crowd grew quiet in expectation of the dictator's acceptance of the crown. However, as soon as it was placed on his head, Caesar removed it. The crowd was divided, some wanting him to accept but others approving of the clear rejection:

'Those who were standing at some distance applauded this action, but those who were near at hand clamoured that he should accept it and not repel the people's favour. Various individuals held different views of the matter. Some were angry, thinking it an indication of power out of place in a democracy; others, thinking to court favour, approved; still others spread the report that Antonius [Antony] had acted as he did not without Caesar's connivance. There were many who were quite willing that Caesar be made king openly. All sorts of talk began to go through the crowd. When Antonius crowned Caesar a second time, the people shouted in chorus, "Hail, King"; but Caesar still refusing the crown, ordered it to be taken to the temple of Capitoline Jupiter, saying that it was more appropriate there. Again, the same people applauded as before.'[53]

The *Lupercalia* did not have the desired effect. What mattered was not what was happening but what many thought was happening. Cicero would later claim that Antony signed Caesar's death warrant by placing the crown on his head.

The conspirators used their misinformation campaign to claim that Caesar only rejected it when the crowd showed its disapproval, whilst other rumours suggested that Antony had presented it on his own initiative to gain Caesar's favour by offering what he most desired. Nicolaus of Damascus believed that this one act convinced many that the rumours were true: 'Of all the occurrences of that time this was not the least influential in hastening the action of the conspirators, for it proved to their very eyes the truth of the suspicions they entertained.' The ambiguity of the scene is evident in the confusion of the crowd. The rumours continued, and Caesar, in utter frustration, decided to remove himself from the machinations of the capital, announcing that he would depart on 18 March for a three-year campaign on the Danube and then against Parthia.[54] Time now became the conspirators' enemy. After leaving on campaign, he would be surrounded by his soldiers and there could be no doubt he would return with the victor's laurels.

Another rumour was quickly propagated and allowed to grow: 'At the next meeting of the House (it was further whispered), Lucius Cotta would announce a decision of the Fifteen who had charge of the Sibylline Books, that since these prophetic writings stated clearly: "Only a king can conquer the Parthians," the title of king must be conferred to Caesar.'[55] Cicero knew it to be false, but some believed it. Aware of the allegation, Caesar intensified his preparations to leave. [56]

Caesar's behaviour made an attempt upon his life inevitable. His approachability without the precaution of a bodyguard invited an attempt. Furthermore, his preoccupation with status led to charges of arrogance and possessing the superiority of a king. Another miscalculation only added fuel to the fire. Caesar had made a show of not attending a Senate meeting that voted him unprecedented honours. Instead, he sat in his gilded chair in his newly constructed Forum, hearing petitions and dispensing justice. He knew there would be little open resistance to the senatorial proposals, Cassius standing almost alone in opposition.

After the vote, the whole Senate, led by former consuls and the magistrates, gathered before Caesar, framed as he was by the Temple of Venus. A huge crowd filled the space. Caesar sat in deep conversation with some of his advisors, dealing with the issues before him and seemingly unaware of their approach. One of his *amici* informed him of the senators' presence and he put down his papers. However, he remained seated instead of rising to show his respect to the august body of men that stood before him. As dictator, his powers and status were greater than that of the former consuls, but they were shocked and indignant at this perceived contempt. He quickly realized his error. Etiquette demanded he immediately dispense with the business at hand and rise, but it looked like an arrogant claim to supremacy. His *amici* later claimed that he had an attack of diarrhoea, which incapacitated him. However, it was noted that he had no problem walking home later.[57]

Until this moment, there had existed disparate groups of fractured conspirators who baulked at murdering a man whom they admired and feared. Cassius's *amici* were reluctant to act, offering advice that the figure of Marcus Brutus could unite them all. Cassius's genius lay in his political realism. The conspirators centred on Cassius were all known to have personal grudges against Caesar, which undermined their claim to be acting from noble motives in defending the constitution from a tyrant. Brutus stood outside that circle, but neither was he a Caesarian, even though he had benefited from the favour of the dictator. Furthermore, he had fought for Pompey at Pharsalus. He united the two groupings in the conspiracy – the Pompeian and Caesarian factions – but belonged to neither.[58] Cassius knew he needed to appeal to both the disillusioned who had been supporters of Caesar and to former supporters of Pompey who had been reconciled to him.

Brutus was, like Cassius, a philosopher of some renown,[59] but unlike his brother-in-law, he had embraced the Stoicism of Cato, his surrogate father and now considered a martyr of the Republic. There was little in his philosophy that advocated tyrannicide. He followed a branch of Stoic philosophy called the Old Academy that sought to modernize the views of Socrates and Plato. These founders, along with Aristotle, thought that there were only three forms of government: rule by one person, rule by the few and rule by the many in a democracy, each of which were subdivided into good and bad forms. The worst of the six was a lawless monarchy, which Plato equated to a tyranny; life under such a regime was the worst kind of slavery. Brutus adopted '*Libertas*' as the watchword of the conspiracy, in contrast to the slavery that they had to endure under Caesar's tyranny. Liberty, though, did not mean equality. It meant the pre-eminence of the 'best men', the nobility, in the management of the state. There is no better example of this than in the actions of the leading 'liberator' himself. In 48 bc, Brutus ordered his agents to charge 48 per cent interest on a loan he had given to a small community in Crete, his high status having provided the freedom to extort and exploit in the name of the state.[60]

Slavery, to a Stoic, was the moral condition of the unwise, whilst the wise were free, even under a tyranny. This was because they had freedom of choice, even if they chose to exit life to preserve their integrity. Under Stoicism, there was no moral imperative to murder the oppressor. The model was Socrates, who chose to drink hemlock rather than agree to compromise his principles, a model followed by Cato. Marcus Junius Brutus, however, did not look to his illustrious uncle, but instead to his legendary ancestor, Lucius Junius Brutus. His appeal to Stoicism to embrace murder was to resonate down the subsequent generations.[61]

Cassius judged Brutus's character to perfection. He knew that if he rejected his approach, the conspiracy was doomed as an unjust vendetta against their ruler and benefactor. The signs were evident to all. Whilst serving as *tresviri monetales* in 54 BC, Brutus had issued coins commemorating his family heritage, with Lucius Brutus on one side and *Libertas* on the other, or in another issue, Servilius Ahala. Any visitor to his house will have seen a family tree drawn on the wall of his *atrium* tracing his line back to the tyrannicides. This had been constructed at his request by Atticus, Cicero's close friend. Brutus called it his Parthenon, his temple to all the gods.[62] Cassius understood Brutus's primary motivation was his family history, which he exploited in preparation for their first meeting after the breach in their friendship.

Every morning, as Brutus ascended his praetor's tribunal in the Forum, he found it covered with 'such writings as, "Brutus, are you bribed?" "Brutus, are you dead?" "Thou should'st be living at this hour!" "Your posterity is unworthy of you," or "You are not his descendant."'[63] Also written on the pedestal of Lucius Brutus's statue on the Capitol was 'If only you were alive now!' and on that of Caesar himself, 'Brutus was elected Consul'. Rumours were also circulated that Brutus was not descended from the tyrannicide, as Lucius's two young sons were executed for conspiring to restore the monarchy before they had offspring of their own.[64] The burden fell on Marcus to prove by his actions that he was whom he said. Cassius thus played his brother-in-law, who, despite his philosophical claims to personal freedom, was a slave to his pride.

Cassius now invited Brutus to a meeting, where they embraced, their mutual hostility diffused and then redirected at Caesar. Plutarch's account, probably based on the biographies of Bibulus and Emphylos, details Cassius's inciteful approach. He asked Brutus 'if he were determined to be in the Senate-house the first day of the month of March, because he heard say that Caesar's friends should move the council that day, that Caesar should be called king by the Senate'. None of the ancient sources refer to this meeting of the Senate or any discussion by it of this proposal. This is no doubt because the rumour was false, its origin lying in Cassius's intrigues. Brutus said he had no intention of attending. However, Cassius pointed out that both of them were praetors and so could be summoned. What would he do then? Brutus replied: 'I mean not to hold my peace, but to withstand it, and rather die than lose my liberty.' At that moment, Cassius knew that Brutus would join the conspiracy. Cassius claimed he knew who had invoked his illustrious ancestor on the tribunal and bronze statue crowning the Capitol. He said these people were not the base rabble but the noblest and best of Rome, who 'specially require (as a due debt unto them) the taking away of the tyranny, being fully bent to suffer any extremity for thy sake, so that thou wilt shew thyself to be the man thou art taken for, and that they hope thou art'. Brutus was ensnared; they embraced, and within a month Caesar was dead.[65]

The ranks of the conspiracy rapidly expanded due to the diligence of Brutus. He only approached those amongst his *amici* whom he trusted implicitly, either due to their personal loyalty (*fides*) to him or their individual grievances. Nevertheless, each approach was initially ambiguous as he tested the waters without disclosing the plot. Q. Ligarius was a man almost guaranteed to join, being an embittered former Pompeian and close associate of Brutus. After the Battle of Pharsalus, Ligarius chose to fight on until defeat at Thapsus ended his hopes of a Republican victory. Caesar spared his life but refused to allow him to return to Italy. Ligarius feared for his life and fell into a deep depression. Caesar was petitioned by Cicero on his behalf, but the dictator despised him. Eventually, the dictator relented and recalled him from exile. Ligarius, however, felt no gratitude for this clemency, but instead bitterly resented fearing for his life and having had to contemplate a life in exile, away from family and friends. Time was pressing, so when Brutus visited him on his sick bed, he still sought out his support in an ambiguous statement that transmitted the urgency of the situation without disclosing his hidden intentions. Brutus entered his friend's chamber and 'said unto him: "Ligarius, in what a time art thou sick?" Ligarius rising up in his bed, and taking him by the right hand, said unto him: "Brutus," said he, "if thou hast any great enterprise in hand worthy of thyself, I am whole."'[66]

The conspirators discussed who they could approach – nobles whom they knew well and who belonged to their network of *amicitiae* but would accept their leadership without question, and were willing to risk their lives for the cause. For this reason, they discounted Cicero, who would have agreed with their purpose but, in their perceptive judgement, was a flawed individual who would question decisions and valued his own life above liberty.[67]

Instead, Cassius agreed that Brutus recruit three of his *amici*, who were carefully chosen. The nobility liked to demonstrate their education and learning by holding debates on literature or philosophical questions after a sumptuous dinner as the drink flowed and the lanterns burned low. A theoretical debate could be used as a cloak to ascertain their attitude to tyrannicide. Pacuvius Labeo was a man distinguished by his learning, while his two companions were disciples of Cato, Brutus's uncle.[68] Statilius was an Epicurean, so the Stoic Brutus may have consulted Cassius as to the likelihood of him joining the plot. His background suggested he would, as he had fought alongside Cato in Africa, and then, wishing also to commit suicide, he was saved by his friends.[69] The final guest was Favonius, a 'devoted follower of Cato', but he was 'more impetuous and frenzied than reasonable in his pursuit of philosophy'.[70]

The debate followed the traditional form of a dialectic, where one person poses a question to one of the guests, who in turn are given the opportunity to respond before it opens to a general discussion. Brutus, as the chairman, did not have to volunteer his views. This formal structure suited his requirements perfectly. It is evident from their different replies that the question considered whether a monarchy was a legitimate or tolerable form of government. Favonius was asked first, and as a Stoic he considered civil war worse than an illegitimate monarchy. All were aware that the murder of Caesar would probably result in civil war. Statilius disagreed with traditional Epicurean principles, as he suggested 'it did not become a wise and sensible man to be thrown into turmoil and peril for the sake of feeble and foolish folk'. His search for tranquillity was not to be risked by supporting those who lacked philosophical knowledge and enlightenment. Labeo, however, disagreed with both, which implied a potential to agree to the assassination. Brutus kept his peace but later approached Labeo in private, who eagerly enlisted.[71]

Surprisingly, the conspirators agreed to recruit one of Caesar's closest friends, a man so favoured that the dictator named him in his will as his heir should his nephew, Octavian, predecease him: Decimus Junius Brutus.

Decimus held no grievances against Caesar, and the closeness of their relationship ensured his position as a foremost man in the state. A loyal Caesarian general in Gaul and in the war against Pompey, he had been made a praetor in 44 BC, then delegated the governorship of Cisalpine Gaul with the promise of a consulship to follow in 42 BC.[72] His breach of trust with Caesar lay in the influence of Marcus Brutus, his relative and close friend. He was also descended from Lucius Brutus, the tyrannicide, but there is no evidence that this familial link dominated his reasoning.

Remarkably, it was Cassius and Labeo who first arranged a private meeting with Decimus, but he refused to commit himself until he met Marcus to confirm he was the leader of the plot.[73] His recruitment was vital for two reasons. Firstly, as a prominent Caesarian, his presence would help to enlist other disaffected supporters of Caesar; Trebonius, Minucius, Cimber and Casca may thereafter have joined. Secondly, he had purchased a large number of gladiators. Caesar would have been escorted in public by an armed retinue of *amici*, clients, freedmen and slaves. More of a concern for the assassins was the large number of Caesar's veterans in the capital awaiting transfer to the colonies and lands they had been allocated. They had no ties to the Republican senators, whose confiscated estates they expected to settle on. Antony oversaw the seizures, which fired the hatred of former Pompeians. Furthermore, it was feared these veterans might seek to avenge the murder of their former general who had led them to victory after victory. The gladiators were an insurance policy against this.[74]

The rapid expansion of the conspiracy had increased the risk of discovery. Caesar was informed of the existence of various plots against his life, but chose to disregard them:

> 'They came very near to being detected for two reasons. One was the number of those who were privy to the plot, although Caesar would not receive any information about anything of the sort and punished very severely those who brought any news of the kind. The second reason was their delay; for they stood in awe of him, for all their hatred of him, and kept putting the matter off, fearing, in spite of the fact that he no longer had any guard, that they might be killed by some of the men who were always with him; and thus, they ran the risk of being discovered and put to death.'[75]

The problem for Caesar and future emperors was not a lack of information, but too much. *Amici* might try to undermine the position of a rival by questioning their loyalty to the ruler. Allegations had to be supported by trustworthy evidence, and that was lacking. No state police or spy network existed. As he was unable to discern which allegations were credible, Caesar rejected them all. It would prove a fatal mistake. Days before his death, several people warned him that Brutus was planning his murder, to which he replied after laying his hands on his body: '"Brutus will wait for this skin of mine" – implying that Brutus certainly had the qualities which entitled him to power, but that he would not, for the sake of power, behave basely and ungratefully.' Caesar felt the offices and respect he had bestowed on Brutus obligated him under the rules of *amicitiae*. However, he did not trust him or Cassius. In a *concilium* with his advisors, Caesar asked them what they felt Cassius was planning, as he thought 'personally I am not too fond of him, he is much too pale'.[76]

Furthermore, some rumours that were relayed to Caesar were misinformation to undermine the validity of evidence of the real plot. It was reported to him that Antony and P. Cornelius Dolabella were plotting against him. Events were to show that Dolabella was a devious individual, but Antony's loyalty was unassailable. However, all were aware that the pair both hated each other and so would never conspire together. Caesar doubted neither, but responded that '"I'm not much afraid of these fat, long haired people. It's the other type I'm more frightened of, the pale thin ones" – by which he meant Brutus and Cassius.'[77] The conspiracy was so large that discovery was becoming inevitable. Suetonius puts the numbers of plotters at more than sixty, although this probably refers to those who knew about it but did not necessarily take an active part in the assassination itself. Nicolaus of Damascus refers to eighty members, but only twenty are known by name. This number, though, only constituted about 7 per cent of the Senate. Over 300 senators had been appointed by Caesar as censor, and many others owed their careers to him.[78]

The group was so large that they would have been unable to all meet at once, creating communication problems. While they agreed on the removal of Caesar, they disagreed on almost everything else. Many, led by Cassius, wanted to kill Antony as well, but Brutus objected. He argued that they stood on the moral high ground, and the murder of Caesar's deputy would undermine their noble act. Furthermore, they stood as constitutionalists, despite their many personal grievances, and the assassination of Antony, the consul, would weaken that position. He seems to have believed that the leading Caesarians would co-operate with him to restore the Republic once Caesar was dead, but in this he was utterly delusional. In June, Brutus and Cassius would blame Decimus Brutus for mistakes made after the assassination. Decimus possibly claimed he could persuade Antony and Lepidus to avoid a civil war by accepting Caesar's death in return for a prominent role in the new regime.[79]

Time was their enemy, yet they could not even agree on how to kill Caesar. There were special elections planned to confirm Caesar's choices for future offices in late February or early March, and it was suggested that when he stood on the bridge that electors passed to vote, some of them should push him off, whilst another group waited below with daggers. Others proposed attacking him on the Sacred Way, as his official residence as *Pontifex Maximus* was located there. However, they had taken an oath before the gods to Caesar's safety, and to kill him in such a place would be considered especially sacrilegious. Others dismissed these suggestions and advocated assaulting him at the entrance to the Theatre, probably during a gladiatorial combat, where the presence of Decimus Brutus's gladiators would not raise suspicions, nor would the presence of weapons. The issue with all was surviving the attack, as Caesar would have been surrounded by his armed friends in every instance. Many would inevitably be killed or injured. It would thus not be a pure and noble act, but probably a pitched battle. There were by this time only about three weeks left before Caesar's planned departure from Rome.[80]

Ironically, it was Antony who provided the solution. Caesar had proposed to resign his consulship when he left Rome on his campaign on 18 March and make Dolabella consul instead. Antony objected, so Caesar called for the issue to be debated at a meeting of the Senate in the Theatre of Pompey, not wanting to alienate either of his supporters. The date set was 15 March, the Ides of March.[81] The location appeared providential. The Senate would gather in the assembly rooms built into the Theatre, where a huge statue of Pompey gazed down to witness the murder of his nemesis. The setting for his death would symbolize the restoration of the Roman state. There were other advantages as well. Caesar's armed escort of *equites*, freedmen and slaves would be prohibited from entering the Senate, and other senatorial supporters would be sat a distance away on the benches. As consul, Antony would be sat next to him, so had to be delayed from entering the chamber. All the conspirators would be present and the whole Senate could witness the glorious restoration of the Republic. Finally, there were gladiatorial games taking place in the Theatre complex, so Brutus's gladiators could help if required.[82]

Almost immediately, parts of the plan became widespread knowledge. At the beginning of the month, the *haruspex* (seer) Sparinna warned Caesar of imminent danger that came 'no later than the Ides of March'.[83] Like other warnings, Caesar dismissed it.

As the Ides approached, Brutus became increasingly absorbed and preoccupied. His dreams turned into nightmares and conversations were replaced with silence. This anxiety was transmitted to his wife, Porcia, although he refused to discuss his concerns with her. Brutus would never doubt the righteousness of his actions, but the dread of betrayal and failure was ever-present, with 'no lack of informers against him'.[84] His attitude, like that of most Roman male aristocrats, was that a woman's role was restricted to the home, and they were too weak to carry the burdens associated with public life, especially the possible consequences of what he was planning. His intransigence drove her to desperation; sending away her slaves from her bedchamber, she stabbed herself in the thigh. The wound bled profusely and then became infected. At first, she too refused to tell her husband what was wrong. Eventually, she gave way and implored him to share his troubles. She invoked her father's resolute spirit to persuade Brutus to divulge his worries: 'I know that men think women's natures too weak to be entrusted with secrets, but surely a good upbringing and the company of honourable men can do much to strengthen us, and at least Porcia can claim that she is the daughter of Cato and the wife of Brutus.'[85] She then showed him her wound to demonstrate her strength and fortitude. Brutus raised his hands to the heavens, praying he would succeed and prove a worthy husband. He then told Porcia everything.

On the night before the fateful meeting of the Senate, Caesar dined at the house of Marcus Aemilius Lepidus with Decimus Brutus. The after-dinner discussion took the form of another dialectic, with an unknown person asking the questions. Caesar was listening as he signed letters and read petitions. The discussion centred on the most desirable manner of death. The chosen topic is too much of a coincidence to be accidental. Was this person trying to warn Caesar, knowing Decimus Brutus was part of the conspiracy? Caesar's response became infamous: it had to be sudden.[86] Decimus Brutus knew his fellow conspirators would grant his wish.

For Caesar and his wife, Calpurnia, the night was troubled by bad omens. Sleep was fitful. Caesar was ill for part of it, whilst Calpurnia dreamt that the carved pediment of their mansion that the Senate had voted him collapsed, and then that her husband lay stabbed in her arms. Caesar himself awoke as the doors were blown open by strong winds and looked down to see her wrapped in disturbed sleep, muttering to herself.[87]

Caesar rose well before dawn, having official business to perform in his capacity as *Pontifex Maximus*. He called at the nearby house of Cn. Domitius Calvinus. Spurinna was also there to make public observations on the sacrifice. Caesar, upon meeting the haruspex again, could not resist using the opportunity to point out that the Ides had come and he had met with no misfortune, to which Spurinna replied that they had come but not gone. The sacrifice of a white ewe was made to Jupiter on the Ides of every month. Calvinus, probably a *pontifex*, lived on the next street to the *Via Sacra* (Sacred Way), and from there they went in procession up to the Temple of Jupiter Optimus Maximus on the Capitoline. His religious duties completed, Caesar planned to return to his home, the *Domus Publica*, and there receive his *amici* and clients in the morning *salutatio* at dawn. There would be time to take a little food before attending the Senate meeting between 8 and 9 o'clock.[88]

The conspirators also met before dawn at the home of Cassius, ostensibly to celebrate his son assuming the *toga virilis*. This ceremony marked his son entering manhood, so he was aged around 16. Traditionally, this would have taken place on the *Liberalia* (the festival celebrating Liber, the Roman god of wine and fertility), but Cassius was not sure he would be alive to see it if he waited until the 17 March. Cassius's close family and *amici* witnessed the event, which evidently consisted of most of the plotters. Brutus would also have been present as the boy's uncle. He had secretly hidden a dagger beneath the folds of his toga, witnessed only by his wife. Most of the others had weapons in their document boxes or intended to use the stylus they used to write with.[89]

Once Brutus arrived at Cassius's house, they escorted the young boy down to the Forum for the final part of the ceremony. They may have passed Caesar as he walked up the *Via Sacra* to the Capitoline. The gladiators had been sent on ahead to the Theatre of Pompey, with the excuse that they were there to abduct a gladiator who was performing in the games as he had been contracted to fight in their troupe. They waited in a room off the portico of the Theatre. The conspirators then left the Forum for the Theatre of Pompey in case Caesar arrived early. It was the job of Decimus Brutus and Trebonius to delay Antony outside with pressing business, condemning Caesar to face his assailants alone.[90]

Some of the conspirators were magistrates; both Brutus and Cassius were praetors, and others were tribunes. They started to hear petitions and appeals whilst waiting under the huge portico. Nerves of steel were required to listen to the cases whilst awaiting the arrival of the man they intended to murder in cold blood. At one point, one of the litigants became angry at Brutus's decision and started shouting that he was going to appeal to Caesar. Brutus calmly replied: 'Caesar does not prevent me from acting in accordance with the laws, nor will he do so at any future time.'[91] However, Caesar had still not arrived.

Tensions rose. A man walked up to Casca and took him by the hand, saying: 'You kept this a secret from us, Casca, but Brutus has told me everything.' Casca was taken aback; this stranger appeared to know about the imminent murder of Caesar. Who else also knew? Casca, frozen with panic, was unable to reply. The stranger then smiled and said: 'You must tell me, my dear fellow, how you made a fortune so quickly that you can stand for the aedileship.' Casca had been just about to ask him how he knew of the plot to murder Caesar.[92]

Cassius and Brutus were standing together when they were greeted enthusiastically by a senator they hardly knew, Popilius Laenas, who whispered to them so as not to be overheard: 'My prayers are with you. May your plan succeed, but whatever you do, make haste. Everyone is talking about it now.' He then walked away. Knowledge of the plot seemed to be widespread. Was the failure of Caesar to arrive at the meeting he had called due to the plot's discovery? At this very moment, a messenger ran up to Brutus from his house to tell him his wife was dying.[93]

Porcia had risen before dawn to support her husband in what might be his last hours, watching as he secured the dagger beneath his clothes and left the house. She was beside herself with anxiety and worry, rushing outside at any unusual noise or cries. Not daring to send servants to the Theatre of Pompey, she instead sent them to the Forum to gather any information. The time for the meeting of the Senate passed and there had been no news. Her worries and fears overwhelmed her. Her strength drained away and, knowing she could not make it to her private chamber, she remained with servants in the *atrium* until she collapsed, unable to speak. Her attendants screamed and panic set in, drawing a crowd of neighbours and strangers who assumed she had died. Assuming the worst, one ran to inform his master that his wife had passed away. Porcia had actually only fainted, but Brutus, awaiting the arrival of Caesar, would have been distraught upon hearing the news yet still determined to perform his 'duty' to the state.[94]

Consequently, Brutus remained, surrounded by many senators who were not involved in the plot and who must have questioned why he did not return home. The rumour was that Caesar would not be attending the Senate session.

Slaves, assuming at this late hour that the dictator would not arrive, had started to remove his gilded chair from the assembly hall. Lesser men would have abandoned hope and contemplated how they could save themselves. News then arrived that Caesar was concerned about repeated ill omens and was going to cancel the meeting, whereupon it was decided to send Caesar's close friend, Decimus Brutus, to his house to find out what was happening.[95]

Caesar had arrived home from completing his religious duties at the Capitol to find his wife's anxiety had heightened in his absence. Normally calm and composed, this was unlike her. She clung to him and begged him not to go to the Theatre of Pompey. His *amici* who had greeted him at the *salutatio* waited to escort him to the Senate. He performed sacrifices to the gods in response to the ill omens, but the auspices were bad. His friends now urged him to remain at home. Caesar was probably still feeling lightheaded from the illness he suffered after the banquet at the home of Lepidus, and his doctors recommended that he rest. The Senate meeting had not been called to discuss an urgent matter, the debate forced by Antony being something he did not relish. Indeed, Caesar was about to summon Antony as consul to cancel the meeting when Decimus Brutus arrived.[96]

This was the moment when the course of history changed. Caesar had decided he was not going to the meeting, and Decimus Brutus anticipated the impending betrayal of the conspiracy: either Caesar went to the Theatre of Pompey and died, or Decimus would be executed as a traitor rather than being lauded as a hero. Decimus was desperate. However, Caesar trusted him implicitly and valued his opinion. Decimus reminded Caesar of the need to respect the dignity of the Senate and his dismissal of superstition:

> '[T]hough he was at that time thought to be one of his most intimate friends, [Decimus] came up to him and said, "What do you say, Caesar? Are you going to pay any attention to a woman's dreams and foolish men's omens, a man such as you? Are you going to insult the Senate which has honoured you and which you yourself convened, by not going out? No; if you take my advice you will dismiss from your mind the dreams of these people and go, for the Senate has been in session since morning, and is awaiting you." He was persuaded and went out.'

If he was set on postponing the meeting, Decimus said that so as not to further antagonize the senators, it would be best for Caesar to do it himself. With that, he took him by the hand and led him out.[97]

A huge crowd had gathered to escort the dictator to the meeting, including his slaves, freedmen, friends and strangers. Caesar got into his litter and, with difficulty, made his way across the city. Many pushed towards him, trying to pass on written requests and petitions, but were mostly kept away. Amongst them was a slave from the household of one of the conspirators. He tried to reach Caesar with evidence about the plot to murder him, but was prevented from doing so by the crowd. Instead, as the throng moved off, he forced his way past the doorkeeper and pleaded to be taken to the mistress of the house. He was taken to Calpurnia and begged to be kept safe until Caesar's return as he had important information for her husband. There he waited. The Fates had turned their faces away from Caesar.[98]

News arrived at the Theatre of Pompey that Caesar was on his way, but he was coming in person to postpone the meeting as he was feeling ill.[99] The conspirators' relief was replaced with fear. Caesar's litter then arrived, and as he got out, he was met by Popilius Laenas, who had just inferred to Brutus that he knew of their plan. The conspirators looked on, assuming the worst. Laenas spoke to Caesar for a few minutes whilst the dictator listened. Through silent gestures, each of the plotters prepared to die fighting. They placed their hands on their daggers, ready to kill themselves or make a desperate attempt to kill Caesar despite his guard of friends and clients. However, Brutus realized from Laenas's actions and body language that he was actually pressing a petition, not making accusations. Brutus could not speak to his fellow plotters as he was surrounded by those who were not involved. Instead, he became extravagantly cheerful, laughing and joking. They now realized that they were safe. Laenas eventually kissed Caesar's hand and moved away.[100]

Caesar then moved towards the altar to make the traditional sacrifice before the commencement of the senatorial meeting. Unseen by the conspirators, another informant attempted to intercept Caesar before he entered the building. Artemidorus, a Greek Stoic philosopher, had been admitted to the household of Brutus. He had become aware of the plan, either because he had been told by Brutus or he had overheard conversations. Everything was written on a note that he pressed into Caesar's hand. As written petitions were constantly given to Caesar, Artemidorus told him to read this one immediately and alone. To press upon him that it was not a request, Artemidorus told him that 'it concerns you personally'. Caesar did not pass it on to his attendants but kept it in his hand, intending to read it. However, the opportunity never presented itself. Artemidorus watched as he entered the Theatre holding the document, the only one he kept with him. It remained unread.[101]

The sacrifice was made but the omens foretold death. Another and another were performed, but with the same outcome. Caesar's *amici* again tried to dissuade him from entering the building, with only one dissenting voice, that of Decimus Brutus. At that moment, an attendant came forward to inform

Caesar that the Senate was quorate and awaiting his arrival. Antony should have entered with him, but Caesar, glancing round, saw his consul deep in conversation. He entered alone.[102]

Antony, a large, strong and burly man, would have put up fierce resistance to the murder of Caesar. Brutus had already decided that Antony should not die, much to the anger of his fellow plotters. To save him, Decimus Brutus and Trebonius had the task of delaying his entry. Both, as fellow Caesarians and long acquainted with Antony, would demand the respect of the consul and could not be easily dismissed.[103]

Brutus, Cassius and the rest of the plotters had entered the chamber, passing the huge statue of Pompey the Great. Cassius looked up and invoked the great man as though he was a god, asking for his favour in the murder of Caesar.[104] The Senate rose as he entered. Caesar walked towards his golden chair, around which a group of senators had gathered. He sat and was immediately pressured by Cimber for the recall from exile of his brother. He was aggressively insistent, yet Caesar remained calm, saying he would make his decision on another occasion. Others surrounded him on all sides as though supporting Cimber in his request. As planned, Casca stood behind the chair, waiting for the signal to stab Caesar, who would not see the blow. The dictator was obscured from the view of those sitting around the perimeter of the chamber.[105]

As arranged, Cimber grabbed hold of Caesar's shoulders and pulled down his toga. This was to remove any clothing that might inhibit the first blow and hold Caesar so he could not move. Caesar, angry at this assault, cried out, 'This is violence', and turned. Casca's dagger missed his throat and penetrated the shoulder. Caesar, groaning in pain, then forced himself up and grabbed Casca's arm with his left hand, stabbing him with the stylus in his right hand. Shouting at his assailant, he cried: 'Casca you villain, what are you doing?' Casca, in his fright, shouted to his brother in Greek to help him. Caesar looked around to see that he was surrounded. Another blow came in and Caesar leapt back to avoid it, but received another unseen strike from the side. Grievously wounded, Caesar now accepted his fate. He let part of his toga fall to cover his legs and pulled the top of it over his head. This was not to blot from sight the ring of daggers around him but to ensure he died with dignity. He stood, awaiting the end. The blows then came in like a feeding frenzy. Caesar made no sound. Some of the thrusts were true, unlike the men who dealt them. Others, in their orgiastic state, stabbed each other. As it was agreed that every active conspirator should stab him, Brutus stepped forward and directed his blow into Caesar's groin. Cassius had aimed his strike at the face. Twenty-three wounds pierced the body of the man they had sworn to protect, and he died under the silent gaze of Pompey.[106]

Only two senators had tried to help Caesar, but they were unable to reach him, such was the crush of men trying to kill him. The rest of the Senate sat as a stunned audience to a horror show. Brutus then stepped forward to address the noble fathers. He was covered in blood; some was his own, as he had been stabbed in the hand, but much of it was Caesar's. Pandemonium now broke out. Hundreds of senators ran in terror to the doors, with many injured and some crushed to death. Brutus called for Cicero to join them and then abandoned his attempt to make a speech. The status and eloquence of the great orator was needed to sanitize their actions.[107] Caesar's body lay in a pool of blood whilst chaos broke out all around it.

Panic spread, the crowd that was watching the games emptied onto the streets fearing massacre at the hands of soldiers or gladiators. Shouts rose for people to bar their doors and shutter the windows. Many took to their roofs to defend their homes from attack using roof tiles. Some saw an opportunity in the chaos and ransacked the markets. Antony fled, pretending to be a slave, and fortified his house. Lepidus, Caesar's deputy as Master of Horse, was in the Forum when he received the news of the assassination. He rushed to the island in the Tiber where Caesar's soldiers were lodged. The conspirators collected Decimus Brutus's gladiators and marched to the Capitol, which they intended to fortify. They invoked Liberty, symbolized by a slave's cap of manumission raised high on a spear, held their bloody daggers aloft and cried freedom. Few heeded their call, but some did, including Dolabella, wearing the trappings of the consulship Caesar had promised him, and later Cicero.[108]

Caesar's body was left in the Theatre of Pompey. The conspirators had initially planned to dispose of it in the Tiber like the corpse of a common criminal, but they feared the reaction of Antony and Lepidus, who commanded a large body of Caesarian soldiers.[109] This was their second mistake, the first having been when they acquiesced in Brutus's naïve decision to let Antony live. Nobody now dared to remove the body of Rome's greatest general: his killers had barricaded themselves on the Capitol, protected by their armed slaves and gladiators, while his friends hid in their houses, not daring to risk the streets. Instead, it was left to three of Caesar's slaves to gather the courage others lacked and return to the scene of the crime. They placed his corpse in the litter that he had arrived in, and with difficulty, as there were only three of them, carried it back to his home. A bloodied arm hung down through the flowing curtains, which gave glimpses of his mutilated face. As they travelled with their burden through the narrow streets and into the Forum, wailing and cries of anguish filled the air from the doorways and rooftops. Caesar had been the people's dictator. Calpurnia received her husband, distraught, his death having been foretold.[110]

As the remainder of the day passed and the conspirators survived the night without attack, they grew in courage. However, they had relinquished the initiative to Antony, who soon realized they had no plan. The tyrannicides believed they would be acclaimed by the people. Brutus felt confident enough to summon an assembly in the Forum, and he and his fellow conspirators went down to address the crowd from the Rostra. His friends may have acclaimed his rhetorical gifts, but Brutus completely misjudged the mood of the people. The aristocracy may have flocked to him in his splendid isolation during the night to acclaim the restoration of their privileges, their rights to offices of state and lucrative governorships, but the vast multitude of poor, the veterans who had survived numerous battles and the tenant farmers felt very differently. Amongst them, the conspirators had paid for some to shout for peace, but even they knew that their cries were futile. Brutus justified breaking the oath to protect Caesar by claiming that no oath could be binding if made to a tyrant, saying their duty to their country was greater. He also assured the veterans that they would receive their promised lands, but criticized Caesar for confiscating the property and estates of the rich without compensation. He was met with silence. Then Cinna, a conspirator, came forward and denounced Caesar. The crowd grew increasingly agitated, then angry, and hurled abuse at them. The people had no love for the Republic. The 'liberators' fled back to the Capitol, fearing the vengeance of the citizens.[111]

Antony was prepared to wait for his vengeance. A politician of consummate skill and daring, he advocated compromise but planned for war. During the night, he secured from Calpurnia all of Caesar's papers and sent messages around to call a meeting of the Senate near his house. He also sent his son as a hostage to the Capitol, as did Lepidus. Then, in their separate houses, they entertained Brutus and Cassius. They appeared amenable and conciliatory, guaranteeing the safety of the conspirators. In the Senate on 17 March, he proposed that Caesar's will be ratified, as well as all his previous acts, and that he be granted a public funeral. Despite the objections of Cassius, Brutus saw no threat in agreeing and the Senate gave its consent. This was the moment the conspirators lost control of events. Brutus had suffered a total and overwhelming defeat; he just did not know it yet.[112]

Antony and Lepidus flooded Rome with their soldiers and Caesarian veterans. On 16 March, a mere day after the murder of Caesar, Decimus Brutus wrote to Brutus and Cassius advising them to not only leave Rome, but Italy itself. The safety of the conspirators could not be guaranteed. Caesar's funeral on 20 March was carefully choreographed. Antony knew the contents of Caesar's will and he had Caesar's body. A gilded shrine had been constructed in the Forum, just in front of the Rostra. It had been built to resemble the temple of

Venus Genetrix, from whom he had claimed descent. An ivory bier held his corpse, draped in purple and gold cloth, the colours of power. It was carried by the most eminent supporters of Caesar, magistrates and nobles. A huge crowd had gathered, burning with anger at his killing. Antony was determined to spark the flames. On top of the bier, a tall pole carried Caesar's toga, ripped by dagger thrusts and covered in blood. Antony ordered a herald to read the recent senatorial decree granting Caesar divine honours, followed by the oath they had all sworn to his safety.[113]

The herald then read Caesar's will. He had adopted the grandson of his sister Julia, Octavius, who now bore the name Caesar. History knows him as Augustus. The crowd were next informed that Decimus Brutus was named his secondary heir. Their indignation rose. He donated his gardens on the banks of the Tiber to the public, and each male citizen was to receive three gold pieces from his estate. Antony then began his speech slowly, calmly, until, sensing the rising mood of the crowd, he seized hold of the bloodied toga and held it up, pointing out each of the rents in the cloth as a wound that killed Caesar. The mob erupted into a wave of violence, first building a huge pyre to cremate his body and then crashing through the city, attacking the homes of the conspirators, wanting blood themselves. The 'liberators' fled and the Roman world descended into its bloodiest yet civil war.[114] All the conspirators would be engulfed in its flames.

The conspiracy had begun as several fragmentary, disparate groups. These were based around a small number of *amici*, with the most important centred on Cassius. The majority appear to have withered on the vine. Cassius made little progress in expanding his supporters, as many were reluctant to join men well known for their antagonism to Caesar. However, Caesar's determination to leave Rome for the Danube and the East forced him to act rapidly. Brutus was enlisted a few weeks before the assassination, at the suggestion of Cassius's own *amici*. His presence encouraged those former Pompeians who had made an accommodation with Caesar and disaffected Caesarians to join the conspiracy. All, with the possible exception of Brutus, were motivated by grievances and perceived insults to their *dignitas* or status. Brutus, though, was consumed by his family heritage, and his political naivety cost his fellow conspirators their lives. Under his leadership, the plot came within minutes of discovery, and Caesar's murder was as much down to his refusal to countenance evidence of conspiracy as it was to the preparation of its leader.

Cassius, for all his flaws, was a realist, an experienced general capable of strategic thinking and ruthlessness. He thought as much about the days after the battle as the fight itself. By May 44 BC, it was clear to all that they had erred in letting Antony live. Cicero wrote to Atticus: 'That deed was done with the courage of men but the strategy of children. Who did not realise this: an heir had been left to the monarchy?'[115] The heir Cicero meant was Antony. He guilelessly dismissed Octavian, who would go on to use Caesar's name to seize power greater even than that held by Caesar.

In June, Brutus, his family and *amici* met at their villa near Antium. Brutus sought advice as to whether he should return to Rome or leave Italy. The man who refused to listen to other opinions, the man unhindered by self-doubt, the man who never questioned the righteousness of his actions, now sat conflicted, seeking guidance. Cicero launched into a monologue on securing the safety of Brutus, but was interrupted by Cassius entering the room. The latter looked resplendent in his armour, ready for war. He had no doubts: he was travelling to Greece. Cassius felt Rome was already lost to Antony and Gaius Julius Caesar Octavian, but that the East would provide the resources to sustain the Republican cause.[116] The most astute and skilful leader of that cause had stepped forward three months too late. It was Cassius, not Brutus, whom Antony feared in the war that followed. He was competent, experienced and energetic. However, just over two years later, Cassius took his own life after defeat at the Battle of Philippi. Brutus mourned over his friend's body, a man he believed so noble that he was the last of the Romans.[117] Three weeks later, Brutus too lay dead.

2

Crisis and Conspiracy

The Conspiracy of Caepio and Murena (23–22 BC)

'The tall trees fall in the tempest and the thunderbolt strikes the high peaks.'

(Horace, *Odes*, 2.10.9, dedicated to L. Licinius Murena, imploring him to choose the 'golden mean' – in philosophy, the desirable middle ground between two extremes)

To Horace, the perfect life was one spent pursuing moderation. It was wise advice that his friend should have heeded.[1] However, Murena did little with restraint. The conspirator was viewed by the senatorial sources as a deeply flawed character who could have risen to great heights had he made different choices and avoided the political storm that engulfed him. He 'could have passed for a good man',[2] yet in the face of perceived wrongs, 'he was immoderate and unrestrained in his outspokenness toward all alike'.[3] He spoke and acted with a freedom that no longer existed under Augustus's Principate. He also had a reputation for enjoying his drink. Horace uses his name, one that must have been well known to his readers, to exhort: 'Don't wait: drink to the new moon, boy, to the midnight hour, to the augur, Murena: the wine is mixed in three measures, or nine, depending which of the two is fitting.' A noble of impeccable Republican ancestry, he embodied old-fashioned *libertas*, as envisioned by an aristocracy increasingly disillusioned by Augustus's dominance of the state, especially his monopoly of the consulship.[4]

Augustus had controlled the machinery of the state through perpetual possession of the consular office, along with members of the imperial family or loyal adherents. He had held the supreme post that conferred the highest honour on its recipient continuously from 31–23 BC, twice with his close *amicus* M. Vipsanius Agrippa. In late 24 BC, a Murena was elected as his colleague for the following year, according to the *Fasti Capitolini* inscribed in the previous autumn. However, municipal and collegial records for the year begin with Cn. Calpurnius Piso as the emperor's consular partner. There is a frustrating gap in the *Fasti Capitolini* describing the fate of this Aulus Terentius Varro Murena, which modern historians thought referred to his removal or abdication following the failed conspiracy against Augustus. However, it is now believed the gap instead recorded his death before taking office. Furthermore, the name inscribed in the *Fasti Capitolini* does not include the name Licinius, by which the conspirator is referred to in some of the written sources, making it highly likely the conspirator was the brother of the deceased consul designate.[5]

The full name of our plotter takes a little construction. Horace and Cassius Dio name him as Licinius Murena, Velleius Paterculus as Lucius Murena, whilst to Tacitus and Suetonius he is Varro Murena.[6] He was closely connected to Augustus's inner circle of advisors. As well as the deceased consul, another half-brother was Gaius Proculeius, and a sister, Terentia, was married to Maecenas. A second sister of the same name married M. Seius, whose son became a Praetorian Prefect under Augustus and whose grandson was the infamous Sejanus, Tiberius's Praetorian Prefect.[7] Several historians have argued that he was born L. Licinius Murena and was adopted into the Terentia *gens*, becoming A. Terentius Varro Licinius Murena. Both were illustrious and ancient families who had supported Pompey the Great in the civil war against Julius Caesar. For this, his family had been impoverished by confiscations, but were rescued by the generosity of Proculeius, who was a close friend of Augustus. Murena's name alone would have carried him to the consular office in the footsteps of his brother.[8]

An inscription from Lanuvium shows he held extensive estates in the area and that he was a patron of Ptolemais in Cyrene, whilst another from the city refers to a man of his name holding the office of *aedile*. Horace also spent a night at another of Murena's estates at Formiae as he journeyed to Brundisium.[9] He possessed the *dignitas* inherited from two families of unblemished Republican heritage and, through Terentia and Proculeius, connections to the inner circles of power around the emperor. He was a man who felt entitled and empowered to act to express his *auctoritas* (authority) without restraint.

He was not alone. Augustus sought to placate the aristocracy with a series of concessions, culminating in the constitutional settlement of 23 BC. Firstly, Terentius Varro Murena was replaced as consul by Cn. Calpurnius Piso. This illustrious noble had fought against both Julius Caesar and then his adopted son. Twice pardoned, he had retired from public life to his country estates but was unexpectedly appointed as the emperor's colleague. His acceptance marked a reconciliation with the political realities of the Principate. At the same time, his nephew Marcellus, the son of his sister, Octavia, was made *aedile* and gave spectacular games to the people. He had been married to Augustus's only daughter, Julia, two years earlier and had also received the rank of a former praetor with the right to stand for consular office ten years before the legal age.[10]

Augustus's health had been poor for several years, but now it broke down and he deteriorated to the point of death. The world watched and waited, fearing a civil war should he die. Some, however, waited with hope. Many expected him to name his nephew, 19-year-old Marcellus, as his political heir, which would have been a public declaration of a monarchy that was hidden behind the facade of Republican institutions. Furthermore, Marcellus was too young and inexperienced to hold the reins of government. Instead, Augustus handed over his state papers to the consul Piso and his signet ring to his great general and close friend, M. Vipsanius Agrippa, signifying his position as his heir. The political situation was fluid and fragile. He was saved by his doctor, who prescribed a course of cold baths, but the suspicion that he had named Marcellus as his successor to his position in the state forced him to bring his will into the Senate and dramatically offer to open and read it to prove he had not subverted the legal powers and authority that could only be granted by a senatorial decree. The senators, fearing for their political futures, demanded he keep his will sealed. The crisis had passed, but it revealed the precarious constitutional position Augustus held and the veiled opposition waiting for the opportunity to reassert the supremacy of the Senate over the Princeps.[11]

Augustus decided to place his absolute control of the state on a firmer foundation whilst offering a concession to the old Republican aristocracy. In late June, he travelled to the Alban Mount outside the city to attend the Latin Games, and there gave up his consulship for L. Sestius. Replacement, or *suffect*, consuls were rare under the Republic, but were increasingly used by Augustus and his successors to reward loyal supporters. The two prestigious 'ordinary consuls' who gave their name to the year were normally the preserve of the aristocracy. The new *suffect* consul in 23 BC was a loyal former Republican who idolized Marcus Brutus: another response to the discontent of the nobility.[12] To replace his consular powers, the Senate voted Augustus the powers of a tribune without holding the post itself, *tribunicia potestas*, as well as those of proconsul in the form of *imperium maius*. This gave him greater authority than those powers held by a serving consul, or any provincial governor, and he retained this authority in Rome itself. He was also permitted to introduce one matter before the Senate at each meeting and retained control of the imperial provinces, which contained the majority of the Roman Army. He governed these through imperial legates whom he appointed.

The readjustment of Augustus's constitutional position confirmed his place as supreme head of the state, but also fully restored the highest social prize in the *cursus honorum* (literally 'course of honours', the sequential order of offices held by Roman politicians) to the aristocracy. He hoped this would placate most to the Principate, but all realized this was merely a sop to Republican sentiments as he 'was reluctant to take the style of king or dictator, yet desirous of some title indicating his pre-eminence over all other authorities'. Many resented the numerous 'new men' who populated the emperor's inner circle to the exclusion of the old Republican aristocracy.[13] This year of crisis continued. Agrippa had departed to the East to settle several disputes, but rumours spread that he was angered by the unprecedented promotion of the young Marcellus and that his official appointment was a cover for his disagreement with Augustus. Furthermore, plague and famine decimated Italy and Rome itself, causing popular unrest. The River Tiber then flooded in the autumn, adding to the physical distress around the capital and probably ruining the grain stored in the huge warehouses that lined its banks. The gods were clearly showing their disfavour. Augustus was forced to make twelve distributions of free grain to alleviate the suffering of a quarter of a million people entitled to it. The population of the capital, though, was probably around a million, so many were left at the mercy of private landowners and merchants. Popular discontent continued to grow into 22 BC and beyond. Then Augustus's plans for the succession were thrown into disarray by the death of Marcellus in the autumn.[14]

Augustus's misfortune offered an opportunity to his opponents. In the autumn of 23 BC, Marcus Primus, the former governor of the senatorial province of Macedonia, was charged with making war without authorization on the client Thracian kingdom of the Odrysae in the spring of 25 or 24 BC. He may have been responding to border raids into his province.[15] Primus was probably a new man (*novus homo*) whose career was entirely reliant on the favour of the emperor rather than a noble name. He was probably a praetor in 26 BC, suggesting he entered the Senate around 35 BC, when Augustus flooded it with his supporters as a reward for loyal service in the civil wars. Furthermore, the governors of the senatorial provinces were allocated by lot from a list approved by the emperor.[16] Surprisingly, Primus chose Murena as one of his advocates in court. He possibly hoped his forceful and forthright manner might sway the jury when his guilt was obvious, and it is unlikely he would have sought the support of his advocate had he made public any opposition to Augustus.

The courts were the political battlegrounds of Rome. Grudges could be avenged, with reputations made or destroyed. The Odrysae would have required a patron to support their claim in Rome and find suitable men willing to impeach the former governor. Although the prosecutors are not known, a powerful patron can be identified in M. Licinius Crassus, grandson of the *triumvir* and consul in 30 BC as a colleague of Augustus. He was a former supporter of Mark Antony and Sextus Pompey. He was Primus's predecessor as governor of Macedonia, and had waged a successful war in Thrace against an invasion by the Bastarnae. A man of his social standing would not have acted as a prosecutor, but employed his *amici* instead.

In 29 BC, Crassus had crushed the invasion, throwing the Bastarnae back across the Danube. He had been awarded a triumph when he returned to Rome. However, Augustus added this triumph to his list of honours. Furthermore, Crassus had killed the Bastarnae king in single combat and so claimed the *spolia opima*, which was the armour, weapons and decorations stripped from the body of a slain opponent. They were usually ceremonially dedicated to Jupiter Feretrius in Rome. This was the greatest honour a Roman commander could acquire and brought comparisons with Romulus, Rome's legendary founder, who defeated and killed a king in revenge for the Rape of the Sabine Women. He also recovered Roman standards lost to the Getae in 59 BC, and inscriptions from Athens and Thespiae hail him as *imperator*. Before he returned to Rome to press his demands, Crassus awarded land captured from defeated tribes to the Odrysae, who became his clients. He returned to Rome as a hero in 28 BC, but was met with hostility from Rome's new Romulus, Augustus, who wanted to monopolize all military glory to minimize threats from potential rivals. The Princeps claimed that only a serving consul could be awarded the *spolia opima* and his triumph was delayed until 27 BC. Augustus made sure he was not in Rome to witness it, and the silence that engulfs Crassus's career after this date suggests it came to a sudden halt. Crassus was a noble of impeccable ancestry, deprived of his rightful honours and treated with disdain by the emperor.[17]

Crassus was duty-bound as patron of the Odrysae to support their case, and the invasion of their lands would have been impossible to deny. A delegation of the leaders of the tribe was no doubt in Rome with witnesses and evidence. Murena chose the only defence open to him. Primus had been ordered to attack the Odrysae. However, Macedonia was a senatorial province and no senatorial decree had been issued to allow him to attack a client state. Instead, Primus 'declared at one moment that he had done it with the approval of Augustus, and at another that of Marcellus'.[18] There were problems with this line of defence. Firstly, Augustus had been in Spain in 25 BC, so it would not have been possible for him to meet with Primus in Rome. Clearly, there were no written instructions, as none were produced in court, and the claim was probably fictitious anyway. The 17-year-old Marcellus was in Rome but held no official or constitutional office in 25 BC. No doubt faced with the prosecution questioning this assertion, Primus asserted that the command was given by Marcellus acting on written instructions from the Princeps in Spain. This would explain in court why there was no written evidence, and Marcellus was now dead. Furthermore, Augustus was not permitted to give evidence in court unless summoned by the defence or prosecution.

Neither Primus nor Murena would summon Augustus, as he would undermine their case. However, it was clearly in the interests of the prosecution to hear evidence from the Princeps. Nevertheless, there was now a huge opportunity for Augustus's enemies – men such as Crassus – to publicly humiliate the emperor and undermine his position. In 25 BC, Augustus mainly used his constitutional powers as consul to control the state. He controlled the imperial provinces allocated to him through his legates, but his control of the senatorial provinces was constitutionally ambiguous. In theory, he could issue commands to these proconsular governors as consul, but this was almost unheard of as it insulted the dignity of both the Senate and the governor. Furthermore, if he used his nephew Marcellus as a conduit to pass on instructions, the dynastic implications were clear as he had no constitutional authority. The Republican facade would crumble, revealing the monarchy that stood cloaked behind it. Augustus's opponents would have flocked to witness the trial, knowing the political implications of an acquittal were colossal. [19]

Murena would only have taken this position if he knew the prosecution would not undermine his case. This implies collusion between the two sides. The case of the Odrysae was thus of secondary importance in a greater political game, one in which Augustus was forced to act. Despite not being summoned, he presented himself to the praetor supervising the trial. Although he had no legal right to do so, he was allowed to give evidence. When the praetor asked him 'whether he had instructed the man to make war, he denied it'.[20] Within minutes, Murena's case had collapsed. He now completely lost his temper. Frustrated and outraged at the illegal actions of the emperor, Murena, 'in the course of some rather disrespectful remarks that he made to him, enquired: "What are you doing here, who summoned you?" Augustus merely replied: "The public weal."' He placed himself above the law and Rome's institutions, including the Senate. He used his personal *auctoritas* to intervene and protect his recent settlement. However, Murena's aggressive response overtly questioned this authority and sullied his *dignitas*. More importantly, he undermined Augustus's claim that the Republic had been restored.[21]

Augustus's position and his authority had been publicly challenged by Murena; he would not allow this to do unpunished. Furthermore, despite Augustus's public denial that he gave authorization for Primus to attack the Odrysae, a significant number of the jurors voted in the secret ballot for acquittal. This was another public affront. Either they did not believe Augustus's testimony or they voted in response to his illegal attendance in court. The *lex Acilia* explicitly prohibited any magistrate possessing either *imperium* or *potestas* from interfering in a case unless summoned by one of the parties involved. A third of the jury were senators, a third *equites* and the remainder were wealthy property owners.

Some of the elite sought to curry imperial favour by praising his 'good sense' and voted him a further 'right to summon the senate as often as he pleased'. However, 'some of the others despised him' because the precedent was now set by his actions. Indeed, the emperor Tiberius would sit in on trials next to the Rostra in the Forum.[22]

Murena knew his position was precarious. Malicious charges were likely to follow, laid by Augustus's allies or those hunting rewards. Soon after, he joined a conspiracy to murder the emperor. The Roman historian Velleius Paterculus dates the conspiracy to three years before the plot of Egnatius in 19 BC and shortly after the death of Marcellus. This implies that both the trial and conspiracy occurred in late 23 BC, although Dio includes it in his narrative of 22 BC in an attempt to link together the trial, the conspiracy and its aftermath. The capture and execution of the conspirators possibly took place in early 22 BC, which would account for the erroneous chronology.[23]

The plot was led by Fannius Caepio. He is described as 'young', so it is unlikely he had held any offices of state. Fired by youthful ideals and moral certainties, he 'was the instigator of it, but others also joined with him'.[24] He may have been the son of the Republican general C. Fannius. Furthermore, Marcus Junius Brutus, the leader of the conspiracy against Julius Caesar, was also known as Q. Caepio Brutus, so there may have been some kind of familial link, possibly through adoption.[25] Fannius Caepio's nobility must have been greater than that of Murena, otherwise leadership of the plot would have passed to him. He is described as 'the worst type of scoundrel'.[26] The timing of the plot implies that he was motivated by the constitutional settlement of 23 BC that set Augustus above the Senate, as powerful as any king or dictator, meaning his powers were now personal and not bound to the control of the state. Augustus's illegal intervention in the trial of Primus provided the impetus and recruits such as Murena. Many other senators were also hostile to this new statutory arrangement.[27]

The plan was to murder the emperor, probably in the Senate, as the leaders were themselves senators but known to be hostile to Augustus, so access to him would have been difficult.[28] No doubt the assassination of Julius Caesar provided the blueprint for their plans. The murder of Augustus would create a political vacuum in Rome, as his nephew, Marcellus, was dead and his only daughter, Julia, was an unmarried widow. His wife Livia's children by her former husband were not members of the Julian *gens*, but were Claudians. The 19-year-old Tiberius had little administrative experience, having just been appointed to the minor office of quaestor, whilst his younger brother, Nero Claudius Drusus, had none. Augustus's close friend, M. Vipsanius Agrippa, possessed proconsular *imperium* similar but inferior to the powers granted to Augustus and held command over forces in the East, but he was in distant Lesbos, off the coast of Asia Minor. It was winter, so the seas were no longer navigable, meaning news of Augustus's death would take time to arrive and he would have to return by land with his forces. The Senate would therefore take up the reins of government, headed by two consuls of impeccable Republican sentiments. There is no indication that Cn. Calpurnius Piso and L. Sestius were involved, but by nature and through expediency they would be forced to govern in the name of the Senate in the absence of any other constitutional or political alternatives.

The conspiracy was betrayed by a certain Castricius. A few years later, Augustus was obliged to again intervene in a court case, where 'he made a personal appeal to the plaintiff in the presence of the judges' as he 'was indebted for the disclosure of Murena's conspiracy'.[29] Castricius appears on an inscription from Lanuvium, where he had gained the epithet *Myriotalentus* (millionaire). His motivation for betraying the conspiracy is thus laid bare. He was rewarded with the ancestral estates of Varro Murena and also placed the emperor in a debt of gratitude.[30]

Augustus summoned his advisors to consult their views as to his next steps. Maecenas was present, but on his return home he was caught in a moral dilemma. What had a greater claim on his loyalty: his family or his emperor? Discussions in the imperial *concilium* were state secrets, but Murena was his wife's brother. She was unlikely to forgive him if he kept his silence, so he told her about the discovery and that Murena needed to flee. For this 'inability to hold his tongue',[31] Maecenas fell from imperial favour.

Murena and Caepio escaped the city. The plot had progressed slowly and was not yet a serious threat to the emperor.[32] Augustus ordered Tiberius, who was a quaestor in 23 BC, to act as a public prosecutor and secure their conviction on a charge of treason.[33] They were convicted in their absence, their guilt being assumed by their failure to attend the court.[34] Despite the serious nature of the charge, 'some of the jurymen voted to acquit even these conspirators', their courage fortified behind the secret ballot.[35] They either did not believe the accused had conspired or their vote represented opposition to Augustus's position as supreme head of state.

The punishment for treason under the *maiestas* law was exile and the confiscation of estates. Traditionally, those who fled were assumed to have voluntarily gone into exile. There was no death penalty. However, praetorians were ordered to pursue the plotters and execute them. The Senate had sole authority for such a command, but no source refers to the issuing of a senatorial decree, so the order likely came from Augustus himself. This was another subversion of senatorial authority. There were some precedents for this, but the order strained the boundaries of legality beyond breaking point. Another legal precedent was set.[36] Both Maecenas and Murena's brother, Proculeius, attempted to intercede, probably questioning the legality of Augustus's command, but they failed.[37] Maecenas was not able to sway the opinion of the enraged emperor, while Proculeius's influence had long since waned as he had been too close to Gallus, the disgraced former prefect of Egypt.[38]

Caepio and his father planned his escape. As the gates of the city were guarded, it was decided that the barges on the Tiber offered the least risk of detection. Caepio was hidden in a chest and carried to the docks by a reliable slave. There, the human cargo was taken downriver to the busy port of Ostia. When it became dark, they travelled to his father's estates near Laurentum, a coastal town southwest of Rome near Lanuvium, where they remained until they could board a small coastal trading ship. The captain must have been paid well to risk the open sea in the stormy winter months. Inevitably, a storm rose and sank the ship, but they survived and came ashore near the great metropolis of Naples. Here, they were joined by another slave, who probably looked after one of his master's properties in the city. Nevertheless, the young man now met his death. An informer disclosed their location and a centurion apprehended Caepio, although his trusted companion – who had protected him for their whole journey – prepared to die defending his master. His survival implies that Caepio persuaded him not to surrender his life in vain. Even then, the slave could not be persuaded by threats or the promise of rewards to betray his complicity in the plot. Notwithstanding, Caepio was executed. The other slave used the confusion as an opportunity to run away, but he was later captured.[39]

Caepio's father, no doubt struck down with grief, was unable to take his vengeance upon the emperor. Instead, the disloyal slave felt the full force of his anger. He 'led him through the midst of the Forum with an inscription making known the reason why he was to be put to death, and afterwards crucified him'.[40] The other slave, who demonstrated both bravery and loyalty to his lost son, was freed. Augustus, already facing severe criticism for his subversion of the law, felt it best to ignore the elder Caepio's implied criticism of the emperor and the unwelcome publicity this very public execution exposed him to.

Murena had also successfully made his escape from Rome. He had sought the help of an *amicus*, a philosopher called Atheneaus who was the leading citizen of Seleucia on the borders of Cilicia Aspera in Asia Minor.[41] He had probably moved to Rome to enhance his reputation, and there 'had fallen into friendship with Murena'.[42] He was not a conspirator, as he was later tried but acquitted. This was highly unusual in a charge of *maiestas*. It is likely that Murena was his patron and so felt duty bound under ties of *amicitiae* to support him. Murena may have travelled with him disguised as one of his students and remained hidden on his estate. They were, however, captured together, probably in early 22 BC.

Athenaeus was returned alone to Rome for trial, Murena probably being executed away from the capital. The philosopher managed to prove his innocence and was released. When his *amici* visited him to congratulate him on his good fortune 'and question him, he repeated the following from Euripedes: "I am come, having left the vaults of the dead and the gates of darkness." But he survived his return only a short time, having been killed in the collapse, which took place in the night, of the house in which he lived.'[43]

The events of 23 BC revealed the vulnerable position of Augustus and the opposition to his supremacy. His treatment of the conspirators was meant as a warning to others who might choose a similar path. The seriousness of the threat is evident in Augustus's reaction, ordering a celebration commemorating his triumph over Caepio and Murena as though he had won a tremendous military victory over a dangerous enemy of Rome itself. The Senate voted for sacrifices to the gods, offering thanks for his survival.[44] Furthermore, Augustus extended his control over the courts and Rome's legal system, making 'a law that in trials at which the defendant was not present the vote should not be taken secretly, and the defendant should be convicted only by a unanimous vote'. The latter proviso was mere window dressing, as no juror would openly vote to acquit a man accused of treason. To do so was to invite a similar charge and inevitable condemnation. By the end of his reign, all trials for treason involving senators were held in the Senate itself, culminating in an open vote. The judicial system was by then completely under imperial control, with justice a weapon to be used against the enemies of the imperial regime.[45]

The relentless famine continued into 22 BC. The starving mob demanded Augustus become a dictator, being ignorant of the subtleties of his constitutional position – he already held powers greater than any dictator. However, the demands were similar to those made of Caesar to undermine his political support, and Augustus was sure not to make the same mistake as his predecessor. He made a great show of rejecting their demands, tearing his toga in two and begging them to withdraw their request. Instead, he took personal charge of the grain supply administered by two former praetors.

Augustus left Rome in mid-22 BC, firstly for Sicily and then Syria. Rome continued to be blighted by unrest and conspiracies, so his absence from the seat of power is difficult to explain.[46] His personal supervision of the Sicilian grain harvest at a time of famine is understandable, but a visit to Africa or Egypt – Rome's bread baskets – would be expected. In such circumstances, a tour of Greece and the East, including Syria, is surprising, as Agrippa was already in the East with explicit responsibility for this province.

The conspiracy must have involved a larger number of senators than Caepio and Murena, but no further arrests, trials or executions are recorded. The informer

Castricus may have been on the periphery of the plot, being unable to name more than its two principal ringleaders. Knowing whom to trust was a perpetual, insolvable problem from Julius Caesar onwards. Rome was a dangerous place, and Caesar's reluctance to take sensible precautions in the face of persistent information of a plot led to his death. The actions of Maccenas proved to Augustus that even his closest advisors were not to be entirely trusted. Augustus decided to remove himself from the nest of vipers that inhabited the capital and journey to safer climes, surrounded by soldiers and *amici* of his choosing.

The selection of another heir to his name would also place the Principate on stronger foundations, and he turned to Vipsanius Agrippa to solve his political problems. In 21 BC, his friend – who had been at his side from his youth – was compelled to divorce Marcella and marry Augustus's daughter, Julia. This union would provide further heirs in Gaius and Lucius Caesar, who were both adopted and raised by their grandfather. All were pawns in his dynastic machinations. It was this successional and political ambition that fired the resentments of Caepio and Murena, with the latter further angered by the illegal intervention of Augustus in his court case. The constitutional settlement of 23 BC was not one that appealed to all. However, few possessed the courage to act upon their convictions, whilst many feared a resumption of civil war should Augustus die. For this reason, the murders of Caepio and Murena could be ignored, but in hushed discussions between trusted friends and family, there existed the muted 'criticism of those who were not pleased with what had been done'.[47] The conspirators were secretly admired, but publicly denounced. In the prescriptive, febrile atmosphere of Imperial Rome, Murena was denounced by the cowed as a brave but bad man.

3

Adultery and Treason

The Conspiracy of Julia the Elder and Treason of Julia the Younger (2 BC and AD 8)

'When a woman has parted with her virtue, she will refuse nothing.'

(Tacitus, *Annals*, 4.3)

Rome's male elite believed women to be fickle slaves to their emotions, requiring the protection of firstly their fathers and later their husbands. Tacitus distrusted assertive, confident women, but transcended the attitude of his sex and class by recognizing the bravery and fortitude of some women in times of crisis. However, female members of the imperial house inevitably became immersed in politics because the blood of Augustus ran in their veins. They were expected to be mute compliant pawns in the dynastic planning of their male relatives, but many refused to acquiesce to this role and asserted their authority, thereby drawing the criticism of the male sources. Both Julias, both Agrippinas and Caesonia, the wife of Gaius – all-powerful, intelligent and forceful – suffered the posthumous hostility of those writers who came after.[1]

Augustus had no son, and instead used his only daughter, Julia, to establish a personal line of succession through marriage.[2] Her mother, Scribonia, had been divorced by her father on the day of her birth so that he could marry Livia. Julia was raised in the household of her father, as was traditional.[3] Her contact with her mother would have been limited. Julia was brought up in the customary manner for the aristocracy, with an extensive education in the classics but with the expectation of marriage and running the household. Consequently, 'the education of his daughter and granddaughters included even spinning and weaving, they were forbidden to say or do anything, either publicly or in private, that could not decently figure in the imperial daybook. He took severe measures to prevent them from forming friendships without his consent.' After a youthful P. Vinicius, the future consul in AD 2, visited Julia in the imperial palace at Baiae, the young man received a letter from the emperor reprimanding him for behaving 'with too little modesty'.[4] Constrained in her youth, she later took pleasure in the company of young, similarly well-educated aristocrats with literary pretensions.

Julia was married at 14 to Marcellus, Augustus's anointed heir. This was considered the proper age for marriage, as 30 was the average age of death, even amongst the elite.[5] She was a widow by 16.[6] Allowed a couple of years' respite by her father, she was married to the next heir presumptive, M. Vipsanius Agrippa. Ten years later, she was again bereaved, but had produced four children and was pregnant with a fifth. Augustus adopted her two eldest boys, Gaius and Lucius, as his own, leaving Julia the Younger, Agrippina the Elder and Agrippa Postumus outside his dynastic manoeuvrings for the present.

The death of Agrippa brought another dynastic crisis, and Julia was again used as the solution, being married to the cold and austere Tiberius, the son of Augustus's wife, Livia. The decision was cruel to both. Tiberius was happily married to Agrippa's daughter, Vipsania, with whom he already had a son. However, 'at first he lived on good terms with Julia, and dutifully reciprocated her love; but gradually conceived such a loathing for her that, after their child had died in infancy at Aquileia, he broke off marital relations.'[7] The feelings were mutual, with Gaius and Lucius, Julia's children and Augustus's adopted heirs, hating him with a passion. [8]

Suddenly, in 6 BC, Tiberius announced his retirement to Rhodes. Rumours circulated that his unhappy domestic affairs were the catalyst for this drastic decision, although it was also said that he resented the accelerated promotion of Gaius and Lucius as Augustus's chosen heirs, or that he was angered by his recent commission to travel to distant Armenia to settle affairs in the turbulent client kingdom. Tacitus suggests that Julia 'despised him as her inferior; and this in reality, was the inner reason for his retirement to Rhodes'. The proud Claudian would have burned with resentment at this treatment. Probably a combination of all these factors influenced his decision, but although initially voluntary, Augustus would make clear his exile had become mandatory.[9]

Julia must have been overjoyed to escape her husband. She had already written a letter to her father complaining about her husband's treatment of her. Her lover, Tiberius Sempronius Gracchus, helped draft the letter and encouraged her to seek the emperor's sympathy. The letter no doubt asked her father, as head of the family, to support a formal divorce. However, the emperor refused. He did not want her to become eligible for marriage, as any husband would automatically become a threat to his plans for the succession. She was a virtual widow again, with her husband banished from her mind. Tiberius, never one to forget or forgive, would have his revenge upon becoming emperor. The liaison with Gracchus was believed to have begun when she was married to Agrippa, and would only end with their exile. He was the bearer of a great name, a descendant of the revolutionary tribunes of the second century BC, a man 'of high birth, shrewd wit and perverted eloquence'.[10] They were well matched.

At a banquet, the conversation turned to her children's close resemblance to their father, Agrippa. Julia replied: 'I only take a passenger on board when I have a full cargo.'[11] Her coarse humour was taken literally by her enemies, but her joke was based on a line from a Greek comedy or epigram.[12] She was well known for her sense of humour, flamboyant personality and luxurious lifestyle. One day she appeared before Augustus in an extremely revealing dress. Her father, clearly disapproving, refrained from passing comment. The next day,

'to his delight, she wore a different kind of dress and greeted him with studied demureness. Although the day before he had repressed his feelings, he was now unable to contain his pleasure and said: "This dress is much more becoming in the daughter of Augustus." But Julia had an excuse ready and replied: "Yes, for today I am dressed to meet my father's eyes; yesterday it was for my husband's."'

This was more likely to have been for Marcellus or Agrippa rather than Tiberius. She was probably wearing a see-through Coan silk dress which had been associated with courtesans but by the first century was commonly worn by married women.[13]

She surrounded herself with young men of shared enthusiasms, who likewise drew criticism for their lifestyle. Augustus repeatedly commented on 'the extravagance of her dress and the notoriety of her companions and had urged her in language at once tender and grave to show more restraint'. However, despite his use of her as his pawn in the dynastic scheming, their relationship remained relaxed and amiable. Her father once arrived in her private quarters to find her maids pulling out grey hairs. They chatted for a while before Augustus asked whether she would rather be grey or bald in old age, to which she replied 'grey'. 'Why, then,' said her father, thus rebuking her deceit, 'are these women of yours in such a hurry to make you bald?'[14]

Augustus was paternally tolerant of her extravagant tastes, but there are hints that Livia used criticism of her amongst the socially conservative male elite and matrons to play politics.

'[At] a display of gladiators, the contrast between Livia's suite and Julia's had caught the eye, for the former was attended by a number of grown-up men of distinction but the latter was seated surrounded by young people of the fast set. Her father sent Julia a letter of advice, bidding her mark the difference between the behaviour of the two chief ladies of Rome, to which she wrote this neat reply: "These friends of mine will be old men too, when I am old.'"

The comparison between the two parties was surely Livia's.'[15] She was desperate to engineer the recall of her son, Tiberius, possibly inferring he could moderate her errant ways.

Away from the shadow cast by her husband, Julia's light shone fiercely. This sophisticated and highly intelligent woman had finally gained her independence, and she seized this freedom with a firm grasp: 'she had a love of letters and a considerable store of learning – not hard to come by in her home – and to these qualities were added a gentle humanity and a kindly disposition, all of which won for her a high regard.' She drew into her orbit noblemen of similar disposition and interests. The wives and children of emperors played a central role in court life, and power groupings formed around them consisting of ambitious senators, imperial freedmen and *equites*.[16]

Apart from Gracchus, there was the patrician T. Quinctius Crispinus Sulpicianus, the consul of 9 BC. Consequently, he was roughly the same age as Julia. He had the distinction of sharing this office with the brother of Tiberius, Nero Drusus Claudius, who died in the same year whilst campaigning in Germany. His name denotes he was adopted by a Quinctius, whose last consulship was in 123 BC, but he was a Sulpicii, another noble family. His son or brother by adoption, T. Quinctius Crispinus Valerianus, a consul in AD 2, was praetor in 2 BC, the year of Sulpicianus's exile. His career was not affected.[17] Sulpicianus possessed a 'stern demeanour', a surprising quality in the company of the frivolous imperial daughter.[18]

Gracchus himself was tribune in 2 BC, a lowly but non-compulsory office in the *cursus honorum*, chosen in honour of his famous ancestors. Did he consider himself a revolutionary? His friendship with Julia had begun whilst she was married to Agrippa, suggesting he was of an age to have been at least a praetor by this time, or even a consul. He is also included in Ovid's list of contemporary poets, like others in Julia's group. Augustus had clearly stifled his career. He was, though, an accomplished orator and poet, being greatly appreciated by his imperial patroness.[19]

Other aristocrats who sought her friendship included Appius Claudius Pulcher and Cornelius Scipio, the latter probably related to Julia through her mother's first husband. Appius Claudius may have been the grandson of another revolutionary tribune, the notorious P. Clodius. If so, the nature of Julia's group emerges. Scipio was a close friend of Propertius, who led opposition to Augustus's adultery law.[20]

In 18 BC, Augustus promulgated two laws that established in his mind the moral regeneration of Rome. One encouraged marriage and rewarded the procreation of children. [21] The other was far more contentious. The *lex Julia de adulteriis coercendis* made adultery a public crime, to be prosecuted in a state court rather than in private through a family tribunal. The law only classed adultery as being committed by a wife and her lovers. A husband's unfaithfulness was not considered illegal. Those found guilty were exiled to an island and had part of their property confiscated. The purpose was to reinforce the strict moral standards upon women expected by conservative society. Furthermore, as Rome possessed no state prosecutors, Augustus made it the husband's responsibility to prosecute his wife and her lover. If he failed to do so within two months, then any citizen could prosecute both parties and the husband on the charge of prostituting his wife. A significant section of Roman society commended Augustus's law, and the Senate eventually honoured him in 2 BC with the title *Pater Patriae* (Father of his Country) in recognition of his efforts to restore moral rectitude. [22]

There was, however, a significant group of the elite who opposed these laws and their underlying implications. Firstly, many aristocrats were angry that Augustus had weaponised adultery in the charged atmosphere of Roman politics. Political enmities were fought in the courtroom, and now a *delator* (informer) could accuse his opponent of failing to take the required legal action despite the infidelities of his wife. Witnesses could be bought and prosecutions amply rewarded. [23] Others rejected the moral and ethical absurdities of the restoration of a moralistic golden age that never existed. They read the poetry of Propertius and later Ovid, both claiming to be the poets of love. The resistance to Augustus's moral legislation became the hook to attract supporters to Julia's group through advocating an alternative lifestyle of love without boundaries and personal freedom. [24]

The most prestigious member of Julia's entourage was Iullus Antonius, another blossoming poet, whom Horace mentions composing a Pindaric Ode to celebrate one of Augustus's triumphs. [25] He was the son of Mark Antony, whom Augustus – then known as Octavian – had defeated. When his father committed suicide with Cleopatra, Augustus ordered his elder brother, aged 17, to be executed, but spared Iullus. He was favoured with marriage into the imperial family, his wife, Marcella, being the daughter of Augustus's sister, Octavia, who had brought him up after the death of his father. He was praetor in 13 BC, then consul in 10 BC and chosen for the prestigious governorship of Asia in 7 BC. [26] However, all this imperial generosity would never compensate for the loss of his father and brother.

The final named *amicus* of Julia was Demosthenes. Identified by some as an actor or musician, he was more likely a Greek philosopher. All those named in her circle were members of the elite, keen to demonstrate their classical education. An actor or musician was unlikely to gain access to this circle.[27] Others were involved in Julia's circle, but they are dismissed as 'men of lesser name and of both orders', along with many other women.[28]

Julia led her entourage in their decadent excesses. Like her, they believed their names and her status protected them from criticism. They were naturally supporters of Gaius against the interests of Tiberius and Livia. When a 'serious minded *amicus*' was dispatched 'to persuade her that she would be better advised to order her life to conform to her father's simple tastes she replied: "He forgets that he is Caesar, but I remember that I am Caesar's daughter."'[29] Her response is key to understanding her character. She felt empowered by her position as Augustus's daughter and the mother of his two designated heirs. Gaius was 17 in 2 BC, Lucius three years younger, whilst Augustus was 61, a very old man by Roman standards. Time was on her side. Although completely hostile to Julia, as his work was written in Tiberius's reign, the historian Velleius Paterculus describes her arrogance in 'claiming as legitimate whatever took her fancy'. It is a rare insightful glimpse of a woman who had the confidence to openly operate in the male world of politics.[30]

In the autumn of 2 BC, Julia made a catastrophic mistake, progressing beyond the boundaries of the permissible to embrace the unacceptable. The emperor was informed that his daughter had nightly been defiling the Forum, the hallowed political centre of Rome. It was reported, according to Seneca,

> 'that she had invited adulterers in crowds and scoured the city in nightly escapades; that his daughter had chosen the forum itself and the platform from which her father had carried his law against adultery for her fornications; that there had been a daily gathering by the statue of Marsyas when she turned from adultery to prostitution and claimed the right to every kind of licence with any unknown adulterer.'[31]

Dio confirms this account, saying the events happened when she 'was so dissolute in her conduct as actually to take part in revels and drinking bouts at night in the Forum and on the very *Rostra*'.[32] Pliny elaborates that the allegation derived from a letter of Augustus to the Senate.[33] The sources suggest this highly intelligent woman had taken leave of her senses, and rather than pursuing her indiscretions in the privacy of her many houses, she craved the publicity of the Forum, not once but on several occasions.

Her actions were indeed a public statement, but her real political purpose is hidden in the allegations of serial adultery and self-prostitution disseminated to discredit her character and destroy her reputation. Charges of adultery also allowed Augustus to try her associates privately and exile them according to his law. The whole investigation appears to have been completed in this private capacity, directed by Augustus, in which the imperial slaves and freedmen and women of those accused were tortured to elicit possibly fabricated evidence of serial adultery and other crimes.[34] This was the fate of Demosthenes, whose freedman Aesopus, 'who was privy to his late master's adultery with Julia, was for long put to the torture but steadfastly refused to betray his patron, until Demosthenes convicted by the evidence of others who also knew the facts, himself confessed'.[35] Few were able to resist torture for long and many crumpled at the mere sight of the instruments. Furthermore, slaves had little to gain from protecting their owners and would often be willing collaborators.

The key to this mystifying episode was the way the Rostra was treated and the crowning of the statue of Marsyas. A few months earlier, Julia's father had been honoured with the title *Pater Patriae* for his restoration of the established political, social and moral order. His new accolade was inscribed in the vestibule of the palace, in the *curia* where the Senate met and in his new Forum. The honour was announced to the public from the Rostra, the same platform where his marriage and adultery legislation was announced. Ovid wrote a poem in celebration, praising the 'father of the world. You have the name on earth which Jupiter holds in highest heaven; you are father of men, and he of gods.' The poet went on to include in his emperor's achievements the command for women to be chaste, his destruction of wickedness and the establishment of the rule of law. The establishment of women's secondary status in his marriage and adultery laws was offensive to many, as was allowing the charge of adultery to be used in the febrile political atmosphere of Rome's legal system. The use of the Rostra for a scene of debauchery was a very public declaration of opposition by his daughter and her supporters.[36]

The little statue of Marsyas had stood for 300 years near the *comitium* where the people voted or possibly close to the Rostra itself. Marsyas was a satyr who served the god of revelry and wine, Dionysus, who was now worshipped by the aristocratic revellers. He carried a wineskin from his left shoulder and held up his right hand in greeting. He was closely associated with the welfare of the people, and in particular *Libertas* and free speech. The statue was used as a meeting place for litigants and at night for prostitutes. The later association was emphasized in the 'official' account. The ecstasies experienced by these worshippers of Dionysus acquired a political meaning when they crowned him with a garland.[37] The criticism of Augustus was evident to those who witnessed

Julia's party, and, as the acts were repeated, they were planned rather than a result of drunken spontaneity.

The emperor was enraged by their actions. The violence and horror of his reaction imply he was taken utterly by surprise at Julia's betrayal. He 'refused to see visitors for some time' and even considered executing his daughter.[38] All bar one of her circle was charged with adultery under the *lex Julia* and exiled to different islands. The trial of Sempronius Gracchus was deferred until his term as tribune was completed, and then he spent the remainder of his life on the island of Cercina off the coast of Africa. Iullus Antonius, however, was indicted under the *maiestas* law of conspiring to murder the emperor. He was sentenced to death, but was allowed to commit suicide. His young son was exiled to Massilia, where he would die many years later.[39] According to Dio, 'other prominent persons' were also executed whilst Antonius had 'designs upon the throne'.[40] Pliny elaborates on Julia's role in aggravating her father's grief through her adultery 'and the revelations of her plots against her father's life'.[41]

Ovid may also provide a glimpse of Julia's conspiracy in his poem *The Fasti*, completed around AD 8. He retells the story of Tullia, the daughter of Rome's second king, Servius Tullius. She plotted to murder her husband and her father so she could marry Lucius Tarquinius. Ovid's lines could not have been read without reference to Julia. Servius is made to cry out, 'Hide my features, so they may not behold the abominable face of my daughter.' She also urges Lucius to act, declaring that 'Crime is royal business. Seize power by killing your father-in-law and dip our hands in my father's blood.' Ovid would expect his readers to remember Julia's offence. The poet was exiled this year for two crimes, one being a poem.[42] Julia's life as a pawn in her father's dynastic calculations had taught her much. The pursuit of unlimited power required the rejection of all boundaries: love, family, happiness and morality were secondary to survival. She drank deeply upon the lessons her life had shown her, and drew her own conclusions.

The puzzle is understanding why Julia would plot to kill Augustus when she could have waited for nature to take its course. Her father was elderly by Roman standards and her son, Gaius, the imperial heir, was 17. Nero was 17 when he ascended the throne, but was guided by his mother, Agrippina the Younger, Seneca and his Praetorian Prefect, Burrus. The emperor Gaius was 25 and ruled without support. Did she hope to become her son's counsellor before he became old enough to rule on his own? This may explain the need to hasten the death of Augustus. Tiberius would have undoubtedly never left his island exile on Rhodes, but Livia would present a problem. However, women had to act in Rome's political landscape through their husbands, and Livia would be deprived of one. Julia's relationship with Iullus Antonius implies she considered him her future partner, no doubt after divorcing his wife, Marcella. However, his own son may have clouded the succession as he was related to Augustus through his mother, who was the daughter of Augustus's sister, Octavia. His claim, though, would not be as strong as that of Gaius and Lucius Caesar, who already bore the imperial name. There was also the question of whether either of her children would be amenable to a regency that was also reliant on the cooperation of leading supporters of Augustus in the Senate and the army.[43]

Augustus sent a letter to the Senate, which was read out by his quaestor. Julia's crimes were officially announced: serial adultery and desecration of the Rostra and imperial Forum. To publicly charge his daughter with attempted parricide was too politically embarrassing. The charge of serial adultery destroyed her reputation, and that of her supposed lovers, but also impacted the imperial claims of Gaius and Lucius. However, their adoption by Augustus as his own sons negated their ties to Julia. The Senate was no doubt informed of the punishments he had already imposed on the accused. This was an unconstitutional abuse of his legal powers, but who would dare object and become associated with those already convicted?[44]

The fact that Augustus made the accusations public surprised many contemporaries, who suggested that the emperor's rage deprived him temporarily of rational thought. Seneca wrote that he was

'led away by his passion, he divulged all these crimes which, as emperor, he ought to have kept secret with as much care as he punished them, because the shame of some deeds asperses even him who avenges them. Afterwards, when by lapse of time shame took the place of anger in his mind, he lamented that he had not kept silent about matters which he had not learned until it was disgraceful to speak of them, and often used to exclaim, "None of these things would have happened to me, if either Agrippa or Maecenas had lived!"'[45]

No matter how much these charges made him look foolish, they helped to distract attention away from her real crime in planning his murder.[46]

Julia's household, like those of all arrested, were questioned, many under torture. It was believed that slaves would only tell the truth in these circumstances. However, one of her female servants chose death. Augustus was told that 'one of Julia's accomplices, the freedwoman Phoebe hanged herself about this time, he said he would have preferred to be Phoebe's father'.[47] The use of the word 'accomplices' may suggest she had already been incriminated in the conspiracy and chose suicide so as not to further implicate her mistress when tortured. The aged emperor's personal involvement in the investigation would have been mentally exhausting as well as deeply upsetting. This probably explains the reason why he appointed the first two Praetorian Prefects in 2 BC. As well as taking responsibility for the administrative tasks associated with the Praetorian cohorts, they oversaw his safety. It was for this reason that men of administrative rather than military ability were appointed to the post. In future, they would handle investigations and supervise the questioning and torture of the accused.[48]

Julia was banished to the island of Pandateria. This was a prison island, where she was 'forbidden wine and male company, even slaves'. She also suffered *damnatio memoriae*, with her name erased from inscriptions and her images mutilated, which highlights the political nature of her crime.[49] Her punishment exceeded those sanctions set by Augustus's adultery law, as noted by Tacitus: 'For designating as he did the besetting sin of both the sexes by the harsh applications of sacrilege and treason, he overstepped both the mild penalties of an earlier day and those of his own laws.'[50]

As an emperor possessing absolute power, Augustus was above the law as there existed no checks upon his power, apart from assassination. He was also acting as head of the family, exercising his *patria potestas* (power of a father), as her husband was effectively exiled on Rhodes. However, her punishment was seen as more befitting treason than adultery. Her mother, Scribonia, volunteered to join her daughter and so was free to bring her own household, providing some comfort to her daughter. This was a declaration of maternal love and a public affirmation of her daughter's morality.[51] Augustus also informed Tiberius that he was divorced from his wife, although Tiberius sent letters to the emperor pleading clemency on her behalf and asking that she be allowed to retain any gifts he had given her. This was more likely political calculation than sympathy for his ex-wife's fate. Her fall and his divorce severed his concrete link to the imperial family, and the two designated heirs of the emperor despised him. It had brought no benefit to Tiberius or his mother. He was now cast adrift awaiting his fate, with Livia his sole protector.[52]

Pandateria, modern Ventotene, lies 25 miles off the coast of Italy, northwest of the Bay of Naples. This island, 2 miles in length, would be her home for the next five years.[53] Augustus had built a huge villa complex at its northern end, with panoramic views across the sea enjoyed from an *ambulatio* (pathway). The villa also possessed a theatre, an *exedra* (living room), baths and a *triclinia* (dining area), and gardens covering 32,000 square feet. There was also a smaller, more sheltered villa which was probably used in the winter months. Despite these luxuries, the island was a prison, with the seas patrolled by imperial galleys from the naval base at Misenum. Access to the island was restricted to a small port built into the cliff face. Praetorians would be an ever-present reminder of the precarious nature of her existence.[54]

Julia was probably already on the island before Augustus made her fate public. She remained hugely popular with Rome's populace and there were frequent demonstrations demanding her recall. However, 'nothing would persuade him to forgive his daughter; and when the Roman people interceded several times on her behalf, earnestly pleading for her recall, he stormed at a popular assembly: "If you ever bring this matter up again, may the gods curse you with daughters and wives like mine."'[55] Livia had probably earned his anger for urging the recall of her son, Tiberius. There were some magistrates willing to endure the emperor's anger by bringing the proposal before the people. These must have hoped to gain the favour of Julia's children, Gaius, and Lucius Caesar. Many would have looked to the rising son to secure their future position. Julia also knew her exile would end when her son succeeded, so she played a waiting game. Then on 20 August AD 2, Lucius died, followed by Gaius on 21 February AD 4. Her hopes were crushed and to add to her pain, Tiberius was recalled to Rome.

The deaths of Gaius and Lucius had left Augustus's dynastic plans in ruins. He was left with no choice; the Fates had forced him to 'nominate Tiberius as his successor only for want of a better choice'.[56] Tiberius was a Claudii, so upon his adoption by Augustus, he was compelled to adopt Germanicus, the son of his brother, Drusus, but the grandson of Octavia, the emperor's sister. Germanicus was married to Agrippina the Elder, the daughter of Julia, so the throne would eventually revert to the Julian line. Tiberius already had a son, but he was immaterial to the emperor's planning. Finally, Augustus also adopted the 16-year-old Agrippa Postumus, Julia's remaining son. Tiberius was awarded *tribunicia potestas* and *imperium maius*, and then sent to wage war in Germany. Postumus received nothing. These adoptions precipitated a vicious struggle between the supporters of Tiberius and those who worked for the restoration of Julia and the claims of her surviving son and daughters, Julia the Younger and Agrippina the Elder.[57]

Agrippa Postumus existed merely as an insurance policy should Tiberius die before ascending the throne. He lived on the Palatine, surrounded by a nest of vipers. Foremost amongst these was Livia, who worked to remove any threats to the succession of her son. Julia the Elder was also moved to the coastal town of Rhegium at this time. She was confined to the city but allowed to leave the house. However, she remained under close surveillance, with Praetorians undoubtedly present. The city also had an active naval base and was settled with veterans from the fleet, and it was bound to Augustus by a debt of gratitude.[58] This was not a softening of her father's heart towards his errant daughter, but a reaction to increased popular protests against Julia's exile.

These protests were well organized and calculated:

'The people urged Augustus very strongly to restore his daughter from exile, but he answered that fire should sooner mix with water than she should be restored. And the people threw many firebrands into the Tiber; and though at the time they accomplished nothing, yet later on they brought such pressure to bear that she was at least brought from the island to the mainland.'[59]

The timing is significant. Many feared the restoration of Tiberius, having sought the favour of Gaius and Lucius by offending him and even urging his execution. He was not a man to forget, nor forgive. The adoption of Agrippa Postumus and leniency towards his mother offered hope when, in reality, there was none.

By the spring of AD 5, it was evident that Agrippa Postumus's political advancement was being hobbled as his coming-of-age ceremony was deliberately delayed. At the latest, he might expect to assume the *toga virilis* at the *Liberalia* on 17 March AD 4. He was 17 but still legally categorized as a child. He finally entered adulthood in the second half of AD 5, but without the honours granted to Marcellus, Gaius and Lucius. Marcellus had been made *aedile* and given the right to stand for the consulship ten years early. Agrippa Postumus's frustration and anger were natural responses. His fall quickly followed. In AD 6, he had been banished to his villa in Surrentum on the Bay of Naples, and during the following year he was disowned by Augustus and exiled to the island of Planasia, near Corsica. His crimes were insolence, stubbornness and a violent temper. He had also spoken 'ill of Livia as a stepmother, while he often reproached Augustus himself for not giving him the inheritance his father had left him'.[60]

At 18, he would have expected to receive the estates left to him in the will of Agrippa, but Augustus retained them as the head of the family and his adopted father. Furthermore, he had not been given the usual honours bestowed on an imperial prince, and when Tiberius was sent reinforcements for his campaign in Illyria, it was Germanicus who led them, not him. His father had died before he was born and his mother, whom he had barely seen, was exiled to a distant city and her very memory was suppressed. He lacked the political acumen to stifle his resentments, but allowed his anger and frustration to surface and boil. The historian Tacitus, although echoing the faults of Agrippa's character, stresses Livia's role in his fall, saying she 'secretly undermined her stepchildren while they flourished'.[61]

It was only natural for Agrippa Postumus to become the focus of all those resentful, angered or who feared the succession of Tiberius. This was especially true of all those who had bet their political futures on the succession of Gaius or Lucius. Furthermore, the years were hard for many in Rome after AD 5, which saw food shortages and a devasting fire, which may have been the result of arson. The wars in Pannonia and Illyria led to forced conscription and increased taxes. Rumours circulated that Tiberius was deliberately prolonging the conflict for his own advantage. Natural disasters added to those that were man-made. Consequently,

> 'the masses, distressed by the famine, an outbreak of plague and the tax and the losses sustained in the fire, were ill at ease, and they not only openly discussed numerous plans for a revolution, but also posted at night even more numerous bulletins. Word was given out that all this had been planned by one Publius Rufus, but suspicion was directed to others; for as Rufus could neither have devised nor accomplished any of these things, it was believed that others, making use of his name, were planning a revolution.'

Dio uses the word Ομιλος for 'masses', which implies a very large group of people. Elections were so disrupted that Augustus had to appoint the magistrates himself. The disturbances were both organized and extended over a considerable period of time, their primary targets being Tiberius and his mother. Rewards were offered to informers, and gladiators along with surplus slaves were removed from the capital. Tiberius was also forced to return repeatedly to Rome whilst campaigning in Illyria and Dalmatia, as 'he was afraid that Augustus might take advantage of his absence to show preference for somebody else'.[62]

This conspiracy, headed by Publius Rufus, is probably the same referred to in Suetonius as being led by 'Plautius Rufus and Lucius Paulus (the husband of Augustus' grand-daughter)'.[63] In AD 7, a Junius Novatus circulated 'a most damaging libel on him [Augustus] under the name of Agrippa Postumus'.[64] This is likely to have been part of the materials distributed by Publius Rufus and linked to the treatment of Agrippa which led to his transfer from Surrentum to the closely guarded island of Planasia.[65] The imperial claims of Julia the Younger's husband, Lucius Aemilius Paullus, were also probably promoted by Rufus, as he was exiled around this time. This scion of two great noble houses could claim descent from the consul Aemilius Paullus, who fell at the Battle of Cannae fighting Hannibal in 216 BC, and the Carthaginian's final nemesis, Cornelius Scipio. He was also the grandson of Scribonia, the mother of Julia the Elder, through an earlier marriage. Scribonia's voluntary exile would have added to his grievances and sense of injustice. However, this great patrician had been honoured by Augustus in sharing the consulship of AD 1 with the emperor's adopted son and his brother-in-law, Gaius Caesar, whilst his brother was consul in AD 6. He married Julia in 4/5 BC, and their daughter, Aemilia Lepida, was engaged to the future emperor, Claudius, but when her 'parents offended Augustus, her engagement was broken off'. Clearly, Paullus was condemned and Julia suffered some form of sanction. In the enforced absence of Agrippa, his illustrious ancestry and marriage connections to the imperial family made him a more credible successor than Tiberius. The popular discontent in Rome provided an opportunity to try and force Augustus to make alternative plans. Consequently, Tiberius was forced to regularly return to Rome and Augustus to consolidate his position.[66]

A list of the Arval Brethren dated to AD 14 records the replacement of a L. Aemilius Paullus, which only occurred upon the death of a priest, suggesting Julia the Younger's husband was not executed until after the death of Augustus. This would also explain why she was charged with adultery rather than *stuprum* (sexual relations outside of marriage) in AD 8, as her husband was still alive, although banished to a distant part of the Empire. To confuse matters, the Scholiast on Juvenal claimed Julia was relegated after Paullus was condemned for treason, but then recalled and then exiled again for immorality. The source is not entirely reliable, but Suetonius does confirm that Julia was associated with her husband's crime. However, it would be surprising for Augustus to have been so forgiving of his granddaughter and recalled her. It is possible that he decided her guilt was through association rather than complicity in Paullus's conspiracy.[67]

Julia's remission was only to be short-lived. In AD 8, she was permanently exiled by her grandfather to the island of Trimerus in the Adriatic in another private trial. She would die there twenty years later. She was pregnant, but Augustus ordered the baby to be exposed (left on a mountain to die) when she had given birth. Her lover, D. Junius Silanus, merely forfeited the imperial friendship; realizing that he was expected to go into voluntary exile, he removed himself from Italy. This was a social and political death for the noble, but he escaped with his life. The penalty for adultery was banishment, not death.[68] Ten years later, Tiberius allowed him to return while keeping Julia the Younger on her island prison. The hypocrisy in the comparative treatment of those associated with Julia the Elder, as well as his daughter and granddaughter, is staggering. Their different treatment might be explained by their association with an attempt to murder Augustus, whilst Julia and her lover were not charged with treason.[69]

Another prominent Roman who received no forgiveness from Augustus or Tiberius was the poet Ovid. He was exiled to distant Tomis on the Black Sea coast due to a poem and an error, according to the poetical defence he set out in his second book of *Tristia* and the *Ars Amatoria*. His sexually explicit poetry and promotion of tolerant morality had always run counter to the moralizing social programme promoted by Augustus, and he had sailed close to destruction in his thinly veiled allusions to Julia the Elder's wrongs.[70] In *Tristia*, he uses the word 'error' thirteen times, and comes close to admitting his mistake:

'Why did I see something? Why did I make my eyes guilty?
Why was a crime discerned by me, all unawares?
Unintentionally Actaeon saw Diana divested of her clothes:
No less was he the prey for his own dogs.
It is clear that among the gods even misfortune must be atoned for,
And when a divinity is injured an accident receives no pardon.
To be sure, on that day on which a bad mistake carried me away,
A house small but without a stain perished.'[71]

Ovid saw something treasonous, and from another line it is clear he failed to report it. In the myth, Acteon was hunting and inadvertently saw the goddess Diana naked whilst bathing in a pool. In revenge, the goddess transformed him into a stag, so he was torn to pieces by his own hounds. These lines imply that he accidentally saw Julia the Younger naked with her lover, no doubt Junius Silanus. Imperial slaves probably revealed Ovid's presence, because they were tortured for evidence. As an added incentive towards the procurement of evidence, a decree in AD 8 allowed for rewards to be granted to all informers, whether slave or free, for information supporting a charge of *maiestas*. The anger of the god Augustus is reflected in the dogs tearing their master apart. Ovid lauded illicit love in the *Ars Amatoria* and he now suffered for the very actions he praised. However, the first two books of this poem were written around AD 1 and provided instructions for men looking to seduce women. Abandoning all caution, he wrote a third book instructing women to do likewise, effectively encouraging women to break Augustus's adultery law. He had in effect joined the illicit opponents of the regime, distributing nightly propaganda supporting the claims of Agrippa Postumus. Like Julia, he would die in distant exile.[72]

There were several attempts to rescue Julia and Agrippa Postumus from their islands and take them to the legions. As Augustus grew increasingly frail, Tiberius's supporters gradually filled the most important offices of the state. Many of these came from families who had opposed Augustus in the civil wars and consequently lost influence and access to offices in the early and middle years of his reign, but they now sought the friendship of Tiberius Caesar. His opponents grew increasingly desperate. Epicadus, part Parthian, and an elderly forger called Audasius were arrested for attempting a rescue. They probably hoped to use fake documents bearing the seal of Augustus ordering the pair's release.[73] Upon the death of Augustus, a similar plan was adopted to rescue Agrippa and take him to the army led by Clemens, a former slave of Agrippa Postumus. He took a merchant ship bound for Panasia, but was delayed by the weather. When he eventually arrived on the prison island, he discovered his master had been executed and his body cremated. He took the ashes and, as he closely resembled the former heir, secretly gained a considerable following.[74]

Clemens evaded capture for two years. He even 'went to Gaul and won many to his cause there and many later in Italy'.[75] It was rumoured that Agrippa Postumus had survived and was returning to Rome via Ostia. Huge crowds gathered in anticipation, and Clemens was secretly received by powerful backers. Tiberius was forced to employ a ruse to capture him, Praetorians being disguised as intermediaries from prominent Romans who offered him money for his cause. He was then apprehended by a large force of soldiers and brought to the palace for interrogation by the emperor himself. Tiberius asked him 'how he had turned himself into Agrippa, he is said to have answered: "As you turned yourself into a Caesar."'The support for this imposter of Agrippa was so strong that a public execution was impossible, so he was killed in a secluded part of the palace. The interrogation had also been brought to a premature end by the fears over what Clemens might reveal. A hunt for his powerful supporters would only destabilize the regime. These were the supporters of Gaius and Lucius, who then looked to L. Aemilius Paullus, Julia the Younger and Agrippa Postumus. Because 'many of the imperial household, as well as *equites* and senators, were said to have given him support of their wealth and the benefits of their advice, no investigation followed'.[76]

The orders to murder Agrippa Postumus may have been left in secret instructions by Augustus, or by Livia or Tiberius. He was a focal point for all who opposed the succession of Tiberius. The historian Tacitus is clear in his opinion as to who was culpable, saying that his treacherous stepmother and Tiberius, 'actuated in the one case by fear, and in the other by stepmotherly dislike, hurriedly procured the murder of a youth they suspected and disliked'.[77]

Agrippa was a strong man and met his end bravely, raging against the fate prescribed to him by those demonstrating the same brutish violence they charged him with. Although unarmed, he fought back against the Praetorian centurion sent to kill him, and it was only with great difficulty that he was able to end his life.[78] Tiberius and Livia were ruthless in removing those who had stood against them. The timing of the death of L. Aemilius Paullus raises suspicion, but the murder of Julia the Elder's lover, Sempronius Gracchus, was motivated by an avenging, unforgiving new emperor. Cercina had been his home for fourteen years. He saw the imperial warship in the distance and walked to the harbour to meet his assassins. 'As they landed, he asked for a few minutes grace, so that he could write his final instructions to his wife Alliaria. This done, he offered his neck to the assassins, and met his death with a firmness not unworthy of the Sempronian name from which his life had been a degeneration.'[79]

Augustus had failed to include in his will the continuance of the allowance that had supported his daughter, Julia the Elder. This allowed her vengeful ex-husband to cut off all support. She was imprisoned inside her house and kept under close guard in case another attempt was made to free her. Her mother, Scribonia, continued to support her, but she was broken, bereft of hope, with her last son, Agrippa Postumus, murdered and Julia the Younger set to see off the remainder of her life on the prison island of Trimerus. Tiberius left her 'to perish of destitution and slow decline'. She died of starvation a few months later.[80]

Tiberius was so plagued by plots in the first few years of his reign that he often complained 'that he was holding a wolf by the ears'.[81] He, like Augustus, was a wolf surrounded by other wolves. Survival in the rabid atmosphere of politics in imperial Rome required wolverine savagery and remorseless brutality to survive. The family of the Julio-Claudians would devour itself as its principal leaders systematically destroyed potential rivals within the group, just as Augustus sacrificed his daughter and grandchildren, with some of them also conspiring in the pursuit of power, influence and, ultimately, their survival. Many were caught and ruined in this dangerous power play. Drawing on his own bitter experiences, Ovid offers this advice to Rome's elite: 'If in anything you believe a friend, live for yourself and flee far away from great names.'[82] Great names, he was saying, possessed great ambition. It was a valuable suggestion that continued to be ignored by many.

The problem of safeguarding the succession and thereby avoiding civil war was a continuing problem for emperors. The maintenance of a facade of Republican democracy hiding the reality of a hereditary monarchy created political and social problems. The use of daughters and marriage alliances to establish the position of the designated heir meant imperial women became powerful centres of influence, attracting their supporters. Consequently, adultery was a political act providing a form of legitimacy to the imperial claims of a lover, and therefore falling under the *maiestas* law. This was especially so as the lines of imperial succession were personal, not official.[83]

The nobility could accept a Principate headed by a descendant of Augustus, but none of the emperor's blood flowed through the veins of Tiberius. Many of the old Republican families – especially descendants of the Scipios, the dictator Sulla and Pompey the Great – would feel they had an equal claim to command the state. A Cornelius Scipio was part of Julia the Elder's group, and a Cornelia was the mother of L. Aemilius Paullus, the husband of Julia the Younger.[84] The emperor Claudius would face the same issues, with many nobles questioning his right to the throne, leading to his fateful marriage to Agrippina the Younger. The divorce of Julia the Elder undermined Tiberius's claims, just as her potential marriage to Iullus Antonius would bolster his. She looked to be the arbiter of the succession and her own fate, rather than her father, who had used her in his own schemes, without the slightest regard for love, family or simple human compassion.

The Plot of the Three Daggers

The failed conspiracies to take the life of Gaius (Caligula) in AD 39

'Let them hate me, so long as they fear me.'

(directed by Gaius to his enemies, Suetonius, *Gaius*, 30)

The Principate was born in one act of blood and another of denial. The murder of Julius Caesar resonated through the decades in the minds of conspirators and emperors alike. They lived knowing that some wanted them dead, and the greatest threat came from both those close to their person and distant military revolts. However, they were expected by the nobility to maintain a facade of Republican conventions and traditions, in particular direct access to the imperial person.[1] Despite holding supreme power, the 'good' emperor, such as Augustus, was expected to maintain the illusion of social equality with senators and Rome's elite. They faced a choice between reward and repression. Gaius (Caligula) initially adopted the former, only to discover multiple plots against his life, and consequently embraced fear and terror as the better defence against treachery.

The reign of Gaius started in a fanfare of expectation. The malignant and vindictive rule of Tiberius was over, and Gaius promised an end to the terror unleashed on the former friends and clients of Sejanus. He was the son of the Roman hero Germanicus, who died, allegedly poisoned, before he could ascend the throne. Indeed, his family was beset with tragedy. His two brothers, Drusus and Nero, as well as his mother, Agrippina the Elder, fell victim to the court machinations of Sejanus and suspicions of Tiberius. He was raised by Livia, the wife of Augustus, then Antonia the Younger, before being summoned to Tiberius's pleasure palace on the island of Capri. There, at the mercy of the man who destroyed his family, he said little and did even less. Sejanus had fallen but his terror was surpassed by that of the new Praetorian Prefect, Macro. Informers (*delatores*) denounced many with the most tenuous links to the former prefect, whereupon they were dragged before the emperor for a perfunctory trial, often preceded by torture, and then thrown from the cliffs that the imperial palace surmounted. This was the world of Gaius for six years. He held no offices, had no experience of government and few social dealings with Rome's nobility.[2]

Gaius entered Rome to be greeted with unprecedented joy on 27 March AD 37: '[T]he memory of Germanicus and compassion for his family that had been practically wiped out by successive murders, made most provincials and soldiers, many of whom had known him as a child, the entire population of Rome itself, show extravagant joy that he was now Emperor.'[3] The young man courted the approval of all. He gave the funeral speech for his adopted father, Tiberius, weeping profusely, then brought the ashes of his family to be interned in Augustus's mausoleum beside those of his biological father.

He was devoted to his surviving sisters, Drusilla, Agrippina the Younger and Livilla, but especially Drusilla. Their bonds were so close that they were accused of incest in the salacious reporting of Suetonius, but this is doubtful. Their long years of anxiety and the loss of their two brothers drew them close together. No such charges are repeated in the near-contemporary accounts of Philo, Seneca and Tacitus. Gaius made it clear they were part of the imperial house by modifying the annual oath of allegiance to the emperor to the following: 'I will not value my life or that of my children less highly than I do the safety of the emperor Gaius and his sisters.'[4]

One of his first acts was to end the terror that had been unleashed on the former *amici* and clients of Sejanus. Many remained, protected by their nobility, their position or their bonds of friendship to the powerful. Hundreds, though, had already died, charged with treason (*maiestas*) and suffering gruesome deaths.[5] Gaius had more reasons than most to want to pursue a vendetta on those who had supported Sejanus, but instead he sought to end the virtual civil war that raged amongst Rome's elite.

Some senators knew their lives were in danger, having made accusations against the new emperor's mother and brothers or provided 'evidence' of their treason. Instead, he flattered the Senate, promised to share power with them and looked for their protection as their son and ward. He ended the *maiestas* trials and the use of informers, as well as ordering the immediate release of all former supporters of Sejanus who remained in prison or exile. Finally, he produced all the witness statements in huge batches, the testimonies and other supposed evidence that senators had produced to destroy his family, and having sworn that he had not read a single sheet, had them publicly burnt in the Forum. He announced: 'I have done this in order that, no matter how strongly I may desire to harbour malice against anyone for my mother's and my brothers' sake, I shall nevertheless be unable to punish them.'[6]

The news would have reached Mogontiacum (Mainz) on the Rhine about two weeks later. The governor of Upper Germany, Gnaeus Cornelius Lentulus

Gaetulicus, had lived there as a virtual exile from Rome. The relief he felt that he might be able to finally leave his province is reflected in a history of Gaius's life that he wrote.[7]

In AD 34, Gaetulicus was accused by his former legate of *maiestas* because his daughter had been betrothed to a son of Sejanus. However, Gaetulicus was in an incredibly powerful position, which he had exploited by anticipating such an accusation. He commanded four legions in Upper Germany, with an equivalent number of auxiliary soldiers. He had cultivated the loyalty of these men by relaxing discipline and granting extraordinary freedoms. The soldiers' loyalty to Tiberius was undermined, as the governor 'had gained an extraordinary hold on their affections as an officer of large clemency, chary of severity, and, thanks to his father-in-law Lucius Apronius, not unacceptable even to the next army'.[8] This 'next army' was the three legions of Lower Germany, which had been under Apronius's command since AD 28, when he was defeated by the Frisians but surprisingly remained in his post.[9]

The neighbouring province of Pannonia, with its three legions, was governed by C. Calvisius Sabinus, with whom Gaetulicus shared the ordinary consulship in AD 26. Sabinus had also been charged with *maiestas* in AD 32, but was saved when one of the informers absolved him.[10] Their common bond was cemented with the marriage of Cornelia, identified as Gaetulicus's sister. Gaetulicus now effectively controlled ten legions and an equivalent number of auxiliaries. From this position of strength, Tacitus says he wrote to the emperor, pointing out that

> 'his connection with Sejanus was not begun by his own will but upon the advice of Tiberius. It had been as easy for himself to be deceived as for Tiberius; and the same error should not be treated as harmless in one case and fatal in the other. His loyalty was inviolate, and, if he was not treacherously attacked, would remain so: a successor he would not take otherwise than as indicative of his doom. Best would be to ratify a kind of treaty, by which the emperor would be supreme elsewhere, while he himself kept his province.'

The aged Tiberius did not want to fight a civil war in his twilight days and the accuser was himself condemned and exiled from Rome.[11]

Since AD 29, Gaetulicus was virtually an emperor on the Rhine but lived an exile from Rome. He had replaced his brother in the post, so many of the soldiers were steadfastly attached to his family. Their loyalty to him was reinforced by ready requests for leave, easy duty and relaxed discipline.[12] His 'capital' was Mogontiacum, which stood on the confluence of the Rhine with the Main. The fortress, high on the hill that dominates the area, held two legions.

A large civil settlement had grown between the river, its port and the camp. It was populated by locals serving the large number of soldiers and veterans whom Gaetulicus could draw on. A large stone bathhouse and theatre had been constructed, but it remained a largely wooden settlement, a pale reflection of the grandeur and splendour of Rome. He thus might cherish the memory of his mansion in the capital or numerous estates he could never visit, or the *amici* he was unable to see.[13]

Gaetulicus was born into a powerful patrician family which had held five consulships between AD 24 and his own in AD 26. His father was a close *amicus* of Tiberius and was City Prefect from AD 33–36. He inherited the cognomen Gaetulicus from his father, who gave it to him rather than his older brother, as he probably fought alongside him in the African campaign against the Gaetuli in AD 6. He was a praetor in AD 15, and as a noble was guaranteed to be an ordinary consul. Ironically, he did not need to seek the support of Sejanus, but his enemies used any links to the fallen Praetorian Prefect as a weapon to destroy him.[14]

He was a man of great learning, not only writing a work – possibly a memoir – that encompassed the life of Gaius, but also composing poetry in both Greek and Latin on erotic themes, praised for their use of free verse by Martial.[15] The accession of Gaius and the subsequent amnesty gave him fresh hope of returning to a life of learned retirement (*otium*), surrounded by his vineyards and libraries. He might also see his three children, one of whom had been adopted by D. Silanus, the lover of Augustus's granddaughter, Julia the Younger. His confidence rose further when the emperor honoured his nephew, L. Apronius Caesianus, by sharing the ordinary consulship with him in January AD 39.[16] However, events in Rome were to destroy these dreams.

Gaius attempted to make concessions upon his accession, but he was intent to live life to the full. His life of danger on Capri surrounded by the vipers of court, the cruelty he witnessed and the ostentatious demonstration of power in the opulence of Tiberius's pleasure palace warped his understanding of how to rule in the manner of a *Civilis Princeps*, where power is hidden by constitutional facades and social etiquettes. He demonstrated his supremacy in sumptuous banquets, where luxury was paraded without equal. Dishes were served covered in gold leaf and drinks with dissolved pearls, whilst the emperor was dressed in silks and tunics embroidered with precious stones. Furthermore, his passion for the theatre, chariot races and gladiatorial games was evident to all, and the crowds loved him for it.[17]

Gaius embraced a life without limits. He enthusiastically appeared as a gladiator, a singer and a dancer, drove a chariot and sometimes 'could not resist the temptation of supporting the tragic actors at public performances; and would repeat their gestures by way of praise or criticism'. The aristocracy was offended by his lack of *dignitas*, saying he behaved 'like one of the crowd'. Whilst his luxurious extravagance relegated them to a secondary status, his behaviour undermined their assertion that rank was manifested in education, deportment and manners.[18] Even their access to the emperor as his advisors was weakened. In October AD 37, Gaius became seriously ill. His Praetorian Prefect, Macro, and former father-in-law, M. Junius Silanus, prepared for his death and the succession of Tiberius Gemellus, the grandson of Tiberius who had been adopted by Gaius upon his accession. From his sick bed, however, Gaius named his sister, Drusilla, as his heir, despite having an adopted son. Constitutionally it was not in the emperor's remit to transfer the legal powers associated with the emperor, but that of the Senate, nor was it considered possible for a woman to hold office. Gaius was effectively naming Drusilla's husband, Marcus Aemilius Lepidus, as his successor.[19]

The Aemilii were steeped in Roman history. An ancestor had fought and died at the Battle of Cannae in 216 BC, whilst another had conquered Macedon and added it to the Empire in 168 BC. The busts and masks in their *atrium* would also have included Pompey the Great and Sulla, the dictator. The *triumvir* M. Aemilius Lepidus, supporter of Julius Caesar, was another relation. Marcus Aemilius Lepidus was the son of the consul of AD 6, who was held in such high esteem by Augustus that, in one of his last conversations, he considered him a potential heir to the throne, yet he was too contemptuous to desire it. He was a man of high intelligence and possessed a political acumen that enabled him to remain close to the throne under Tiberius, successfully navigating the currents of political division that decimated the elite after the fall of Sejanus. His brother, L. Aemilius Paullus, lacked all the skills necessary to carry a noble name and survive the intrigues of the court. He had been married to Augustus's daughter, Julia the Elder, but was exiled and executed for conspiracy. His family were distinguished beyond measure, but the son of Marcus, who carried the same name, did not inherit the skills of his father, instead acquiring the delusions of his uncle.[20]

The relationship between Gaius and the young Lepidus was so close that it was believed that they were lovers.[21] They were the same age and shared the same pursuit of pleasure. Soon after he came to power, the emperor ordered Drusilla to divorce her husband of four years and marry his friend. Lepidus was five years younger than his new wife. Their friendship is surprising, as Lepidus's sister, Aemilia Lepida, had spied on Gaius's brother, Drusus, on behalf of Sejanus. Sejanus had used this information to imprison Drusus on the island of Pontia, where he was starved to death. His wife was protected by her father until his death, when she was accused of adultery with a slave and committed suicide.[22] Her brother drew no lessons from his sister's fate.

Gaius demanded complete loyalty from those he trusted. He recovered from his illness and took the actions of Macro and Silanus as evidence of deceit. He owed his throne to Macro, but present transgressions outweighed past services. Gaius was ruthless with any who crossed him. It was extremely dangerous to remove a Praetorian Prefect, as they commanded thousands of troops. Macro was therefore promoted to the governorship of Egypt, and was then moved out of office charged with *maiestas*. He chose suicide, as did his wife and Silanus. The young Tiberius Gemellus was killed by a tribune of the guards. The orator and historian Philo has little sympathy for his fate, as Gaius 'being the stronger promptly did to the weaker what the weaker would have done to him. This is defence, not murder.'[23] The post of one Praetorian Prefect was replaced with two. One remains nameless, the other was Marcus Arrecinus Clemens. Their power was a pale reflection of that wielded by Macro or his predecessor Sejanus. Instead, Gaius drew on his family, whose loyalty he did not question.

Augustus and Tiberius had invited the aristocracy to offer advice on his *concilium*. Gaius dispensed with this. If it was summoned, its role was merely to listen and ratify. When Philo met the emperor on his embassy from Alexandria, Gaius was alone.[24] If advice was needed, he listened to his sisters and Lepidus. A set of statue bases in the *sebasteion* at Aphrodisias reflects the influence of this young aristocrat. Alongside those for the emperor, Germanicus and Agrippina the Elder is a base for Lepidus. Many nobles had married into the imperial family, but none had been included in the imperial cult to be worshipped with those born into the Julian clan. Furthermore, Lepidus was permitted to stand as consul five years before the legally permitted age, an honour normally reserved for princes of the imperial house.[25] There were no male descendants of Augustus left apart from Gaius, as Claudius, Germanicus's brother and Gaius's uncle, was a Claudian. He also suffered from a stammer and walked with a limp, probably due to cerebral palsy. Consequently, although highly intelligent, Claudius had been hidden from public view by Augustus and Tiberius, and his abilities dismissed. This suited him as he avoided the merciless intrigues of court, and instead he pursued academic interests.

On 10 June AD 38, Drusilla died at the age of 20. Gaius was devastated. Unable to give her funeral eulogy, it was her husband who addressed the crowds. She was given all the posthumous honours granted by Augustus's wife, Livia, and was also deified. The emperor sought solitude in his grief. He first stayed in the imperial villa in the Alban Hills and grew his beard in the symbolic act of mourning. He then wandered through Campania before taking a ship to Syracuse in Sicily to supervise the construction of granaries. The emperor had lost the love of his life.[26]

Marcus Aemilius Lepidus remained powerful. He was able to use his influence with Gaius to save the life of Avillius Flaccus, who had been summoned from the governorship of Egypt to face trial in Rome. He was a supporter of Tiberius Gemellus, and probably, like many who had done the same, faced an ominous future. Lepidus ensured his friend was spared execution and instead exiled to the more hospitable island of Andros rather than the barren waste of Gyaros.[27]

Upon his return to Rome, Gaius began preparations for a massive campaign into Germany to continue the war of his father, Germanicus. Two new legions were recruited from the two German provinces and Gaul: the *XV* and *XXII Primigenia*, their numbering suggesting they were twinned with Gaetulicus's legions at Mogontiacum. Recruitment and training were probably supervised by centurions from the legions of Upper Germany, further extending the military power of its governor. The legions were named 'First Born', no doubt in honour of the birth of Gaius's first child, a daughter, with Milonia Caesonia.[28]

The provincial historian Josephus, free from the baggage that accompanied the judgements of Rome's elite, recognized that Gaius 'administered the empire quite high-mindedly during the first and second years of his reign. By exercising moderation, he made great advances in popularity with the Romans themselves and with their subjects.'[29] Many nobles might not agree. However, the emperor had ended the internecine warfare that had torn apart the elite after the fall of Sejanus, and sought compromise and accommodation. This continued into AD 39 with the appointment of Apronius Caesianus as his consular colleague. Following custom, he resigned his office after thirty days, and made the City Prefect, Q. Sanquinius Maximus, consul. This was possibly a symbolic act, as in AD 32 Maximus had intervened in the Senate to detoxify the conflicts between opponents and former *amici* of the infamous Praetorian Prefect.[30] Within weeks, the political equanimity was shattered. It was not to return.

A plot had been discovered shortly after Gaius lay down the consulship, and consequently,

'many of the foremost men perished in fulfilment of sentences of condemnation (for not a few of these who had been released from prison were punished for the very reasons that had led to their imprisonment by Tiberius) and many others of less prominence in gladiatorial combats. In fact, there was nothing but slaughter; for the emperor no longer showed any favours even to the populace, but opposed absolutely everything they wished, and consequently the people on their part resisted all his desires.'[31]

These 'foremost men' were former consuls. They were Rome's nobility. Furthermore, they had been imprisoned in the previous reign and accused of being associated with Sejanus. Gaius's rage went deep. These conspirators had been integral to the imprisonment and executions of his mother and brothers, they had been imprisoned for this and then Gaius released them. They were consequently obligated to him, having received his mercy,[32] and yet instead of loyalty, they had plotted the murder of their emperor.

Gaius would not forgive a second time. They were charged with treason, *maiestas*, and tried before the Senate. Guilty verdicts were inevitable, and they were sentenced to death. The emperor then read the documents detailing the evidence used against his mother and brothers, the evidence he had previously announced he had burned. It was clear that many of the senators had acted as informers, witnesses or provided information at Sejanus's behest. It was their actions that had condemned his family. Gaius summoned the Senate and gave a speech of which they had never heard the like. He told them the truth.

He entered with batches of the documents carried by his freedmen. He then began by praising Tiberius, the emperor who had persecuted his family, and then accused all those who sat before him of *maiestas*. He denounced their hypocrisy in criticizing Tiberius and Sejanus when they had been the ones who made the charges, provided the evidence and passed the condemnations. Dio had access to his words, preserved in the senatorial records. He said Gaius then 'took up separately the case of each man who had lost his life, and tried to show, as people thought at least, that the senators had been responsible for the death of most of them, some by accusing them, others by testifying against them, and all in their votes of condemnation'. He had his freedmen read out the supporting documents. He accused the Senate of turning Tiberius and Sejanus into monsters by honouring them, puffing up their pride and arrogance. Finally, he imagined Tiberius standing before him and advising his successor:

'Therefore, show no affection for any of them and spare none of them. For they all hate you and they all pray for your death; and they will murder you if they can. Do not stop to consider then, what acts of yours will please them nor mind if they talk, but look solely to your own pleasure and safety, since that has most just claim. In this way you will suffer no harm and will at the same time enjoy all the greatest pleasures; you will also be honoured by them, whether they wish it or not. If, however, you chose the opposite course, it will profit you naught in reality; for, though in name you may win an empty reputation, you will gain no advantage, but will become victim of plots and will perish ingloriously. For no man living is ruled of his own free will; on the contrary, only so long as a person is afraid, does he pay court to the man who is stronger, but when he gains courage, he avenges himself on the man who is weaker.'[33]

With that, he restored trials for *maiestas* and reinstated the use of informers. For their part, the Senate did as he predicted and honoured him with sacrifices towards his mercy and an ovation as if he had defeated a foreign enemy. In the emperor's eyes, he had done so. The Senate would learn to fear and hate him.[34] The speech was a turning point. The Senate had been humiliated for its hypocrisy, but so had the idea of a *civilis princeps*. The Empire was now a monarchy, and they his subjects. The resentment of the aristocracy at their loss of status and power was laid bare by the speech. The nobility's only recourse to the situation was either blatant sycophancy or plotting murder. Gaius had also reignited the conflict within the aristocracy, knowing they would tear themselves apart. It was now open season on all those who had co-operated with Sejanus, Macro or Tiberius, and Gaius demonstrated what he expected.[35]

Maiestas charges were made by the emperor himself against Domitius Afer, the greatest orator of the age. A 'new man', Afer had risen to consular office and great wealth through acting as a *delator*, laying charges of *maiestas* and claiming a quarter of the estates of the condemned after a successful prosecution. The accused's real crime was to have prosecuted a cousin of Agrippina the Elder for adultery and use of magic against Tiberius. For this, 'Gaius hated him.'[36] He now stood accused of implied criticism of the emperor when he set up a statue of him referring to his second consulship in his twenty-seventh year. Gaius took this as a pointed comment on his youthful rise to this office. After listening to the emperor's prosecution speech before the senators, Afer knew better than to defend himself. Instead, 'he pretended to be astonished and overwhelmed by the ability of Gaius, and repeating the accusations point by point, praised it as if he were a mere listener and not himself on trial'. He then prostrated himself on the floor as if more fearful of his powers of oratory than those of emperor. Gaius was supposedly melted by this display and acquitted him. Entertaining as all this was, the real reason for his acquittal emerged later. Afer had meticulously cultivated the patronage of Callistus, the emperor's powerful imperial freedman. No doubt it was pointed out that he was too useful as an informer and *delator* to discard. When Gaius was asked why he pursued the prosecution, he answered: 'It would not have been right for me to keep such a speech to myself.'[37]

Another to suffer for their association with Sejanus was the governor of Pannonia, C. Calvisius Sabinus. He had survived in AD 32 when charged but then absolved of *maiestas*, but now the charges had the full support of the emperor. He was recalled from his governorship and, along with wife Cornelia, indicted for *maiestas*.[38] It was alleged she had committed adultery with legionaries, including in the headquarters building. The charge was not doubted by Tacitus. Both committed suicide before the case was heard by the Senate. Gaetulicus, on the distant Rhine, not only knew he could not return to his family or the capital, but had lost his sister and brother-in-law. Nor would he acquiesce to a recall from his province, knowing he would be sanctioning his own death. Only the end of Gaius would give him a new beginning.

The emperor attempted to secure his position by marrying for a fourth time, but to a woman of proven fertility. His previous marriages were barren, resulting in his divorcing them. Caesonia had three children from a previous marriage and already carried Gaius's baby. They were married in the summer of AD 39, and his daughter, Julia Drusilla, was born soon after. Named after the sister he had lost, he loved both his wife and daughter without limit.[39] Jokingly, 'he even threatened to torture Caesonia as a means of discovering why he was so devoted to her'.[40] She was neither beautiful nor young, but both possessed a fervent nature with a ruthlessness to match.

The birth of Julia Drusilla ended Marcus Lepidus's imperial ambitions. The birth of a boy would inevitably follow. Rather than accept his role as the closest advisor to the emperor, he dreamed of being emperor himself. Pride and ambition poisoned rational thought. To repair his position, he entered into affairs with both of Gaius's sisters, Agrippina the Younger and Livilla. Both were married, Agrippina to 'a wholly despicable character' in Gneaus Domitius Ahenobarbus.

As a young man, Ahenobarbus had killed one of his freedmen who refused to drink as much as he commanded. On another occasion, he deliberately ran over a child with his chariot and when criticized for this by an equestrian in the Forum, he gouged out his eyes. However, as if through karma, he visibly suffered from poor health. He had heart disease, resulting in swelling from fluid retention. An odious husband might have been reason enough to enter into a relationship with Lepidus, but Agrippina had more pressing motives. She had a son, born in AD 37, Lucius Domitius Ahenobarbus, known to history as Nero. Should Gaius die without an heir, he would be able to claim the throne. Marriage with Lepidus was an attractive proposal, but it would require two deaths: those of her husband and her brother. In Roman law, a divorced husband kept the children. This was not an option for Agrippina.[41]

The motivations of Livilla are difficult to reconstruct. She was married to M. Vinicius, described as a mild and gentle character as well as an elegant orator. His father and grandfather were consuls, but his nobility paled in comparison to the heritage of Lepidus. However, his nephew, L. Annius Vinicianus, was a close friend of Lepidus. Ahenobarbus, Vinicius and Vinicianus were to survive the conspiracy, indicating they were not involved, otherwise the emperor would have destroyed them. Livilla had no children, and her position would not have improved had Lepidus ascended the throne with Agrippina as his consort. She possibly hoped he would marry her, instead of her sister.[42]

The details of the conspiracy are vague. Successful plots are written about in detail, the conspirators ready to publicize their role and gain credit for their actions in overcoming 'tyranny'. Nobody wanted to be associated with failure or face execution for treason, so the facts were buried or distorted to protect the guilty. Lepidus and the two sisters planned to murder Gaius with their own hands, each keeping a dagger with which to deal the fatal blows. He was the leader of the conspiracy, as it was described by Suetonius as being 'headed by Lepidus and Gaetulicus', the pair clearly placed in order of importance.[43]

The greatest threats to an emperor always came from those in close physical proximity to him and from military commands. The sisters and their former brother-in-law aimed to cement their pact in blood, like the murderers of Julius Caesar. They were presenting themselves as 'liberators'. However, Agrippina would never be part of a conspiracy whose aim was to restore the Republic. Her power and influence lay in being a princess of the imperial house. According to Tacitus, she entered into this 'illicit relationship with Marcus Aemilius Lepidus as a means to power'. Lepidus would have prospered under a restored Republican constitution, but it is highly unlikely he would have risked all for the benefit of other members of the aristocracy. However, his influence with the emperor was on the wane. Gaius decided that he had been too lenient with Avillius Flaccus, whom he had exiled to Andros, and instead ordered his execution. Lepidus was unable to save his *amicus* a second time.[44]

The legions under Gaetulicus would provide military support for their claim, but Calvisius Sabinus no longer controlled the Pannonian legions and it is unlikely Apronius was still governor of Lower Germany; he disappears from the historical record after AD 34. Plans would need to be in place for the German legions to march on Rome through the Alps in case opposition was encountered. The Praetorian Prefects and the guard must have been expected to support them, possibly with the incentive of a donative. The emperor's German bodyguard of Batavians, commanded by a Thracian gladiator, was more of a problem as they had pledged their loyalty to him alone, and had no allegiance to the Roman state or its constitution. Furthermore, they spoke little Latin and so were isolated from the political manoeuvrings of court society.[45] The conspirators knew that the legal powers of the Princeps could only be granted by the Senate. Most of the aristocracy would rejoice at the murder of Gaius, but the consuls would have to introduce the necessary proposals.

In September AD 39, Gaius travelled to Agrippina's villa, at Mevania in Umbria on the Via Flaminia, 'to visit the river Clitumnus and its sacred grove'. The campaigning season was ending, so the journey was made for pleasure, as indicated by his retinue. The court was on the move. Actors, gladiators, racing horses, women 'and all the other trappings of luxury' accompanied the imperial party in preparation for an extended stay. However, his plans soon lay in ruins.[46]

It was here that the emperor was informed of the plot. His sisters and Lepidus had accompanied him, and it was possibly here that they planned to murder him. The full extent of the conspiracy was not immediately clear. The two consuls were immediately relieved of their office and their *fasces*, the symbols of office, smashed, supposedly – if Dio is to be believed – for not celebrating his birthday. Gaius was born on 31 August, indicating their removal was at the start of September. One is unknown, although the other may have been Cn. Domitius Corbulo, the father of the famous general. One subsequently committed suicide. For three days, Rome had no consuls until Gaius appointed the ambitious Aulus Didius Gallus, along with Domitius Afer.[47]

The appointment of Afer, a man the emperor hated, is astonishing even if the *delator* had the ear of Callistus. Gaius must have trusted him completely, knowing there was a plot against his life, and he would probably have to leave Rome. The most likely explanation is that it was Afer who had disclosed evidence of the conspiracy through Callistus. Possibly he had been approached on the premise that he was an enemy of the emperor, having nearly lost his life in the senatorial trial. The honour of a consulship would be a suitable reward. Tacitus enigmatically stated that as Afer grew older his oratorical skills diminished, 'but not his inability to remain silent'. The other consul appointed with Afer was Aulus Didius Gallus. He was also a new man, ennobled by his evaluation to this office, and his loyalty was bought. He was probably well known by Gaius, as he had been constructing two aqueducts for the emperor.[48]

Investigations were started, probably led by the Praetorian Prefects. Letters were discovered written by Lepidus, Livilla and Agrippina, incriminating them in both adultery and conspiracy. These were acquired by 'trickery and seduction'.[49] Three daggers were also found. Still, Gaius did not know how far the plot had progressed. Torture was then employed. Lucilius Junior was later praised by his *amicus*, the Stoic philosopher Seneca, for he 'did not tear away his loyalty in the matter of his friendship with Gaetulicus'. Seneca's language indicates that Gaetulicus was still alive at this time.[50] Lucullus also held a procuratorship in Alpes Penninae and Graiae, which commanded the Little and Great Bernard passes over the Alps linking Gaetulicus's German legions and Italy.[51] It was important for Gaius to ascertain what potential opposition he faced when marching to Mogontiacum.

It would have been vital to suppress any news of the arrest of Lepidus and the sisters. Gaetulicus would revolt if he knew the conspiracy had been discovered, as he would if Gaius approached with an army. It would also be too risky for the emperor to arrive at Mogontiacum surrounded by soldiers whose loyalty was suspect. It is likely the emperor sent an advance force of trustworthy troops and agents to the Rhine. *Speculatores* were specialists in such underhand activities, including acting as spies, messengers, assassins and executioners. The Praetorians had a dedicated branch of these soldiers. Their cover was a mission to recruit more Batavians from the Rhine Delta for the German bodyguard.[52]

The man selected for this dangerous mission was probably Servius Sulpicius Galba, who would replace Gaetulicus as governor of his province. The choice is surprising as his aristocratic credentials were exemplary. His ancestors populated the consular lists of the Republic from 200 BC. He claimed descent from the king of the gods, Jupiter, but took the greatest pride in his links to the poet Catullus. His grandfather had joined the conspiracy against Julius Caesar, and his wife, Lepida, may have been a sister of the leader of the present conspiracy. Gaius's trust in him probably derived from a shared childhood spent in the guardianship of Augustus's wife, Livia.[53] That trust was to be repaid well.

Once Galba and his men had left Mevania for the Rhine, Gaius followed, after a suitable delay. His departure was sudden and rapid in an attempt to outpace news of his journey north and arrive at Mogontiacum to crush any revolt before it had time to take root. Dio, in presenting the actions of the emperor as erratic and irrational, strips away the historical context, merely stating that 'he did not openly announce his expedition beforehand but went first to one of the suburbs and then suddenly set out on the journey'.[54]

Suetonius, employing a similar writing strategy, ignores the real reason for his sudden departure and instead refers to the publicized reason for Galba's move to the Rhine:

> '[S]omeone reminded him that he needed Batavian recruits for his bodyguard, which suggested the idea of the German expedition. He wasted no time in summoning regular legions and auxiliaries from all directions, levied troops everywhere with the utmost strictness, and collected military supplies of all kinds on an unprecedented scale. Then he marched off so rapidly and hurriedly that the Guard cohorts could not keep up with him except by breaking with tradition: they had to tie their standards on the pack mules.'[55]

The plans for an invasion of Germany were already well advanced, but again, facts are recorded out of chronological order. He had also summoned auxiliary units from the surrounding provinces to meet him at Mogontiacum to overwhelm any sparks of revolt.

A large proportion of the Praetorians marched with him. Normally, they carried their standards in front of each cohort, but their weight slowed down the advance, so they were carried on pack mules with the other equipment. Gaius 'travelled in a litter borne by eight bearers; and, whenever he approached a town, made the inhabitants sweep the roads and lay the dust with sprinklers'.[56] This was not due to conceit, as Suetonius suggests, but to keep the dust out of the mouths and eyes of the soldiers so as not to hinder their pace. Some of the Guard will have been left at Mevania with his sisters and Lepidus, whilst others would have been needed to secure Rome.

Callistus, Caesonia and Domitius Afer would have been trusted to safeguard the capital. However Gaius was concerned about the legion controlled by the senatorial governor of Africa, L. Calpurnius Piso. He was the son of the noble who was accused of poisoning his father, Germanicus. The legion was allotted to a separate legate, an arrangement that all subsequent emperors continued.[57]

Once Galba reached Mogontiacum, he executed Geatulicus. Unlike many nobles who conspired from base motives, Gaetulicus was a man who possessed a nobility of character and of purpose. It appears, though, that he had been caught completely by surprise. According to Dio, his death was ordered because 'he was endeared to the soldiers'.[58] The governor was indeed loved by his men, but this was not the reason for his death. Galba quickly set about restoring the loyalty of the soldiers to the emperor, under the guise of reimposing discipline – 'the day after taking up his command he put a stop to applause at a religious festival, by posting a notice to the effect that "hands will be kept inside cloaks on all occasions".' The legionaries soon resented his authority as songs made the rounds recalling the relaxed rules of his predecessor:

'Soldier, soldier, on parade,
You should learn the soldier's trade,
Galba's now commanding us –
Galba, not Gaetulicus.'

Parades, drills, and manoeuvres restored the effectiveness of the soldiers. The German army hated Galba, a hatred that would endure until AD 69, when they rebelled against him after he ascended the throne. When the emperor arrived, he held competitions and military exercises to demonstrate his control over the rebellious units. Gaius was particularly impressed, especially when Galba ran beside his chariot as he continued to direct manoeuvres. Praise and prizes were used to win over the ranks, but many of the officers were not trusted.[59]

The senior centurions were cashiered, but they were granted a pension.[60] Those implicated in the plot were executed. Some of the units Gaius had summoned to meet him at Mogontiacum had arrived late. Gaius had their commanders summarily dismissed as their loyalty was suspect.[61] News of the upheaval amongst the Roman garrisons must have reached the Chatti, who seized on the opportunity to cross the Rhine and plunder the affluent province beyond. Galba's prompt response checked the raid, and Gaius, at the head of the German army, counterattacked into barbarian territory.[62]

Once the threat of a revolt on the Rhine had been dealt with, the emperor informed the Senate. On 27 October, the Arval Brethren performed a sacrifice and gave thanks that 'the nefarious plans of Gnaeus Lentulus Gaetulicus against Gaius Germanicus were detected'. No mention was made of Lepidus or Gaius's sisters, which suggests their complicity in the conspiracy was not made public as investigations continued.[63] The Senate condemned the memory of the governor to *damnatio memoriae*. He was thus removed from history, his name erased from all records and inscriptions. His children, however, survived and were allowed to enjoy a senatorial career, the eldest becoming consul in AD 55, and all three had children of their own.[64] If, as seems likely, Gaetulicus was caught off guard, his private correspondence probably fell into the hands of Galba and Gaius. This would account for Gaius's move to Lugdunum (Lyons), the capital of Gallia Lugdunensis.

Although the campaigning season was over, with winter setting in, Gaius had a pressing reason for choosing to bring the imperial court to Lyons. It was the location of the imperial mint and had a large store of precious metals. Investigations continued, resulting in many executions of the leading men in the Gallic provinces. According to Dio, Gaius 'murdered some men on the ground that they were rebelling, and others on the ground that they were conspiring against him; but the real complaint was one and the same for the whole people – the fact they were rich'.[65] Those convicted of treason, with evidence incriminating them from documents seized at Mogontiacum or as a result of details elicited from Gaetulicus's officers, would have their estates confiscated. Dio also refers to 'a crowd of prisoners' and orders for the wealthiest citizens of the province to be put to death. It is reasonable to assume that Gaetulicus planned to seize the mint to raise a donative for the soldiers that were supporting him, especially as many veterans from his legions were settled there.[66]

Gaius summoned Ptolemy of Mauretania to Lugdunum from his kingdom in North Africa. Once he arrived, he was put to death. Ptolemy's past association with Gaetulicus when they had fought side-by-side against the nomadic Gaetuli was enough to convict him.[67] As a young man on Capri, Gaius had seen how Tiberius and Macro had destroyed anyone connected with Sejanus's network of *amici* and clients. Debts of loyalty and obligation made them suspect. This observation was now applied to many of those linked to Gaetulicus, Lepidus, Agrippina and Livilla.

The Senate was informed of the involvement in the conspiracy of his former brother-in-law and sisters. A trial was then held, where letters were presented as evidence of their treason and adultery, as well as the three daggers with which they planned to kill him. They were condemned by the very people who had longed for their success. Gaius sent a Praetorian tribune named Dexter to cut Lepidus's throat. The sisters were condemned to exile on the Pontine islands, where Agrippina the Elder had been starved and beaten to death. Gaius then warned the princesses that he had swords as well as islands. Agrippina was made to walk back to Rome carrying the urn containing Lepidus's ashes. This implies they had been kept at Mevania when Gaius had travelled to the Rhine. The order was a deliberate parody of their mother, who had carried the ashes of their father, Germanicus, from Brundisium to Rome; hers was an act of piety and love, in comparison to her daughter, whose impiety and betrayal had humiliated him. The three daggers were then placed in the Temple of Mars Ultor, Mars the Avenger. The temple stood in the middle of the Forum, a monument in honour of vengeance. The long walls were adorned with the statues and busts of famous Romans, culminating in that of Augustus himself, who avenged his adopted father and ended the rule of the Senate. Gaius walked in his footsteps.[68]

Once Agrippina arrived in the city, the praetor Vespasian, the future emperor, curried imperial favour by proposing that Lepidus's bones be denied proper burial in a tomb and instead be scattered outside the gates. He also proposed the emperor be granted a triumph for his German victory. For this, he earned an invitation to dine with the emperor when he returned to Rome, as well as the hatred of Agrippina. Nevertheless, Gaius demanded that the Senate not pass any future honours on himself or members of the imperial family; such actions suggested the primacy of the Senate over his constitutional powers.[69]

The informers and senatorial *delators* were now let loose on the friendship networks of the condemned. Charges of *maiestas* brought certain judgment, none possessing the courage to vote for an acquittal as this would invite a treason charge against themselves. Many enthusiastically embraced the feral atmosphere, hoping for a quarter share of the estates of the condemned or attempting to save themselves from a charge. Consequently, 'many trials were brought against them, as a result of their friendship they had shown toward his sisters and toward the men who had been murdered; even some aediles and praetors were compelled to resign their offices and stand trial'.[70]

Many men feared for their lives. Agrippina's husband, Gnaeus Domitius Ahenobabus, disappears from the records of the Arval Brethren in Rome. He took his son and retired to the coastal port of Pyrgi, where he died a year later. Livilla's husband also survived, and his sister's son, L. Annius Vinicianus, remained at court but considered his life at risk. The latter had been an *amicus* of Lepidus and harboured thoughts of revenge. He would be a leading figure in the successful plot to murder the emperor. The Annii had been involved in treason under Tiberius, and would be in the reigns of Claudius and Nero. Tigellinus Ofonius, Nero's future Praetorian Prefect, escaped his poor origins by becoming an *amicus* of both Ahenobarbus and M. Vinicius, but he was condemned and exiled towards the end of AD 39 for having had improper relations with Agrippina. Another charged with adultery with Agrippina was Seneca. He was sentenced to death, but escaped as an unnamed female told Gaius that he was already close to death. Seneca was recalled after Gaius's murder, but later fell under imperial suspicion from Claudius and Nero due to his close association with both sisters.[71]

The widespread conspiracy fed Gaius's paranoia and suspicions. Since Augustus, anyone charged with treason could be tortured, their rights forfeited by the act of betrayal. Gaius used it as a weapon. Showing increasing ruthlessness, he used terror to satisfy his need for revenge and intimidate opponents. His infamous cry was to demand that the condemned were made to feel they were dying.[72] This only fed the desperation of the Senate, whose sycophancy only angered the emperor more. Despite the imperial command, the Senate voted Gaius an ovation and granted his uncle the honour of leading a delegation to inform him of the award.

The Senate's embassy was stopped before it entered Gaul. Not only had the Senate not followed his order, but he did not trust those selected. He suspected some were spies or sent to murder him. Only a few were allowed to proceed. When they arrived at Lugdunum, the emperor vented his anger, the focus of his rage being his uncle, Claudius. He reminded him that no member of his family was to be honoured by the Senate in any way, yet he had acquiesced to the demands of his enemies. He threatened to throw his uncle into the river. Claudius, highly intelligent, though believed by many to be a fool, excused his mistake by pretending to be naïve and stupid. It saved him, but he was punished by a loss of *dignitas* in being made the last man of consular rank called to speak in the Senate. Later, a second delegation of senatorial envoys was allowed an audience. They requested the emperor's return to the capital. Gaius's reply was a promise he intended to keep. He shouted: "'I am coming, and this," tapping the hilt of his sword, "is coming too!" He was only returning to those who really welcomed him; namely, the *equites* and the people; so far as the senators were concerned, he would never again consider himself their fellow citizen, or their emperor, and forbade any more to meet him.' He had declared war on the Senate and the aristocracy.[73]

The emperor's suspicions were cast far and wide. The Guard received a large donative for their devotion, but the loyalty of the two Praetorian Prefects who would have supervised the investigation and torture of suspects was openly questioned by the emperor. There was no direct evidence incriminating them, otherwise they too would have been executed. However, Gaius must have wondered how Lepidus and his sisters had intended to escape arrest and death after they had killed him.[74]

The aristocracy disappeared from the inner circle of the emperor. Gaius relied instead on the advice of his wife, Caesonia, and a small group of imperial freedmen. These were former slaves emancipated by members of the imperial family. The reciprocal nature of Roman society meant their loyalty to Gaius was assured; or so he thought. Callistus probably played a central role in hunting the conspirators, and his power now knew no bounds. He amassed great wealth and inspired terror. Helicon, a former slave from Egypt, acted as a bodyguard, never leaving his master's side, exercising with him, attending him in the baths and sleeping in his private chambers. The most terrifying figure of all was Protogenes, who 'assisted the emperor in all his harshest measures'. He carried around two books called 'Dagger' and 'Sword', which contained the names of all 600 senators and the punishment they would receive if they failed to display sufficient loyalty.[75]

Gaius now displayed all the trappings of an absolute monarchy, modelled on the successor states of Alexander the Great in the Hellenistic East. This was the brutal reality of imperial power placed on display to all. He expected to be treated as divine. The aristocracy lived in fear and was removed from access to the emperor. Favours, requests and petitions, which they expected to be made on a personal and private basis, had now to be made through his freedmen. This was an inversion of social order, with nobles petitioning former slaves. Their status and dignity were offended; the nobility refused to accept this humiliation. The Stoic philosopher, Epictetus, a former imperial freedman himself, sneered at their discomfort. He addressed their shame: 'When you kiss the hands of other people's slaves, making yourself a slave of the slaves, all for the sake of these great and glorious honours and offices – what can you expect then?' The nobility could countenance no infringement of their privileges or dignity. Plots multiplied, fed by fear and hate.[76]

On his twenty-eighth birthday, 31 August AD 40, Gaius re-entered Rome to receive the ovation awarded by the Senate. Five months later he would be dead.

5

The Murder of a God

The Assassination of Gaius (24 January AD 41)

'"How am I a slave?" he wants to know. "My father is free, my mother is free, and there is no deed of sale for me. Add to which I'm a senator. I'm a personal friend of Caesar, I've been a consul and I own many slaves personally." In the first place, senator, your father could have been slavish in the same respect as you, along with your mother, your grandfather and all your ancestors down the line.'

(Epictetus, *Discourses*, 4.6–10)

Stoics believed that personal freedom existed in renouncing the political ambitions that forced the elite to serve the emperor, to flatter him and propose exorbitant honours. Gaius despised this dialogue and the aristocracy's craving for public displays of wealth, titles and offices of state. He made public his disdain for their obsession with status, rank and standing by threatening to make his favourite horse a consul. The joke was pointed and vicious. He ordered the animal to be stabled in a palace with a marble stall, fed from an ivory manager, warmed with blankets dyed purple and served by a household of slaves. A banquet was given in the horse's honour, where guests toasted him with goblets of gold whilst the animal ate golden corn. This parody of the fixations of the nobility was not an act of insanity but a hatred that by AD 40 had turned the emperor into a monster.[1]

His return to Rome was marked by an increased ferocity as he became aware of plots being formed against him.[2] Seneca, whilst omitting the context of his actions, describes the fate of a group of plotters. Gaius, upon being informed of a plot when attending an evening festival, took immediate action:

'[He] flogged and tortured Sextus Papinius, whose father was a consular [senator], Betilinius Bassus, his own quaestor, and several others, both senators and equestrians, on the same day, not to carry out any judicial inquiry, but merely to amuse himself. Indeed, so impatient was he of any delay in receiving the pleasure which his monstrous cruelty never delayed in asking, that when walking with some senators and ladies in his mother's gardens, along the walk between the colonnade and the river, he struck off some of their heads by lamplight.'[3]

In his parallel account, Dio does not doubt their guilt but also mentions an Anicius Cerialis, whom he identifies as Papinius's father, who was also tortured and put to death. This is another error by Dio, as Cerialis was still alive late in Nero's reign, hated by all for betraying the conspiracy against Gaius. Papinius had been promised his life if he denounced others, which he did. The emperor was not a man to break his word.[4]

Gaius was ruthless in extinguishing the flames of opposition. He sent Praetorian centurions to the houses of the victims' fathers and had them slain as well. Betilinius Bassus, however, was singled out for punishment, probably because he had been honoured as the emperor's own quaestor, who represented him in the Senate. He ordered Bassus stripped and tied to the ground so the Praetorians could gain a firmer footing as they wielded the whip.[5] His father, Betilinius Capito, a procurator, was dragged to the imperial gardens to witness his son's death. When he asked for permission to close his eyes, the emperor ordered his execution too. With his death inevitable and seeking revenge, the father pretended to be a conspirator himself and started to name some of the emperor's closest confidants as fellow participants, and he would have succeeded in his trick if he had not included Callistus, the Praetorian Prefects and his wife, Caesonia. Capito then joined his son in death.[6]

The loyalty of his wife was beyond question in the mind of the emperor, but the seeds of doubt planted in his mind germinated and grew, fed by his increased paranoia. His anxiety manifested itself in insomnia and drinking. Gaius grew increasingly erratic:

'[He] privately summoned the prefects and Callistus and said to them: "I am but one, and you are three; and I am defenceless, whereas you are armed. If, therefore, you hate me and desire to kill me, slay me." As a result of this affair, he believed that he was hated and they were vexed at his behaviour, and so he suspected them and wore a sword at his side when in the city; and to forestall any harmony of action on their part he attempted to embroil them with one another, by pretending to make a confidant of each one another separately and talking to him about the others, until they understood his purpose and abandoned him to the conspirators.'[7]

He trusted no one apart from his wife, and they in turn knew there was nothing to be done to discourage his suspicions. All three concluded that their executions were inevitable so long as Gaius lived.[8]

The problem for any courtier was trying to predict the responses of their ruler to their words and actions. Consequently, it was important for the emperor to act in a rational, predictable way so that they could foresee and calculate his reactions. Gaius's behaviour, though, became increasingly erratic, violent and unpredictable. Their trust in him was undermined by his lack of trust in them. Flattery of him was seen by both as mere performance, lacking integrity.[9] Gaius no longer believed his advisors' words were motivated by loyalty and respect, for as the Greek orator and philosopher, Dio Chrysostom, noted, if you 'praise a tyrant he takes no pleasure in it. For he thinks that those who praise him feel otherwise.'[10] Their dilemma was complicated by how to guarantee their own survival after the death of Gaius. The Praetorian Prefects had taken a solemn oath to safeguard the life of their emperor and his family. His successor was not only unlikely to retain them in office, but their very survival would encourage others to disregard their oaths and plot murder. Their best hope lay in dismissal from office, but with their lives and wealth intact. This could only happen if the successor of Gaius was indebted to them. Nevertheless, the Praetorians' soldiers remained loyal to the emperor, the son of Germanicus and great-grandson of Augustus.[11]

Callistus's position was even worse. He was hated by the aristocracy as a freedman, a man of lowly rank whose friendship they had been forced to seek for offices, honours and titles. His wealth, partly acquired from gifts from these aristocrats, was legendary. He advertised his riches as a reflection of his power and influence. His palace, for it could not be described as a house, contained a dining room decorated with thirty onyx columns. In comparison, the Theatre of Balbus, constructed in 13 BC at great expense, was praised for including just four columns built from this stunning stone.[12] The nobility despised the status of Callistus but also his role at the side of the emperor, having helped to crush previous plots and supervised the investigations that followed. According to Josephus:

'[Callistus] was the only man that had arrived at the greatest degree of power under him – such a power, indeed, as was in a manner equal to the power of the tyrant himself, by the dread that all men had of him, and by the great riches he had acquired; for he took bribes most plenteously, and committed injuries without bounds, and was more extravagant in the use of his power in unjust proceedings than any other.'[13]

The death of Gaius would likely lead to his fall, yet the emperor's survival would probably lead to the same outcome.

Gaius knew he had only captured those on the fringes of the conspiracies, suspecting that many more senators were involved. His solution relied upon the propensity of the elite to tear itself apart in seeking its own survival. It was carefully planned. The emperor convened the Senate and made a great speech granting its members impunity, saying he knew only a few of them still bore a grudge against him. He then waited. Many dreaded they were amongst the unnamed few whilst desiring imperial favour. Another session was called, attended by Gaius's feared freedman, Protogenes, the keeper of the emperor's two books listing the fates of all senators who might oppose him. The Senators flocked around him to offer good wishes when one of their number, Scribonius Proculus, who had been implicated in an imperial investigation, approached. Protogenes asked him: 'Do you, too, greet me, when you hate the emperor so?' The crowd of senators immediately fell upon the unfortunate man, stabbing him with their pens, being joined by the rest of the senators, who lynched him before tearing the corpse limb from limb. The horror continued outside the chamber, his dismembered organs and shattered body being dragged through the streets and placed at the feet of the emperor.[14]

The Senate, its prestige and dignity as soiled as the emperor's morality, then voted that Gaius could sit on a high platform in their meetings so nobody could approach him, and be guarded by Praetorians in the building. The emperor praised their demonstration of loyalty but then sponsored a law allowing slaves to testify against their masters. Both demonstrated the poison in their relationship: the Senate recognized that many in their number wished Gaius dead, so he was to be protected in their meetings, whilst the emperor sought evidence that could be used to destroy his opponents.

The emperor's uncle, Claudius, was then tried in front of the Senate, the charges based on evidence provided by one of his slaves. Gaius officiated at the trial.[15] Although acquitted, Claudius had to suffer the indignity of defending himself against the accusations of a slave. He no doubt feared for his life. The message was also broadcast to the senators: no one was safe from the informers and now their own homes were no longer secure, just like the palace where Gaius lived. Nobles would have hundreds of slaves in their houses, silent witnesses to their conversations at banquets, in their *atrium*, bedroom or taking a stroll in the gardens. The more explicit plans of any plot would have been made in secret gatherings, away from the public gaze but still inhabited by slaves. Furthermore, most slaves had suffered abuse and now had a weapon to gain their revenge and their freedom.[16]

In early AD 41, another conspiracy came to light. The consular senator Pomponius was accused of treason by Timidius, and he named the senator's freedwoman and mistress, Quintilia, as a witness.[17] Timidius is described as the senator's *amicus* in Dio, but his enemy in Josephus, which suggests that either their one-time friendship had turned sour or he anticipated the rewards for turning informer. This explains how he had access to information on the plot. The witness, however, refused to talk. Josephus suggests this was because the charge was false, but Suetonius refers to 'her patron's guilt'.[18] Quintilia was an actress, renowned both for her youth and beauty. At Timidius's suggestion, she was tortured, but as she was led away 'she trod on the foot of one of those involved, as a sign to be brave and not fear her interrogation; she would bear it with the courage of a man'.[19] This presupposes the existence of a plot, and the unnamed conspirator must have been a close advisor to the emperor. The Praetorian Prefects would have been present at an investigation into a threat against the emperor, but Clemens was only approached after this event. Callistus would also have been summoned to the *concilium*. The text suggests this conspirator was the Praetorian tribune Cassius Chaerea, who escorted her.[20]

Cassius Chaerea was a soldier of proven courage and integrity. When the German legions mutinied in AD 14, he was serving as a young and reckless centurion. The legionaries reacted to the severe discipline imposed by their centurions by whipping each officer sixty times and throwing their mangled bodies in the Rhine or over the ramparts. Chaerea, although surrounded by armed assailants, cut his way through the crowd and escaped.[21] Over the next twenty-seven years, he had risen to the command of a cohort of Praetorians in the imperial guard. He was no longer young, but rightly proud of his career and record. Dio describes him as 'an old-fashioned sort of man to begin with, and he had his own special cause for resentment'.[22] The historian is no doubt alluding to his attitude towards his sacred oath made to serve and protect the emperor. He had refused to join the revolt in AD 14, but was now willing to murder his emperor. He is named by the sources as the architect of the plot that ultimately succeeded where so many others had failed.[23]

Chaerea burned with a hatred for Gaius, mainly because the emperor publicly humiliated him in front of his fellow officers and men. Chaerea was very effeminate and had a high-pitched voice, which Gaius exploited with his cutting sense of humour, to the amusement of those around. The tribunes received the watchword from the emperor at each change of the palace guard. Gaius would call Chaerea 'a wench, though he was the hardiest of men', and chose watchwords that questioned his *virtus*, such as Venus or Love.[24] Chaerea was furious each time he received it, 'and even more so when he passed it on and was laughed at by his colleagues. Other officers joined in the game at his expense, discussing in advance, when it was his turn to bring him Caesar's password, which of the usual amusing words he would come back with.'[25] Furthermore, when the tribune had been granted a favour, Gaius would offer his middle finger to be kissed, which he then wiggled obscenely.[26]

This treatment was not the only grievance Chaerea harboured. Praetorians were used by the emperor to collect arrears of taxes to the imperial treasury, but Chaerea 'took his time over the exactions, acting in his own way and not as Gaius ordered'. The tribune felt the full force of the emperor's anger and was accused of being spineless. His daily contact with Gaius left him in danger, and the emperor had started to suspect his loyalty after the false confession of Capito.[27] Chaerea was also used as the emperor's torturer, Gaius calculating that he would be more brutal in exacting information to compensate for the slurs he had to endure.[28]

Quintilia was aware that Chaerea was involved and stood on his foot as she was led away to reassure him that she would not break during the torture he was ordered to inflict on her. Chaerea would certainly have admired her courage, yet he submitted her to horrendous torment. Despite the agonies, she refused to talk. He must have admired her bravery, whilst being angry and resentful at his role in the emperor's oppression. Quintilia was dragged before the emperor, her face destroyed and her body broken. Gaius was so moved that he released her with a gift of 8,000 gold pieces to mitigate his guilt. This act only compounded Chaerea's distress, as the monster had shown mercy whilst he had given none.

After Gaius declared his trust in the Senate had been restored after the brutal murder of Scribonius Proculus, and as a further gesture of his goodwill, he granted clemency for Pomponius, who was released despite his hidden guilt. The shaming and humiliation of the Senate was complete.[29]

The plot led by Chaerea would gain momentum, spurred on by the near exposure of another. There were several conspiracies at first, existing in isolation from each other. One group was centred on a Spanish senator from Corduba in Spain, Aemilius Regulus. He was motivated by a sense of injustice, for 'he hated unjust deeds with the hot temper of a free man'. He recruited to his cause his *amici* and others whom he considered motivated by similar aspirations. Yet his plot disappears from the historical record.[30]

L. Annius Vinicianus engineered another conspiracy.[31] A close *amicus* of the conspirator Marcus Aemilius Lepidus, he sought revenge for his execution. He also probably feared that his close association with his fallen friend placed his own life in danger. He was the nephew of M. Vinicius, the husband of Gaius's sister, Livilla.[32] Vinicius remains in the shadows of this conspiracy but had reason to wish the emperor dead, as his wife languished in exile under the constant threat of death. He had survived her fall, but like Annius Vinicianus, had cause to be worried by Gaius's suspicious nature. Both secretly craved the throne, as events after the murder of Gaius were to prove.

Another noble whose role in the conspiracy is shrouded in ambiguity was Decimus Valerius Asiaticus. Like Vinicianus, he was considered one of Gaius's closest friends, but he secretly hated him. He had suffered public humiliation whilst attending an imperial banquet. Whilst in a heavy drinking session, the emperor loudly 'reproached this man with the way his wife behaved in bed'. The shame touched this 'proud-spirited man' to the core, nor was he 'one hardly likely to put up with another's insults quietly'.[33] Asiaticus, a native of Vienne in Gallia Narbonensis, was a 'new man', lacking the ancestry of many other old Republican families in the Senate. Yet he possessed great wealth and an extensive network of senatorial *amici* and clients who would support his dreams of founding an imperial dynasty.[34] He was later accused of being 'the prime mover in the killing of Gaius Caesar'[35] and his actions at the time of the murder suggested he knew of the plot at the very least. However, Chaerea appears to have been unaware of his complicity, and Vinicianus later blocked the attempt by Asiaticus to be chosen emperor by the Senate, suggesting he was playing his own game, using the assassination to his advantage.[36]

Chaerea knew that time was against him. Not only was it increasingly likely the conspiracy would be discovered, but Gaius had announced he was leaving Rome to visit Alexandria on 25 January.[37] The tribune had considered acting on his own, killing the emperor when receiving the watchword or standing guard at the games. However, clear 'calculation made him hold back'.[38] The German bodyguard or other Praetorians would have defended their emperor, increasing the risk of failure. Chaerea was willing to give his own life to satisfy vengeance, but only if his attempt ended the life of the emperor. Therefore, he took the risk of approaching other members of the guard whom he knew held grievances against Gaius.

He firstly approached a fellow tribune who he knew would be receptive to his aim. Papinius was probably related to Sextus Papinius, who was tortured and executed by Gaius. Chaerea must have been sure of his reaction, as he was the first officer he approached. Next, Chaerea and Papinius met with the Praetorian Prefect, Clemens. This was a great risk because Chaerea clearly did not trust the Prefect. Although his speech in Josephus is fictional, the logic behind it was undoubtedly feasible. Chaerea understandably regretted their role as torturers, but Clemens failed to respond. However, the Prefect did not prevent him from continuing. Chaerea then mentioned the dangers to both their lives, but pointedly remarked that should Gaius die at someone else's hand, they would exact revenge on his enablers, with Clemens at the head of the list. This was undeniable. Clemens was ambiguous in his response, urging Chaerea to wait upon events whilst commending his purpose. He pleaded old age and rejected the opportunity to become actively involved, but his inaction was vital for the plot's success.[39]

Both Suetonius and Dio are clear that the Prefect was involved in a plot against Gaius, but it evidently was not the one led by Chaerea.[40] Later, after the murder of the emperor, Annius Vinicianus fled the scene of the crime and was brought safely to Clemens 'along with many other senators'. They had managed to avoid the rampaging German bodyguards and were escorted unharmed by certain Praetorians to their headquarters in the palace. Clemens released them after praising the courage of the conspirators and the justice of the deed.[41] All this points to a preprepared plan by men aware of Chaerea's plot and ready to exploit the assassination whilst minimizing the risk to themselves. The prefects and Vinicianus would also want to minimize their roles as the soldiers had sworn on oath to protect the emperor, whilst the senator aspired for the throne himself and consequently did not want to stain his integrity with the blood of his predecessor.

Chaerea's conversation with his commanding officer only increased his anxiety. His apparent ambiguous response and lack of commitment suggested he was calculating where his best interests lay. Consequently,

> 'he hurried to Cornelius Sabinus, a fellow tribune whom he knew to be an excellent man – a lover of liberty and therefore hostile to the present state of affairs. Chaerea wanted to get the plan quickly under way and thought it good to have Sabinus as an ally. He was afraid that Clemens might talk; and in any case, delaying and putting off the moment seemed appropriate only to procrastinators.'[42]

Both Suetonius and Dio give Sabinus equal status with Chaerea in the execution of the plot. Sabinus, as a soldier, may have had a different concept of *Libertas* to the nobility. He appears to have been disgusted by Gaius's lack of *virtus*, but his motivations are unclear in the sources. He had been unsure whom to approach and unwilling to take the initial risk of initiating a conversation that might rapidly end in his execution. Silence hindered the progress of any conspiracy. Chaerea's hatred of the emperor and fear of imminent discovery made him more reckless. Chaerea took a huge risk in approaching Sabinus, but he had made a wise choice in selecting his angry colleague.[43]

They next approached Annius Vinicianus, 'who was congenial to them in excellence of character and devotion to noble beliefs'.[44] This is a rather idealized interpretation of his nature: in a matter of months after the accession of Claudius, he would plot this emperor's murder too as he 'was one of those who had been proposed for the throne after the death of Gaius, and it was partly fear inspired by this circumstance that caused him to rebel'.[45] Similarly, Vinicianus feared Gaius due to his close relationship with M. Aemilius Lepidus. The Praetorian tribunes were aware that Vinicianus's vulnerability made him a prospective ally, so they understood each other's unhappiness at the state of affairs. Though 'for fear of danger they did not openly speak their mind about how they hated Gaius, they knew it in other ways and thus stayed on good terms with one another'. However, the tribunes appear to have been completely unaware of his separate plot.[46]

Understandably, the meeting went well. Sabinus's recruitment made the Praetorian conspirators plan for events after the assassination to ensure their survival. They also hoped Vinicianus and his senatorial supporters would be indebted to them for the removal of their tyrant, further ensuring their safety. There would be no need for a Praetorian Guard if the Republic was restored, so they possibly hoped the senator would ascend the throne himself or, through ancient nobility deriving from the Annii, would command the leading role in the Senate.[47]

Vinicianus, as an *amicus* of Gaius, had probably seen Chaerea suffer the indignities and humiliations for the amusement of the emperor. It was also widely known that he was publicly shamed at court. Consequently, Vinicianus asked the tribune what watchword he had received that day. This cleverly enflamed and embarrassed the tribune, but also tested his loyalty as this should have been secret information. This tentative questioning or in the circles of the educated elite, a philosophical debate, appeared to be the safest route in ascertaining the commitment of potential recruits at initial meetings. Chaerea deferred to the nobility of the senator, who assumed leadership of the group. Vinicianus clearly saw himself as another Brutus and chose *Libertas* as the password for the conspirators.[48]

The numbers actively involved or aware of the conspiracy now exploded. The disciplined tribunes, however, appear to have restricted recruits to several centurions and possibly some guardsmen. These were probably in the cohorts they commanded.[49] However, Vinicianus appears to have been less careful in his recruitment of fellow senators, risking all. As Chaerea was escorting the emperor into the Curia, a voice from the crowd of senators called out, 'urging him on and telling him to do what had to be done with the help of divine power'. He was at first completely shaken, thinking the conspiracy had been revealed, but then realized it was a voice of support from a fellow plotter or, less plausibly, from the gods themselves.[50]

Like the conspiracy against Julius Caesar, the numbers involved had become unmanageable; the fact it was not discovered was extraordinary. However, any reports would have come to the attention of those either involved in it, already aware of it or invested in its success from their very silence. Josephus reports that news of it 'had now reached many people. All of them – senators, *equites*, and those soldiers who knew about it – were ready and armed, since no one was in any doubt that the removal of Gaius was a blessing.'[51]

This is supported by Dio:

'There were a good many, of course, in the conspiracy and privy to what was being done, among them Callistus and the prefect. Practically all his courtiers were won over, both on their own account and for the common good. And those who did not take part in the conspiracy did not reveal it when they knew of it and were glad to see a plot formed against him.'

Just as in the conspiracy to murder Caesar, there was a small core of active conspirators and a much larger contingent who took a passive, risk-averse position.[52]

Callistus was aware of the plot against his ruler, and as a freeman owed a debt to the family which had freed him. This was not so much a moral debt, but a social contract where his loyalty was expected in return for his liberty. Furthermore, he was a pragmatist who always erred on the side of prudence, for he 'believed power to be held more securely by cautious than by vigorous counsels'. However, Gaius's increasing paranoia, impulsiveness and suspicions forced the powerful advisor to risk his position, wealth and life. Yet most Romans would rejoice at Callistus's death, especially the nobility, who hated and despised him due to his influence and low status. Gaius's death brought its own complications. A successor would not leave his predecessor's assassins alive, as it set a dangerous precedent. Callistus needed to distance himself from the murder or any knowledge of it. He knew he needed to manage the political consequences of the murder to secure his position.[53]

Callistus sought salvation in a marginal and derided figure, the emperor's uncle, Claudius. He did not share the blood of Augustus, and so was not considered a Julian. He was descended from Mark Antony and Octavia, Augustus's sister, through Antonia the Younger and Tiberius's brother, Nero Drusus. His brother, Germanicus, added some lustre to his imperial claims, but he had been adopted by Augustus. Claudius suffered the prejudices of the time that surrounded disabilities and so was considered stupid, which he played on to survive the machinations that surrounded the courts of Tiberius and Gaius. He had come close to death when he was denounced by his slave and tried before Gaius and the Senate. Most of the conspirators discounted any potential claim he had to the throne and underestimated his fierce intelligence; most, but not all.

Like so many, Claudius felt his life was endangered by Gaius. Callistus pushed against an open door by claiming he had been ordered by the emperor to poison him. As Josephus points out, if that had been the case, either Claudius would be dead or Callistus would be, having failed to carry out the imperial command. Claudius, though, was ready to believe it. The freedman had placed him in his debt. There can be little doubt that he was made aware of plots to murder his nephew. Plans were then set in motion to secure the succession of Claudius upon the murder of Gaius. He could count on the support of those senators who had prospered under Gaius and feared prosecution under a restored Republic or unsympathetic successor. Furthermore, the Praetorians would be against any restoration of senatorial rule.[54]

With the date of Gaius's departure for Egypt rapidly approaching, Chaerea was eager to strike, but he had to be restrained by his fellow plotters. They only had one chance and it needed to be carefully planned. Chaerea saw this hesitancy as timidity, not prudence. In the meantime, the emperor was celebrating the five-day festival of the *Ludi Palatini*, inaugurated in commemoration of Augustus, starting on 17 January. Gaius subsequently extended it to the 24th so he could incorporate his own mystery cult, where he performed.[55] Chaerea and Sabinus decided this was their final opportunity to kill him. A temporary theatre had been constructed in the *Area Palatina* between the portico of the Temple of Magna Mater and the imperial palace of Augustus. This large open area was dominated by statues of Mars and Venus, the ancestors of the Julii, and another to the genius of Augustus, which was fronted by two altars to this divine emperor.[56]

The plan was to murder Gaius on the first day of the festivities. It was Chaerea who 'first worked out how it could be done and set about it long before all of them'. Only the nobility was invited to the event, along with their wives, children and attendant slaves. There would be thousands crowded into a narrow space with only two entrances: one public from the city and the other leading into the palace and restricted to the emperor and his entourage. The chaos would be exacerbated by the emperor's refusal to allocate seats, with nobles sitting next to slaves and men sitting next to women. The emperor enjoyed watching the confusion and the indignant gestures of the privileged who had expected to sit near the front. The assassins would make their move when Gaius used the narrow entrance, as the crowds would separate him from his German guard and allow time for them to strike. However, the first day passed without a suitable opportunity, then the second, then another and another. Chaerea, despairing at the hesitancy of his fellow conspirators, called a meeting.[57]

A large gathering was sure to raise suspicions. Annius Vinicianus, as the nominal leader of the conspiracy, would have been present, along with the three Praetorian tribunes involved. Only a few others were probably invited. The problem was the presence of the Germans, as most of the courtiers surrounding

Gaius were either involved or aware of the plot. A strategy was thus devised to separate these loyal troops from the emperor as he left the imperial box. Many of the rank-and-file Praetorians also remained loyal, so the attack would have to occur away from the corridors lined by these men. The emperor's private residence within the palace complex lay towards the Forum, and he was in the habit during the week of using a shortcut along a covered corridor next to the House of Germanicus to get there. This was not guarded, as it was away from the public areas of the palace. This was where it was agreed he would die. Chaerea and Sabinus's cohorts were allocated for palace duty on the final day of the *Ludi Palatini*, probably deliberately by Clemens. The safety of Vinicianus in the immediate aftermath of the murder would also have been considered. The date was set, the very last one possible: 24 January.[58]

The night before the fateful day, the emperor attended a banquet, ate to excess and drank heavily. He awoke feeling nauseous, but he was determined to not let it spoil his enjoyment of the day ahead.[59] Chaerea collected his cohort, marching at dawn to the palace to receive his watchword from the emperor for what he hoped was the last time. He carried his long cavalry sword, denoting his rank, at his side. The area in front of the theatre was already busy, the nobility jostling with equestrians, freedmen and slaves to try to lay claim to the front seats that should have been theirs by right. The crowd rose in the auditorium as people took their seats or defended their right to remain.[60]

The imperial procession soon arrived. Gaius moved to the altar to sacrifice a flamingo to Augustus, but as his knife made the fatal cut, blood sprayed the senator P. Nonius Asprenas, who stood near him. Gaius laughed at the man's discomfort, his pristine toga soiled red. Asprenas took it as a portentous omen, for he too was involved in the conspiracy. The emperor was soon in good humour, his mood lightened and he talked affably to those around him. However, most were aware that the spilling of blood was an omen of imminent death, their only consideration whether it signified that of Aprenas or Gaius. The Fates decided it would be both.[61]

Gaius took his seat alongside the most prominent members of the nobility in the box. Behind stood Praetorian tribunes and his German bodyguards. One of the consuls, Q. Pomponius Secundus, demeaned himself by laying at the emperor's feet, occasionally bending over to shower them with kisses. This was an exceptionally humiliating act, the action of the defeated begging for mercy or a powerless underling requesting a favour. He had only recently been appointed to this office by the emperor, and his servility was evident to all. Gaius, still feeling queasy, probably abstained from the abundant food and wine, but the consul made sure to take his fill.[62]

Some members of the audience had two plays to amuse them. One was the performance to celebrate the divine Augustus, whilst the other was ever so real and brutal – the assassination of an emperor. Many in the crowd knew this was the allotted day; senators appeared incapable of acting in secret. Bathybius, a Praetorian senator, sat next to the ex-consul Cluvius Rufus, a historian of some note whom Josephus probably used to write his account. Bathybius leaned in to ask him if he had heard any news of the revolution. Cluvius replied that he hadn't, to which Bathybius told him: 'Well, Cluvius, today's contest is a tyrannicide.' Concerned that they would be overheard, Cluvius, quoting Homer, urged him to be cautious: 'Friend, hold thy peace, lest other of the Greeks should hear thy word.'[63] There would have been many informers in the crowd. News of the conspiracy had reached many, so Chaerea was right to worry that their discovery was merely a matter of time.

The crowd had settled once Gaius had taken his seat, only to erupt again when fruits were thrown into the throng, along with expensive birds that ran amok as people tried to grab them. Arguments over seats that had only recently been extinguished now ignited again over the prizes. Fights broke out, much to the amusement of the emperor.[64]

The morning's scheduled entertainment involved the shedding of much simulated blood: another ill omen to the superstitious and credulous. The first performance was a mime called *Laureolus*, where the leader of a gang of bandits is crucified, leading to a gory death. This was followed by the play *Cinyras*, about the founder of Paphos in Cyprus who commits suicide, presenting the opportunity for yet more gore. The actors were so keen to demonstrate 'their proficiency with dying that they flooded the stage with blood'.[65] The emperor's already-delicate constitution was probably made worse by the spectacle.

Around midday, Gaius normally retired to take lunch and bathe. However, the previous night's overindulgence was taking a heavy toll on his wellbeing, and he was undecided on whether to remain or rest in the palace.[66] The delay was causing untold agonies to the waiting Chaerea, who left the imperial box to consult with the other tribunes outside. Vinicianus, concerned that the impatient Chaerea would act recklessly, rose to go after him. He was sat next to Gaius, who grabbed his toga and asked where he was going. Vinicianus sat down again. He stayed a few moments before rising again. The emperor decided that, like himself, his *amicus* was suffering from the aftereffects of the banquet and allowed him to depart.[67]

Time passed; it was mid-afternoon and still the emperor remained in his seat. The conspirators had remained at their allotted posts, but they had finally decided to go into the imperial box together and murder Gaius there. The German bodyguard and those Praetorians not involved in the plot were sure to defend him, so Chaerea and his comrades knew that many would die in the attempt. However, there was then a sudden noise behind the doors as the imperial party rose to leave the theatre. The urgings of Asprenas had persuaded Gaius to retire to his private chambers. The guards started to clear the petitioners away for Gaius to leave, but in reality to isolate him from any potential saviours.[68]

The doors opened and out came Claudius, Marcus Vinicius and Valerius Asiaticus. Josephus writes: 'The conspirators would have liked to block their way, but respect for their dignity made this impossible.' Under normal circumstances, respect would have been shown to the emperor in allowing him to leave first, but circumstances were pressing, all three probably wishing to distance themselves from the murder about to take place. They did not want to get caught at the back and be at the mercy of Gaius's German bodyguards. Chaerea and his colleagues, unaware that these prominent nobles knew of their plot, were surprised and frustrated by their hurried departure. Claudius rushed down the main thoroughfare lined with imperial slaves and guards towards his quarters, probably the House of Germanicus adjacent to the covered passageway Gaius normally took to his rooms nearer the Forum. Vinicius had no doubt been informed of the need to leave as quickly as possible by his nephew, Vinicianus.[69]

Gaius walked down the corridor with his litter bearers and a group of prominent senators, all conspirators. Chaerea was at his side. However, other Praetorians blocked the exit from the theatre behind him. The soldiers 'shut everyone out, pretending he wished to be alone'. The German bodyguard was unable to follow due to the press of bodies in front of them as this was the only exit into the palace. This avoided a confrontation between the Praetorians preventing the senators and *equites* from leaving the theatre and the Germans. This explains the later fury of the German guard directed at the senators rather than the Praetorians, as they were probably unaware of who caused the initial disruption.[70]

Gaius turned from the main corridor down the covered walkway, where he found some boys from noble families of Asia Minor practising a Trojan War dance for the festival. The emperor stopped to watch and was so impressed that he was about to return to the theatre to watch their performance, when the lead dancer declined, complaining of a cold.[71]

At this moment, Gaius was approached by Chaerea and Sabinus for the watchword for the change of the cohorts on duty in the palace. The sources provide a number of versions of the events that followed. According to Josephus, Chaerea asked for the watchword from the emperor, and receiving another derogatory response, struck the emperor a blow between the neck and shoulder. The blow was not fatal and Gaius attempted to run away, but was felled by Sabinus.[72] However, doubt can be cast on this version as Chaerea had commanded the cohort on duty in the morning, meaning Sabinus would have requested the watchword as his unit was taking over.

Suetonius preserved two versions, in one of which Sabinus asked for the watchword. Gaius replied 'Jupiter', and then Chaerea struck him down from behind crying, 'Mark this', which is the traditional command of a priest performing a sacrifice. In the other account, Chaerea attacked Gaius whilst the emperor was talking to the boys. All versions then agree that there followed an orgy of stabbing as the retinue of senators used their hidden daggers to inflict their own revenge. Gaius lay writhing on the ground before 'he succumbed to thirty further wounds, including sword thrusts through his genitals'. Vinicianus is described by Josephus as one of the assassins, rather than a conspirator, suggesting he too plunged his dagger into the body of his emperor.[73] Seneca, in a different account, reports that Chaerea cut through his neck with one blow, and then his body was attacked in vengeance 'for public and private wrongs'.[74] It was not only Valerius Asiaticus who wanted revenge for the emperor's sexually predatory behaviour.

Some were sated and quickly left the scene as the emperor's litter bearers belatedly arrived to try and defend him with their poles. Others, however, had not had their fill and, according to Dio, even ate his flesh to prove he was not a god. Some arrived to revel in his bloodied body and spit upon it.[75] The majority of the assassins then headed for the House of Germanicus, where Claudius was hiding.[76] It was adjacent to the passage where Gaius had been murdered, meaning they could avoid the German guards advancing from the theatre. They knew they were safe there for a time. Chaerea was concerned for the safety of Annius Vinicianus, whose stature and nobility would be used to orchestrate events now Gaius was dead. Chaerea probably believed he would also protect them during the political maelstrom they anticipated would follow. He then left the House of Germanicus to rejoin his cohort, ordering the guardsmen to find Vinicianus. He was found and taken to Clemens, the Praetorian Prefect, who released him after praising his actions.[77]

Meanwhile, the Germans found the body of their emperor. Their anger boiled, for they had failed in their sacred oath to protect him with their lives. They had 'loved him, and when they heard of his murder, they felt it deeply'. Many of the Praetorian guardsmen who were not involved in the conspiracy also rioted, seeking the murderers of Gaius.[78] Groups of soldiers rampaged through the palace, hunting the guilty.

The target of their rage was senators. Asprenas was the first to die. He had blood on his toga from the mishap whilst sacrificing the flamingo at the start of the day. He was cut down, marked as guilty, although he was indeed involved in the plot. Next, they came across the well-built L. Norbanus Balbus, who was descended from military men of great renown. Balbus died bravely, attacking one of the soldiers and wrenching his sword from him before being surrounded and falling 'beneath a hail of blows'. Another, Anteius, had foolishly gone to enjoy the bloodied spectacle of the emperor's corpse, the man who had exiled his father and then sent Praetorians to execute him. His pleasure was cut short. Several of the assassins were slain, alongside some others who had the misfortune to fall into the path of the vengeance-seeking soldiers.[79]

Some of the Germans had returned to the theatre, which was still packed with members of the nobility awaiting the start of the afternoon session. The news of the death of the emperor had just reached them. It was met by a stunned silence, shock and, for some, grief. This reaction was probably not due to their fear this was a test of their loyalty or the rumour that he had survived the attack. Such a calculation would have taken time to process, but their reaction was immediate. The ancient sources dismiss this reaction as the simple expression of short-sighted disappointment by the women, children and slaves at the inevitable curtailment of their enjoyment. However, the murder of Julius Caesar would have been foremost in their minds, and the horrors of the civil war that followed. There was no public rejoicing. Nevertheless, the Germans wanted vengeance. They had surrounded the exterior of the stadium, and those inside could hear the tumult of the rampaging soldiers across the Palatine. None attempted to leave, but sat awaiting their fate. Then some of the German guards entered, carrying the heads of the senators they had killed and placed them on the altar of Augustus. At this the audience erupted, pleaded their ignorance, fell on their knees in supplication and begged for mercy.[80]

The rumour that Gaius was still alive gave hope to the Germans. Meanwhile, the conspirators were desperate to stop a massacre. One brave individual volunteered to enter the theatre. Arruntius Evarestus was a wealthy auctioneer who had a powerful voice. He put on mourning clothes and, wearing a face bearing a picture of grief, he entered, announcing that Gaius was indeed dead. He had no hold over the soldiers, but they now knew their future actions would not be rewarded or sanctioned by Gaius, but by his successor. Still, they could not completely believe what they had been told.[81]

An officer who had their respect was needed, but their commander, the Thracian gladiator Sabinus, was leading the unrest.[82] Instead, Arruntius Stella and other Praetorian tribunes informed the Germans the emperor was dead, telling them they should put away their weapons.[83] Arruntius was a man of authority, probably the joint Praetorian Prefect. He also knew of the plot to murder Gaius, but calculated it was in his interests to disregard it. The command was now obeyed. The Praetorians were attempting to discover who had conspired, not something the Praetorian Prefects wanted to continue. Valerius Asaiaticus then resurfaced from his hiding place to be questioned by the troops. He had emerged from the theatre ahead of the emperor, alongside Claudius and Vinicius, and disappeared into the palace, probably concealing himself in the House of Germanicus. Accused of murdering Gaius, he held his nerve, and as he stood he 'quietened them in a remarkable manner; he climbed up to a conspicuous place and cried: "Would that I had killed him!"'[84]

The duplicity in this statement fooled the soldiers. He had indeed not been present at the murder, but had plotted the death of the man who raped his wife. He was not going to admit his role in front of the enraged guard, as he too would then have been killed. However, his very public declaration requires some explanation. He was publicizing his part in the conspiracy, as news of his grand announcement would spread to the senators. The people who mattered would thus be aware of his role. A tyrannicide was sure to gain support in the *curia*, as a leading man in either a Republican Senate or the Empire.

Claudius would appear to have had a lot of guests in his house. We are meant to believe that he retired to his Hermaeum after leaving the theatre and then, upon hearing the tumult outside his house, hid trembling behind a curtain on the balcony. A guardsman named Gratus saw a pair of feet sticking out from the curtain and brought him out. Claudius expected death, but instead was apparently acclaimed emperor.[85] This is the story publicized by official imperial propaganda after Claudius ascended the throne. No mention is made of the other conspirators who escaped to his house. The Praetorian who discovered him was suspiciously named 'Thankful' in English, and it stretches credibility that a man of such lowly rank would possess the necessary poise to acclaim an emperor.

It is more likely that Claudius's 'capture' by a group of soldiers was prearranged. Claudius or Callistus had the wealth to reward these men later. Many Praetorians had gathered in the open area in front of the palace. It was evident to all that they were redundant in a restored Republic. They needed an emperor who would be in their debt, who 'would probably honour them for it and reward them with handouts. That was the plan.' The two Praetorian Prefects and those tribunes involved in the conspiracy had departed to address the Senate. A vacuum now existed, which was about to be filled. The soldiers flocked around Claudius, placed him in a litter and carried him to the Praetorian camp, where they declared him emperor. Onlookers who saw Claudius rushed through the streets, mistakenly believing he was being taken to a certain death. A military coup had thus been successfully completed whilst the senators gathered to rejoice at their reborn freedoms and the restoration of liberty.[86]

The same naivety, arrogance and lack of planning that beset the conspirators after the murder of Julius Caesar, now destroyed the diminishing chances of success of the plotters after the assassination of Gaius. As Cassius, a realist in the art of politics, deferred to the *dignitas* of Brutus, so Chaerea submitted to the nobility of the senators who talked, made speeches and passed decrees whilst Claudius consolidated his position.

The consul, Q. Pomponius Secundus, convened the Senate 'in the name of freedom' on the Capitol, and not in the Senate House as it bore the mark of the imperial family. The Capitol, raised above the Forum, was also easier to defend. The state treasury was transferred there, guarded by the three Urban cohorts commanded by the City Prefect. Some Praetorians also joined Chaerea and Sabinus there, along with both Praetorian Prefects. News of Claudius's acclamation had reached them, but they felt safe, supported by their soldiers and protected by their nobility.[87]

The meeting began with a speech from the consul, Gnaeus Sentius Saturninus. He described all *princeps* as tyrants and compared the assassins to the heroic tyrannicides of Julius Caesar. As he began, calling for the restoration of the Republic and praising Chaerea, a senator noticed a ring on the man's finger which was engraved with a portrait of Gaius. These were given by the emperor to his most esteemed *amici*. The senator stood and pulled it from the consul's hand, and then threw it on the floor. Just as Pomponius had fawned at the feet of Gaius only hours before, so Saturninus had been a major beneficiary of imperial favour.[88]

Others stood, offered grandiose speeches and made proposals, all to be voted on, and all out of touch with reality. Some wanted to condemn all members of the Julian family, including Julius Caesar and Augustus. This *damnatio memoriae* would have involved the destruction of all their temples, inscriptions and the palace itself, constituting the complete dismantling of the imperial cult. Others, however, wanted the imperial system to continue, but with the emperor elected by the Senate. Prominent members of the aristocracy no doubt backed this proposal. They met in a spirit of arrogance, believing mistakenly that they already held the reins of power, united by hatred of Gaius but divided in their motivations and aims.[89]

The session was only completed when all had had their say and night had fallen. Chaerea then asked the consuls, as the supreme military commanders in the Republic, for the watchword. In imitation of the famous tyrannicides Brutus and Cassius, they gave it as 'Liberty'. This had been the secret code word for the conspirators. The Urban cohorts then marched off to guard the Capitol and take control of the Forum.[90]

The leaders then met to decide the fate of Caesonia and her baby daughter. They had planned in detail the murder of Gaius, but little thought had been dedicated to controlling subsequent events. This is probably because Chaerea took the lead in planning the murder, as the risks were mostly his after he had submitted to the nobility of Vinicianus. Vinicianus had his own plans, which did not involve the restoration of the Republic. Yet other conspirators wanted to return to the rule of the aristocracy, whilst some dreamt of the imperial throne themselves. Divided in purpose, they would fall.[91]

Chaerea possessed a soldier's attitude to the situation. They were at war with the Julian *gens*. He urged that Caesonia and her child must die, as the line would present a continued threat to the Republic, and, incidentally, his life. Whilst Antony had been spared, Caesonia must die. Others considered it too cruel to kill a woman and baby who were blameless. Such a comment produced objections that Caesonia had turned Gaius mad by giving him an aphrodisiac or that she was his enabler, using her influence to consolidate support for the emperor. It was eventually decided that they should die, but none of the conspirators wanted the ignominy attached to committing the act. Instead, they approached another Praetorian tribune, Lupus, who wanted the glory of being part of the successful restoration of freedom. He was also related to the Praetorian Prefect Clemens, and Chaerea calculated that the prefect would protect him from any consequences.[92]

Lupus hurriedly left with some centurions, eager to complete his task. They found Caesonia lying over the body of her husband, covered in his blood. Her daughter lay beside her. In her misery, Caesonia cried: 'I warned you, I warned you again and again.' Some said that she was condemning her husband's behaviour, which appears unlikely in their close, devoted relationship. More likely, she had urged Gaius to act against those whom they suspected, but he was restrained by a lack of evidence. When she heard the footsteps of the approaching soldiers, she looked up and told them to come close to see what they had done to their emperor. She then noted their resolute stance and realized their intent. She met her end with courage, urging Lupus to make hers a quick death. 'Don't wait,' she told him, 'finish the act of the drama you have written for us.' Mercifully, she died before seeing her baby picked up and smashed against a wall.[93]

It was decided to send a delegation to Claudius, asserting the supremacy of the Senate and stressing their willingness to use force to defend freedom. Two tribunes of the people headed the party, as they were legally sacrosanct from any form of violence whilst in office. The senators requested Claudius leave the Praetorian fortress and attend the Senate, where he could present arguments to support his claims and, if necessary, have the legal powers conferred on him by the sovereign authority. They warned him that he was not a descendant of Augustus, so had no greater right to the throne than others sat in the Senate. The two tribunes, surrounded by thousands of Praetorians, knew where true power lay and fell on their knees before Claudius to deliver a personal message, begging him not to bring civil war to the streets of the city. They were later amply rewarded for this show of deference. Q. Veranius was made praetor, probably in AD 42, followed by consul in AD 49. His colleague, Sertorius Brocchus, was made a governor in an eastern province by Claudius.[94]

Claudius was never a fool and knew he held the position of strength militarily, if not politically. However, he did not want to start his reign stained by the blood of the Senate or innocent civilians, so he consulted his advisors as to how he should respond to the Senate's request. The most prominent of these men was Herod Agrippa, the king of Judea and grandson of Herod the Great. He was a close friend of Gaius and so, upon hearing of his murder, he recovered the body, quickly cremated his remains on an improvised pyre and buried it in a shallow grave in the Lamian Gardens on the Esquiline Hill. However, if he had hoped to appease the emperor's restless spirit, he failed. Agrippina and Livilla, on their recall from exile, exhumed his remains and entombed them, probably in the Mausoleum of Augustus. Subsequently, the area was to be avoided at night, for 'all the city knew that the Gardens had been haunted until then by his ghost, and that something horrible appeared every night at the scene of his murder until at last the building burned down'.[95]

Herod Agrippa then calculated who was going to win the confrontation between Claudius and the Senate. The retention of his kingdom probably depended upon this choice. He firstly quickly made his way to the Praetorian fortress, determining that Claudius was in effect already emperor, having 9,000 Praetorians willing to fight for him.[96]

Claudius declined the Senate's invitation to join them. There, isolated from his support, it is likely Chaerea would have ended Claudius's claim with the edge of his sword. Instead, Claudius claimed he was kidnapped by the Praetorians and held against his will. Consequently, he was unable to attend the meeting. Herod Agrippa was delegated to return with the envoys to report back to the Senate. Immediately, a huge donative of 15,000 sesterces was promised to each member of the guard, whereupon Claudius received their oath of loyalty. The donative was sure to undermine the loyalty of the Urban Cohorts to the senatorial cause. A new Praetorian Prefect was appointed in Rufrius Pollio. Clemens and Stella remained with the Senate, commanders without a force to command.[97]

The embassy returned to the Senate and gave Claudius's response. Herod Agrippa was asked his opinion, which was that the Senate needed 'soldiers and weapons to protect them'. He was told the Urban Cohorts were at their disposal and they intended to train and arm slaves in return for their freedom. This was delusional, as Herod Agrippa made clear. The Praetorians were disciplined, well-armed soldiers who would easily overcome a rabble. Indignant, the Senate sent another delegation with Herod Agrippa, threatening war unless Claudius relinquish his claims. However, Claudius knew the Senate's position was untenable. He offered peace or war. If the Senate chose peace, then he promised to rule with the aristocracy, a monarchy in name only. However, should there be war, he only asked that it be fought outside the city to avoid a massacre.[98]

As the night drew on, Claudius's position strengthened whilst the Senate was drained of support. The donative had its effect. Six thousand *Vigiles* of the Night Watch marched into the Praetorian camp, as did the rowers of the imperial fleet based on the island in the Tiber and many gladiators. Many senators quickly realized the impossibility of their situation. The Forum had been filled by a hostile crowd, demanding the murderers of Gaius be punished. They 'resented the Senate, they saw the emperors as a curb on its rapacity and a protection for themselves. They were delighted at the seizure of Claudius, believing that if he became emperor, he would save them from the sort of civil strife there had been in the days of Pompey.' During the night, most of the senators went into hiding in the city or fled to their country villas. When the Senate was recalled at dawn, only 100 returned; over 500 had abandoned the cause of liberty.[99]

The support of the Urban Cohorts had also collapsed. They faced certain death in the looming conflict with the Praetorians and their military allies. They demanded that the Senate choose a single commander-in-chief, an *imperator*. Chaos ensued as the aspirations, greed and ambitions of the leading nobles overflowed in desperate bids to win support. They stood on their illustrious nobility and marriage connections, considering themselves better candidates for the throne than Claudius.

M. Vinicius's claim was frustrated by the two consuls, who used various procedures to counter his move. With the death of Gnaeus Domitius Ahenobarbus, the husband of Agrippina, Vinicius was now the only male with strong links to the imperial house, through his wife, Livilla. He was no doubt supported by Vinicianus, who in turn was proposed but, unsuccessful, managed to undermine the claims of Valerius Asiaticus, who admitted his part in the assassination and 'claimed the glory for it'. The Senate was paralyzed by division, impotent before the ambitions of the leading nobles. Rivalries left it powerless. There were others on the distant frontiers of the Empire who had a greater claim, but they were unaware of the murder of the emperor. Ser. Sulpicius Galba in Upper Germany had an impeccable lineage and a proven military record, as did Appius Junius Silanus in Hispania Citerior. Of more recent nobility was the family of A. Plautius in Pannonia. Another descendant of great Republican families was the highly ambitious L. Arruntius Camillus Scribonianus in Dalmatia. Both Galba and Camillus were urged to seize the moment, but much to Claudius's relief, they all acquiesced in his seizure of the throne, knowing any move on their part would inevitably lead to civil war.

However, it was the donative promised by the new emperor to their troops which was probably a greater factor in curbing their ambitions.[100]

Chaerea assumed the leadership that was lacking amongst his supposed superiors. He called for the Urban Cohorts to assemble so that he could address them. The ranks should have been respectfully silent when he raised his hand, but the soldiers shouted him down. This was mutiny. He must have recalled his brush with death at the hands of rebellious legionaries in Germany in AD 14. He was furious. The soldiers, understandably frustrated with the inaction of the Senate, demanded an emperor. The tribune thundered that 'If they wanted an emperor, he'd give them one' and asked someone to bring the password from Eutychus, a charioteer from the Green faction which Gaius had supported. This was an insult as they had been ordered by the emperor to carry out the demeaning task of building stables for his horses, including the great Incitatus, who was nearly appointed a consul. They had been humiliated then and would be again if they abandoned the Senate. Chaerea then challenged them to bring him the head of Claudius. How monstrous it was, he declared, to kill a madman and replace him with an idiot.[101]

The Urban Cohorts knew they would be massacred if they followed this order. One of their number drew his sword and addressed his comrades, declaring that he would not fight his fellow soldiers in the Praetorian fortress. He marched through the Senate, bringing all the cohorts with him. They too drew their swords and raised the standards. The prospective donative must also have been at the forefront of their minds.[102]

The remaining senators fell into a panic, blaming one another for their ineptitude. Abandoned, their delusions stripped bare, their only hope was to beg for mercy from Claudius. At this, Sabinus stepped forward, denouncing them as a 'government of slaves' and stating that he would rather commit suicide than serve Claudius. He accused Chaerea of cowardice, saying he wanted 'to test Claudius' intentions thoroughly'. Chaerea defended himself, saying he had always been resolved to die to end tyranny.[103] The end of the conspiracy was undignified and shameful, each now looking to their own survival.

The senators now rushed to the Praetorian fortress to pay their respects to Claudius, led by the consul Q. Pomponius Secundus. At the gates, they were met by a force of furious Praetorians. The focus of their rage was the consul, who had initially 'summoned the Senate in the name of freedom'. They drew their swords and were about to kill him when Claudius, alerted by Herod Agrippa, came out and saved him. To calm the situation, he sat Pomponius next to him on the tribunal. He was a consul and so had to be treated with respect, even if they did not believe he deserved it. The remaining senators received a cold reception. They were shoved and punched as they attempted to approach

Claudius, who watched, enjoying his victory. One of their number, Aponius, was so badly beaten he had to withdraw. Some were close to death.[104]

It was Herod Agrippa who brought Claudius back to his senses. The murder of the leading members of the Senate would undermine his objective of seeking compromise. The whole Senate was thus summoned to the meet on the Palatine, the embodiment of empire. There, they fawned before Claudius, granting him the legal powers of his predecessors and praising him for his clemency. Claudius had seized power in less than twenty-four hours, a well-planned and executed operation. Callistus remained at Claudius's side in the influential post of *a libellis*, with responsibility for petitions. The new Praetorian Prefect, Rufrius Pollio, ordered Chaerea and Sabinus confined to barracks. However, they appeared on the Palatine. Claudius sought counsel from his advisors before making his decision on their fate.[105]

Chaerea was sentenced to death. He had broken his oath to protect the emperor and his execution would serve as a deterrent against future disloyalty. However, Sabinus, as guilty as Chaerea on these counts, was spared and allowed to remain as a tribune in the guard. The two Praetorian Prefects, as guilty of treason as those who wielded the daggers, were merely dismissed. Clemens's son also served as Praetorian Prefect in AD 70, a post his father held 'with distinction', according to senatorial historian Tacitus. His daughter was chosen as a wife by the emperor Vespasian for his son, Titus. The difference in the conspirators' fates lay partly in Chaerea's determination to kill Claudius. Lupus was also to die. Following Chaerea's orders, he had brutally murdered Caesonia and her baby. Many others were sentenced, including other tribunes, centurions and Protogenes, Gaius's feared agent of death.[106]

Chaerea died as he had lived. It was freezing as they were led out before a public excited at the day's entertainment. Lupus broke down and cried at his fate, but Chaerea reminded him of his dignity. They walked to the place of execution, followed by a huge crowd. They were told to strip. Lupus shook with fear, attempting to save face by complaining of the cold. 'The cold never did a wolf any harm,' was Chaerea's curt reply, the name 'Lupus' meaning wolf. When Chaerea's turn came, he asked the Praetorian if he had any practice at killing. He then felt the blade and told him to get his sword, the one he had used to murder Gaius. He saw himself as Cassius reborn, who committed suicide with the same dagger he used on Julius Caesar. Chaerea then knelt and stretched his neck out as far as he could to offer a larger target. He died in one blow. Lupus, however, lost his nerve and 'made a bad exit; he had not the courage to stretch his neck out firmly, and it took several blows to kill him'. The pardoned Sabinus kept his word, and rather than serve Claudius he chose death by falling on his sword.[107]

The nine-day festival of *Parentalia*, where Romans remembered the shades of the dead, began on 13 February. On the last day, offerings were made at the family graves and a midnight feast was held in the tomb of their relatives to placate the vengeful spirits. Places were left vacant for the deceased to attend and enjoy the hospitality of the living. The guilt-ridden also made votive offerings in honour of Chaerea, 'appealing to his ghost to be gracious to them and not be angry at their ingratitude'.[108]

6

The Claudian Civil War

Conspiracy of Annius Vinicianus and revolt of Camillus Scribonianus, AD 42

'Clemency has commanded every vice that wears the disguise of peace to betake itself afar: she has broken every maddened sword-blade. No more shall the funereal procession of a fettered senate weary the headsman at his task; no more will crowded prison leave only a senator here and there for the unhappy Curia to count.'

Calpurnius Siculus, *Eclogues*, 1.56–61, on the hope offered by the accession of Nero and the end of Claudius's reign

Claudius's reign was born in bloodshed and wrought by an almost perpetual conflict between an emperor with a tenuous claim to the throne and a nobility whose more illustrious members felt they possessed a greater right to the imperial purple. Many more felt vulnerable due to their involvement in the murder of Gaius, their support for the restoration of the Republic or their pursuit of the throne, believing the Julian house had been eradicated. Claudius, ironically, also needed to dissociate himself from the murder of his nephew when many knew he was as guilty as they were. Belatedly, Cassius Chaerea realized his mistake in overlooking the Claudian, but by then his safety had been secured by the Praetorians. Just as Gaius had publicly declared war on the Senate, so the Senate had declared war on Claudius in those heady hours after the death of Gaius. Claudius made a great show at reconciliation with the aristocracy. However, as the contemporary poet Calpurnius Siculus was aware, the civil war at the heart of the state continued, with the prisons full and the executioner repeatedly employed. More than thirty-five senators were killed during his reign, along with 221 *equites* and 'other persons, as many as the sands on the seashore'. Siculus warned all to be wary of the false smile of the 'Claudian peace'. Conciliatory gestures and imperial favour masked secret trials and sudden death.[1]

Claudius's main concern was simply to stay alive. He survived the reign of Tiberius and Gaius by hiding behind his books, cultivating a reputation for docility blended with abject stupidity. As the 50-year-old emperor was now the centre of power, he could no longer bury himself in academia, but he still fostered the image of a man dominated by his wife, Messalina, and the freedmen. This image was carefully worked and was preserved down the ages. A late fourth-century work condemns him as 'obedient to his stomach, wine, vile lust; simpleminded and almost doltish; lazy and tremulous; subject to the dictates of his freedmen and wife'.[2] These others took the blame for the imperial executions and judicial murders, where the accused were tried in the private chambers of the emperor, often without a defence. Seneca has Augustus warn the other gods in an imaginary trial on Olympus: 'This man, gentlemen, who seems to you incapable of shooting a fly, killed men as easily as you get a low roll of the dice.'[3] Fear made him ruthless. He had been complicit in the murder of his nephew, Gaius, whilst his brother, Germanicus, was believed by many to have been poisoned in AD 19 by the aristocrat, Gnaeus Calpurnius Piso.

Despite his professed desire to reign in the manner of Augustus, Claudius knew his right to rule was not derived from any blood relationship to the first emperor but rather came from the point of a sword. His first issue of gold coins openly acknowledged his debt to the Praetorian Guard. An *aureus* shows the Praetorian fortress in the background with a guardsman holding a standard below the legend 'Commander Received' (i.e. into the guard's loyalty). No other emperor so overtly advertised the fact he owed the throne to the Praetorians. The coin was probably minted as part of the issue to pay the huge donative of 15,000 sesterces to each member of the guard. The *aureus* was normally the preserve of the senatorial class, who would have resented the implication of its message as constitutionally the legal powers associated with the emperor were decreed solely by the Senate.[4]

The emperor's fear of assassination was extreme. Armed guards attended his banquets and accompanied him into the Senate, searched all those entering the imperial presence, served his food and searched the premises of those favoured with an imperial visit. Remembering the murder of Caesar, he even had the stylus case removed from every caller's attendant or secretary. Such behaviour was likely to cause great offence. Praetorians were also forbidden to visit the houses of senators.[5] He trusted few senators but relied heavily for advice on those whose interests lay in preserving his life: his wife and freedmen including Callistus, Narcissus and Pallas. The presence of a woman and men of low status controlling access to imperial *beneficia* further fuelled the resentment of the aristocracy.

Messalina married Claudius in AD 39. He was a grey-haired 50-year-old in perpetual poor health. She was possibly only 14 or 15 at the time, and their daughter, Claudia Octavia, was born soon after. A son, Britannicus, was born in AD 41. Had Messalina been a man, she would have had a greater claim to the throne than her husband. She was the great-granddaughter of Augustus's sister, Octavia, through both her mother, Domitia Lepida, and her father, M. Valerius Messalla. She worked to secure the succession for her infant son, and that meant keeping her sickly husband alive as long as possible. Fifty was considered old when the average age of death was around 30.[6]

Despite the initial hostility of the Senate to his ascent to the throne, the new emperor sought to conciliate the opposition. He immediately ordered the destruction of 'all records of those two days when there had been talk of changing the form of government. He ordered a general amnesty and forgetfulness for what had been done.'[7] However, neither he nor those involved forgot. To add lustre to the illusion of legitimacy, his grandmother, Livia, the wife of Augustus, was raised to divine status. His brother, Germanicus, had been adopted by Tiberius and married Augustus's granddaughter, Agrippina the Elder. However, he could make no claim on the Julian line, unlike other noble families such as a branch of the Junii Silani through their links to Julia the Younger.[8]

He recalled all those exiled under Gaius, including his predecessor's sisters, Agrippina the Younger, Livilla and Seneca. Domitius Ahenobarbus, the future emperor Nero, was restored to his mother's care. Also, Appius Junius Silanus returned from the governorship of eastern Spain, with its three legions, on the pretext of marrying Messalina's mother, Domitia Lepida. This was clearly because his loyalty was questioned. The marriage was an obvious attempt to ally him with the new regime.[9]

Despite these attempts to nullify the threats, plots soon emerged. Livilla's recall was brief in the extreme. Her presence around the court was a threat to Messalina. According to Dio, the granddaughter of Augustus pointedly failed to pay the emperor's wife the respect that she felt was her due. However, she also used her beauty to draw the attention of Claudius, even though she was his niece. They were often found alone together. Livilla was married to M. Vinicius, but a divorce and marriage to the emperor would improve his legitimacy. Roman law prohibited marriage between relations that close, but in AD 49 her sister, Agrippina, would marry her uncle after the Senate changed the law. Consequently, if Dio is to be believed, Messalina 'secured her banishment by trumping up various charges against her, including that of adultery (for which Annaeus Seneca was also exiled), and not long afterwards even compassed her death'. Livilla was starved to death, sharing the same fate as her mother.[10]

Seneca, however, appears to contradict this account. In *The Apocolocyntosis*, he explicitly blames Claudius for the death of Livilla.[11] Seneca had previously been exiled by Gaius for complicity in the assassination plot of Lepidus, Agrippina and Livilla. The charge of adultery was often used to attack the integrity of the accused, in association with an indictment for treason. Livilla was tried in private before the emperor, but Seneca was tried before the Senate. Dio initially asserts that the charge of adultery made against Seneca was false, only later to suggest it was true. A public trial would involve some form of evidence and statements by witnesses. A sentence of death was passed on him rather than exile, suggesting he was accused of *maiestas*. The emperor commuted his punishment to exile in Corsica.[12] Seneca later took pride in his refusal to save himself by implicating others. He wrote:

'I risked my life for loyalty: no word was forced out of me that I couldn't speak in good conscience. I feared everything for my friends, but nothing for myself, except that I may not be a good enough friend. I wept no womanly tears, I did not kneel down low and grasp anybody's hands to beg my life. I did nothing undignified, nothing unbefitting a good person, or a man. I rose above the dangers that faced me, and I thanked fortune that she had wanted to test how highly I valued loyalty.'[13]

The implication is that he knew a secret that incriminated his friends. Livilla's husband, M. Vicinius, appears not to have been involved. Messalina attracted much criticism for the fall of Livilla and Seneca, which suited Claudius, who escaped any direct responsibility for the death of his niece.[14]

Another conspiracy emerges from the narrative in AD 42. Appius Junius Silanus was executed, apparently as a result of the scheming of Messalina and Narcissus. Dio reports that after Silanus's recent marriage to Domitia Lepida, the mother of the empress, his stepdaughter took offence at his refusal to make love to her, and, supported by imperial freedman Narcissus, they concocted a story that they had separately dreamt that Silanus planned to murder Claudius. They had previously arranged for Silanus to attend an early-morning meeting with the emperor. Upon his arrival, they reported that he was attempting to force his way into the emperor's private quarters. Claudius then believed their dreams to be true and accused him of attempted murder, sentencing him to death. The Senate was informed the next day of his summary trial, conviction and execution. The story of the dreams of Messalina and Narcissus also allowed the emperor to escape full responsibility for the illegality of his action and the removal of a perceived threat to his throne.[15]

However, the demise of Silanus and the conspiracy of Annius Vinicianus were linked, for 'after his death the Romans no longer cherished fair hopes of Claudius, and Annius Vinicianus with some others straightaway formed a plot against him'.[16] Appius Silanus had many reasons to hold a grievance against imperial control of the state. His father had been convicted in AD 22 for corruption during his governorship of Asia. To this was added a charge of treason to prevent his *amici* from coming to his defence. His treatment is described by Tacitus as brutal. Tiberius himself questioned the former governor and ordered the family slaves to be bought by the state so they could be questioned under torture. The emperor thereby injured his defence beyond repair. He was found guilty and exiled, and the son lost his father. His uncle, Decimus Silanus, the lover of Julia the Younger, had also gone into exile, but had been controversially allowed to return in AD 20. Another uncle, C. Junius Silanus, had been publicly humiliated in the Senate by Gaius, charged with treason and forced to commit suicide. Added to those familial grievances were deeply personal ones. Factionalism quickly developed after the reign of Augustus, where family grievances against imperial power were passed down the generations to imperil the lives of emperors and noble alike.[17]

In AD 32, Appius Junius Silanus had been accused of *maiestas* along with a number of other senators, including Calvisius Sabinus, who was probably married to the sister of the conspirator Gaetulicus, with whom he shared the consulship of AD 26. His fellow accused also included Annius Vinicianus and his father, Annius Pollio, who was married to the sister of M. Vinicius. Appius and Sabinus were saved by one of the informers, who absolved them. However, the fates of Annius Vinicianus and the others awaited the decision of the emperor Tiberius, who wanted to personally attend the trial, though he remained in pampered seclusion on the island of Capri. He never returned to Rome, and their lives were placed on hold until Tiberius died in AD 37. The joint accusations against this group were probably based on a shared bond of *amicitiae*.[18]

After surviving the charge of *maiestas*, Silanus was surprisingly given the strategically important Spanish province of Tarraconensis, only to be separated from his control of its three legions through the promise of marriage into the imperial family. The private trial of Silanus suggests there was no concrete evidence against him that could be employed to build a material case in the Senate. There were suspicions and questions concerning his loyalty.[19] Silanus may have thought that his marriage to Messalina's mother, with her links to Augustus' sister, would provide enough support to remove Claudius and gain recognition as either emperor or allow the Senate to appoint the ruler as they had discussed after the murder of Gaius. Domitia Lepida's relationship with her daughter was strained, so he may have believed that she would support him. In any case, she survived her husband's fall and could take comfort in her connections to the imperial heir, Britannicus.[20]

The proximity of the death of Silanus and the conspiracy of Annius Vinicianus may imply that they were involved in the same plot. The execution of Silanus spurred Vinicianus into action. He had also become aware that the governor of Dalmatia, Furius Camillus Scribonianus, was planning to revolt. Vinicianus considered himself a doomed man. He had been a leader of the conspiracy that led to the murder of Gaius and was put forward as a potential emperor in the senatorial debates that followed. It was 'partly fear inspired by this circumstance that caused him to rebel'. He probably anticipated another charge of *maiestas* or a more private examination in the seclusion of the palace. If he had been inspired 'partly' through fear, then his aspirations for the imperial throne must account for additional motivation.[21]

Another prominent conspirator was Quintus Pomponius Secundus, who as consul in AD 41 had convened the Senate after the assassination of Gaius and advocated a restoration of the Republic. Upon receiving the news that Claudius had been proclaimed emperor by the guard, he had instead demanded that the Senate vote for an individual who was worthy of leading the nation. For this and his support for a renewal of the Republic, he had nearly been torn apart when he came to the Praetorian camp to beg for Claudius's mercy, only to be rescued by the newly acclaimed emperor and placed next to him on the tribunal in the place of honour. Yet he too, inspired by fear, joined the plot. He faced a relentless series of prosecutions by his half-brother, Publius Suillius Rufus, a notorious *delator* who worked hand in glove with Messalina. Many believed that he had 'driven Quintus Pomponius by a relentless prosecution into the extremity of civil war'. A further twist was provided by another brother, Publius Pomponius Secundus, who had protected him after the fall of Sejanus but remained a loyal adherent of Claudius. For placing loyalty to his emperor above that to his brother, he was awarded a *suffect* consulship in AD 44, followed by governorships of Cyrenaica with Crete and then Germania Superior. Claudius decided Quintus's reasons for joining the plot were personal.[22]

The indictment of Quintus Pomponius Secundus was in direct contravention of Claudius's proclamation ordering a general amnesty and forgetfulness of those events in the hours following the murder of his predecessor. The emperor's word was shown to be worthless. Many of those who supported a change of government or opposed the claims of Claudius realized they shared Secundus's fate. The evidence was overwhelming. They were all destined to be convicted by the very senators who a year earlier had cheered them on. The punishment was likely to be exile and confiscation of their estates, or even death.

Annius Vinicianus had widespread support amongst the elite, but he knew that the Praetorians and Urban Cohorts would remain loyal to their emperor. The news that the governor of Dalmatia was already planning to revolt would have been greeted with relief, Annius sending trusted adherents 'to enlist his support'. The aims of Camillus Scribonianus appear contradictory. He joined Annius because 'he had already been spoken of for emperor'. This desire is supported by later evidence presented at the trial before the Senate of his freedman, who was asked by Narcissus what he would have done if his patron had become emperor. However, when he publicly raised the standard of revolt and appealed to his soldiers, 'Camillus held out to them the hope of seeing the republic restored and promised to give back to them their ancient freedom'.[23] The mistakes made after the assassination of Gaius were repeated. Two separate conspiracies led by men who wanted to be emperor were united only by their common desire to replace the ruling emperor. A compromise position was probably agreed upon where the Senate would vote on their respective claims, restoring primacy to this institution. This was a fatal mistake as it undermined the support of the soldiers, who had no desire to restore a system that proved exploitive and corrupt, purely serving the interests of a small number of wealthy nobles.

Lucius Arruntius Camillus Scribonianus was the very incarnation of the privileged aristocracy. The consul of AD 32 was the natural son of the patrician Marcus Furius Camillus, who was descended from the legendary Furius, who reputedly was granted a triumph four times and became dictator for five years in the fifth century BC. He was honoured as the second founder of Rome for defeating a Gallic invasion after they sacked the capital. Their house then fell into obscurity, but their fame was revived by Camillus's 'unassuming' father who, as governor of Africa, was awarded triumphal insignia for defeating the Numidian rebel Tacfarinas in AD 17. His son, immodest in both his name and ambitions, was adopted by the prestigious Lucius Arruntius, who had been considered by Augustus as possessing the ability and prestige to become emperor. His adopted father opposed the Praetorian Prefects Sejanus and Macro, choosing suicide in AD 37 rather than submitting to tyranny. Camillus could also claim descent through the Scribonii to both the dictator Sulla and Pompey the Great. An inscription recording his career and ancestry recognizes his renown as the great-grandson of Pompey. This was important to him. Furthermore, the name of the Furii was so distinguished that his sister had once been betrothed to the young Claudius, but she had tragically died on their wedding day. Along with an illustrious lineage, Camillus inherited a family tradition of opposition to tyranny and defence of Republican values.[24]

Camillus sent a demand to the emperor and invited him to resign his power and become a private citizen. He 'felt sure that Claudius could be frightened into abdication and retirement merely by an impudent, threatening and insulting letter, without the need of declaring war; and Claudius did indeed summon his leading advisers and ask them whether he should comply with Camillus's demands'.[25] The letter was published by the rebel, constituting a public denigration of the emperor's character and martial abilities. The rumour that he was a coward was hoped to undermine the allegiance of the Praetorians. However, there was never any doubt that Claudius would decide not to relinquish the throne, as his death would inevitably follow.

News of the revolt led to a flight from the capital. 'Many senators and knights flocked to him', with some being 'of the highest birth'.[26] They took their wives, freemen and household slaves with them. Amongst this exodus was the *suffect* consul of AD 37, Caecina Paetus, and his wife, Arria, who was a close friend of Messalina.[27] They would have caught a ship to Salona, the provincial capital, and then to the legionary base of either the VII Legion at Tilurium (Gardun) or the XI Legion at Burnum (Ivoševci). Both were only a short distance away. As well as the two Dalmatian legions, Camillus could draw upon a large number of auxiliary soldiers. He had probably been in post for two years and had focused on winning over the support of the officers, but appears to have assumed the rank and file would merely follow their orders. There is no mention in the sources of a promised donative, probably as Camillus claimed he was acting in support of the restitution of senatorial government. If this was the case, it constituted a serious error, as the soldiers knew they would be rewarded by the emperor if they returned to his standards. The revolt only lasted five days.[28]

The soldiers were already angered by Camillus's declaration that they were to restore the Republic, and they 'suspected that they should have trouble and strife once more',[29] an unusual concern as the rebellion would surely lead to civil war and a confrontation with the Praetorians and Urban Cohorts. However, other forces were probably expected to join them, but these remained loyal to Claudius. The most obvious were the three legions in Pannonia, who could block their route into Italy through the Julian Alps. The imperial fleet at Ravenna also remained loyal, preventing Camillus from transporting his forces across the Adriatic. The soldiers soon started to refuse to obey orders: '[O]n being ordered to march off and rally around their new emperor, they found that some divine intervention prevented them from dressing the Eagles with garlands and perfumes, and that the standards resisted all attempts to pull them out of the ground.'[30]

Divine intervention may be discounted. More probable is the growing realization by some that the revolt was condemned to failure, with many of the soldiers regretting their actions and needing a pretext to justify breaking their oath to Claudius and then Camillus. The *sacramentum*, or military oath, was sworn to the gods 'to value the safety of the emperor beyond everything'.[31] Second-century sophist and writer Philostratus gives the following advice to any governor who 'intends to use force against the man who appointed him to his command and in whose best interests he swore to give advice and act, [that] he first of all must prove to the gods that he is breaking his oath without impiety'.[32] Soldiers believed their oath had divine power, and breaking it without just cause invited divine retribution.[33] The rumour circulating the camps implied the gods did not recognize the imperial claims of Camillus, nor the oath the soldiers had sworn to him.

The governor fled with his wife and supporters, probably to the port of Scardona (Skradin), which served as the main harbour for the fortress at Burnum. The counter-revolt probably started with the XI Legion garrisoned there, as Claudius later built a huge amphitheatre for the garrison. From there he sailed to the island of Issa, modern Vis. The island lies far from the coast and Camillus's ship may have been forced there in a storm.[34] The situation was hopeless. Indeed, one of his soldiers saw an opportunity to gain imperial favour and killed his commander, who died in his wife's arms. The lone assassin was well rewarded, rising 'from the ranks to the highest posts in the army'.[35] Claudius ordered that other soldiers who had led the revolt against their officers be promoted as a reward.[36]

The extent of the rewards for the soldiers of the two legions who returned to their original allegiance reflects the emperor's relief at the ending of the revolt and avoidance of civil war. Both legions gained the appellation *Claudia Pia Fidelis* (Claudian, Loyal and Patriotic), and their veterans were allocated land plots in Siculi and Aequum on a bay to the west of Salona, where they could settle after their years of service. Detachments of the VIII Augusta Legion stationed at Burnum may also have been involved in the revolt, as an officer was recorded as being honoured with a golden crown 'on return from service', a subtle understatement of previous disloyalty and subsequent return to the emperor's standards.[37]

A new governor was sent to the province with a reputation as a harsh disciplinarian: L. Salvius Otho, the *suffect* consul of AD 33. The father of the future emperor Otho, he was ordered to restore order in Dalmatia and hunt down supporters of the revolt. However, he was overly diligent in the application of this command:

> '[He] went so far as to carry out the execution of those soldiers who, having repented of having been led by their officers to join Camillus' rebellion killed them and they were put to death in his presence in front of his headquarters; though he knew well enough that the Emperor Claudius himself had rewarded these same men with promotion for the act.'[38]

These men had probably executed their superior officers, who had led the rebellion, and consequently undermined army discipline, at least in the estimation of their new commander. As a result, Otho fell from imperial favour. Whatever his justification, he appeared to have placed his justice above that of his emperor.

Furthermore, his actions seemed to be motivated by a desire to remove any incriminating evidence against himself.

Although the revolt had been rapidly crushed, many conspirators who had remained in Rome were undiscovered. Events would force them to act quickly and attempt to murder Claudius before they were themselves exposed. Many of those senators and *equites* who had been captured in Dalmatia were transported back to Rome for interrogation, torture and then trial. Their convictions were a certainty unless they turned informer and revealed others. Caecina Paetus was captured with his wife, Arria. They were taken to the coast and he was put on board a ship bound for Italy:

> '[Arria] begged the soldiers to take her with him. "This is a senator of consular rank," she insisted, "and of course you will allow him a few slaves to serve his meals, dress him and put on his shoes; all of which I can do for him myself." Her request was refused. She then hired a small fishing smack, and the great ship sailed with her following in her tiny boat.'[39]

Surprisingly, she had not been arrested. It is unlikely the new Dalmatian governor had already interrogated her and decided her innocence before the investigation headed by the emperor. Her freedom instead points to the intervention of Messalina. The empress and freedmen working for Narcissus later stood accused of taking bribes 'from some of the most guilty'.[40] The freedmen may have, but the empress was already fabulously wealthy. Those who had plotted to murder Messalina's husband would also have planned to kill her and her children. Arria was completely loyal to her husband, which did not constitute a crime, despite his choices.

Rome was subsumed in a ferocious investigation. Many conspirators remained free. Despite the emperor's promise at the start of his reign to refuse to accept evidence from slaves and freedmen, their testimony was encouraged and readily accepted. The households of the accused were put to torture. Some senators and *equites* were also tortured, when the law explicitly prohibited men of their rank from suffering the same indignities as a slave. Senators were tried in front of their peers. However, their guilt was already assumed, as Claudius himself 'read the charge seated between the consuls on a chair of state or on a bench; then he would go to his accustomed seat and chairs would be placed for the consuls'. The prosecutors included the Praetorian Prefects and imperial freedmen, led by Narcissus.[41]

In this manner, Caecina Paetus was found guilty and sentenced to death. As an act of mercy, emperors allowed the convicted to commit suicide in anticipation of a guilty verdict. This 'clemency' preserved the estates of the accused for their children, which would otherwise have been confiscated by the state with a portion allocated to the successful prosecutors. Arria managed to gain an audience with the emperor, either to persuade him to reduce the sentence to exile or allow him to kill himself. There she found Camillus's wife, Vibia, bargaining for her own life by 'volunteering to give evidence of the revolt. "Am I to listen to you," she cried, "who could go on living after Scribonianus died in your arms?"'[42]

Her husband was allowed to take his own life, but understandably, his courage started to wane when it came to accomplishing the deed. His wife then again demonstrated a fortitude and loyalty that became famous down the ages. She took the dagger that Caecina Paetus had chosen but could not bring himself to use, and instead plunged it into her own chest. She then 'handed it to her husband with the immortal, almost divine words, "It does not hurt, Paetus."' At this, he finally ended his own life. Then, determined upon sharing his fate despite the understandable opposition of her son-in-law, Thrasea Paetus, who had her watched and guarded, Arria hit her head against a wall and fell senseless to the floor. Coming round, she explained: 'It is no good. You can make me choose a painful death, but you cannot make it impossible.'[43]

No one doubted that many of those convicted were guilty of conspiracy and treason. However, the deaths and executions served to create martyrs to imperial tyranny that helped to inspire others to oppose the emperor, whomsoever they may be. Arria's son-in-law and her relatives became the centre of the Stoic opposition to Nero. Her nobility of purpose inspired Pliny, Cassius Dio and the poet Martial, who cherished her memory:

'When the chaste Arria handed to her Paetus the sword which she had with her own hand drawn forth from her heart, "If you believe me," said she, "the wound which I have made gives me no pain; but it is that which you will make, Paetus, that pains me."'[44]

Even the dead were put on trial. Camillus was known to have been killed on Issa, but Claudius wanted the conspirators' guilt proven to his enemies sitting on the Senate benches. His end was to be used as a warning to those listening and watching. For this reason, Camillus's freedman was brought before the Senate and interrogated by Narcissus. Galaesus's inevitable fate liberated his tongue, and he used the opportunity to exercise a 'great freedom of speech'. The spectacle of two freedmen sparring before the assembled Fathers would have been a curious spectacle, with many secretly sympathetic to the defendant and others covertly guilty of the crime he stood accused of. Galaesus had probably faced questions by the Prefects and senatorial prosecutors, then Narcissus took the floor 'and said to him: "What would you have done Galaesus, if Camillus had become emperor?" He replied: "I would have stood behind him and kept my mouth shut."[45] The implied criticism of the emperor who sat before them, and his most powerful freedman, secretly delighted the assembly, but their freedom of expression was limited to clandestine discussions in private. Galaesus's posthumous fame spread.

The blood continued to flow, with further revelations. However, progress towards apprehending the conspirators was slow until L. Otho extracted key information from a group of slaves, no doubt belonging to one of the senators who had fled to join Camillus in Dalmatia. He 'contrived to uncover a plot against the emperor's life' and was restored to favour. The importance of the material is reflected in the honours Claudius gave Otho, for his family were raised to the status of patricians and his statue was placed in the palace. The emperor felt that he owed his life to Otho, whom he praised 'as one whose loyalty I can hardly dare hope that my children will emulate'. The imperial panegyric was probably delivered in the Senate, to contrast his governor's actions with some of his peers.[46]

Claudius was set upon vengeance, and this resolve was transmitted to the two people he trusted above all, Messalina and Narcissus. Both sought out enemies of Claudius and destroyed them: '[They] and all the latter's fellow freedmen seized the opportunity for their direst vengeance. They employed slaves and freedmen, for instance, as informers against their own masters.' The emperor had made a solemn promise upon his accession to never allow slaves to provide evidence against their owners. To avoid charges of hypocrisy, the blame was passed onto his lieutenants. Rewards were offered for information, the households of those incriminated were put to torture, and their slaves, freedmen and sometimes their senatorial and equestrian *amici* all suffered.[47] Claudius was driven in his desire for revenge. The watchword he repeatedly gave the Praetorian tribunes was invariably the same verse from Homer about it being necessary 'to avenge yourself upon one who first injured you'. It was the same line he repeatedly used in the Senate; the threat was understood by all. Gaius had made the same threats, although more direct and forceful, but the sentiment was the same. Seneca had labelled Gaius a madman for attempting to rule without the aristocracy, but then condemns Claudius as a fool for attempting a reconciliation with them. The discovery of the conspiracy ended this attempt, with more members of the elite executed by Claudius than by his predecessor.[48]

Many of the plotters realized their time had come. The leader, Annius Vinnicianus, chose his own death.[49] Q. Pomponius Secundus also perished. There is no mention of a trial, so his brother may have used his influence with the emperor to allow him to commit suicide. The Senate, though, passed a *damnatio memoriae* erasing his name from all inscriptions, eradicating his life from historical memory. His hopes of living on after death were thereby destroyed.[50] Dio provides a graphic description of the slaughter that followed:

> '[M]any men, therefore, and women, too, were executed at this time, some of the latter even meeting their fate in the very prison itself. And when they were to die, the women, too, were led in chains upon a scaffold, like captives, and their bodies, also, were thrown out upon the Stairway; for in the case of those who were executed anywhere outside the city, only the heads were exhibited there.'

The dead included a serving tribune and praetor who had to resign his office before his trial and execution.[51]

The corpses were thrown onto the Gemonian Steps, which rose from the Forum to the Capitoline and Temple of Juno Moneta. They were close to the *Carcer*, Rome's underground prison, where many were strangled. The bodies were left exposed to abuse before the remains were dragged like those of a criminal to be thrown into the River Tiber. Romans believed that the souls of the dead bore the wounds that were inflicted on them at the time they died. Denied a proper burial, their disfigured souls were cursed to wander the earth for eternity. Furthermore, there would be no tomb to record their deeds, where their friends and family could remember their lives and respect their memory.[52] Some families whose loved ones suffered this fate cried for vengeance. They would not forgive, nor would they forget.

The body of one convicted senator was rescued from the Gemonian Steps and given a proper burial by his wife, Cloatilla, who was then prosecuted under the law of *maiestas* and found guilty but pardoned by Claudius. She was later prosecuted by her own family as she had arranged a loan from her brother to cover the debts incurred by her husband, but defaulted, probably when he was absent in Dalmatia. She had, however, secured the monies against her dowry. The brother then sued his sister to reclaim the money. The infamous *delator* Cn. Domitius Afer defended her in court, arguing that it was in the social interest for dowries to remain inviable. He turned to her sons and directed them to keep their obligation to her as she had to their father. He recognized their loss but asserted: 'Nonetheless, it is your duty boys, to give your mother burial.'The law was clear, so Afer played upon the pity of the jurors for her destitute children and their religious and moral duty that they may have been unable to fulfil.[53]

The case is important for two reasons. Firstly, historians should not assume all families acted with one accord from ties of filial loyalty. The varying fates of Pomponius Secundus and his brother act as a further warning against making this assumption. M. Vinicius twice survived the condemnation of his wife, Livilla, under Gaius and Claudius, and the fall of his nephew, L. Annius Vinicianus. Clearly, there was no evidence to implicate him in any involvement. Motives and allegiances were complex. Secondly, there can be little doubt that some conspirators were driven by financial gain, balancing the risks of failure against the prospect of rewards from supporting a successful aspirant for the throne.

Other families were embittered by the treatment of their mothers, fathers, brothers and sisters. Claudius attempted to break this cycle of inherited enmity by granting immunity to all the sons of those put to death, and some were given money after their family estates had been confiscated to allow them to pursue a public career.[54] This spirit of imperial conciliation was another false smile. The son of Camillus Scribonianus was allowed to replace his father in the Arval Brethren, but nine years later he was exiled and probably poisoned. His crime was to consult astrologers on the future health of the emperor. His mother, Vibia, was also implicated.[55]

Certain families revelled in their opposition to the tyranny of imperial rule, their fervour fuelled by martyrdom. After assisting his mother-in-law, Arria, the wife of Caecina Paetus, attain a noble death in the manner of Socrates, Cato, Brutus and Cassius, Thrasea and his family became the centre of the Stoic opposition to Nero and later Domitian. He was charged with factionalism under Nero and sought an honourable death, whilst his son-in-law, Helvidius Priscus, was exiled for treason. They and their *amici* did not join plots to murder the emperor, but instead signalled their opposition to tyranny through a refusal to cooperate with imperial rule.[56] Other relations who inherited enmities and political allegiances contrary to imperial interests took a more direct route. The sons of L. Annius Vicinanus would plot against Nero in AD 66. The Annii were involved in treason in the reigns of Tiberius, Gaius, Claudius and Nero. Asinius Pollio would be involved in the Piso Conspiracy and exiled in AD 65, and his brother, Annius Vinicianus, would lead a plot in the following year.[57]

The inquisition headed by Messalina and Narcissus was hugely effective. There was no repeat of a widespread conspiracy involving a significant number of senators and equestrians. Claudius sought to strengthen his position by removing potential rivals to the throne with links to the imperial house. Julia Livia, the daughter of Drusus, son of the emperor Tiberius, was accused of incest by the *delator* P. Suillius Rufus, no doubt at the bidding of Claudius and Messalina. At the same time, the Praetorian Prefect Catonius Justus was also executed. He had been closely associated with her father. The other Prefect, Rufius Pollio, appointed by Claudius upon the assassination of Gaius, was taken by Claudius to Britain, but was executed afterwards. These men were replaced by Lusius Geta and Rufius Crispinus, both of whom were 'faithful to Messalina's memory and bound to her children'. Messalina used her position as the instrument of Claudius's terror to strengthen her position and that of her young son and daughter.[58]

The Claudian invasion of Britain was born from the failed conspiracy. The emperor and his advisors must have decided upon it in late AD 42.[59] Conquest would raise the morale of the army after the revolt and add to the emperor's *auctoriatas*, so recently undermined by the widespread conspiracy amongst the elite classes. He was following in the footsteps of Julius Caesar. Yet it was a massive risk to leave Rome for distant lands, even though most of the plotters had been caught, exiled or executed. Claudius's visit to the war zone was to be very brief. His army was to be led by the governor of Pannonia, Aulus Plautius, who had already proven his loyalty by not joining the revolt in neighbouring Dalmatia. Rome was left in the loyal and capable hands of L. Vitellius, who probably also took command of the Praetorians garrisoning the capital. The emperor also took with him an entourage of nobles whose loyalty was questionable. Among them were M. Vicinius and D. Valerius Asiaticus. The former was alleged later to have been poisoned by Messalina, even though 'he was contriving to save his life by keeping quiet and minding his own business'. He was unlikely to join a plot involving Pomponius Secundus, as he had opposed his candidacy for the throne after the murder of Gaius. Despite rumours to the contrary, it is likely he died of natural causes, having been honoured with consular office for a rare second time, and was given a state funeral.[60]

Not so Valerius Asiaticus, who was proud and arrogant.[61] He too had been honoured with a second consulship in AD 46, but he stood down from the office, claiming that as he was so wealthy he would be in less danger if he resigned it.[62] The insult to the emperor was deliberate and calculated. He would have known that it invited a response. Asiaticus was a new man, ennobled by his consular office in AD 35. His career had been supported by his patroness, Antonia, mother of Claudius. However, his lack of a noble pedigree was counterbalanced by his immense wealth. In Rome, he owned the fabled Gardens of Lucullus, which, rumour had it, was the cause of his downfall as they were wanted by Messalina.[63] His wealth extended from his native city of Vienne in Gaul to encompass lands and debts of gratitude over most of the province. Any financial loan required repayment, not necessarily financial, but more often political in nature. He presented a significant threat. He had been actively involved in the murder of Gaius, then openly boasted about it. His candidacy for the throne was opposed by Annius Vinicianus, which probably explains his absence from the plot against Claudius. However, he retained a large body of supporters in the Senate and amongst the Gallic provincials.[64]

The imperial *concilium* met in AD 47. The plot of Vinicianus and the rebellion of Camillus remained at the forefront of their minds and fed the paranoia of the emperor. Claudius's closest advisors were few in number, but their advice was trusted. The imperial freedmen would have been present, including Callistus, Polybius, Pallas, Narcissus and Sosibius, who brought the first charges. Also involved were Messalina and the few senators allowed into this inner circle, Lucius Vitellius and Claudius's *amicus* and *delator*, Suillius Rufus. Sosibius warned Claudius:

> '[T]he prime mover in the killing of Gaius, Caesar, Asiaticus had not trembled to avow his complicity in a gathering of the Roman people and even to arrogate the glory of the assassination. Famous, in consequence, at Rome, with a reputation that pervaded the provinces, he was preparing an excursion to the armies of Germany; for the reason that, born as he was in Vienne and backed by a multitude of powerful connections, he had every facility for creating trouble among the people of his native land.'[65]

The speech, although fictional, does appear to be based on factual information. Asiaticus had been using his money and connections to undermine Claudius's control of Gaul. The proximity of the armies along the Rhine made this potentially disastrous. Claudius would soon afterwards allow many of the aristocracy in Gallia Comata to enter the Senate, binding these men in loyalty to himself when they had previously been bound to Asiaticus. In admitting these senators into the Senate, the emperor would ascribe to 'Asiaticus the vile name of that brigand, that portent of hate from the wrestling school, who brought home the rank of consul before his colony acquired the full benefit of Roman citizenship'. His son retained his father's influence and joined the Gallic revolt of Vindex in opposition to Nero. Claudius had just been informed of a plot against him, but chose to publicly demonstrate his composure by dismissing it as irrelevant: 'It is not necessary to ward off a flea in the same way one wards off a beast.' His choice of language closely resembles the words he later uses to describe Asiaticus. Claudius and his advisors believed there existed a significant plot led by Asiaticus.[66]

The Praetorian Prefect Crispinus was dispatched to Baiae on the Bay of Naples to arrest Asiaticus with a large body of soldiers.[67] Crispinus was later rewarded with one-and-a-half million sesterces and the honours associated with a senator who had attained the praetorship.[68] The threat was real, with significant opposition anticipated. Possibly they feared Asiaticus would arm his slaves to escape arrest. Instead, he was thrown in irons and brought back to Rome.

A trial was held in the palace before the emperor. Suillius Rufus charged Asiaticus with providing loans to corrupt army officers 'who, he alleged were bound in return' by adultery and homosexuality. The last charge 'was too much for the defendant's taciturnity: "Question thy sons, Suillius," he broke out, "they will confess me man."[69] According to Tacitus, it was alleged that Suillius's son 'played the woman's part in that foulest of intercourse'.[70] The charges were familiar and well used to undermine the credibility and character of the defendant. Asiaticus was allowed to answer the charges and the emperor appeared to doubt his guilt. The emperor asked for advice from his *amici*. Then Vitellius intervened to destroy him, suggesting that Asiaticus be allowed to choose the manner of his death in light of his distinguished service to the state. The emperor was saved from taking responsibility.

Asiaticus went home and his *amici* gathered around him. They suggested he starved himself to death, but he rejected it. There would be no lingering ignoble death for him. Instead, he went through his normal gymnastic exercises, bathed and then dined with his friends. There, he observed 'that it would have been more respectable to perish by the subtlety of Tiberius or the onslaught of Gaius Caesar than to fall by the female fraud and lecherous tongue of Vitellius, [and he] opened his arteries: but not before he [had] visited his pyre and given orders for it to be moved to another site so that his trees with their shady leafage might not be affected by the heat'.[71] Ironically, the Gardens of Lucullus that witnessed the last rites of its past owner, Asiaticus, would also witness the last breath of its new owner, Messalina. Both were victims of the Claudian civil war.[72]

The Marriage of the She-Wolf

The Adulteries of Messalina and Conspiracy of Narcissus, Autumn AD 48

'Preferring a mat to her bedroom in the palace, she had the nerve to put on a nighttime hood, the whore-empress. Like that, with a blond wig hiding her black hair, she went inside a brothel reeking of ancient blankets to an empty cubicle – her very own. Then, she stood there naked and for sale, with her nipples gilded, under the trade name of "She-Wolf" putting on display the belly you came from, noble born Britannicus.'

Juvenal, *Satire*, VI.118–123

Messalina used sex as a weapon. Juvenal's story of the She-Wolf, a fable written over sixty years after her death, was based on a kernel of truth. Similar accounts are replete in Dio, Tacitus, Pliny the Elder and Suetonius, and were probably based on a presentation made to the Senate to justify her death. Juvenal wrote the poem as a warning to a friend who was contemplating marriage. The poet was brim full of the Roman male bias against powerful, intelligent women acting in the male world of politics. He weeps for the supposed decline in female virtues and focuses his ire upon several infamous examples. This is mirrored in Tacitus's account, which saw her as a usurper of masculine power. There is no doubt that Messalina pursued affairs, but not to the extent the ancient sources alleged, yet surprisingly she was unconcerned that knowledge of these was in the public domain. The fates of Augustus's daughter and granddaughter served as a warning that she chose to ignore.[1]

Messalina has been characterized as a sexually promiscuous young woman in her late twenties who used her position of power to experiment with young men rather than seek faithful solace with her husband, who was three times her age. According to Tacitus, she drove the renowned beauty Poppaea Sabina to suicide as she was a competitor for the affections of court actor Mnester. Poppaea previously had been charged with adultery with Asiaticus but escaped condemnation. Her true crime was her beauty. A regular at court, Messalina decided to remove a potential rival for the affections of her husband. Livilla had been exiled for this very reason.[2] Claudius loved and trusted his wife, and employed her and Narcissus as his instruments of destruction to crush his enemies. However, in the Roman world, adultery was a female preserve – men could acquire as many mistresses as they liked without suffering condemnation or legal peril. Claudius took full advantage of this attitude.[3]

Messalina sought to control the imperial court, protect her position as the wife of the emperor and ensure the succession of her young son, Britannicus. Her gender made this extremely difficult. Instead, she used sex to build a network of allegiance and used Augustus's adultery law to her advantage. She had her own court and rooms in the palace, where she held lavish banquets followed by unrestrained parties at which married couples were encouraged to avail themselves of all their desires. The wives of the elite were, like her, made

'to show themselves equally unchaste. She made many of them commit adultery in the very palace itself while their husbands were present and looked on. Such men she loved and cherished and rewarded them with honours and offices; but others, who would not offer their wives for such business, she hated and brought to destruction in every possible way.'[4]

According to the adultery law, the wives and their lovers were liable to prosecution in the public courts and punished with exile and confiscation of estates, whilst their husbands were compelled to prosecute them within two months or be charged with prostituting their wives and face similar punishment.[5] Both husbands and wives were bound to her through her knowledge of their crimes and her ability to support any allegations with witnesses. Messalina ensured Claudius was kept entertained by selecting concubines whose loyalty to her would be well rewarded.[6]

It was these parties that led to allegations of the empress prostituting herself. Juvenal reports popular rumours circulating years later that she regularly attended public brothels, whilst Pliny the Elder believed she outlasted prostitutes in twenty-four-hour sex marathons. The later epitome of Dio distorts the accurate account of her motivations in hosting these romps to pander to the image of her as a sex-crazed nymphomaniac, saying that 'as if it were not enough for her to play the adulteress and harlot – for in addition to her shameless behaviour in general she at times sat as a prostitute in the palace herself and compelled the other women of the highest rank to do the same – [she] now conceived of a desire to have many husbands, that is men really bearing the title.'[7] The sources are indignant at her subversion of the traditional male role, daring to control the court by employing a heady combination of sex, power and influence.

Messalina, Claudius's elite freedmen and courtiers used their position as brokers of imperial benevolence to reward those who cooperated. They 'kept offering for sale and peddling out not merely the franchise and military commands, procuratorships, and governorships', so 'Messalina and his freedmen were puffed up with conceit. There were three of the latter in particular who divided up the power among themselves: Callistus, who had charge of Petitions; Narcissus, who was Chief Secretary, and hence wore a dagger at his side; and Pallas, who was entrusted with the administration of the Finances.'[8] Narcissus and Messalina, in particular, shared a close alliance, and nothing was done without consulting her first. Other powerful freedmen included Polybius, who had been the emperor's researcher for his historical writings and had become so powerful that he was allowed to walk between the two consuls.[9] It was in the reign of Claudius that the official titles for the imperial offices of the state became established as *a studiis* (secretary for documents), *ab epistulis* (for correspondence), *a libellis* (for petitions) and *a rationibus* (for finance). Each built up their own network of alliances at court and amongst Rome's elite, and ultimately competed with each other for influence with the emperor.[10]

All had used their position to accumulate vast wealth. Narcissus amassed a fortune worth 400,000 sesterces and was courted by cities and kings. Claudius joked that when the state ran short of funds, he could ask for a loan from Narcissus and Pallas. Their houses reflected their wealth and power, those of Callistus and his fellow freedman, Posides, standing amongst the wonders of Rome.[11] Access to the emperor in private informal settings, rather than the public *salutatio* or imperial banquets, was the key to power. Many of the senatorial and equestrian elite could only gain imperial bequests and favours through these gatekeepers. The emperor's fear of assassination isolated him from the aristocracy, who bridled at having to approach social inferiors such as former slaves or the emperor's wife. This increased the pressure to cooperate with them, and by kissing the hands of former slaves, they too became slaves. The social inversion cut deep to those who prided themselves on their noble blood, their education and one-time access to the emperor himself.[12]

Claudius, like Tiberius before him, isolated himself in a pleasure palace. Tiberius had established himself on the island of Capri; Claudius's palace was perched high above Rome on the Palatine. Messalina worked to ensure all those with access to him were beholden to her in one way or another. She was said to have slept with Polybius, whilst the other foremost freedmen knew of her adulteries but had not informed the emperor. The withholding of such information was an act of treason. Those who thought to inform Claudius would suffer a sudden disastrous fall. The Praetorian Prefect Catonius Justus, an *amicus* of Livilla, was about to inform Claudius of his wife's adultery, but Messalina ensured his destruction. He was replaced by two loyal adherents of the empress, Lusius Geta and Rufius Crispinus.[13] The infamous *delator* Suillius Rufus was bound to her through the indiscretions of his son, no doubt at the parties she arranged, where Suillius Caesonius was observed committing homosexual acts that were known to all apart from the emperor. Valerius Asiaticus used this information to attack his accuser, Suillius Rufus, but to no avail. Claudius chose to ignore the accusations because Rufus was vital in his role as a *delator*.[14]

Those senators who remained close to the emperor were also caught in her network. The consummate courtier and politician, Lucius Vitellius, the father of the future emperor Aulus Vitellius, carried around Messalina's slipper, which he took out and kissed from time to time, as well as keeping images of Narcissus and Pallas amongst his household gods.[15] He played a key role in ensuring the conviction of Valerius Asiaticus, despite them being close friends from childhood. His tears at his friend's emotional defence and final sentence at his own suggestion were probably genuine. Asiaticus went to his death cursing this abuse of the bonds of friendship. However, Messalina had privately approached him during a break in the proceedings as they collected themselves and dried their tears. warning him 'not to let the prisoner slip through their fingers'. This was no idle threat. Both of his sons became consuls the following year: a bittersweet reward for an act of personal treachery. The court was a battleground of conflicted and shifting loyalties.[16]

For Messalina, the risks were great and the threats were many. Firstly, there were the wandering affections of the emperor. Then she had to consider her husband's age and health. He was considered old by Roman standards, and his health had always been bad. His demeanour added to an impression of fragility, which further increased the anxieties of those whose power and influence lay with his survival.[17] The fates had 'cut from the imperial line one doddering life' who, according to Seneca, 'began fighting against his breath' from the very moment of his birth. He walked with a limp, and when angry, he stammered, his nose ran and he drooled. However, when calm and seated, he presented a fine figure, although the precariousness of his life during the reigns of three emperors had turned his hair white. His health had improved since he ascended the throne, but he suffered from excruciating stomach pains, probably an ulcer brought on by his excessive drinking. Appearances counted in the minds of the prejudiced, so he was considered frail in both mind and body. Such was the expectation of the emperor's imminent death that Rome's astrologers had 'been burying him off every month of every year'.[18]

These concerns dominated Messalina's thinking. Britannicus, the heir, was only six in AD 47, and in the event of Claudius's death, her position and the life of her son would be at risk. Despite her efforts to remove potential successors to the throne, one remained. Agrippina the Younger, the emperor's niece and granddaughter of Augustus, had been recalled from exile in AD 41 with Livilla. Unlike her sister, she appears to have removed herself from the court and probably remained on her new husband's estates. Sallustius Passienus Crispus, one of the foremost senators of his day and close friend of the emperor, fortuitously died before AD 47, leaving her two hundred million sesterces and the opportunity to rebuild her network of supporters. Those with grievances against Messalina would naturally gravitate towards her and her 9-year-old son, Domitius Ahenobarbus, the future emperor Nero. He had a greater claim to the throne than either Claudius or Britannicus. Dio describes Claudius as 'the son of Drusus, the son of Livia', with no mention of any links to Augustus, whilst Tacitus labels Britannicus as 'the last of the Claudii'.[19]

Agrippina saw the fate of her sister and knew to stay well away from court. She instead looked to forge alliances from a safe distance. The fact she did not look to remarry would also have heightened Messalina's suspicions. Despite being the emperor's niece, Livilla had been seen as a threat. Indeed, Agrippina would eventually marry Claudius, requiring a senatorial amendment to the law on incest. Slowly, Agrippina worked on enhancing the popularity of her son and attacking the reputation of Messalina. Rumours were spread that

'Messalina, realizing that Nero would become a rival to her son Britannicus, had sent assassins to strangle him during his siesta. They were driven away in terror, people said, by a snake which suddenly darted from beneath Nero's pillow. Agrippina persuaded him to have this skin set in a golden bracelet, which he wore for a long time on his right arm.'[20]

The rumour took hold and grew, propagated no doubt by her supporters. It was said that serpents watched over him, which Nero later confirmed, but that it was only one.[21]

The need for divine protection was seen as clear evidence of the righteousness of their cause when facing the menace of the evil empress. Agrippina presented her son as the one true male heir of Germanicus, diminishing Claudius's link to his heroic brother. The mother, meanwhile, took on the posture of wronged innocence, eliciting 'growing pity' in light 'of her persecution by Messalina'. The threat to the empress's position appeared to be confirmed at the ancient equestrian parade of *Lusus Troiae* (the Trojan Game) in AD 47, which was performed by boys of noble birth. The imperial family looked on as 'a cavalcade of boys from the great families opened the mimic battle of Troy, among them being the emperor's son Britannicus, and Lucius Domitius, soon to be adopted as heir to the throne and to the designation of Nero – the livelier applause given by the populace to Domitius was accepted as prophetic.'[22]

Claudius, ever mindful of strengthening his weak claims to the throne, would have taken note. His main concern was his own survival, not the succession of his son. The applause for Agrippina's son was probably augmented by a hefty distribution of the monies she had recently inherited. Messalina's position and that of her son had been publicly challenged. The empress prepared her assault upon Agrippina, 'who, always her enemy and now, more than usually excited', looked to gather suitable accusers armed with incriminating allegations and witnesses to guarantee her rival's fall. [23]

The empresses's suspicions now turned to the members of the court. Agrippina was sure to have acquired supporters close to the emperor. Messalina's fears led her to question the loyalty of the freedman Polybius. Seneca, exiled in Corsica, wrote his *To Polybius on Consolation* hoping the *a libellis* would support his petition to return.[24] Seneca was a close friend of Agrippina and would secure his wish when she married Claudius. The choice of Polybius rather than the other members of the imperial bureaucracy or court would have been carefully considered by Seneca. The choice certainly sparked Messalina's doubts, especially if Polybius acted upon the request and approached the emperor. Consequently, 'she falsely accused Polybius and caused his death'. The execution of a fellow freedman undermined the trust of Narcissus, Pallas and Callistus in the loyalty of the empress. The cabal she had carefully constructed around the emperor had started to fracture.[25]

The threat posed by Agrippina, along with Claudius's age and fragile health, forced Messalina to prepare for the eventuality of his death before Britannicus came of age. However, the death of Valerius Asiaticus aroused huge resentment amongst many senators. His secret trial within the palace and dignified death made him a martyr whose memory could be exploited to foster and maintain opposition. This hostility was conveyed in the prosecution of Suillius Rufus.[26] This unscrupulous *delator* had agreed to defend Samius, a distinguished equestrian, for 400,000 sesterces, but he colluded with the prosecution, probably for another payment. His client, facing conviction and ruin, stabbed himself in the house of Suillius Rufus.

The outcry was led by the following year's designated consul, Gaius Silius, who demanded the emperor enforce the Cincian law, which forbade any payment for pleading a case. Suillius, and others like him, had made a fortune from payments and rewards from the emperor for successful prosecutions for *maiestas*. Most of the Senate rose to support Silius's proposal, but then those senators who sought to lose began to protest. In a state lacking both a police force or a prosecution service, emperors relied heavily on these senators, maligned as *delators* or informers, to uncover conspiracies and ensure a successful conviction. Claudius was forced to intervene and set a compromise figure of a maximum of 10,000 sesterces for acting for the defence or prosecution.[27]

Before his daring intervention, Silius had merely drawn the sympathy of his peers. Both his parents had been accused of treasonous complicity with the Gallic rebel, Sacrovir, in AD 21; his father was forced to take his own life, whilst his mother was exiled and most of their family estates confiscated. Their real crime was their close friendship with Agrippina the Elder, whose network of *amicitiae* was destroyed by Tiberius's Praetorian Prefect, Sejanus.[28] Silius's family were not drawn from the ancient nobility, but were ennobled for loyal service by Augustus. However, nothing more demonstrated his *nobilitas* than his attack upon the duplicity of the imperial *delator* Suillius. Silius may have been spurred into this action by a prosecution of one of his clients, but many patrons would not have dared to incur the wrath of the emperor and his wife. He now had the admiration of many prominent figures in the Senate.[29]

His actions certainly caught the attention of Messalina; but instead of a threat, she saw an opportunity. Silius now held considerable influence in the Senate, which could be used to counter the support Agrippina the Younger had gathered. The empress drew him into her circle of supporters, using her familiar tactics. However, she fell madly in love with him, burning with a desire 'verging upon insanity'. Tacitus describes her as becoming inflamed (*exarserat*), drawn to 'unknown passions' (*incognitas libidines*), and Dio dismisses her weak female constitution as becoming overwhelmed by an insatiable craving.[30] Both historians considered women as lacking in self-control, being driven and often destroyed by their own sexual desires, making them unsuitable for public life. Messalina was, to them, the epitome of female corruption, justifying male dominance of the political arena. She was the very opposite of a domesticated, homely, compliant Roman wife so lauded by Roman writers. However, the most able and consummate players of the courtly game were women, in Livia, Caesonia, Messalina and her nemesis, Agrippina the Younger. Just as Claudius should not be dismissed as a fool, nor should his wife be regarded as overwhelmed in her lust for Silius. She remained at all times very capable of political calculations and understanding of consequences. However, she was in love.[31]

Gaius Silius was only a few years older than Messalina, unlike her husband. He was also the 'most handsome of Roman youths'. To Juvenal, he was 'the finest and most handsome man of the patrician race',[32] an unusual description of a man in his early thirties but perhaps an attempt to dismiss a man's desire as the naivety of the young and immature. Their affair was open and known to all, thus incriminating all with their failure to report it to the emperor. Silius at first recoiled from the risks involved, but felt he had little choice, for 'refusal was certain death, since there was some little hope of avoiding exposure, and since the rewards were high, he consoled himself by closing his eyes to the future and enjoying the present'. As their liaison progressed, Messalina forced him to divorce his aristocratic wife, Junia Silana, so she could enjoy the privacy of his home. This she filled with gifts, including imperial slaves, freedmen, palace furnishings and statues of members of the imperial family. Possession of these items was treasonable, so guests would have been well aware of the implication, but remained silent. Indeed, Messalina, 'with no attempt at concealment, went incessantly to the house with a crowd of retainers; abroad she clung to his side'. She would have an escort of the Praetorian Guard as she travelled in her carriage through the streets, drawing attention to herself yet despising the consequences, confident in her control of Claudius's gatekeepers.[33]

By AD 48, they were planning for a future together. They were said to have been 'reduced to waiting upon the emperor's old age: deliberation was innocuous only to the innocent'. The imputation is clear: there was no desire to kill Claudius, only to wait upon the natural and inevitable course of events. He was already, by Roman standards, old and in questionable health. Upon his death, they planned to marry, and Silius, who was childless, wished to adopt Britannicus. Messalina would rule through her new husband, who would act as regent until Britannicus came of age. The safety of her son would be assured, as would the succession. Silius had all to gain, as he was already committed to her, wedded by their adultery.[34]

Narcissus and the other imperial freedmen, however, were increasingly concerned by the level of risk she was taking. They met in secret and 'discussed the chances of diverting Messalina from her amour with Silius by private threats while suppressing their knowledge of all other circumstances'. However, she refused to break off her liaison with Silius. To approach her with this request was a risk in itself. The death of Polybius stood as a testament to those who lost her trust. For this reason, Pallas gave up, 'lest failure involve their own destruction'. Callistus was a man who habitually took the route of less resistance, having 'had expert knowledge of the last court as well and believed power to be held more securely by cautious than vigorous counsels'.[35]

The problem in informing Claudius was attempting to explain why they had kept the knowledge of her adultery from him for months. Furthermore, they would have to procure witnesses and evidence of Messalina's adultery. The two Praetorian Prefects were loyal to her, as were many of the imperial officials and senators close to Claudius. The empress herself could be very persuasive. Despite this, plans had started to take shape as 'the very pliancy of the emperor gave ground for confidence that, if they carried the day thanks to the atrocity of the charge, they might crush her by making her condemnation precede her trial'. They knew they needed to deprive Messalina of an opportunity to mount a defence in front of the emperor, no doubt because some of the charges they planned were not true. Failure to do so would mean their deaths. However, they were prepared to allow her one final chance to see reason, warning her that they were prepared to inform the emperor of her infidelity unless she agreed to abandon Silius.[36]

Callistus and Pallas balanced the risks and abandoned their plan. They could, after all, simply deny any knowledge of the affair. Furthermore, the heir was Messalina's son, and when Britannicus ascended the throne, he was sure to seek vengeance on those who had plotted against his mother. Narcissus was in a more complex and vulnerable position. His close association with Messalina in their shared suppression of conspiracies and prosecutions meant that he could not plausibly deny knowledge of her adultery. Her fall would encompass his. But he had also taken the lead in urging her to reject Silius. He no longer trusted her, and with Agrippina and her allies waiting for an opportunity to destroy Messalina, it appeared the empress was openly facilitating their plans with her public and carefree relationship with the young noble. Narcissus calculated that he would be absolved by the emperor if he took responsibility for revealing her adulterous behaviour. Although the charge of adultery was serious, the emperor's response would be more fearful and his gratitude far greater if Narcissus uncovered a plot to murder him, even if one did not exist. Claudius had always been ready to believe in assassination plots, having experienced so many. He was a man understandably consumed by fear, meaning it would be pushing against an open door.

Silius had also been considering his position. If his relationship with Messalina was discovered by the emperor, his death was assured. He wanted a greater commitment from the empress to safeguard his future position and insure against future rejection, so he 'began to press for the mask to be dropped'. The phrase is ambiguous and provides little indication of his thinking. Messalina, unencumbered, logical and calculating, 'took his phrases with a coolness due, not to any tenderness for her husband, but to a misgiving that Silius, with no heights left to scale, might spurn his paramour and come to appreciate at its just value a crime sanctioned in the hour of danger'.[37] The crime was not murder, but a bigamous marriage.

All the sources agree that the two lovers did indeed marry. Tacitus, appreciating the disbelief of his reader, confirms the accuracy of his account.[38] Even Seneca in his *Octavia*, which is generally sympathetic to Messalina, accepts the marriage ceremony as genuine, with Octavia's daughter lamenting that 'Pitiless Venus first exacted punishment for the madness of my wretched mother who was united in incestuous marriage, regardless of me, of her husband, and forgetful of the laws.'[39] However, Messalina was not forgetful of the laws. They remained as ever at the forefront of her thinking. Just as she utilized Augustus's law on adultery to her advantage, so too did she use the law on marriage.

No source mentions that Messalina divorced her husband before participating in the marriage ceremony with Silius. A wife was legally entitled to divorce her husband. Nor did she have to inform him that he was divorced, although it was customary to do so in the form of a legal note. This is why Narcissus was able to inform Claudius that he had been divorced by his wife, when in fact he hadn't. A legal divorce entailed the repudiation of the spouse in front of seven witnesses. This did not happen. The law was clear: if there was no public statement of divorce, the marriage was not dissolved, so Messalina remained married to the emperor.[40] Silius had his public expression of commitment from Messalina, but the agreement of the empress to this wedding ceremony is difficult to explain. Possibly Silius threatened to break off their relationship and 'spurn his paramour', which is hinted at by Tacitus. He must have considered himself a dead man walking, so such a threat held no fear of retribution from his lover. To her, it was merely a gesture made in front of select guests, empty of legal value.

The ceremony had to wait for Claudius to leave Rome for a few days as he travelled to Ostia to inspect the port and granaries that were being built at imperial expense. These trips would have been regular occurrences and announced well in advance. Messalina feigned illness and was left behind to recuperate. Tacitus struggles to believe the audacity of the couple who

> 'could have felt so much security; far more so, that on a specific day, with witnesses to seal the contract, a consul designate and the emperor's wife should have met for the avowed purposes of legitimate marriage; that the woman should have listened to the words of the auspices, have assumed the veil, have sacrificed in the face of Heaven; that both should have dined with the guests, have kissed and embraced, and finally have spent the night in the licence of wedlock.'[41]

Juvenal, writing many years later, uses his poetic licence to embellish the scene as he addresses an imaginary Silius:

> 'She's been sitting there, waiting for a while now, with her bridal veil ready and a purple marriage couch set up the gardens in full view. Following ancient custom, a dowry of a million will be paid, and the augur and witnesses will be there. She will not get married unless it's done lawfully. What's your decision? If you are not prepared to obey her, you'll die before the lamps are lit. If you go through with the crime, there'll be the briefest

delay, until the matter that's known to Rome and the people reaches the emperor's ear. Comply with her command, if a few days of life are worth it. Whichever you decide is easier and better, you'll have no choice but to offer your lovely white neck for execution.'[42]

Tacitus is clear that the marriage was demanded by Silius, rather than Messalina. The garden ceremony was probably performed at the house of Silius, although the palace cannot be discounted.[43] A sumptuous banquet followed, continuing into the night, before the two lovers retired.[44] News of the proceedings was soon public knowledge in Rome. Narcissus realized his opportunity had arrived. He had carefully planned his approach to the emperor, but had been forced to wait until Claudius was separated from his wife. The ceremony itself was a gift that could be embellished to support other allegations. There would be no warning, as previously planned. Surprise was crucial in denying Messalina the opportunity to defend herself.[45]

Two of the emperor's favourite concubines had already been persuaded 'by gifts, promises, and the demonstration of power which would accrue to them from the fall of the wife, to undertake the task of deletion [denouncer]'. Claudius was to be found regularly in their embraces, so the freedman knew that an evening request to join the emperor would not be refused.[46] Ostia lay 15 miles from the capital. It is likely the small party travelled along the Tiber, as the roads would have slowed down carriages. Narcissus knew that the emperor's party was populated by Messalina's supporters. The Praetorian Prefect, Lusius Geta, owed his appointment to the empress, and the senators L. Vitellius and Caecina Largus were her *amici*. Narcissus would be on his own.

The two concubines were admitted to the emperor's private chamber in the palace at Ostia. Calpurnia, as one was called, fell at Claudius's knees in an act of supplication. She then 'exclaimed that Messalina had wedded Silius. In the same breath, she asked Cleopatra, who was standing by ready for the question, if she had heard the news; and on her sign of assent, requested that Narcissus should be summoned.' They had been well drilled, their actions and responses prepared and practised. Narcissus had avoided the risk of giving the news himself; standing outside, he could gauge the emperor's reaction and allow the two women to bear the full brunt of the emperor's rage. However, Claudius appears to have been thrown into a panic. The freedman then seized the opportunity to beg forgiveness for not informing the emperor of his wife's infidelities sooner. The moment of danger had passed, and Narcissus could now fan the flames of imperial fury.[47]

Narcissus told the emperor about the imperial property that decorated the house of the consul designate, a truth, followed by a lie: Claudius was informed that he had been divorced. Another truth was that the ceremony had been public and the Praetorians were aware of the situation but had failed to intervene. Another lie followed: Claudius was in danger of being deposed, and unless he acted quickly, Rome would have a new emperor. Thus, 'by frightening him with the idea that Messalina was going to kill him and set up Silius as ruler in his stead, he persuaded him to arrest and torture a number of persons'.[48]

Such was the emperor's panic that Narcissus even persuaded him that his Praetorian Prefect, Lusius Geta, was not to be trusted as he remained loyal to Messalina. Consequently, Narcissus was made Praetorian Prefect for the following day. This was vital for his deception so he could arrest known associates of the empress and personally supervise their torture to ensure they provided the evidence he needed to support his claims. There could be no public trials; all would die on the morrow. With the emperor emotional and stricken, Narcissus took the opportunity to name some of Messalina's alleged adulterers, including the famous doctor, Vettius Valens, and Plautius Lateranus, the nephew of one of Claudius's commanders in Britain. A wider conspiracy appeared to be emerging, which justified their imminent arrest. Narcissus had delivered a consummate, choreographed performance, culminating in a masterful deception. He knew that his master was 'slow to discover deception – but quick to anger'. He also knew from his reaction to the revolt of Camillus that the emperor's first reaction would be blind panic. He played Claudius perfectly, knowing that 'at the slightest hint of danger he would take instant precaution and vengeance against his supposed enemy, however insignificant, once he began to feel all uneasy'.[49]

Narcissus knew that Claudius would ask his councillors whether the information was true. All they could confirm was his wife's adultery, not what had allegedly occurred in Rome during their absence. The imperial *concilium* was called from those present. Turranius, who was prefect of the corn supply, was asked for his knowledge of these events, then Lusius Geta. They 'admitted the truth' that they were aware of, which appeared to confirm the lies with which Narcissus had laced his account. The remainder of his advisors urged him to first secure the loyalty of the Praetorians before seeking vengeance. They were keen to demonstrate their loyalty by loudly expressing their outrage.[50]

As a new day dawned, the emperor hastily returned to Rome. Narcissus had to ensure that Claudius was kept ignorant of the truth. He firstly demanded a seat in the imperial litter along with the consuls L. Vitellius and Caecina Largus, who might use the privacy of the journey to cast doubts in Claudius's mind concerning the veracity of the account. Secondly, he needed to deprive Messalina of the opportunity to plead her case and demand a hearing. So far, Narcissus had 'carried the day thanks to the atrocity of the charge', but he had to 'crush her by making her condemnation precede her trial'.[51] As Praetorian

Prefect, he could order the guards escorting the emperor to keep her away from the imperial litter. This was another reason he had to depose Lusius Geta for the day, even though he was making an enemy for life. The stakes were too high to care about that.

Inside the litter, the atmosphere was tense. The emperor was agitated, absorbed in conflicted thoughts. At one point he 'inveighed against the profligacies of his wife, and, in the next, recurred to memories of his wedded life and to the infancy of his children'. Narcissus hoped his presence would deter his travelling companions from expressing doubts, but he was also desperate for them to commit to his story. To commit was to take a side, but this they steadfastly refused to do. Messalina might survive to destroy any disloyalty, and they clearly distrusted the freedman. Instead, Vitellius hid behind ambiguous exclamations: 'Ah, the crime – the villainy.' But whose? Narcissus urged him to clarify his remarks and tell the emperor the truth. Instead, he 'responded with incoherent phrases, capable of being turned to any sense required, and his example was copied by Caecina Largus'. Their equivocation implies that both thought Claudius was in no immediate or real danger, despite Narcissus's attempts to question their loyalty.[52]

To survive at court – and L. Vitellius was a consummate survivor – the courtier needed to watch and wait upon events, evaluating who was rising and whose influence was on the wane. Claudius's vacillation indicated that Messalina's fate was not sealed. Vitellius was not going to be forced into taking a side yet. This attitude is illustrated by the reaction of the guests to the poisoning of Britannicus by Nero during an imperial banquet in AD 55. The young Britannicus quickly lost his sight, and he started gasping for breath. He then collapsed, causing 'a stir among the company; some, taken by surprise, ran hither and thither, while those whose discernment was keener, remained motionless, with their eyes fixed on Nero, who, as he still reclined in seeming unconsciousness, said that this was a common occurrence, from a periodical epilepsy'. Agrippina, innocent of the crime as she was by then supporting Britannicus's cause, knew immediately what was happening; 'her terror and confusion, though her countenance struggled to hide it, so visibly appeared, that she was clearly just as ignorant as was Octavia, Britannicus's own sister.' Octavia too understood, but 'had learnt to hide her grief, her affection, and indeed every emotion'. The banquet soon resumed with forced laughter and obligatory mirth. It was vital to conceal one's thoughts whilst anticipating the judgements of others.[53]

As the imperial party moved rapidly towards Rome, the two lovers rose to a new day. As conspirators, it would be expected that they rapidly put their plans for the murder of the emperor and seizure of Rome into action. Possibly the gates of the city could be closed, barred and guarded to prevent Claudius re-entering his capital. The consuls could have been summoned to muster the Senate to announce the restoration of the Republic, or Messalina and Silius, with the Praetorian Prefect Rufrius Crispinus, could have entered the Praetorian fortress to announce the deposition of the old, infirm and foolish usurper with no legitimate claim to the throne and receive the oath of loyalty to Silius. Alternatively, the emperor and his escort could have been ambushed by units of the Urban Cohorts, *Vigiles* (Night Watch) or gladiators in the narrow streets of the city and cut down. But instead, Messalina, Silius and a small group of companions travelled to the *Horti Maecenatis*, an imperial garden on the Esquiline Hill, with its adjacent vineyards on its western slope. There they continued their revelry in a celebration of the autumn grape harvest, the *Rustica Vinalia*.[54] They had no thought of Claudius, an assassination plot or seizing control of Rome.

Silius took on the role of Dionysus, the god of wine, orchards, fertility and revelry, whilst Messalina re-enacted the role of the god's wife, Ariadne. Her choice of character was particularly nuanced, as according to one myth, she was abandoned by her first husband, Theseus, only to be found and wed by a greater husband in Dionysius. So, in her playful performance, she had been abandoned by Claudius, who had left for Ostia.[55] The guests and servants had been given roles to perform, and the show began

'through the grounds of the house. Presses were being trodden, vats flowed; while, beside them, skin-girt women were bounding like Bacchanals excited by sacrifice or delirium. She herself was there with dishevelled tresses and waving thyrsus; at her side, Silius, with an ivy crown, wearing buskins and tossing his head, while all around him rose the din of a wanton chorus.'[56]

The doctor, Vettius Valens, demonstrated his knowledge of the myth as told by Euripides, climbing a tree to imitate Pentheus, who hoped to spy on the frenzied rites, eager to see an orgy, but being seen and torn to pieces. The revellers called up to him, asking what he saw. He replied prophetically: 'A frightful storm over Ostia.'[57] Their comforting assumption that the emperor remained in the port city inspecting the grain supply was soon to be proven false.

Messalina's fellow merrymakers were men of note, but not nobles, with apart from Silius only one senator. She wanted to relax and enjoy the day without pandering to sensibilities or precedence. There was an ex-praetor, Iuncus Vergilianus, the Prefect of the *Vigiles*, Decrius Calpurnianus, and Sulpicius Rufus, a procurator of a gladiatorial training school. The Prefect did not summon his 7,000 firefighters, nor the procurator his gladiators. The remaining equestrians were Pompeius Urbicus, Saufeius Trogus, Traulus Montanus – who had a one-night stand with Messalina – and Titius Proculus, who is described as her custodian. These appointments were common as guardians of premarital fidelity and reflect the commitment she had made to Silius, just as he had demonstrated his loyalty to her by divorcing his wife. 'Autumn was at the full', the world was good and they gathered simply to enjoy the festival with cheerful abandon.[58]

The celebrations were interrupted by rumours emanating from Ostia that Claudius was returning. The rumours were soon replaced by messengers 'hurrying in from all quarters that Claudius knew all and was on his way, hot for revenge'.[59] What did he know? There was no panic; instead, the party acted as though they could calmly deny all by acting normally. It was not the reaction of conspirators suddenly discovered in the middle of their crime. The party broke up. Messalina went to the imperial Gardens of Lucullus on the Pincian Hill, where she could see the whole of Rome clustered below. Silius travelled to the Forum to conduct personal business. Soon it became clear that they, not Claudius, were in the eye of the storm. Narcissus, the temporary Praetorian Prefect, had sent orders on ahead for the officers of the guard to take their men and arrest the known associates of the empress, who 'were melting away by one road or another, when the centurions appeared and threw them into irons as discovered, some in the open, some in hiding'.[60]

It was only now that Messalina realized she was in deep trouble. Passivity was abandoned for a frenzied activity. She decided to meet Claudius with their children before he entered the city, to avoid meeting him surrounded by his freedmen and advisors. She would appeal to him as a father. If this was refused, she asked for Vibidia, the chief Vestal Virgin, to support her pleas as a wife and mother who had the right to be heard by her husband. Claudius, as Pontifex Maximus, could hardly refuse to hear the views of the highest priestess. Messengers were sent to the palace to summon her children, and also to Vibidia to meet at the gate into the city. Speed was vital and the narrow, crowded streets would impede the journey of any litter. Instead, she set off on foot across Rome with only three companions to the Ostian gate. The poor walked, but dignity and symbols of status were now of secondary importance to saving her life.[61]

Once Messalina reached the road from Ostia, she boarded a refuse cart to meet the emperor on the road.[62] When his litter came into view, she dismounted and cried out 'to the emperor to hear the mother of Octavia and Britannicus'. The guard must have prevented her from approaching the covered litter. From inside came the voice of Narcissus, shouting over her, listing all the details of her relationship with Silius and his understanding of the wedding ceremony. At the same time, he distracted Claudius with a document he had prepared earlier detailing her alleged infidelities. The imperial escort continued its journey with Messalina walking alongside, crying, calling out to her husband not to orphan their children. At the city gate, her two children ran forward to greet their father – Britannicus was 7 and Octavia 9. They would have known something terrible was happening and seen their mother distraught, calling out to their father. Narcissus, as the day's Praetorian Prefect, ordered their removal.[63]

At this, the senior Vestal Virgin stepped forward. It was a capital offence to obstruct a Vestal, so there was nothing Narcissus could do as she approached the emperor. Vibidia demanded 'in indignant terms that a wife should not be given undefended to destruction'. Narcissus replied that 'the emperor would hear her and there would be opportunities for rebutting the charge: meanwhile, the Virgin would do well to go and attend to her religious duties'.[64] He had no intention of allowing Messalina this chance to meet her husband and undermine his account of events.

Messalina, her hopes fading rapidly, retired to the Gardens of Lucullus. However, the whole affair had greatly upset Claudius, who had retreated into himself. He sat there, hidden behind the curtains of the litter, listening to his wife and children, whilst his freedman was allowed to treat them with disdain: 'Throughout the proceedings Claudius maintained a strange silence, Vitellius wore an air of unconsciousness: all things moved at the will of the freedman.' The episode was surreal. Common humanity and compassion were left destitute in the gutter. Narcissus knew Claudius was wavering, and he needed to fire his rage again. He would take Claudius to Silius's townhouse, with its imperial adornments. There was no need to rush to the Praetorian camp to secure the loyalty of the guard as he knew there was no plot. He did, though, send officers to the camp to summon the guardsmen to a parade. Some were no doubt bribed to demand the execution of the accused. Messalina's *amici* had been rounded up and taken there. These supposed lovers were her political allies. They knew this was their last day. There would be no trial. The emperor was indebted to the Praetorians, and he would not risk their loyalty. When they demanded their death, then death would come.[65]

The gates of Silius's mansion were locked. Within minutes they were opened, and Claudius entered. Narcissus knew what was there and what effect it would have on the emperor: 'First he pointed out in the vestibule an effigy – banned by senatorial decree – of the elder Silius.' His father had suffered *damnatio memoriae*, so it was a treasonous crime to display his mask amongst those of his other ancestors in the *atrium* of his house. As they moved through the rooms and corridors, the freedman 'demonstrated how the heirlooms of the Nerones and Drusi had been requestioned as the price of infamy'. These were statues and property of Claudius's own ancestors, taken from the palace by Messalina and given to her lover as gifts. This all had the desired effect and the 'emperor grew hot and broke into threats'.[66]

Claudius was now brought to the Praetorian camp, where the ranks of guardsmen had been waiting to be addressed by their emperor. Narcissus, as acting Praetorian Prefect, addressed the soldiers. It would have been brief, as they would have resented a former slave taking command. Next, Claudius stood on the tribunal. His speech was also short: the adultery of his wife reflected badly upon him, as a strong husband controlled his spouse, 'for just as his resentment was, shame denied it utterance'. He then shouted out: 'Am I still emperor?' This he asked time and again. The ancient sources report this as an example of his abject terror at losing the throne. However, it was probably delivered with a loud, rhetorical flourish, to which the soldiers repeatedly shouted back; as prearranged, 'there followed one long cry from the cohorts demanding the names and punishment of the criminals'.[67] The deaths of many followed, a visual confirmation to emperor and Praetorian alike that he remained in power. There would be no trial, just the edge of a sharpened blade to deliver Claudian justice.[67]

Silius was the first to be dragged up to the tribunal. He had come to terms with his fate, but he did not want the slow death by a garrot in the underground, fetid chamber in the *Carcer*. A quick end was all he asked for. The threat of further torture and his bravery inspired other *equites* to dispense with futile pleas for mercy, nor offer a confession. A Praetorian's sword beheaded M. Helvius, a Cotta and a Fabius. Titius Proculus attempted to bargain for his life by turning informer. He misread the situation, as Narcissus wanted no investigation. He was executed, then the prefect of the Vigiles, Pompeius Urbicus and Saufeius Trogus. The doctor, Vettius Valens, offered a confession, hoping for clemency. His declaration was gladly accepted before the bloodied sword fell on him, followed by the senator Juncus Vergilianus and the procurator of the gladiatorial school. Narcissus, as Praetorian Prefect, supervised their deaths.[68]

One of the last to be dragged before the emperor and Narcissus was the pantomime artist, Mnester. He would have to give the performance of his life to save himself. He appealed to the emperor's mercy, tearing his clothes and calling upon him 'to look at the imprints of the lash and remember the phrase by which he had placed him at the disposal of Messalina'. Years earlier, Claudius had instructed him 'to do whatever he should be ordered to do by Messalina'. Accordingly, he had lain with the empress. His words elicited sympathy from Claudius, especially when he rightly claimed that 'others had sinned through a bounty or a high hope, he, from need'. He pointed out that if Silius had become emperor and married Messalina, he would have been one of the first to die. Claudius was wavering. He asked for the opinions of Narcissus and the other freedmen who had joined him, who pointed to the error in granting clemency to one of such low status when others of higher rank had already been despatched. Furthermore, his crime was so great that even if he had been compelled to act, its very heinous nature required the ultimate punishment. There could be no evidence to counter Narcissus's claims. So Mnester died 'for the sake of appearances'.[69]

Another young man, in the prime of life, attempted a similar argument, to no avail. Traulus Montanus was 'a modest but remarkably handsome youth, he had within a single night received his unsought invitation and dismissal from Messalina'. What these lacked were relatives who had placed the emperor in their debt through loyal service. The *delator* and prosecutor Suillius Rufus was able to save his son, but then little was heard of him. He clearly fell from imperial favour. Aulus Plautius was another powerful figure who used his influence to intervene successfully on behalf of his nephew, Plautius Lateranus. This general had remained loyal as governor of Pannonia during the revolt of Camillus and had led the invasion of Britain. Instead of sharing the fate of most of Messalina's *amici*, Lateranus lost his senatorial status until it was restored by Nero.[70] He would die bravely many years later, refusing to expose others after the failure of the Pisonian conspiracy. Many others, not worthy enough to be named in the historical record and lacking the necessary status and connections, were not spared.[71]

Sated, Claudius and Narcissus retired to the palace. The freedman had one more task to perform to complete the plan. He had to persuade the emperor to kill his wife. Messalina had remained in the Gardens of Lucullus, where she was composing a petition, in hope but also in indignation. She had been joined by her mother, Domitia Lepida. The relationship between mother and daughter had fractured after the enforced suicide of her husband, Appius Junius Silanus. However, in Messalina's hour of need, Domitia buried her grievances and joined her in the imperial gardens. Claudius, meanwhile, had indulged himself with an early banquet and diluted his anger with wine. He was starting to reconsider his decisions. Consequently, he

'gave instructions for someone to go and inform "the poor woman" – the exact phrase which he is stated to have used – that she must be in his presence next day to plead her case. The words were noted: his anger was beginning to cool, his love return; and, if they waited longer there was ground for anxiety in the approaching night with its memories of the marriage chamber.'[72]

Narcissus realized his own life was now in deep jeopardy. The emperor was wavering, his anger dissipated. Messalina would present a plausible and honest case in her defence. She would push against an open door. The freedman had to ensure she died before the morning, for, as Tacitus acknowledges, 'if Narcissus had not hastened her despatch, the ruin had all but fallen upon the head of the accuser'. He even went as far as to order the emperor to execute his wife. The emperor did not commit. The freedman, still in command of the Praetorians, burst from the room to find the tribune and centurions who were on duty. What was one more lie to add to the many others that had fallen from his lips? He pretended that the emperor had ordered the execution of Messalina. Whilst the execution squad was organized, Narcissus commanded his freedmen to hurry to the gardens to make sure Messalina did not escape. He had built his own network of power in the palace, which was now employed to ensure her destruction. Evodus, their leader, was also ordered to ensure she died. He was the insurance that the empress would not have the opportunity to be heard.[73]

Messalina lay on the ground, her mother next to her. The executions of Silius and her *amici* suggested her fate was certain. However, despite her mother's urging to end her life with dignity and not await violence at the hands of the soldiers, she still clung to hope between her tears and anguished sobs. The gates had been locked, but they were soon forced open. The tribune stood over her in silence, with his sword drawn, while Narcissus's freemen plied her with 'a stream of slavish insults'. Messalina took the sword and pushed it to her neck, but she was unable to make the cut. She then placed it on her chest, but again could not pull it towards her. Recognizing that she was unable to deliver the fatal blow, the tribune grabbed the weapon and ran her through. Her mother was granted her daughter's body so it would not suffer the indignity of abuse.[74] Her reputation would be murdered next.[75]

Claudius received the news of his wife's death as he lay on his banqueting couch. The message did not stipulate how she died, nor did he ask. Seneca, in his *Apocolocyntosis*, has Claudius defend himself before Augustus on the charge of killing his wife. He denies all knowledge: "'I don't know about it,' you say, God damn you! Not to know about it is worse than killing her.'[76] His perceived indifference became infamous. Suetonius reports that after her execution, 'he went to dinner, and presently asked: "Why is she not here?"'[77] The emperor's forgetfulness was to be assisted by the Senate, which passed a decree of *damnatio memoriae* casting her memory into oblivion. The greatest detail on Claudius's bizarre apathetic disinterest is provided by Tacitus. Upon receiving the news of Messalina's execution, 'he called for a cup and went through the routine of the banquet. Even in the days that followed, he betrayed no symptoms of hatred or joy, of anger or of sadness, or, in fine, of any human emotion; not when he saw the accusers rejoicing, nor even when he saw his children mourning.'[78] He had learnt to show no emotion, a lesson he taught his daughter, Octavia, through the treatment of her mother. Messalina's error was to surrender cold political logic to one singular emotion: love.

Claudius believed his wife was planning a coup with her lover, yet there was no investigation into the extent of any conspiracy. The Praetorian Prefects would have been eager to disassociate themselves from their former patroness and Narcissus would not want any further inquiries made. However, the supposed plot again revealed the weakness of the emperor's imperial claims and the frailty of his support. When he stood before the assembled Praetorian Guard, he vowed that 'having been unfortunate with his wives, he was resolved to live a celibate life in future – they could kill him if he did not keep his word'.[79] He didn't keep his word. On New Year's Day, AD 49, he married Messalina's nemesis, Agrippina the Younger. Her cause had been supported by Pallas, keen to supplant Narcissus in the imperial favour. The marriage was calculated to buttress his claim to the throne, as she carried the blood of Augustus in her veins. Soon after, he was persuaded to adopt her son, Domitius Ahenobarbus, history's Nero. He sacrificed the future of his own son, Britannicus, for short-term political gains. Claudius died aged 63 in AD 54 and was honoured with divine status, probably having been poisoned by his wife with a plate of deadly mushrooms. His adopted son later quipped that they were the dish of the gods.[80]

Narcissus's position in court never recovered from his deception. He was given the lesser honour of *ornamenta quaestoria* when Otho had received Praetorian status for a similar service in uncovering Annius Vinicianus. He was no longer trusted, and Pallas's influence was strengthened. It was his rival who successfully persuaded Claudius to marry his niece. Just as Narcissus had destroyed Messalina and Silius, he now openly bragged that he would ruin Agrippina and Pallas. Ironically, having destroyed his mother, circumstances forced him to support the imperial claims of Britannicus over those of Nero.[81] For this, the new empress ensured that 'he was slain beside the tomb of Messalina, a circumstance due to mere chance, though it seemed to be in fulfilment of her vengeance'.[82]

The Conspiracy of Piso, AD 65

'Everyone knows the saying of the old courtier, who, when someone asked him how he had achieved the rare distinction of living at court till he reached old age, replied, "By receiving wrongs and returning thanks for them."'

(Seneca, *De Ira*, 2.33.3)

Seneca had reached old age. He had journeyed through the maelstrom of courtly politics tethered to the fortunes of Agrippina the Younger and her sister, Livilla. For this, he had suffered exile twice and come close to death. Gaius considered executing him after he was implicated in the plot of Gaetulicus, Marcus Lepidus and Agrippina in AD 39, but he was saved when the emperor was told the philosopher was close to death. Recalled by Claudius, he was soon tried and exiled again in AD 41, and again charged with adultery and conspiracy with Livilla. A couple of years later, he attempted to persuade the imperial freedman, Polybius, to support his recall by claiming that he was a victim of Fortune, whilst omitting any pleas of innocence. A sympathetic response probably led to the death of the freedman at the hands of Messalina. Her fall led to his recall in AD 49 and, through the patronage of Agrippina, he was appointed praetor and tutor to her son, the future emperor Nero.[1]

Seneca had suffered for his bond of *amicitiae* with Agrippina and her sister, but he was ultimately well rewarded for this loyalty. He became a key advisor on Nero's imperial *concilium*, alongside the young emperor's mother, the Praetorian Prefect Burrus and at times a few select senators such as M. Vestinus Atticus and Marcus Salvius Otho, whose father had been granted patrician status for his information on those who had conspired with Annius Vinicianus and Camillus Scribonianus against Claudius.[2] As well as huge political influence, Seneca accumulated a vast fortune in bequests and gifts. He extended his network of *amicitiae* through granting requests for offices, honours, magistracies and loans. Upon the death of the king of the Iceni, Seneca used imperial procurators to call in his loan of 40 million sesterces. The tribe's inability to pay and the resultant forced exactions were one reason for the revolt of Boadicea and the near loss of the province of Britannia.[3]

Bust of Julius Caesar in the Vatican Museum. (*Musei Vaticani {Stato Città del Vaticano}, Public domain, via Wikimedia Commons*)

Bust of Mark Antony from the Vatican Museum. (*Bust: unknown ancient Roman artist of the first century* AD; *photo: unknown photographer, CC BY-SA 4.0* <*https://creativecommons.org/licenses/by-sa/4.0*>, *via Wikimedia Commons*)

Silver *denarius* of Marcus Junius Brutus, with his bust on the obverse. The reverse shows images of the daggers used to murder Julius Caesar, and a Phrygian cap which symbolized liberty as it was given to manumitted slaves when they received their freedom. It was probably minted just before the Battle of Philippi. It was mentioned by the historian Cassius Dio (47.25.3): 'Brutus stamped upon the coins which were being minted his own likeness and a cap and two daggers, indicating by this and by the inscription that he and Cassius had liberated the fatherland.' (*Classical Numismatic Group, Inc. {CNG}, Public domain, via Wikimedia Commons*)

Bust of Augustus with the Civic Crown. (*Glyptothek, Public domain, via Wikimedia Commons*)

Bust of Julia the Elder, daughter of Augustus. (*Musée Saint-Raymond, Public domain, via Wikimedia Commons*)

Julia the Younger, granddaughter of Augustus. (*Jose Luis Filpo Cabana, CC BY 3.0 <https:// creativecommons.org/licenses/by/3.0>, via Wikimedia Commons*)

Bust of Emperor Tiberius, husband of Julia the Elder. (*Musée Saint-Raymond, Public domain, via Wikimedia Commons*)

Bust of Agrippa Postumus, Louvre Museum. (*Louvre Museum, CC BY 3.0 <https://creativecommons.org/licenses/by/3.0>, via Wikimedia Commons*)

Portrait bust of Agrippa Postumus as a child. The figure has been deliberately damaged due to *damnatio memoriae*. Found in Béziers and located in the Musée Saint-Raymond. (*Musée Saint-Raymond, Public domain, via Wikimedia Commons*)

The ruins of the Curia and Theatre of Pompey where Julius Caesar was assassinated on 15 March 44 BC. Located in the Largo di Torro Argentina, just south of the Pantheon. The square is to be transformed into an open-air museum with elevated walkways and viewing points. (*Jakub Hałun, CC BY-SA 4.0 <https://creativecommons.org/licenses/by-sa/4.0>, via Wikimedia Commons*)

Portrait bust probably depicting M. Claudius Marcellus, nephew and adopted son of Augustus. He was married to his daughter, Julia the Elder, until his death in 23 BC. (*National Archaeological Museum of Taranto, Attribution, via Wikimedia Commons*)

Gaius Caesar, eldest son of Julia the Elder and M. Vipsanius Agrippa. Adopted by Augustus as his son, along with his younger brother, Lucius. He died in AD 4, leading to the emperor's adoption of Tiberius and Agrippa Postumus. (*British Museum, CC BY 2.5 <https://creativecommons.org/licenses/by/2.5>, via Wikimedia Commons*)

Lucius Caesar, son of Julia the Elder and M. Vipsanius Agrippa. Adopted by Augustus, he died in AD 2. Located in the Ara Pacis Museum, Rome. (*Giovanni Dall'Orto, Public domain, via Wikimedia Commons*)

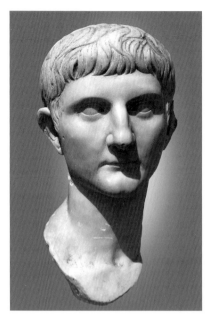

Marble bust of Germanicus, son of Tiberius' brother, Nero Claudius Drusus, and Antonia the Younger, who was the daughter of Augustus' sister, Octavia. Germanicus was adopted by Tiberius as his heir in AD 4 as part of Augustus' dynastic planning, despite Tiberius having a son of his own. Claudius was his brother. Germanicus had won fame in his campaigns in Germany from AD 14–16. Sent to the East by Tiberius, he was allegedly poisoned by the governor of Syria, Gnaeus Calpurnius Piso. He married Agrippina the Elder, with whom he had six children, including Gaius (Caligula), Agrippina the Younger, Julia Drusilla and Julia Livia. (*Musée Saint-Raymond, Public domain, via Wikimedia Commons*)

Marble bust of the Emperor Gaius (Caligula) located in the Metropolitan Museum of Art, New York. (*Metropolitan Museum of Art, CC0, via Wikimedia Commons*)

Marble bust of Agrippina the Younger, daughter of Germanicus, brother of the Emperor Gaius (Caligula) and mother of Nero. (*National Museum in Warsaw, CC0, via Wikimedia Commons*)

Livilla, daughter of Agrippina the Elder and sister of the Emperor Gaius (Caligula). Located in the Altes Museum, Berlin. (© *José Luiz Bernardes Ribeiro*)

Emperor Claudius, son of Nero Claudius Drusus and Antonia the Younger, making him the uncle of Gaius (Caligula). (*Altes Museum, CC BY 3.0*)

Detail taken from a painting by Lawrence Alma-Tadema (1836–1912) showing the discovery of Claudius by a Praetorian soldier after the murder of Gaius. It is likely this story was disseminated after Claudius' accession to exonerate him of any blame in the murder of his nephew. (*Lawrence Alma-Tadema, Public domain, via Wikimedia Commons*)

Marble bust probably depicting Messalina. Located in the Museum of Tongres. (*TimeTravelRome, CC BY 2.0 <https:// creativecommons.org/licenses/by/2.0>, via Wikimedia Commons*)

Bust of Nero at the Capitoline Museum, Rome. (*cjh1452000, CC BY-SA 3.0 <https://creativecommons.org/licenses/by-sa/3.0>, via Wikimedia Commons*)

Portrait of Emperor Domitian. Located in the Capitoline Museum, Rome. (*Steerpike, CC BY-SA 3.0 <https://creativecommons.org/licenses/by-sa/3.0>, via Wikimedia Commons*)

Portrait of Domitia Longina, daughter of Corbulo and wife of Domitian. (*National Museum in Warsaw, CC0, via Wikimedia Commons*)

Portrait bust of Emperor Marcus Cocceius Nerva. Located in the Museo Nazionale Romano. (*Livioandronico2013, CC BY-SA 4.0 <https://creativecommons.org/licenses/by-sa/4.0>, via Wikimedia Commons*)

Oversized head of Emperor Trajan.
Located in the Glyptothek, Munich.
(*Glyptothek, Public domain, via
Wikimedia Commons*)

Double herm of Seneca
with reverse showing the
philosopher Socrates. Located
in the Antikensammlung,
Berlin. (*I, Calidius, CC BY-SA
3.0 <http://creativecommons.
org/licenses/by-sa/3.0/>, via
Wikimedia Commons*)

Gold aureus of Emperor Claudius. Minted in AD 46, this type commemorates the 'reception of the emperor' at the Praetorian Fortress in AD 41 after the murder of Gaius. This was probably one of the yearly issues produced to reward the guard in raising him to the throne and affirm their continued loyalty. A soldier stands on duty above the gate, holding a spear in his right hand, and there is an aquila to the left. (*Classical Numismatic Group, Inc. http://www.cngcoins.com, CC BY-SA 2.5 <https://creativecommons.org/licenses/by-sa/2.5>, via Wikimedia Commons*)

Gold aureus of Nero showing the head of the emperor, and on the reverse Salus, the god of safety, sat on an ornate throne holding a patera in his right hand extended and his left hand by his side. Issued in AD 65–66, probably in response to the conspiracy of either Calpurnius Piso or Annius Vinicianus. (*Classical Numismatic Group, Inc. http://www.cngcoins.com, CC BY-SA 2.5 <https://creativecommons.org/licenses/by-sa/2.5>, via Wikimedia Commons*)

Gold aureus of Nerva issued in AD 97. Shows head of the emperor, and on the reverse two clasped hands with the legend *CONCORDIA EXERCITVVM*, the peace of the army. The need to issue this legend suggests that the loyalty of the army to the new regime was questionable, especially as at least one legion in Pannonia mutinied after the murder of Domitian. (*Classical Numismatic Group, Inc. http://www.cngcoins. com, CC BY-SA 2.5 <https://creativecommons.org/licenses/by-sa/2.5>, via Wikimedia Commons*)

Honorific inscription to the deified Drusilla, with the name of her brother, Emperor Gaius, removed due to *damnatio memoriae* decreed by the Senate after the ascension of Claudius (CIL, XI, 3598). (*Vatican Museums, Public domain, via Wikimedia Commons*)

Bust of Livia, the wife of Augustus and mother of Tiberius. (*Musée Saint-Raymond, Béziers, France, Public domain, via Wikimedia Commons*)

Marble bust of M. Vipsanius Agrippa, second husband of Julia the Elder, c. 25–24 BC. (*Louvre Museum, Paris, CC BY 2.5 <https://creativecommons.org/licenses/by/2.5>, via Wikimedia Commons*)

Bust of Gnaeus Domitius Ahenobarbus, the father of Nero. Located in the Museo Chiaramonti, part of the Vatican Museums. (*Daderot, Public domain, via Wikimedia Commons*)

A marble bust of a Roman noble. Once thought to show Cn. Domitius Corbulo, it is now suggested that it depicts Gaius Cassius Longinus. (*Capitoline Museums, Rome, CC BY 2.5 <https://creativecommons.org/licenses/by/2.5>, via Wikimedia Commons*)

Bust of Servius Sulpicius Galba, who pre-emptively executed Cornelius Gaetulucis in Upper Germany on the orders of Gaius. He later rose in revolt against Nero and became emperor from AD 68–69. Located in Gustav III's Museum of Antiquities in Stockholm. (*Richard Mortel from Riyadh, Saudi Arabia, CC BY 2.0 <https://creativecommons.org/licenses/by/2.0>, via Wikimedia Commons*)

Statue of Claudia Antonia, daughter of Claudius and his second wife, Aelia Paetina. (© *Marie-Lan Nguyen/Wikimedia Commons*)

As a Stoic, Seneca found no issue as an advisor to the emperor or his riches. However, others did. The infamous *delator* Suillius Rufus, pursuing a personal vendetta, assailed him in public and private in AD 58 as 'the embittered enemy of the friends of Claudius, under whom he had suffered a well-earned exile'. He asked his audience how this adulterer who 'polluted the couches of imperial princesses' and sucked Rome, Italy and the provinces dry with his 'limitless usury' was able to justify through his philosophical beliefs acquiring in just 'four years of royal favour, three hundred million sesterces'.[4] There was a considerable degree of truth to these allegations, which made them even more damaging. Seneca had no difficulty in finding accusers and witnesses to prosecute the hated *delator*, such were the multitude of his victims, along with their relatives and *amici*. Suillius was charged with virtually all the crimes of Claudius's reign, including driving Q. Pomponius Secundus to join the revolt of Camillus Scribonianus, along with the deaths of numerous prominent men and women. The case was heard in private by the emperor and he was convicted. He lost half his wealth and was exiled to the Balearic Islands.[5]

The case is significant, as Suillius Rufus would never have dared to challenge Seneca in the pomp of his power and influence. By AD 58, Seneca was struggling to maintain his authority over an increasingly independent and uncontrollable Nero. He and Burrus had abandoned Agrippina, who attempted to steer her son towards a middle course and preserve his marriage to Claudius's daughter, Octavia.[6] Agrippina faced accusations, encouraged by her son, who banished her from the palace and withdrew her Praetorian bodyguard. In response, she supported the aspirations of Britannicus, with tragic results. In AD 59, urged on by his mistress, Poppaea Sabina, Nero arranged for his mother to visit him in his palace on the Bay of Naples. The ship that took her home was designed to collapse and drown her. She miraculously survived; the news being brought to an increasingly panicking son. Seneca and Burrus were roused from their sleep and the emperor told him what he had done. Their dumbstruck response suggests they were innocent of this crime up to this point. Nero wanted to send the Praetorians to kill Agrippina, but Burrus warned him that their loyalty to the daughter of Germanicus 'would flinch from drastic measures against his issue'. Many of the officers had been appointed by her. Instead, Burrus said that the naval officers and their men, who had failed so wretchedly to drown her, were duty-bound to rectify the situation. Agrippina was brutally beaten to death in her bed chamber and her body was hastily buried near the road to Misenum.[7] Her son suffered the anguish of the Furies, being 'hounded by his mother's ghost'.[8]

In AD 62, the Praetorian Prefect Burrus died, leaving Seneca isolated. Burrus was replaced by Ofonius Tigellinus and Faenius Rufus, both of whom had past associations with Agrippina. Tigellinus had been exiled after the failure of the conspiracy of Aemilius Lepidus and accused of adultery with both imperial sisters of Gaius. He came to Nero's attention through a shared love of horseracing and was appointed Prefect of the Vigiles. His colleague, Faenius Rufus, had been Prefect of the Annona thanks to the patronage of Agrippina, a post he performed with rare efficiency.[9] Tigellinus used his unrestricted access to Nero to poison his views of Seneca, whose stock had fallen so low that he needed to make appointments to receive an imperial audience.[10] The elderly courtier, now 65, pleading infirmity and poor health, requested permission to retire to his country estates. Tigellinus knew 'with Seneca brought low, it was a simple matter to undermine Faenius Rufus, the charge in this case being friendship with Agrippina'.[11]

With all restraints now removed, Nero eliminated many of those of imperial descent who through luck or good judgement had managed to survive until then. In distant Asia Minor, Rubellius Plautus was executed by Praetorians sent from Rome. His mother, Julia, was the daughter of Tiberius's son, Drusus. In Massilia, on the Mediterranean coast of Gallia Narbonensis, Faustus Cornelius Sulla was murdered at his dinner table. He was the last of his illustrious name, half-brother to Messalina. Closer to home, Nero divorced Claudius's daughter, Octavia, on the fictitious charge of adultery. She was first exiled, and then the order came to her guard to execute her. Her veins were cut open and she was suffocated in a bath.[12] In her twenty-one years, she had witnessed horrors. Her mother, Messalina, had been executed by her father, Claudius. Her brother, Britannicus, was poisoned whilst she dined with him, and her first fiancé forced to commit suicide so she could be married to Nero. Then, 'as a further and more hideous cruelty her head was amputated and carried to Rome, where it was viewed by Poppaea', the emperor's new wife.[13] The freedman Pallas, who had supported Agrippina, was also poisoned, having been dismissed from Nero's service in AD 55.

Seneca awaited his death. He was charged by a certain Romanus, 'who attacked Seneca, in private informations, as the associate of Gnaeus Piso, but was himself struck down by Seneca, on the same charge. The result was the alarm of Piso and the birth of an elaborate and luckless conspiracy against Nero.'[14] Romanus was almost certainly an imperial freedman, but the nature of the accusation remains obscure. Nero clearly heard the case in the palace with his *amici Caesaris*, which would have included Tigellinus and Rufus, but surprisingly it was dismissed. This was probably due to an elegant defence presented by Seneca, and possibly by Piso too. Both the defendants were evidently close friends and the political attack on Seneca would have endangered his *amicus*. In the circumstances, a defeat in court would have resulted in exile and, more likely, death.[15]

Seneca survived, but he lived a life of fear, travelling between his Italian estates, to Nomentum, Alba, Campania and Baiae on the Bay of Naples. He gave up drinking wine for spring water; not, as his flatters would have people believe, due to aesthetic Stoic beliefs, but to avoid the fate of Britannicus. He restricted his diet to dry bread, figs and other fruit, which made it difficult to hide the taste of poison. He withdrew from society, feigning illness as though he was on the point of death. He devoted himself to writing and Stoicism. In a letter to a friend, he wrote: 'Leisure without study is death, it's burial for a living man.' His thoughts constantly turned to his death, and he planned in detail his last day to mirror that of Socrates. He wished his final hours to reflect his life, one of brilliance and dignity. However, he lived a life that could be extinguished at any moment, at the mercy of another's whim. That, even to a Stoic, was no way to exist.[16]

Gaius Calpurnius Piso counted himself among Nero's friends. The shock of finding himself tried before the emperor brought home the capricious nature of imperial politics. His crime was a bond of friendship with Seneca. He came from a noble and ancient Republican family which claimed descent from Numa Pompilius, Rome's legendary second king. A panegyric, the *Laus Pisonis*, was probably written in his honour by either Calpurnius Siculus or, more likely, Lucan.[17] It praises his character and name:

> 'On the one hand, Piso, comes the summons of your noble rank with the exalted names of ancient Calpus, resplendent among the clans of Rome: on the other, I am thrilled by your own merit, your life in every phase inspiring admiration – such a life as would have been equal to nobility, if nobility had perchance not been yours at birth.'[18]

His father was probably the consul of AD 27, L. Calpurnius Piso, also City Prefect and governor of Africa, whom Gaius deprived of his legion as he 'feared that arrogance might lead him to revolt'.[19] His grandfather was then either L. Calpurnius Piso, the Pontifex, one of the great men of the reigns of Augustus and Tiberius, or the consul of 7 BC, Gnaeus Calpurnius Piso, who was accused of poisoning Germanicus and committed suicide in AD 20. Both were the close confidant to emperors and winners of numerous honours. The grandson had much to live up to, and his first step was admission to the priestly college of the Arval Brethren in May AD 38, followed by consular office.[20]

It was probably soon after holding the highest office in the *cursus honorum* that the *Laus Pisonis* was written. However, the poet struggles to compare his patron's achievements to those of his illustrious ancestors. There were no military victories to applaud, nor advancement as a personal advisor to the emperor.

Instead, praise is restricted to civic virtues, his eloquence at defending his *amici* and clients in court, his lofty oratory in lauding Gaius before a hushed Senate, his generosity to friends and his courtesy to all. He is dignified, moderate and witty in conversation and manners, and physically imposing, tall and handsome. His learning is demonstrated by his poetry and skill with the lyre, whilst his martial abilities are evident when he practices with weapons or plays ball. What is missing are military offices, civilian posts or any career except the consulship, which was his birth right. But, as the poet mentions three times, he was young. There was the hope of future glory, battles won and honours credibly gained. However, disaster then struck.[21]

Piso was betrothed to the aristocratic Livia Orestilla, who was probably descended from Livia, Augustus's wife.[22] However, Gaius intervened at their wedding ceremony and, according to one story recorded by Suetonius, abducted her and 'had the bride carried off to his own home', and then married her himself.[23] The Calpurnii were already too illustrious to be permitted to marry a woman connected to the imperial family, admittedly distantly. Orestilla, though, had no interest in being an empress and remained loyal to the husband of her own choice. Piso and his former fiancée met illicitly, and upon their discovery, Gaius divorced her and exiled both. The emperor 'permitted Piso to take with him ten slaves, and then, when he asked for more, allowed him to employ as many as he liked, merely remarking, "You will have just as many soldiers, too, with you."'[24] The presence of the Praetorians would have been a daily reminder of the precariousness of his existence.

Piso returned to Rome with the amnesty declared by Claudius. However, there were no further offices or honours. He did, however, find love, 'whom low born as she was and recommended only by physical beauty, he had stolen from the bed of one of his friends'. The marriage to Satria Galla meant, according to Tacitus, that 'Piso's infamy was kept alive'. No member of the Satria *gens* had ever become consul, so they were not considered a noble family. Tacitus, admittedly no admirer of Piso, condemns him for abandoning his exclusive lineage in his choice of wife, but even on the point of death his last thoughts were preserving her life and that of his son by leaving a will 'marked by disgusting flatteries of Nero'.[25]

The accession of Nero did provide him with an opportunity to gain imperial favour. He had inherited a fortune from his mother, which he used to beautify his residences and entertain guests with lavish banquets and performances. This embellished his status as one of the foremost nobles in Rome. More importantly, he shared with the emperor a love of Greek culture, but like Nero, he went beyond the usual aristocratic expressions of an elite education by studying the ancient orators and poets, instead making his own contributions to the poetic, artistic and musical genre, as well as acting on the stage. According to the *Laus Pisonis*, 'Greek culture flows forth readily from Roman lips', for 'what lustre, ye gods above, what lustre shines on the fair language of his lips! Here words sparkling in compact splendour have filled out his choice passages; here, decked out with tropes there flies to the hearer from the freed lathe a swift epigram.' He was, like the emperor himself, guided by the patronage of Apollo. This overt philhellenism did not sit well with Rome's aristocratic elite, as it implied effeminacy and a demeaning pandering to the base sentiments of the uncouth crowd.[26]

Consequently, Tacitus, the upholder of traditional Roman virtues, degrades Piso's character and talents, saying he 'enjoyed with the multitude a shining reputation for virtue, or for spectacular qualities resembling virtues'. He continues that, in his opinion, Piso was a superficial and shallow man, whose 'weight of character and continence in pleasure were absent: he gave full scope to frivolity, to ostentation, and at times to debauchery – a trait which was approved by that majority of men, who, in view of the manifold allurements of vice, desire no strictness or marked austerity in the head of state.'[27] Like Nero and Seneca, Piso was a great patron of poets, musicians, actors and artists. The poet Martial commends the generosity of artistic supporters of this golden age: 'Give me back the Pisos and Senecas', he cries, comparing them to the miserly support of his present age.[28]

At the head of this cult of beauty in all its forms was the emperor himself. He lived by a doctrine of aestheticism. His artistic entourage, which included Piso and Seneca, also numbered the future emperor Marcus Cocceius Nerva, whom he hailed as the 'the Tibullus of our time' for his erotic poetry.[29] Seneca promoted the ability of his young nephew, Lucan, who was called to Rome from Athens by the emperor. In AD 60, the gifted poet entered the Neronia, a massive festival encompassing the emperor's loves: poetry, oratory, music and horseracing. Lucan's *Laudes Neronis* was utterly sincere in its praise of the emperor and he won one of the prizes. However, to the horror of those with more traditional values, Nero himself performed, unsurprisingly winning the competitions for poetry and oratory, and then in AD 64 he performed in Naples on the lyre. A cohort of the guard was detached to watch. Many of the soldiers would have been horrified. He drank in public acclaim, freed from the restraints of Seneca and Burrus, liberated by the encouragement of Tigellinus. A Greek aristocrat could win fame and admiration, but not a Roman one.[30]

Lucan revelled in his imperial patronage, soon receiving a quaestorship at a remarkably young age. Nero took immense pleasure from his verses, but gradually their relationship soured. The emperor could not compete with Lucan's towering reputation, and the fall of his uncle added to the strain.[31] Even then he recognized his superior talent, although admiration soon turned to rivalry. The final breach came in a recital by Lucan of his partly finished masterpiece, the *Pharsalia (De Bello Civili)*. The emperor was the principal guest. After an initial introduction lamenting the shedding of Roman blood in the civil war fought by Julius Caesar, and a flattering dedication to Nero, the poem describes the defeat of Pompey the Great and Rome's subsequent loss of liberty under the emperors, commending the murder of Caesar as an example of tyrannicide. The latter part may have only been written after the failure of the conspiracy in AD 65. Understandably, Nero, who was related to Julius Caesar through his adoption by Augustus, rose and left. This was not, the *Vita Lucani* asserts, in a fit of jealous pique, but a public rejection of the political assertions of the elegy. Lucan was then banned from any further recitals or publication of his works. He was not exiled as others would have been under previous emperors, nor prohibited from writing, but the affront was too much for the poet.[32]

Lucan was not to be silenced; his vanity and need for self-advertisement superseded all else. He continued with several satirical attacks upon the emperor and his *amici*:

'Lucan no longer held himself back from words and palpable acts of hostility towards the emperor, so much so that once, in a public lavatory, when he emptied his bowels with a rather loud noise, he shouted out this half-line of Nero's, while the other lavatory users ran off in a panic: "You would think thunder had broken out the earth."'[33]

He got the publicity he desired. The comment was deliberately adroit, and it was soon the centre of secret hilarity in the dining rooms of the wealthy. The line worked on two levels. Firstly, it is base humour associating his own diarrhoea under the toilet seat to thundering underground, but it also equates the emperor's poetry to excrement.[34]

Lucan did not stop there: 'He also lashed out at both Nero himself and his most powerful friends in a slanderous poem.'[35] This was written in response to the horrendous fire that destroyed much of Rome in AD 64. The inferno started in the shops and stalls around the Circus Maximus, and after devouring the high-rise tenements of the poor in the valley bottom, climbed up the Palatine and Caelian hills to engulf the mansions of the rich built on the high ground. Many thousands were burned alive, with many more left destitute. The imperial palace was destroyed, and probably that of Calpurnius Piso on the Caelian Hill. Nero was staying at his villa in Antium when he received the news. He rushed back to Rome to take charge of the fire-fighting, opening the Campus Martius and the imperial gardens to the survivors as well as building shelters for them.

Food was brought in from Ostia and the surrounding towns, whilst imperial funds subsidized the price of grain.[36] The emperor's enemies saw opportunity in the suffering. Rumours were deliberately spread that Nero had sung verses of the destruction of Troy from a balcony or had deliberately ordered the fire to be started so he could build his vast new palace covering huge areas of the destroyed city.[37] Many of the rich were not compensated for the land they lost to Nero's 'Golden House', and they had to pay a large increase in taxes to raise revenue for the reconstruction projects.

Nero was greatly concerned by these rumours, but Lucan as though inviting death, made much of the allegations. In his *De Incendio Urbis* (*On the Burning of the City*, he describes 'the unspeakable flames of the guilty slave-master', meaning Nero, supporting the idea that the emperor himself had set fire to Rome to make room for his new palace.[38] These reports and stories were unfounded, but were meant to undermine the popularity and support for the emperor amongst Rome's poor. He had employed the Praetorians, as well as the Vigiles and Urban Cohorts, to fight the flames and restore order. One of their number, though, was not focused on creating fire breaks or capturing arsonists who were adding to the chaos. Instead, the Praetorian Tribune Subrius Flavus watched the emperor and contemplated his murder.

Subrius Flavus hated the emperor, and at some point in AD 64 he started to plan his assassination. In Naples, Nero had performed in public, the audience augmented with Praetorian guardsmen to encourage a positive response to his recital. In the estimation of a soldier, such an effete act lacked Roman *virtus* and demeaned the dignity of the imperial office. There, Flavus

'had conceived an impulse to attack Nero while he was singing on the stage, or while, during the burning of the palace, he was rushing unguarded from place to place in the night. In one case, there were the opportunities of solitude: in the other, the very presence of a crowd, to be the fairest witness of such an exploit, had fired his imagination; only the desire of escape, that eternal enemy of high enterprise, gave him pause.'[39]

The desire for the glory of a tyrannicide before a captivated audience conflicted with the very human desire to avoid certain death.

The soldier was brave, mirroring the character of Cassius Chaerea, the assassin of Gaius. After his capture and facing imminent execution, Subrius Flavus was dragged before the emperor, who asked him why he had broken his oath to protect his life. After first denying any involvement, the tribune 'embraced the glory of confession' and admitted all: "'I hated you," he answered, "and yet there was not a man in the army truer to you, as long as you deserved to be loved. I began to hate you when you turned into the murderer of your mother and wife – a chariot-driver, an actor, a fire-raiser."'Tacitus is cautious to report his exact words, as, unlike Seneca, who had carefully prepared an audience of friends to witness his death and had written it all down in anticipation of failure, this brave soldier's response came from his soul, unadulterated.[40]

The delay in Flavus's actions was not a reticence to risk his life, but an anxiety caused by whom to approach and trust. He needed to wait for the opportunity to approach comrades in private. The educated elite could hide their intent behind ambiguities and philosophical debates. Not so for a soldier, even though he was an officer. Tacitus, commenting on the recruitment strategy of the senators and *equites*, talks of them 'scattering allusions, therefore, among themselves or their friends, to the crimes of the sovereign, the approaching dissolution of empire, the need of choosing the saviour of an outworn society'.[41] These were vague, ephemeral statements that could be readily denied, in the manner of Brutus's recruitment of his *amici* when planning the murder of Julius Caesar.

Flavus enlisted the support of Sulpicius Asper, a Praetorian centurion who was equally outraged by Nero as he could no longer 'endure his disgraceful behaviour, his licentiousness, and his cruelty'.[42] It is likely he served in Flavus's cohort, so he would have known his character and sentiments well. Further secluded, discreet conversations would have been possible with his superior officer, Faenius Rufus. The political situation of the Praetorian Prefect had continued to deteriorate. His colleague Tigellinus 'persecuted him with calumnies and repeatedly awakened his alarm by describing him as the paramour of Agrippina, still mourning her, and determined upon vengeance'.[43] The Prefect was popular with the soldiers and brought with him further connections to trustworthy officers, many of whom had been appointed through the patronage of the emperor's murdered mother. Rufus now took a leading role in the plot. According to Dio, it was led by Seneca 'and Rufus, the prefect and some other prominent men'.[44]

In all, three out of the twelve tribunes were implicated – Subrius Fulvus, Gavius Silvanus and Statius Proxumus, the latter two joining later – along with the centurions Sulpicius Asper, Venetus Paulus and Maximus Scaurus. A partially preserved inscription records Silvanus's illustrious career. He had risen from the rank of centurion in the legions to a tribunate in the *Vigiles*, then as a Praetorian tribune accompanied Claudius to Britain, where he was awarded a golden crown for killing an enemy in single combat and holding ground to the end of a battle. He was a brave, battle-hardened soldier.[45]

Four further tribunes – Cornelius Martialis, Flavius Nepos, Pompeius and Statius Domitius – would be later stripped of their rank, suggesting they knew of the plot but did not become actively involved. There must have been some members of the rank and file involved, but most were loyal to Nero and the

Julio-Claudian dynasty. Some will have reasoned that they would win either way the dice rolled: if the plot succeeded, they would receive a substantial donative from the new ruler; if it failed, they would be rewarded for their loyalty.[46]

There were evidently a number of dissipated conspiracies which formed after AD 62. One grew within the Praetorian Guard, centred around Subrius Fulvus, in AD 64. Another grew after Romanus's accusations against Seneca and Piso, who were associated with one another. Piso had remained in close contact with his illustrious *amicus*, sending his equestrian client, Antonius Natalis, with concerned messages when he fell sick, but he was often denied an invitation to attend him personally. Seneca lived in social isolation, avoiding any contact with courtiers and potential accusations, nor did he commit any indiscreet communication to paper. Natalis was the only conspirator to name Seneca in the plot, as he limited his association to it solely through the medium of Piso and his envoy.[47] However, the conspiracy did not originate with Piso, as Tacitus makes clear, for, despite not knowing who its original author was, the historian is certain that 'the beginning of the conspiracy did not come from his own wish'.[48]

The problem for Seneca was that he lacked opportunity due to his withdrawal from the court. Piso didn't lack such opportunity, for Nero was a regular visitor to his seaside villa at Baiae, especially after the destruction of their residences by the fire in Rome. Nero loved the sea, travelling out in the Bay of Naples from his own villa on the coast. The resplendent charms of his fellow philhellene's sumptuous property drew him regularly to drop his guard, for 'its charms had a fascination for the Caesar, who came frequently and indulged in the bath or the banquet, dispensing with his guards and tedious magnificence of his rank'.[49] So it was to Piso that Seneca turned, tempting him with the offer of the throne when there were others more qualified through nobility or character to wear the imperial purple. Piso embraced the chance, a slave to ambition and his pride in his nobility.

Apart from Nero himself, the last living male relative of Augustus was Lucius Junius Silanus Torquatus. His father had been poisoned by Agrippina at the start of Nero's reign, so he was brought up by his aunt, Junia Lepida, and her husband, the famous jurist Cassius Longinus, a descendant of Caesar's assassin. Silanus was 'a temperate youth' with an 'exalted lineage and due to the training of Gaius Cassius, with whom he had been educated, stood high enough for any dignity'. Yet the fate of numerous members of his family meant he remained 'vigilant', unwilling to commit, wary and prepared to wait upon events.[50] Nevertheless, Piso knew that many senators would support his candidacy for the throne above his own, fearing that Silanus might 'grasp at the empire; which would be promptly offered to him by the persons who had held aloof from the plot or who pitied Nero as the victim of a murder'.[51] This phrase is significant in its implication that there were many who knew of the plot's existence but were unwilling to risk all by taking an active role. Furthermore, there were many senators who supported Nero and would perceive him as the victim rather than those who had been murdered, exiled or executed during his reign.

Another figure to cause Piso anxiety was the consul Marcus Julius Vestinus Atticus. He had prospered initially due to the influence of his father, who had been Prefect of Egypt from AD 60–62 and a friend of Claudius. His son had been raised to Patrician status through Nero's favour. Another worshipper of beauty, the consul had collected a matching set of handsome slaves who complemented his fabulous furnishings and tableware. Initially a close *amicus* of the emperor, Atticus's bawdy wit and unencumbered liberality of speech had alienated Nero, who had grown to hate him with a passion. Atticus, though, was not intimidated by imperial hostility, 'understanding perfectly, and despising the pusillanimity of the sovereign; the sovereign afraid of the masterful friend who so often mocked him with that rough humour which, if it draws too largely on truth, leaves pungent memories behind'. Consequently, the consul had transformed his house, which dominated the Forum, into a fortress, guarded by a cohort of young men, whilst continuing to fulfil his duties as consul, patron and benefactor to his clients.[52]

He had many admirers, his nobility having sprung from his bravery and willingness to behave as a Republican senator from a bygone age. Such a man of energy, commanding the Senate through his office and a known opponent of the emperor, would have been a valuable asset to the conspiracy. The plotters met to discuss approaching him but then rejected the idea, 'some through old animosities, the majority because they considered him headstrong and impossible as a partner'. Furthermore, Piso considered him a rival who could 'arise as the champion of liberty, or, by selecting another as emperor, convert the state into a gift of his own bestowing'.[53] Piso, although in exile, would have known about the attempt by the consuls in January AD 41 to restore the Republic upon the murder of Gaius, as well as the attempt by others to use a senatorial vote to win the throne. For this reason, Piso postponed and delayed the plan to murder Nero whilst visiting his villa at Baiae. Rome lay 142 miles away, meaning it would take at least two days by road or a dangerous journey by sea, chancing April storms. Piso imagined entering Rome after he had risked all, only to find another had ascended the throne. Nor would he want to taint his claim with another emperor's blood on his hands, the rules of hospitality sacrificed for personal gain. He argued that the murder should take place in Rome in the palace or before a supporting audience in the theatre. Consequently, the plan was delayed.[54]

This meeting of the conspirators was extremely risky. To avoid suspicions, it is likely to have been convened under the guise of a banquet. Consequently, the guests were Piso's own *amici* and clients, just as Cassius and Brutus based their plot around their own networks of *amicitiae*. Natalis, Piso's envoy and 'the partner of Piso in all his secret counsels', would have been present, and as such 'was better acquainted with the conspiracy as a whole'. Seneca would not have risked so public a gathering. Others associated with the plot were probably members of Piso's own network of friends and clients. There was the senator Afranius Quintianus, who was 'a notorious degenerate, had been attacked by Nero in a scurrilous poem, and was now intent upon avenging the affront'. Another senator was Flavius Scaevinus, whose mental powers, according to the critical Tacitus, 'had been wrecked by debauchery, and his life was one of corresponding languor and somnolence'; he was described later by the tribune Subrius Flavus as 'effeminate', a description also applied to Flavus, Quintianus and the equestrian Claudius Senecio. Sceavinus and Natalis appear to have known each other well and 'were on intimate terms with Gaius Piso'. Both now 'took the lead' in the enterprise.[55]

Claudius Senecio was the handsome son of a Claudian freedman, and so probably knew Nero before he became emperor. He was at first a close confidant of the emperor, helping to keep his secret mistress from the knowledge of his mother, Agrippina.[56] By AD 65, his influence had declined, but he 'maintained even then a semblance of friendship and was exposed in consequence to a larger variety of dangers'.[57] Unfortunately, there are no further details of Senecio. He was, however, associated with Otho, the son of the governor of Dalmatia, who replaced Camillus Scribonianus in AD 42 and had been, since AD 59, a virtual exile, acting as governor of distant Lusitania in Spain. His crime was to have been married to Poppaea Sabina, the emperor's wife. Whatever his offence, he clearly felt his life was endangered.

Senecio was also a close *amicus* of Annius Pollio, the eldest son of L. Annius Vinicianus, who had plotted against Gaius and Claudius and paid the ultimate price. However, Pollio's involvement was minimal, as he was only exiled after the discovery of the plot rather than executed. Indeed, all the convicted equestrians, apart from Lucan, were exiled. They appear to be young men hoping for significant rewards from their senatorial patron for their loyalty. The equestrian Glitius Gallus was a military tribune from Falerii and a client of the senator Afranius Quintianus. Another, Julius Augurinus, is recorded on an inscription from Mogontiacum as a cavalry prefect of the *ala Gallorum Petriana*. The motivations of others are dismissed by Tacitus as simply a desire for revolution. Their lowly status precluded a more thorough examination of their rationales.[58]

Another figure of note is the senator Plautius Lateranus, who had been designated consul for AD 66. He had survived his brush with death in AD 48 after the fall of Messalina. His life had been saved by his uncle, Aulus Plautius, the conqueror of Britain. Of all the motivations of the conspirators, his was purely honourable and noble. Like Lucan, he proved to the conspirators his commitment to their cause through 'the vivacity of their hatreds', but his motivation was not through a personal grievance against the emperor but 'by affection for the commonwealth'. Nero had recalled him from his exile imposed by Claudius and had done him no wrong, even nominating him for consular office. Yet he must have harboured a deep hatred of the Principate itself, having come so close to death. Furthermore, it was well known that he had fallen into financial difficulty. Like Piso, he owned a huge house on the Caelian Hill, which would in centuries to come be granted to the Popes as the Lateran Palace. The fire had probably ravaged his property and he would have struggled for the funds to restore it. A tyrannicide could forestall the demands of creditors, knowing that the new emperor was in his debt. Furthermore, a comment he made to Epaphroditus, one of Nero's secretaries, reveals a typical aristocratic hostility to the unrestricted access the imperial freedmen had to the emperor and the power they exercised.[59]

Lateranus would take a central role in the eventual assassination plan, signalling his position amongst the conspirators. Lucan also harnessed his hatred of Nero to ensure his destruction and played a leading part – 'he came out almost as the ringleader of the Pisonian conspiracy, talking a lot in public about the praiseworthy glory of tyrannicide, and full of threats; he was so out of control, that he even bragged about Caesar's execution to all his friends'.[60] Lucan's lack of discretion not only endangered his own life but made the plotters' discovery almost inevitable. Time became imperative, as each passing day brought their destruction closer.

Until the Praetorian Prefect, Faenius Rufus, joined the plot, the conspirators lacked confidence and belief, their discussions merely a talking shop. However, once they were convinced of his commitment, there was a renewed vigour with a realistic opportunity for success. Indeed, 'they began to show more alacrity in debating the time and place of the assassination'.[61] Yet even then, 'while they were still hesitating, reluctant to abridge the period of hope and fear',[62] the frustrations of the more emboldened grew. Piso's reluctance to commit to the original plan to murder Nero at his seaside villa possibly hindered its advancement. Despairing of any further progress, an otherwise unknown concubine took matters into her own hands. Epicharis, 'who had gained her information by means unknown – she had never previously shown interest in anything honourable – began to animate and upbraid the conspirators'.[63] Still, no decisions were made. And as time passed, the risk of discovery increased.

Epicharis is an ephemeral figure who, despite her sex and lowly status, engendered the admiration of Tacitus. He is surprised that a sexually promiscuous woman, like the Julias or Messalina, could be capable of honourable actions.[64] A third-century source identifies her as a mistress of Seneca's brother, Annaeus Mela.[65] Epicharis, increasingly frustrated by these delays, decided to take the bull by the horns. When in Campania, she visited one of the captains in the imperial fleet at Misenum. They clearly had a well-established relationship, as he disclosed some highly sensitive information to her. This captain was Volusius Proculus,

> 'one of Nero's agents in the assassination of his mother, but not (he considered) promoted as the importance of the crime deserved. This person, as a former acquaintance of the woman (or possibly the friendship may have been of recent growth), disclosed what his services to Nero had been, and how thankless they have proved, then proceeded to complaints and to a declared intention of settling the account, should occasion offer.'[66]

Epicharis seems to have been at the centre of the conspiracy, as she was well aware of its progress and was in a position to criticize its members for their risk-averse mentality, even though their status should have precluded such disapproval. She was most likely the concubine of one of its leaders.

The Misenum fleet was ripe for revolt, as in the previous year Nero had ordered it to return to its base from Formiae 'by a given date, [and] no allowance been made for the hazards of the sea'. Consequently, they set out through a raging storm, and as they rounded Cape Misenum many ships were driven onto rocks and lost.[67] The blame was easy to assign. Epicharis saw an opportunity and seized it. Proculus was the ideal target, evidently disaffected and willing to risk all to gain vengeance. She decided to take a risk, as he could win over other officers. Nero often travelled out on the bay, and the ship's crew could be used to overpower his limited guard and kill him. Other possibilities included landing a force of men at Piso's villa whilst the emperor was being entertained without any escort. There was a theatrical and vengeful aspect to this plan, as Nero had attempted to murder his own mother in the bay and had her killed in her villa near Misenum.[68]

Epicharis now encouraged Proculus's rage and

> 'entered upon a catalogue of the emperor's crimes: nothing was left either for the senate (or the people)! But a way had been provided by which he might pay the penalty for the ruin of his country. Proculus had only to gird himself to do his part, bring over his most resolute men to the cause, and look forward to a worthy reward.'

She left out the names of the conspirators, but otherwise revealed enough to make it clear that the plans were well advanced. The naval captain would have little interest in restoring senatorial influence. However, the promise of rewards certainly interested him, and he balanced the risk involved in joining the conspiracy against the certainty of reward with no risk in informing the emperor. He chose the latter option.[69]

Proculus was granted an audience with Nero, but he was only able to provide one name, that of Epicharis. She was summoned and questioned in the presence of her accuser, yet 'in the absence of corroborating evidence silenced him with some ease'. The emperor must have had to evaluate the credibility of numerous allegations. He did remain suspicious, imprisoning Epicharis but not ordering her to be tortured.[70]

The Praetorians involved in the plot will have got messages to their associates that Epicharis had been arrested but not yet tortured. Time was running out for them. Ironically, she had succeeded in putting some steel into the conspirators' resolve. They were now 'moved by fear of betrayal', resolved to kill Nero on the last day of the Circensian Games on 19 April. The emperor, however, took no chances, 'rarely left home and secluded himself in his palace or gardens'.[71] There were no further imperial visits to Piso's maritime villa, so a new plan was required.

The conspirators looked to the successful assassinations of Julius Caesar and Gaius, with an added sense of theatre. Precedent was always important to the Romans. The audience was supplied by the crowd gathered in the Circus Maximus to watch the chariot racing. Theatrical shows had been performed on every day of the festival, apart from the last one. The plotters intended to make a change to the schedule and include their own real-life play centred around a repeat performance of the murder of Julius Caesar. They were poets and artists to the very end. All wore the traditional white for the festival, reflecting the purity of their actions. Nero was due to make libations at the altar before the Temple to the Sun just above the imperial box, and there they would strike the blow for liberty.[72]

It was agreed that Lateranus, who had an imposing muscular build, should approach the emperor as a supplicant petitioning for funds to protect him from his creditors. On his knees before Nero, he would grab his legs and pull him down, then hold him there. Flavius Scaevinus demanded the central role of being the first to plunge the dagger into the pinned emperor, assisted by the tribunes and centurions involved in the conspiracy. For this purpose, Scaevinus had travelled to the Temple of Fortune, or in another version the Temple of Public Safety, in the town of Ferentinum in Etruria. He wore the weapon openly in the days before the planned assassination, 'as the instrument sanctified to a great work'. The theatrical nature of their planning reflected the Stoics' belief that life was a stage and their actions a performance mirroring those of the great tyrannicides involved in the attack on Caesar: Lateranus would be Cimber, with Scaevinus as Casca.[73]

Piso was to wait for a message at the Temple of Ceres that lay next to the Circus Maximus at the foot of the Aventine Hill. It was important for a future emperor and Pontifex Maximus not to pollute his hands in blood or be too closely associated with a treacherous act that broke his religious oath to protect the emperor and the bonds of *amicitiae*. Accompanied by the Praetorian Prefect Faenius Rufus, he was then to parade through the streets of the capital, gathering supporters, towards the Praetorian fortress. The importance of quickly winning the support of the guard had been learnt from the mistakes made in the murder of Gaius and the coup of Claudius. The tribunes and centurions would be vital in winning the acquiescence of the rank and file. The Senate would be then presented with a *fait accompli* and forced to give their assent through fear of the Praetorians.[74]

However, there was clearly some concern that the Praetorians would not support the accession of Piso, as their loyalties remained fixed to the Julio-Claudian dynasty. Consequently, it was suggested that Antonia, Claudius's daughter with Aelia Paetina, would accompany them to 'elicit the approval of the crowd', but also the soldiers. Tacitus took this information from Pliny the Elder, but the historian found it difficult to believe, as Piso remained devoted to his wife, nor would the prudent Antonia have pledged her support to a cause so replete in danger. Piso understood that his claim to the throne was weak, whilst Antonia also knew from the fates of Britannicus and Octavia that her life was in perpetual threat. She did survive the failure of the plot, suggesting there was little evidence to implicate her, or she may have been completely unaware of her passive role and was to have only been approached once Nero was dead.[75]

A later rumour that found widespread credibility further emphasizes Piso's precarious aspirations to the purple. According to Tacitus, the Praetorian tribune

'Subrius Flavus and the centurions had decided in private conference, though not without Seneca's knowledge, that once Nero had been struck down by the agency of Piso, Piso should then be disposed of in his turn, and the empire made over to Seneca; who would thus appear to have been chosen for the supreme power by innocent men, as a consequence of his distinguished virtues.'[76]

The plotters had learnt from the chaos that resulted from not identifying a successor after the murder of Gaius, but that choice had been imposed on them, not agreed upon. The rumour still held traction many years later, as Juvenal repeated it when he asked: 'If a free vote were given to the people, who would be so depraved as to waver in his preference for Seneca over Nero?'[77] Circumstantial evidence suggests the assertion was indeed true.

Firstly, Tacitus reports 'a saying of Flavus in circulation, that "so far as disgrace went, it was immaterial if a harper was removed and a tragic actor took his place"; for Nero singing to his instrument was matched by Piso singing in his stage costume'.[78] Furthermore, when Flavus had been detained by Tigellinus and Nero, he made a convincing defence that 'a man of the sword, like himself, would never have shared so desperate an enterprise with unarmed effeminates'.[79] More incriminating is Seneca's movements. Instead of his usual practice of keeping well away from Rome on his rural Campanian estates, he took up residence on the very day planned for the assassination at his villa near Nomentum, just four miles north-east of Rome on the Via Nomentana. He also invited all his *amici* to his house on the day planned for the murder, witnesses to his accession to the throne perhaps or his glorious and long-planned death scene. The coincidences are far too incriminating to support his innocence and imply guilt.[80]

Nor did Seneca's Stoic beliefs preclude his acceptance of this imperial gift. Stoics believed that the worst form of government was an unjust monarchy, which equated with tyranny, whilst the best form was an enlightened monarchy. This was motivation enough to plot the murder of the tyrant and establish the rule of a philosopher emperor.[81] The conspirators were united in a common aim to replace one emperor with another, not restore the Republic. Conflict lay only in deciding who that person should be. Seneca's own work is replete with examples justifying the removal of a tyrant, but he saw the murder of Julius Caesar as a mistake as it led to the horror of civil war. Silanus had a better claim than him, and there was also the potential threat from provincial commanders such as Domitius Corbulo or Sulpicius Galba. It is difficult to understand how Seneca planned to avoid war in the event of his accession; possibly this was a problem for the future, once the immediate dangers had been extinguished.[82]

If it was Flavus's plan to replace Piso with Seneca, then it is likely Piso would have been murdered in the Praetorian camp away from his escort. There would be no escape, confined behind its imposing walls. His murder could be justified in avenging the death of Nero. Seneca was close by and could be quickly summoned to be presented to both the guard and the Senate. There were plots within plots, as existed in the successful conspiracy against Gaius. The similarities persist in the initial emergence of separate plots amongst groups of disaffected senators with their clients and *amici* and a group of Praetorian officers. The soldiers, though, lacked a successor who would be in their debt, hence their acceptance of the senators Annius Vinicianus or Claudius in AD 41, or Calpurnius Piso now. These men they accepted through force of circumstance rather than free choice.

If the assassination had been left to the Praetorian officers alone, Nero would have died. However, the utter incompetence of the senators and their focus on the theatrical nature of the act, rather than the mechanics of the assassination itself, instead ensured the deaths of them all. The day before the planned attack, Scaevinus visited the house of Piso's close advisor, Natalis. They dismissed their slaves and freedmen and entered a room alone. This was highly unusual, as slaves and freedmen accompanied their masters everywhere, mute witnesses to their daily lives. It certainly piqued the curiosity of Scaevinus's freedman, Milichus, who informed his wife of this unusual event when he returned home. After a considerable period, they both emerged, before Scaevinus returned and embarked on a series of bizarre actions.[83]

That evening, Scaevinus

'sealed his will, and taking the dagger mentioned above, from the sheath, complained that it was blunt from age, and gave orders that it was to be rubbed on a whetstone till the edge glittered: this task he entrusted to his freeman Milichus. At the same time, he began a more elaborate dinner than usual, and presented his favourite slaves with their liberty, or, in some cases, with money. He himself was moody, and obviously deep in thought, though he kept up a disconnected conversation with affected cheerfulness. At last, he gave the word that bandages for wounds and appliances for stopping haemorrhage were to be made ready. The instructions were again addressed to Milichus.'

These were the actions of a man preparing for death when he was very much alive. He appears detached from the realities of the situation, more concerned with the dramatic nature of the murder and perfecting his role than ensuring its success. He now appears as the titular Ajax in Sophocles's play, sharpening his sword before a battle. The Stoics believed that life was a stage, and Scaevinus now prepared to tread the boards.[84]

Milichus was a trusted former slave whose manumission meant he was forever in the debt of Scaevinus. However, the freedman had to balance his obligations to his former master against his own personal safety and that of his wife. If the plot failed, all members of Scaevinus's household would be tortured and executed. Furthermore, the preparations had been witnessed by many of his slaves and freedmen, who might decide to report him to the emperor themselves. There was the certainty of extensive rewards for such information, but his calculation was not as simple as Tacitus asserts. The historian's prejudices rise to the surface once more as he alleges that Milichus was motivated by personal gain, as befits 'his slavish brain', whilst his wife's advice to turn informer was inevitable from a base woman whose instinctive response to her husband's information was one of fear.[85]

At dawn, as the sun banished the dark that made the streets too dangerous to journey at night, Milichus and his wife hurried to the Servilian Gardens, which the emperor had made his residence as the Golden House was being built. They had stolen the ritual dagger to show as evidence. The guards refused them entry, but they were insistent. Eventually, they were taken to Epaphroditus, Nero's *a libellis*, his secretary for petitions. The law stated that any information pertaining to the endangerment of the emperor had to be reported to him. Milichus's difficulty in gaining entry to the palace suggests this was often ignored. The imperial freedman would have known of the naval captain's allegations and the presence of Epicharis in the prison. The emperor was summoned, and the account was repeated for his benefit.[86]

Scaevinus was arrested by Praetorians and brought before the emperor. The senator was questioned, but he delivered a convincing performance, belying Tacitus's judgement of his character. He declared that the dagger had been in his family for generations and was venerated by them. The heirloom was so precious to him that he kept it in his bedroom, but his freedman had stolen it. He said he often examined his will. However, he realised that his debts were about to overwhelm him, and the creditors were circling. He consequently decided to provide grants of money and free his favourite slaves in case his estates were seized to pay his loans and all his slaves sold to other owners. For this reason, he reviewed the contents of his will to make adjustments in case a financial disaster struck. As for the excessive banquet, he did have expensive tastes that those with more conservative and austere opinions may criticize, but that was no crime. This was an excellent touch, as the emperor was often criticised for similar shortcomings. As for the bandages, there simply weren't any. He said his accuser was playing the dual role of informer and witness, which was hardly reliable evidence. He finished with an impressive denunciation of Milichus as an unspeakable villain who could not be trusted. The emperor and his advisors were almost convinced of his innocence, until Milichus's wife remembered the unusual meeting between her master and Natalis and that both men were on intimate terms with Gaius Piso. Clearly, he was a man already under suspicion; his defence now fell apart.[87]

Scaevinus was questioned about the conversation he had with Natalis, as there were no witnesses. When Natalis appeared before the emperor, he gave a totally different account. Their fates were now sealed, and they were both thrown in irons. In a desperate bid to save himself, Natalis turned informer. He said he was at the very centre of the conspiracy. He named Piso, and, as he had acted as an intermediary between his patron and the philosopher, added the

name of Seneca. With Natalis ready to speak, Scaevinus also offered to provide
information, in the expectation of exile rather than death. He named Lucan,
Quintianus and Senecio. These three long denied the charges, but as others
broke, they too looked to their own survival and added further names; Lucan
gave his own mother, whilst Quintianus named his friend Glitius Gallus and
Senecio provided that of Annius Pollio.[88]

The conspiracy had unravelled. Plutarch reveals a complementary rather than
conflicting account of its collapse:

'For but one night remained, after which the tyrant was to die, and all
preparations had been made; but the man who was to kill him saw at the
palace gates when on his way to the theatre a prisoner about to be led
before Nero and lamenting his evil fortune. He approached the prisoner
and whispered to him, "Only pray, my good man, that today may pass by
and tomorrow you will be thankful to me." So the prisoner grasped the
intended meaning, and reflecting, I suppose, that he is a fool who leaves
things close at hand to follow what is out of reach, chose the surer rather
than the more just way of safety. For he revealed to Nero what had been
said to him by the man, who was immediately seized, and tortures and
fire and the lash were applied to the conspirator as he denied, in the face
of constraint, what he had revealed without constraint.'[89]

Unfortunately, the names of the conspirators are not supplied. Evidently, the
prisoner was one of those arrested at the very beginning of the night, for he
was offered hope when it soon became evident that there was none. The man
who approached him would have been a Praetorian officer, as no one else would
have dared to do so. At this stage, Nero was completely unaware of the number
of officers involved as their participation remained hidden. The Praetorian, like
all of his comrades, refused to divulge any information, whereas many of the
senators and equestrians involved broke at the mere threat of torture.[90]

If, as the Stoics believed, their deaths reflected their lives, many had lived
a dishonourable and dissolute existence. Few met their end resolutely or with
their honour intact. Piso himself knew of the plot's discovery due to the arrest of
Scaevinus. He was urged to seize the initiative and either address the populace
from the Rostra in the Forum, to stir up revolution, or hurry to the Praetorian
camp and win over the guard. The Praetorian Prefect, Faenius Rufus, and many
of the officers may have supported him, driven by their complicity to take decisive
action. But Piso was never decisive. Instead, he meekly accepted the situation.
He 'spent a short time in public', probably addressing his *amici* and clients at
his morning *salutatio*, then retired into the interior privacy of his home and

'steeled his spirit against the end, until a body of troops arrived'. There would be no trial; the evidence against him was overwhelming. Torture could not be used on a senator, so he was allowed to choose the manner of his death. He opened the arteries on each arm and bled to death. His last moments were spent with his wife, his love for her second only to his ambition. He was survived by a son, who was allowed to inherit some of his father's wealth and pursue a senatorial career. His house, though, was demolished, its ruins standing testament to his treachery as it had once symbolized his prestige and social status.[91]

In stark contrast to the behaviour of Piso and his closest male confederates, the concubine Epicharis exhibited a bravery that kept her name alive, even after death. She had no need for an elaborate and expensive tomb with an inscription recording forgettable deeds for future generations. Her courage and gift of her life to try to save her undeserving co-conspirators earned the admiration of Tacitus, who inscribed her name in history. Yet the historian was caught in a paradox. Her prominent role and bravery were an inversion of traditional values in Roman society, but he suppressed his alarm, recognizing her deeper worth. Conspiracies, after all, were born in hidden, secret places; the preserve of women, freedmen and slaves. As the first glimpses of a widespread plot revealed itself, Nero ordered her to be tortured. She was taken to the torture chamber under the supervision of Tigellinus, and for a day withstood agony. Fire was used on her, then she was whipped and then racked, her legs dislocated and her sinews snapped. She refused to reveal any names, even though some of those she protected had already betrayed others. As night fell, she was dragged back to her cell.

The next day promised a repeat of the same. A curtained litter was brought to carry her as she was no longer able to walk. Despite the pain, she used this moment of privacy to take her own life. She unwound her breast band and fastened it to the canopy of the litter, whilst pulling herself up and wrapping the other end around her neck. She then allowed the weight of her own body to tighten the noose. This must have been done in utter silence, as those carrying her would have intervened. Tacitus, full of admiration, found it utterly surprising that 'an emancipated slave and a woman, by shielding, under this dire coercion, men unconnected with her and all but unknown, had set an example which shone the brighter at a time when persons freeborn and male, Roman knights and senators, untouched by torture, were betraying each his nearest and dearest'.[92] There was no tomb for her, only an unmarked grave. Her epitaph was not carved in stone to be erased by wind and rain, but was preserved in the pages of Tacitus's *Annals*.

Not all behaved in the manner of Natalis or Lucan. The consul designate Lateranus had been betrayed. He was caught utterly by surprise, suggesting he was one of the first to be named along with Piso. He was not allowed to embrace his wife and children, nor given the opportunity to choose the manner of his death. He was to be questioned. There in the palace, he was approached by the freedman Epaphroditus, who asked him why he had plotted against the emperor. Lateranus bristled at being addressed by a freedman, a former slave, who dared to speak to him, a senator. Epaphroditus was told: 'If I want anything, I'll speak to your master.' The use of 'master' was a deliberate insult. The freedman took a leading role in the investigations, having won Nero's confidence with his astute handling of Milichus. He was to be well rewarded. Another tale, told by Epictetus, who had been owned by the freedman and was a witness to the machinations of Nero's court, reports a member of the elite who had fallen on difficult times and was down to his last million sesterces. The supplicant fell before the imperial freedman to beg for financial assistance. The freedman was horrified, not by the indignity or embarrassment of the situation, but the fact the man had only one-and-a-half million sesterces left. In genuine shock, Epaphroditus asked: 'Dear man, how did you keep silent up to now? How have you endured it?'[93] The petitioner was about to lose his senatorial status, as a million sesterces was set as the minimum requirement by law.

The social inversion of senators begging favours from a freedman was the reason for Lateranus's involvement. Epictetus scorned the humiliation of senators forced to kiss the hands of imperial freedmen, a gesture of inferiority, and of the elite who through cultivating such patrons became 'the slaves of slaves'. As men of low social status became the distributors of imperial *beneficia*, the elite found themselves in a debt of reciprocity to those they despised.[94] This was an inevitable consequence of the almost constant conspiracies and plots spawned by the nobility. The emperor's greatest threats to his personal safety came from those who had personal access to him: his family, his advisors and the Praetorians. As Gaius, Claudius and now Nero found, the aristocracy was a threat and so most were removed from their inner court circle. This only increased the hostility of this class to the imperial freedmen. Lateranus himself had nearly lost his life to the intrigues of Narcissus, who had brought down his patroness, Messalina. He did not forget, nor did he forgive. In his view, though, the fault lay with the emperors who empowered them.

Lateranus met his end bravely, fortified by his pride and *dignitas*, but also his hope that all was not lost. His status precluded the use of torture, but in a calculated insult to his pride, he was taken for execution to the Sessorium, which was reserved for the killing of slaves sentenced to death. His executioner, chosen by fate, was the tribune Statius Proxumus. Only one Praetorian had been implicated so far. Nero had no idea how far his guard had been subverted. Lateranus was silent, knowing that the opportunity to kill Nero had not passed.

Epictetus used Lateranus's bravery as an example of a Stoical acceptance of powers or situations that are no longer under one's control. The philosopher urges his readers in these circumstances to 'hold out your neck the way Lateranus did at Rome when condemned by Nero to be beheaded. He held out his neck willingly to take the blow – but the blow was deficient, so he recoiled a bit, but then he had self-command to offer his neck a second time.' Resolute, he said not a word, but the circumstances evidently preyed upon the mind of his fellow conspirator and executioner.[95]

Nero had some suspicions as to the loyalty of the Praetorians. The arrest of one of their officers, and his determination not to betray others, suggested there were more guardsmen involved. This was the real threat to his life. Tigellinus and the conspirator Faenius Rufus, along with Epaphroditus and Nero's wife, Poppaea, took control of the investigation. The guard around the emperor himself was doubled, and soldiers were sent to close the gates to the city and man the walls to prevent any escaping. The river boats on the Tiber were searched and the hunt extended to the harbour at Ostia. Rome's streets and squares resounded to the noise of hobnails as soldiers filled the city, with patrols even sent out to the surrounding towns and countryside populated by the villas of the rich. However, Nero did not entirely trust the loyalty of these men, with members of his German bodyguard – whose allegiance was beyond question – dispersed amongst the units. Even the Praetorians sent to arrest Piso were carefully selected: only 'recruits or men new to the service, and chosen as such by Nero, the veterans being distrusted as tainted with partisanship'.[96] The role of the Praetorian officers had not been discovered at this time, lending credence to the account preserved by Plutarch.

Another officer involved in the plot was sent to Seneca, such was Nero's unfamiliarity with the danger that existed all around him. Only Natalis had named him, and only to the extent that he had been sent as an envoy to his villa by Piso. Seneca had been ill; he often complained of ailments to keep visitors away. Natalis reported Piso's message and the reply. Piso had asked his friend 'Why did he close his door on Piso? It would be better if they cultivated their friendship by meeting on more intimate terms.' The enigmatic reply suggested they both shared a common cause cloaked by a repudiable distance. Natalis remembered that Seneca recommended that 'spoken exchanges and frequent interviews were to the advantage of neither: still, his own existence depended on the safety of Piso'. Cryptic and enigmatic, the hints of complicity are evident in Seneca's desire to preserve plausible deniability should the plot fail. The phrase itself, in Latin *salute suam incolumitate Pisonis inniti*, was remarkably similar to the oath sworn by soldiers to the emperor. The tribune Gavius Silvanus was sent to Nomentum to ask Seneca whether the reported exchange was true and the meaning of it.[97]

The officer arrived in the early evening and placed a guard around the villa. He then entered and found Seneca dining with his wife and two friends. Seneca partly confirmed Natalis's information. Yes, he had refused to invite Piso to his villa as he was ill and valued his privacy, even though this was uncivil and an insult to the *dignitas* of the great aristocrat. He then denied making the incriminating statement on Piso's safety, as the only person whose safety he ranked greater than his own was the emperor himself. This Nero knew to be true, as he was always frank with the emperor rather than servile. The guards were left in place and Silvanus returned to make his report.[98]

He reported before the imperial *concilium* that included Tigellinus and Poppaea. Faevius Rufus had been sent out of Rome to supervise the units in the outlying towns. Nero dismissed Seneca's explanations out of hand and asked Silvanus whether his former advisor was preparing himself for death. On the contrary, replied the tribune, he observed 'no evidences of alarm, and that he had not detected any sadness in his words or looks'. He was ordered to return and 'pronounce the death sentence' on Seneca, but, in an act of clemency, the order did not extend to his wife, Paulina.[99]

According to one of Tacitus's sources, Fabius Rusticus, Silvanus did not return immediately to supervise the enforced suicide of the Stoic, but instead went to find his commander and leading conspirator. It would have been surprising for a soldier to have hesitated in carrying out the execution of a retired senator, a man of letters and philosopher, no matter how eminent. They lived in different worlds. More likely he was aware of the plan to place Seneca on the throne. Silvanus repeated his orders to the Praetorian Prefect and 'asked if he should obey them; only to be advised by Faenius to carry them out'. He decided that inaction was a harbour of greater safety, and as he had so far escaped the storm that had sunk so many of his fellow conspirators, he recoiled at the risk of allowing Seneca to live.[100]

Once Silvanus arrived at the villa, he sent one of his centurions in to inform Seneca of the imperial command. It must have been deep into the night that the Stoic realized that the death he had so long planned was now to be performed. He had already spent the intervening hours adding the finishing touches to one of his works. He had summoned friends as witnesses and his secretaries to record his final hours, as well as a doctor to supervise. Posterity was to know the glory of his death modelled on that of Socrates, inspired by the great Roman freedom fighters Cato the Younger, Brutus and Cassius. He first asked for his will to add the names of those present as beneficiaries. In doing so, he would obligate them to provide a praiseworthy account of his demise. However, the centurion refused him permission, so Seneca 'left them his sole but fairest possession – the image of his life'. The image of his death was meant to mirror his life. The performance began.[101]

He held a philosophical debate with his *amici*, placing his death into context and urging them to demonstrate the fortitude he now revealed. 'Where,' he asked, 'were the maxims of their philosophy? Where the reasoned attitude towards impending evils which they had studied through so many years? For to whom had Nero's cruelty been unknown?' The scribe was careful to record his wisdom. He divided his copies of his works amongst his friends and asked them to hide them from destruction.[102] Seneca then turned to his wife.

Here the accounts of Tacitus and Dio diverge. The former draws much of his information on Seneca's death from Fabius Rusticus, who, he admits, 'certainly tends to overpraise Seneca, by whose friendship he flourished',[103] whereas Dio uses a hostile source. According to the favourable account, Paulina asked to join her husband in his suicide and he, 'not wishing to stand in the way of her glory, and influenced also by his affection, that he might not leave the woman who enjoyed his wholehearted love exposed to outrage', agreed.[104] It is difficult to perceive what this outrage was, as Nero intervened to preserve Paulina's life. Dio, however, paints a different scene: 'It was his wish to end the life of his wife Paulina at the same time as his own, for he declared that he had taught her both to despise death and to desire to leave the world in company with him. So, he opened her veins as well as his own.'[105]

The difference is important to understand the man Seneca was. They both lay bleeding out in agony. However, the philosopher, keen to add to his glory, called in his secretaries and dictated a long discourse that he asked to be publicized after his death.[106] The ultimate freedom to a Stoic was being able to choose the manner and timing of one's death, the true expression of liberty. Seneca wrote that 'a lancet will open the way to that great freedom, and tranquillity can be purchased at the cost of a pinprick'. Yet his journey was long, so he ordered the arteries in his leg and behind his knees to be cut. He then took hemlock, the poison administered to Socrates as described in Plato's *Phaedo*, and asked to be carried to a hot bath. At its edge, he sprinkled some of the water of his slaves as a libation to Jupiter the Liberator. With that, he was placed in the scolding water, which hastened the blood flow.[107] According to Dio, it was the soldiers who hastened his end to save the life of his wife. Seneca died hard.[108]

Once her husband was dead, Paulina was legally free of his control. The centurion ordered her slaves and freedmen to stop the bleeding and tightly bound her wounds. She lived, as did the image of Seneca, as the Stoic ideal of constancy and ascetic resistance to the violence and immorality of Imperial Rome. He had carefully planned his death, with an audience, props and political stage. Yet reality cut in. His body did not want to reject life, even if he did. His final hours were brutal, painful and lingering until the scene was cut short by a Praetorian's blade.

Lines of men were dragged by their chains to the gates of Nero's gardens, condemned, according to Dio, on the evidence of 'faithless friends and house servants'. By a miracle, none had implicated any further Praetorians. One remained incarcerated but resolute in his determination not to inform on his colleagues, despite the torture. Nero, Tigellinus and Faenius Rufus were pitiless in their cross-examination of the accused, Rufus in particular keen to 'demonstrate his ignorance by browbeating his allies'. The tribune Subrius Flavus stood close by. He knew that their luck, which had held so far, was inevitably going to run out. He knew determined action was their only saviour, rather than a cowardly charade. Placing his hand on the hilt of his sword, he looked towards his commanding officer for a nod of assent, before drawing it and plunging the blade into the body of the emperor. Faenius Rufus, either through cowardice or the hope of a better opportunity, shook his head. The acceptance of commands was ingrained in the tribune. He removed his hand. The final chance had gone.[109]

Soon after, the treachery of the Praetorian Prefect was revealed by his own stupidity. Scaevinus and Cervarius Proculus had been dragged before the emperor's tribunal again, and were receiving a tirade of abuse from Faenius Rufus when Scaevinus rebelled against the duplicity of the man who acted the 'double part of accomplice and conspirator'. With a sneer, he replied to the questions that nobody knew more about the conspiracy than the Prefect himself. Rufus was struck dumb. The silence was a sure indication of the truth in the allegation. Then the man, instead of an indignant and powerful denial, stuttered and tripped over his rebuttal. He was clearly terrified. Proculus then struck to ensure a guilty verdict with further information. Rufus was seized and chained by a bodyguard kept close by Nero for his size and strength. Like Piso, he would pay for his hesitancy.[110]

Scaevinus and Proculus did not stop there in their denunciations. The remaining Praetorians were named and brought before Nero for questioning and condemnation. Flavus at first denied any involvement, but then gave full rein to his hatred of the emperor. He was placed under the custody of another tribune, Veianius Niger, who took him to a neighbouring field. A grave was dug for him, which Flavus criticized as neither deep enough nor broad. It was an example of Niger's lack of discipline or command of the detail. 'Faulty discipline here,' he observed to the Praetorians standing around him. Niger would soon take his revenge. Ordered to kneel, Flavus was commanded to hold his neck out firmly, to which he replied: 'I only hope that you will strike as firmly!' He had observed Niger shaking violently and was concerned his execution would be unnecessarily brutal. It was: it took two blows to sever his head, or as Niger reported to the emperor, keen to demonstrate his loyalty, one-and-a-half.[111]

The violent suppression of the conspirators in the guard was related to how close they had come to killing him. Many of the equestrian plotters were treated with clemency. The centurion Sulpicius Asper was delivered up. Heavily chained, like all his military comrades, he was asked by the emperor why he had plotted to murder him. He replied, giving the Stoic justification replete in the works of Seneca, 'that it was the only service that could be rendered to his many infamies'. He was executed, as were all the other centurions, who met their end bravely, unlike their commander, who met it badly. The tribune Silvanus was surprisingly acquitted, but chose suicide, whilst Statius Proximus was pardoned, probably because he was only at the periphery of the conspiracy and had followed orders in executing Lateranus. Enigmatically, Tacitus contrasts this with the 'folly of his end'. What that was remains an unknown. Three other tribunes were stripped of their rank, probably as they had in some way failed in their duties.[112]

The emperor now decided to use the conspiracy as an opportunity to rid himself of known opponents whose names had failed to emerge in the investigations, questioning and torture. The consul Vestinus Atticus was known for his outspoken views and criticisms of the emperor. No one would dare come to his defence in the circumstances, but as there was no evidence against him, he could not be put on trial.[113] One of the few trusted tribunes, Gerellanus, was ordered to take his whole cohort to enforce Atticus's suicide. Resistance was expected from his personal bodyguard of young men, who could convert his imposing house into a fortress. They arrived to find him hosting a dinner party – a last celebration of life or a desperate attempt to present the image of innocence? No resistance was offered. Instead, Atticus retired to his private chamber with his doctor, who severed his arteries. He was then plunged in hot water and expired. His guests were held in his dining room, surrounded by soldiers, suspended between life and death until, many hours later, an imperial order arrived to release them. When Nero was later informed of their terror, he laughingly dismissed their consternation as 'they had paid dearly enough for their consular banquet'.[114] There was nothing like a little terror to remind the elite of the consequences of disloyalty.

Those with links of *amicitiae* to the plotters were now arrested, tried before the imperial *concilium* and sentenced. Tacitus describes Rome as 'filled with funerals, and the Capitol with burnt offerings. Here, for the killing of a son; there, for that of a brother, a kinsman, or a friend; men were addressing their thanks to Heaven, bedecking their mansions with bays, falling at the knees of the sovereign.' However, the imperial retaliation was muted. Many of the equestrian clients of the convicted senators were exiled rather than executed.

On their return to Rome after the eventual murder of Nero, most were ready enough to advertise their involvement. Among them was Annius Pollio, a son of the conspirator Annius Vinicianus and identified by his *amicus* Claudius Senecio. At least two of the thirteen exiled were allowed to take their wives with them. Most were sent to relatively pleasant islands in the Aegean, such as Andros. Only one, a Stoic philosopher named Musonius Rufus, was sent to the dry, barren rock of Gyaros. His discovery of a freshwater spring brought approval from the locals, whilst he was visited by many eminent scholars eager to drink from his learning. Glitius Gallus, convicted by the word of his friend Quintianus, was a huge benefactor to his new home of Andros. Two inscriptions dedicated by the town commend his generosity and that of his wife, 'on account of their goodness'.[115]

The initial panic was now over, and Nero could decide on the fate of the accused at his leisure. Lucan had been offered impunity in return for information. It did him little good. He too was ordered to take his life, but allowed to choose the manner. The poet 'wrote a note to his father containing corrections for some of his verses, and after eating heartily, held out his arms to be cut by a doctor'. His mother had probably not forgiven him for implicating her. As his hands and feet turned cold, he read some lines from his *Pharsalia* to the audience of friends he had assembled. The lines recalled the glory of a mortally wounded soldier as he awaited the end of his journey. Scaevinus too had hoped his betrayals would save his life. He was to be disappointed, as were Afranius Quintianus and Claudius Senecio. However, some incentive needed to exist for future informers to renounce their accomplices, so Natalis and Cervarius Proculus received a pardon. The conspiracy was primarily uncovered through Milichus. Without his intervention, Nero would have fallen victim to the assassin's dagger. He thus became immensely rich and was honoured with the Greek form of the title 'saviour'.[116]

There were others who were rewarded. The loyal Praetorian Prefect Tigellinus was understandably honoured for his role, supervising the hunt for plotters, especially in the guard. Triumphal statues were raised to him in the Forum, as well as in the palace itself. Additionally, Turpilianus, the consul of AD 61, was awarded with *ornamenta triumphalia*.[117] Yet Cocceius Nerva, poet and future emperor, but in AD 65 merely a designated praetor, was awarded the same honours as the Prefect. His role in uncovering the conspiracy must have been immense, but was suppressed by historians like Tacitus, who were alive in his reign and that of his adopted successor, Trajan. He was clearly approached by the conspirators, possibly members of the disaffected literary circle that encompassed Lucan and Piso. Others propose it was for his legal advice or the production of an epic poem celebrating the destruction of the plot. There is, however, no evidence he was a lawyer, nor do the rewards reflect his implied contribution. His role remains obscure but duplicitous.[118]

Nero was shocked by the numbers involved, but also the participation of many Praetorian officers. He saw threats were everywhere, a fear stoked by his Prefects Tigellinus and Rufus's replacement, the sinister Nymphidius Sabinus. The latter was the grandson of the imperial freedman Callistus and had inherited all his ability for intrigues. His role in the discovery of the conspiracy was significant but enigmatic, as he had been awarded *insignia consularia*. Nero now relied heavily on the advice of these two men, as well as invoking the protection of the divine. After the discovery of Piso's conspiracy, he took comfort in the security offered by a

'statuette of a girl sent him by an anonymous commoner as a charm against conspiracies. It so happened that a conspiracy came to light immediately afterwards; so, he began to worship the girl as though she were a powerful goddess, and sacrificed to her three times a day, expecting people to believe that she gave him knowledge of the future.'[119]

The divinity was to prove a forlorn hope.

Nero's anxieties and fears manifested themselves in increased isolation and outbursts of anger. In late AD 65, his wife Poppaea died, along with his unborn child. It was said her death was caused by his unrestrained rage when he kicked her in the belly during an argument. She miscarried and died soon after. His grief knew no bounds. He had acquired more ghosts to haunt his waking and sleeping hours. He retreated into a fantasy world of art, music and the stage; here he was safe, but others weren't.[120]

After the conspiracy of Calpurnius Piso, Nero considered the nobility drawn from the ancient Republican aristocracy to be his main threat. The *delators* and informers were empowered to bring accusations against any rich individual associated with the condemned. Their accusations were sure to get a favourable hearing, with few prepared to risk their estates or their lives in supporting the defendants or vote in the defendant's favour, especially in charges of *maiestas*. The prosecutor's incentive was a proportion of the estates of those they were able to convict. There were fortunes to be made or grievances to be satisfied, and they were able to exploit the fractured relationship between the emperor and the Senate.

The last male descendant of Augustus, apart from Nero, was Piso's potential rival for the throne, Lucius Junius Silanus. He is described as a 'headstrong individual' who was being trained by his uncle for the throne. He had a strong motive to desire the destruction of the Julio-Claudians. His father had fallen victim to the intrigues of Agrippina and his uncle was forced to commit suicide after an indictment for treason. The young man was charged before the Senate. Tacitus appears to be selective in recounting the charges against him, but Silanus was certainly accused of *maiestas*. Convicted and exiled to Naxos, his journey was interrupted by a centurion. The noble was a strongly built man and he put up a brave but futile fight, though unarmed. All his wounds were to the front. The blood of Augustus proved fatal to all. His uncle, Cassius Longinus, was exiled to Sardinia, accused of secretly keeping a mask of Caesar's assassin and his ancestor, alongside an inscription 'to the leader of the party'. His daughter was married to Domitius Corbulo, which contributed to the emperor questioning the loyalty of the great general.[121]

Nero often retreated to the Greek city of Naples, where he was assured of artistic acclaim from its inhabitants. It was here in AD 66 that the emperor received the Armenian king, Tiridates, who had been reduced to client status by the Roman general Corbulo. The victorious commander had sent his son-in-law and *legate* to escort Tiridates to Rome. This was a gesture of fidelity, as he effectively became a hostage to his loyalty. L. Annius Vinicianus was the second son of the rebel of AD 42 and brother of Annius Pollio. As he joined the imperial party from Naples to Rome, he would have known that his brother had been exiled for his role in the Pisonian conspiracy.

Rome itself was filled with news of the infamous trial of Barea Soranus and his daughter, Servilia. The aristocracy considered the very foundations of Roman society set by bonds of loyalty and *amicitiae* was now threatened by the emperor's advancement of *delators*. Many years later, Juvenal wrote of senators of low status and humble origins gaining imperial favour by judicial attacks on the great and the good. The Syrian, P. Egnatius Celer, a senator of foreign birth, profited from the conviction of his *amicus* Barea Soranus: 'An old Stoic *delator* who was raised on the banks of that river where Pegasus' wing descended, killed his friend and pupil Barea.'[122] Celer received honours and a huge sum from his role as a witness, whilst the prosecutor, Ostorius Sabinus, was granted 1.2 million sesterces. The rewarding of a witness was highly unusual and probably intended to encourage such charges against more of Nero's opponents. The rewarding of *delators* only occurred late in Nero's reign after the conspiracy of Piso.[123]

Barea Soranus was a member of the 'Stoic Opposition', along with Thrasea Paetus. Soranus took a principled stand against tyranny. He was a friend of Rubellius Plautus, whom Nero had executed in AD 62 for conspiracy, although his real crime was being a descendant of the emperor Tiberius. As the governor of Asia in AD 61–62, he refused to allow the art treasures of Pergamum to be shipped back to the capital to decorate Nero's palaces. Furthermore, when the local citizens rioted to protect their heritage, the governor refused to punish them. Sabinus accused him of sedition and failing to act in the interests of Rome. However, the real horror was associating his daughter, Servilia, with his charges. She was accused of consulting astrologers and paying for their spells with her own jewels. The trial took place straight after the conviction of Thrasea Paetus. She admitted that she had used astrologers, but only to know her father's fate and whether the emperor would show him mercy or the Senate pass a harsh sentence. She may also have been indicted as her husband, Annius Pollio, had been exiled the year before for his involvement in the Pisonian conspiracy. Her brother-in-law, Annius Vinicianus, was probably sat in the Senate witnessing the trial, which had an inevitable conclusion.[124]

There were too many coincidences, too many connections to the previously convicted for any other verdict. Tellingly the prosecutor was not hounded down later under the more tolerant regime of Vespasian for providing false evidence against his patron and being the 'betrayer and corrupter of *amicitiae*'. There was no charge against Sabinus suggesting there was concrete evidence of guilt. After the Pisonian conspiracy, Nero's attitude had hardened against any with suspicious ties or familial heritage. Servilia herself had admitted to procuring the use of magic, itself a serious crime.[125]

L. Annius Vinicianus, if present in the Senate, would have witnessed a bear pit of hostility and hatred. His sister-in-law, Servilia, had been summoned as a witness for the prosecution to provide evidence against her own father. She stood, eyes cast down, at one end of the consular tribunal, facing her father, who stood at the other end. She was only 19, aware that her evidence condemned him to death. She pleaded her excuse that she was merely a loving daughter, worried for her parent. Under a fierce barrage of questioning by Sabinus, her father cried out that she was innocent and had not been in Asia with him during his governorship, nor was she aware of the role of her husband in the conspiracy of Piso. He threw himself at his daughter to embrace her, to take away her anguish. She opened her arms, but the lictors rushed forward to stop this expression of humanity. Two witnesses for the defence gave statements as to his exemplary character, only to be exiled after the trial – a warning against others foolish enough to aid enemies of the emperor. Rufus then stood up, and taking the traditional pose of a Stoic, and cloaking his face in the appearance of integrity, provided the evidence to sentence his patron to death and also condemn his daughter. As an act of mercy, they were allowed to choose the manner of their end.[126]

L. Annius Vinicianus wanted revenge. His father had been executed by Claudius, his brother exiled by Nero and now his sister-in-law forced to commit suicide. All had been condemned by a fawning Senate, eager to be seen to be doing the emperor's bidding. However, the tyrant was to pay the price. Nero was due to leave the Senate, Rome and his ghosts behind for an artistic tour of Greece with Tiridates. The usual stop on the journey to Brundisium was at Beneventum, where gladiatorial contests were arranged, as they had been in AD 64. The emperor's entourage understandably contained few senators, but Vinicianus was probably present as he was escorting the Armenian king on his return journey. The loss of Tacitus as a source has left posterity guessing as to his plan. At a date between mid-May and Nero's departure from Italy, the Arval Brethren sacrificed to the gods 'for the detection of a wicked plot'. Annius Vinicianus was captured and executed.[127]

His plot led to the recall of his father-in-law, Corbulo, from the East. He was already under suspicion through his family connections. The senator Vespasian had been given command of three legions to crush the Jewish Revolt. His wife was the daughter of the guardian of L. Junius Silanus, L. Cassius Longinus, who had been exiled. She was also a half-brother of Q. Pomponius Secundus, who died after the conspiracy of Vinicianus in AD 42, and P. Glitius Gallus, recently exiled to Andros. Corbulo met the imperial party in Corinth. There is no evidence that he was involved in any treachery, but Nero saw threats everywhere, tormented by the shadows of his fears, guilt and anxieties. One of Rome's greatest generals was not even granted an opportunity to defend himself, being ordered to take his own life. Taking a sword, Corbulo stabbed himself, crying 'Axios!' ('I am worthy!').[128] Another relative of Corbulo, Servius Cornelius Salvidienus Orfitus, was charged with leasing three shops near the Forum to plot treason. The location was considered strategic in the control of the public space after the murder of the emperor.[129] The two governors of the German provinces, the brothers Publius Sulpicius Scribonius Rufus and Publius Sulpicius Scribonius Proculus, were told to travel to Greece, possibly expecting an appointment to the prospective campaign in the Caucasus. However, unknown to them, they both faced accusations by a *delator*. They were from the elite aristocracy, descended from Pompey the Great. They too were ordered to commit suicide upon their arrival in Greece, a command they dutifully performed. High-born provincial commanders were now replaced by 'new men' who owed their careers entirely to imperial patronage.[130]

The executions of these nobles may have been linked to evidence implicating them in the Pisonian or Vinician conspiracies. After the uncovering of Piso and his allies, Nero collected and published all the incriminating evidence in the form of a speech to the Senate and an edict to the people, for 'he was often distressed by popular talk that he ruined so many innocent citizens of high distinction merely on the grounds of jealousy and fear'. He no longer cared. After AD 66, there was no attempt by Nero or the imperial freedman Helius, his deputy in distant Rome, to reference their summary deaths to reports, creating more martyrs to fan the flames of resistance. Furthermore, Nero's performances on the stage offended the sensibilities of Rome's elite. Isolated and hated by the aristocracy, he used terror to secure his safety. None of the aristocracy could feel safe, so conspiracies spawned and multiplied in Rome and led directly to the revolt of Vindex in Gaul.[131]

Corbulo's death cry, '*Axios!*', was used by spectators to acclaim the winners in athletic competitions in recognition that they had witnessed an excellent performance. The general had led a glorious life and was seen by Nero's enemies as a potential emperor. In his shout, he contrasted his own worthy career fighting Rome's wars to the emperor's unworthy performances on the stage. Nero had retreated into a fairy-tale world of affected acclaim, pleasure, art and beauty. The ugliness of his reality was kept at a distance. The Pisonian conspiracy marked a significant change in his reign. His behaviour and lack of morality now inspired fear and destroyed the unwritten social and political rules by which the elite could navigate courtly politics. He no longer trusted them, and they could no longer trust him, with inevitable results. His government became a life and death struggle in a fight for survival.[132]

Calpurnius Piso, though, was as deluded as his emperor. He was in no immediate danger, but felt insecure having been previously exiled and prosecuted. Ambition, excessive pride in his heritage and the pursuit of power were his undoing. To Tacitus, all those who grasped for the throne were by this act unworthy to hold it. Piso was a man of mediocre talents who felt entitled by his illustrious ancestry to hold imperial power. The core of the conspiracy was centred around his own clients and *amici*. The scarcity of other aristocratic conspirators is an eloquent statement towards his fitness to rule. The choice of Seneca by the Praetorian officers as their preferred successor is significant. Piso was no more than a sanitized version of Nero: repellent to the soldiers in the palace and no doubt to those garrisoning the borders of the Empire. Rome was essentially a military dictatorship, yet he lacked any military office in his *cursus honorum*. Had he succeeded, a civil war would have been inevitable, a view shared by Tacitus and, evidently, much of the Senate.[133]

Many of the educated elite involved in the plot prioritized the dramatic nature of their performance as tyrannicides rather than focus on the practical necessities. Even Seneca, distant in a futile attempt to protect his position, spent his time planning for a ritualized death in the manner of Socrates. To them, life was a show, and they were actors upon life's stage. Their lives were built on false pretences and a driving sense of entitlement. Tragically, it was the realists who struggled to persuade their social superiors to take the necessary steps, who were betrayed by them, who suffered and who died. '*Axios!*' Subrius Flavus and Epicharis.[134]

The Murder of Domitian, AD 96

'He used to say that the lot of emperors was a most miserable one, because no one ever believes in any conspiracy they discover unless it has resulted in their deaths.'

(Suetonius, *Domitian*, 21)

Domitian faced death most of his life. His mother had died when he was a child, and as a teenager he was hunted through the streets of Rome by the supporters of the emperor Vitellius when his father, Vespasian, raised the standard of revolt in distant Judaea. Around the age of 13, his father was absent, serving Nero in Africa and Greece and crushing the Jewish Revolt. It is likely he was brought up in the household of his uncle, Flavius Sabinus, with his son of the same name and niece, Julia Flavia. The future emperor Nerva may also have acted as his guardian whilst Vespasian was in Greece, leading to the later rumour that the older man had debauched his ward. Nerva, the consummate survivor, emerged unscathed from the civil war in AD 69, but Sabinus, Domitian's surrogate father, was not so lucky. Uncle and nephew had been besieged on the Capitol by Vitellean forces, and upon its capture, Sabinus was brutally murdered, Domitian escaping disguised as a worshipper of Isis.[1] This was one of many close acquaintances with death.

Domitian's relationship with his father and elder brother, Titus, was strained. Poignantly, the only people who probably loved him in his entire life, and were loved by him, were his wife, Domitia, his niece, Julia – from his time in the household of Sabinus – and his childhood nurse, Phyllis. His relationship with Julia was so close, despite the execution of her husband for treason, that rumours spread of an affair. However, she was dead by AD 91. Fate and the circumstances of life had detached him from natural familial bonds. The emperor Vespasian died in AD 79, and his elder brother in AD 81, both of whom were deified. Domitian then ascended the throne, the son and brother of gods. However, he looked for divine protection from Minerva, the goddess of wisdom and justice; a motherly figure to replace the one he had hardly known. He kept her statue amongst his household gods and goddesses in his private bed chamber, and she would dominate his coinage between AD 82 and 85. Such was the fragility of an emperor's safety the loyalty of the Praetorian Guard and the diligence of informers were never enough to guarantee survival.

Whatever trust he had in the allegiance of his family was destroyed when his cousin, Sabinus's son, who was married to Julia, conspired against him, along with several senators. The orator Dio of Prusa was exiled at this time for his bond of *amicitiae* with an unnamed man related by blood and marriage to the imperial family, who styled themselves 'Fortune's Favourites'.[2] Yet fortune did not favour them, nor the leaders of another plot in AD 87 known only from an inscription by the Arval Brethren, who made sacrifices 'because of the detected crimes of the wicked', a further revolt on the Rhine in AD 89 and another ephemeral plot in AD 91.[3]

In response, like many of his predecessors, Domitian let loose the *delators*, after initially suppressing their influence at the start of his reign. The elite was to be allowed to tear itself apart in accusations and counter-charges, with the courts a battleground of allegation, recrimination and revenge. Informers, prosecutors and witnesses became his dogs of war. Pliny the Younger writes of a servile war, where slaves were able to denounce their masters. Furthermore, other senatorial sources describe a reign of terror, but it was senators and equestrians themselves who laid the charges against other members of their class. Most senators, however, loyal servants of the Flavian dynasty, remained unaffected. In total, only thirteen senators were condemned to death, at least six of them undoubtedly guilty of treason. Domitian, though, was condemned as a monster, unlike Claudius, who executed thirty-five senators and hundreds of equestrians in a reign covering a similar period. The difference was that Claudius was succeeded by his adopted son, Nero, whilst Domitian was the last of his line and replaced by a new dynast eager to justify his predecessor's murder in the name of tyrannicide and thus legitimatize his claims. Nerva, poet and friend of Nero, an informer of the Pisonian conspirators and close advisor to Vespasian, Titus and Domitian himself, was involved in his emperor's assassination.[4]

The overriding concern for all emperors was their survival, surrounded as they were by threats, duplicity and feigned loyalty. Domitian, an avid reader of the emperor Tiberius's state papers, learned lessons.[5] Tiberius had allowed *delators* free rein to destroy the adherents of his Praetorian Prefect Sejanus, accused of conspiring against him. He also sought safety in distance from the treacherous environment of court in Rome. In the later part of his reign, Tiberius ruled from his pleasure palace on the island of Capri. Gaius and Claudius attempted to isolate themselves from the aristocracy by surrounding themselves with imperial freedmen and restricting access to their person, as had Nero. The last of the descendants of Augustus had also escaped senatorial plots by embarking on a two-year artistic tour of Greece, only to return to Rome and death. Domitian learned from all their fates.

Despite building a huge new palace covering the Palatine Hill in Rome, Domitian spent much of his time in his vast palace complex at Alba, 12 miles from the capital. His visits to Rome were fleeting, much of his reign being spent on the Rhine and Danube in countering barbarian attacks. He felt safe in his villa sat upon an acropolis in the Alban hills. The Senate was never summoned there, and his administration was run by a few select nobles, *equites* and freedmen.

The nobility resented their lack of imperial access, a privilege they perceived as a right. Consequently, they were deprived of the ability to petition for imperial gifts, favours and offices for themselves or their *amici* and clients. Instead, they were forced to approach his freedmen. This situation was inevitable, given the aristocracy's inability to come to terms with the demands of the Principate and their inflated estimation of their heritage and *dignitas*. Many of them felt they possessed the necessary nobility to be emperor themselves. The Flavians promoted the careers of new men, appointing them as governors of the imperial provinces, whilst the nobility was granted the empty symbols of elevated status in ordinary consulships and priesthoods. Real power lay with senators whose careers were not based on their illustrious name but on loyal service. These men had nothing to fear. Trajan, a loyal servant to Domitian, claimed that the emperor was a bad emperor but a good *amicus*.[6]

The imperial freedmen who commanded virtual unrestricted personal access to the emperor held real power and influence under Claudius and his successors. These former slaves, freed by the emperor, were bound to show him loyalty and protect his person and interests as their former master, patron and liberator. They lived in the palace as part of the *familia Caesaris*.[7] Their lowly status precluded any attempt to ascend the throne, but this did not halt their involvement in plots led by senatorial aspirants to the purple. Callistus was behind the rise of Claudius, and Narcissus the fall of Messalina. Domitian understood these men were entirely capable of plotting against him, even in his secluded rural retreat.

Domitian's isolation grew. He enjoyed solitude, relaxing by walking alone in the gardens.[8] To a Roman, this was strange and noteworthy behaviour, as there was little division between public and private life. Social discourse was an expectation, an opportunity to request favours or display social status in demonstrating one's education and learning.[9]

Imperial banquets in the huge audience hall of the Aula Regula on the Palatine were used to demonstrate his elevated, divine status, but the emperor ate little on his raised platform and they ended abruptly with no opportunity for the drink and entertainment that was customary on these occasions. Arrogant and disdaining social etiquette, Domitian abandoned all pretence of an emperor ruling in partnership with the Senate. He was not the social equal of the aristocracy, and the charade of Augustus's Principate was abandoned to reveal the true political reality of an autocratic monarchy based on the support of the Roman Army.

Domitian was addressed as 'Lord and God' and treated as the son of Minerva, the goddess he revered the most, 'in consequence of which he was wont to celebrate the *Panathenaea* on a magnificent scale; on these occasions he held contests of poets and orators and gladiators almost every year at his Alban Villa'. He also established a college of priests to organize games and plays in Minerva's honour. He worshipped her 'with superstitious reverence'. The seriousness of his devotion is reflected in a rumour recorded by Suetonius that no doubt spread soon after his death: Domitian dreamt that the goddess appeared to him in a dream 'to tell him that she had been disarmed by Jupiter and could no longer protect him'. A variation of this story is given by Dio, where the goddess threw away her weapons and plunged in her chariot into an abyss, drawn by black horses.[10]

Roman society and religion were based on the principle of reciprocity. The receipt of gifts or favours placed the recipient in a debt of obligation until their patron or *amicus* asked for a favour in return. The same conditions applied to a mortal's relationship with the gods. Sacrifices were made to obligate the god or goddess; for example, a safe journey across the sea could be ensured through a sacrifice to Neptune. The greater the gift offered to the god, the greater the chance the obligation would be accepted in full. Domitian looked to the protection of Minerva, the goddess of justice. In return, the emperor was fanatical in his protection of the state religion in his capacity as Pontifex Maximus and his battle against corruption and injustice.[11]

In his quest for divine approval, he confronted the exploitation of provincials by rapacious senatorial governors which recommenced after his murder. The prosecution of greedy governors was encouraged, decrees were issued to protect city endowments from corrupt officials and curators were appointed to investigate malpractice. Even Suetonius is forced to acknowledge that 'he was most conscientious in dispensing justice', urging tribunes to prosecute a corrupt *aedile* guilty of extortion, and in fact 'kept such a tight hold of city magistrates and provincial governors that the general standard of honesty and justice rose to an unprecedented high level'. This desire for good government, though, was given as a further example of his tyrannical behaviour. To the senatorial class, *Libertas* was the freedom to exploit without limits. However, the goddess would have appreciated his zeal for justice.[12]

Domitian was equally zealous in upholding traditional morals and defending the state religion, thereby earning divine gratitude, especially Minerva's. He was as ruthless and merciless in his application of Rome's ancient religious and morality laws as he was in imposing its legal codes. At the start of his reign, he took personal charge of an investigation into three of the six Vestal Virgins who had broken their sacred oaths and had affairs, imperilling the wellbeing of the state and the safety of the emperor himself as Pontifex Maximus and devotee of Minerva. In this instance, he showed some mercy in allowing the women to choose the manner of their deaths and only exiling their lovers. The Chief Vestal escaped in the first instance, but around AD 89 she stood accused a second time. Domitian had by then survived assassination plots and armed insurrection. Fear and anxiety had burned his soul, and the help of Minerva was required more than ever in his fight for survival. A trial was held in the Alban villa rather than the Regia of the Pontifex Maximus in Rome. A guilty verdict was inevitable. She was buried alive, as decreed by the ancient religious law, and her lovers beaten to death, apart from one who admitted his guilt and was exiled. Pliny was horrified, not by the horrendous fate of the woman but that senators and equestrians could suffer the same punishment.[13]

Inevitably, the constant threat of sudden death affected the emperor's psychological balance. Initially, Domitian drew approval for a benevolent reign, where 'he gave conspicuous signs of self-restraint and even generosity, treating all his friends with great consideration and always insisting that, above all, they should do nothing mean'. However, over time, 'fear made him cruel'. Anxiety bred mistrust, which in turn was fed by an army of informers looking to gain imperial favour by accusing the guilty and innocent alike of plots against his life. In a court where all things were false, where words were employed by courtiers to utter fulsome praise but a misplaced one may result in a rapid fall from favour, the risks were huge but the rewards greater. As Domitian's insecurities multiplied, his responses became less predictable. The challenge for the courtier was to know the rules of the political game and perform accordingly, but worryingly, they knew that they could 'praise a tyrant and he takes no pleasure in it. For he thinks that those who praise him feel otherwise.' Consequently, his responses to perceived threats became increasingly impulsive, emotional and vicious, which led to increased tensions at court; 'as a result, Domitian was such a prey to fear and anxiety that the least sign of danger unnerved him'.[14]

Devoured by his insecurities, Domitian executed members of his small inner circle of advisors in AD 95, raising the temperature to boiling point. At the start of the year, the emperor honoured his cousin, T. Flavius Clemens, by sharing the consulship with him. A 'man of despicable idleness'[15] who lacked any imperial ambitions for himself, Clemens was now elevated to the side of the emperor. Domitian had adopted his children, making them his heirs. Soon after his term ended on 1 May, Clemens and his wife, Domitilla, also a cousin, were accused of atheism, 'a charge on which many others who drifted into Jewish ways were condemned'.[16] They may have converted to Christianity, as this was seen as a breakaway sect of Judaism at the time. An early Christian catacomb in Rome was named after Domitilla. Clemens was executed and his wife was exiled to Pandateria, their children disappearing from the historical record.[17]

The refusal of Christians and Jews to recognize the pantheon of the gods was perceived as disloyalty to the state and the established religion. Domitian could not expect to retain the favour of Minerva, especially considering the actions of one so close to the throne. The emperor interpreted Clemens's conversion as a betrayal that endangered his own life. The household of the condemned, including their slaves and freedmen, were absorbed into the palace bureaucracy. They included Stephanus, a freedman of Domitilla and the emperor's future assassin. There was, however, no general persecution of Christians. The emperor's reaction was not based on open hostility to the monotheistic claims of these religions or disloyalty to the state, but a personal treachery by two members of the imperial family.[18]

Another member of the emperor's *concilium* was also condemned at this time for religious offences. The aristocrat Manius Acilius Glabrio was 'accused of the same crime as most of the others', implying he too had converted. The Church historian Eusebius refers to the Christian victims of Domitian's cruelty – 'at Rome great numbers of men distinguished by birth and attainments were executed without a fair trial, and countless other eminent men were for no reason at all banished from the country and their property confiscated'.[19] Even allowing for a certain exaggeration in numbers, the accused were of high status. Glabrio was exiled, then later put to death for conspiracy; as Juvenal observed, 'surviving to old age amongst the nobility has long been like a miracle'.[20] Glabrio and his father had been regular guests at the Alban villa and trusted advisors to the emperor.[21]

Another noble who was also exiled after being convicted for conspiring with Acilius Glabrio and then executed was the illustriously named patrician Servius Cornelius Scipio Salvidienus Orfitus.[22] His father had been executed in AD 66 by Nero, implicated in either the Pisonian conspiracy or that of Annius Vinicianus.[23] He was also related to Q. Pomponius Secundus and Domitius Corbulo; enough motive to hold a personal vendetta against imperial tyranny. Yet Philostratus, possibly in dark humour, or more likely through utter naivety, asserts he was no more capable of treason than Nerva. Admittedly, the Greek biographer conceded that Orfitus was considered a suitable candidate for imperial power.[24]

The numbers that attended the emperor's advisory council were small, closeted and intimate. The sudden fall of two of its members and the exile of Domitilla, who probably lived in the Alban palace, would have been stunning. Courtiers, nobles and freedmen alike would have re-evaluated their positions. Consequently, the emperor's relationships with his court officials deteriorated. Throughout his rule, he had demanded the highest standards from them, dismissing two Praetorian Prefects – one probably Casperius Aelianus – in the later part of the reign, possibly around AD 95.[25] An imperial freedman felt the full force of Domitian's anger for offending the gods and breaking the law. Providing 'a lesson that the sanctity of the gods must be protected against thoughtless abuse, Domitian made his soldiers tear down a tomb built for the son of one of his own freedmen from stones intended for the Temple of Capitoline Jupiter, and fling its contents of bones and ashes into the sea'.[26] Effectively, the son was sentenced to *damnatio memoriae* and his soul, deprived of a final resting place, condemned to wander the Earth for eternity. The father's impiety appears not to have been punished. He may have been the recipient of imperial clemency due to his recent bereavement, a small consolation that would fail to counter the bitter anger he felt.

Another freedman was not so lucky. Epaphroditus, who had played an important role in the uncovering of Piso's conspiracy, had risen rapidly under Nero to the office of *a libellis*, responsible for drafting the imperial responses to petitions. He had remained loyal to his emperor until the very end, helping Nero commit suicide. Twenty-eight years later, he was accused of failing his former master and patron because he had not attempted to save his life. The 70-year-old was exiled and later executed. The reason, according to Dio, was that by AD 95 Domitian had become 'suspicious of all mankind, and from now on ceased to repose hopes of safety in either the freedmen, or yet the prefects', consequently he hoped 'to terrify his own freedmen long in advance, so that they should venture no similar deed'.[27]

The charge appears unique and must be questioned. Roman prosecutors often made multiple accusations against a defendant to impugn their character and ward off potential allies. Epaphroditus's role in the suicide of Nero would have been raised because he had helped his emperor cut his throat, possibly leading to its inclusion in the reported indictment. Furthermore, if the emperor had wanted to intimidate his freedmen, why exile Epaphroditus and only later kill him? It is likely he had also retired from court. He is reported to have helped his former slave and Stoic, Epictetus, even though he had retired when Domitian banished philosophers from Italy around AD 95. The poet Martial, when petitioning the close *amici* of Domitian to promote his work, does not mention him, nor does he appear in any of his verses. Instead, he commends Entellus, the then *a libellis*, for his extensive vines and splendid house. Parthenius, the *a cubiculo* in charge of the private quarters of the emperor, also received a poem from Martial on the fifth birthday of his son, whilst the *ab epistulis* responsible for imperial correspondence, Abascantus, received praise from Statius.[28]

Epaphroditus remained a powerful, rich and influential figure, even if he no longer remained at court. As a slave freed by either Claudius or Nero, he would be considered a member of the imperial household with duties and responsibilities. He possessed huge gardens on the Esquiline Hill in Rome and still courted the favour of the emperor. Epictetus remembered his old master, who had sold a slave because he was no good and he was then 'bought by the imperial household and became a shoemaker to Caesar. You should have seen Epaphroditus flatter him then!'[29] His punishment and fate were similar to that experienced by Clemens and Glabrio, and there is some tenuous evidence that the former *a libellis* had also converted to Christianity. Paul, in a letter to the Philippians, refers to a fellow associate named Epaphroditus to whom he sent greetings, and 'especially to those in Caesar's household'. The evidence is admittedly questionable, but contextually it would make sense.[30]

According to our sources, the executions of Clemens and Epaphroditus in April AD 95 led directly to the murder of Domitian in September the following year. A delay of sixteen months suggests there were other, more pressing factors at play. Greed, unfettered ambition and fear were the motivating factors. Domitian had become increasingly dissatisfied with the performance and conduct of many of the imperial freedmen. Bribery was an established component in the administration and society generally. It could be expressed as an act of gratitude or *beneficia*, but legally these requirements had to be moderate. Domitian was determined to impose moderation, but this led to insecurity through the uncertainty in what was deemed acceptable. Freedmen such as Callistus, Narcissus and many more had become the richest men in Rome through their access to the emperor. This emperor had started to reform the bureaucracy by replacing freedmen at the head of the huge administrative departments with equestrians, as well as promoting eunuchs. He also created new posts only open to the equestrian class. He had been away from Rome on five campaigns and probably found equestrians to be more efficient and capable, especially in a travelling court. Abascantus was either dismissed or demoted from *ab epistulis* to *a cognitionibus* around AD 95. The freedmen were hated and knew that once cast adrift from imperial protection, they faced prosecution, conviction and punishment, possibly death. Demotion would also affect their ability to demand favours and money, and loss of influence. The example of Epaphroditus's fate served as an abject illustration of the future they faced.[31]

Imperial displeasure with the elite freedmen also offered opportunities to others who aimed to profit from their misfortune. Accusations were made against some, and they were accepted. Stephanus, the former freedman of Domitilla, used her exile and execution of her husband as his cloak to hide the real reason for his involvement in the plot. He had been accused of embezzlement. He knew how the emperor responded to corruption.[32] The motivations of Parthenius can only be surmised, but he had been greatly honoured by Domitian in the past; as a mark of his trust in him, he was allowed to carry a sword in the emperor's presence. He had recruited two of his junior chamberlains in Satur and Sigerus, as well as one of his own freedmen, Maximus. All these possibly faced the emperor's wrath and merciless judgement, and conspired 'because complaints had been lodged against them and others because they were expecting complaints to be lodged'. Principled motivations were absent; this was a fight for survival.[33]

Parthenius was the instigator, leader and organizer.[34] He recruited the core conspirators from men he knew he could trust from regular contacts or close familiarity and known fears arising from their misconduct. He was joined by the *a libellis*, Entellus. According to Dio, both Praetorian Prefects, Petronius Secundus and Norbanus, were aware of the plot, but from later events it is evident that Petronius took an active role. The only other Praetorian involved was Clodianus, a *cornicularius*, a junior officer serving as an adjutant to a centurion as the chief clerk, in charge of the *tabularium* or records office. However, according to a late source, he joined the conspiracy as he 'expected punishment on account of fraud involving intercepted funds'. His commanding officers would have been able to use the charges to recruit him. The elderly freedmen would not have been able to overpower the 44-year-old emperor and needed men capable of wielding a dagger and striking the deadly blows. It was for this reason that a palace gladiator was also enlisted. As a slave, he would have expected his freedom in return.[35]

Most of this small cabal of conspirators would have been able to meet as part of their role in the palace bureaucracy without raising any suspicions. They had to plan how and when to murder Domitian, but also their survival afterwards. The killing of a former master by freedmen was considered an abhorrent act in Roman society and was treated as parricide. These *libertini* were duty-bound to protect the life of their patron, on pain of death. This had been one of the main points that had been made in the trial of Epaphroditus. Furthermore, there were lessons to be drawn from history. After the murder of Gaius, his guards had rampaged through the palace, slaughtering assassins and innocents alike. After the death of Nero, many of his leading freedmen were victims of a senatorial massacre. Domitian's successor had to be a senator selected in advance by them, indebted to them and trusted by them. The Senate could have no role, especially after the farce that erupted after the murder of Gaius. They would have looked to previous successful plots to draw inspiration. The obvious model to follow was that of Callistus. Furthermore, the freedmen had to hide their role in the murder of their patron as well as absolve the imperial successor of any responsibility, just as Claudius had done.

The involvement of both Praetorian Prefects was vital in ensuring the short-term survival of the assassins. The hunt for their candidate for the throne, though, proved to be a major problem. This future emperor would need to have the nobility and *auctoritas* to command respect, but the Praetorian soldiers were loyal to Domitian, as were the armies on Rome's frontiers. The risks were too great for those they initially approached. Consequently, according to Dio,

> 'they did not proceed to carry it out until they had determined who was to succeed to the imperial office. They discussed the matter with various men, and when none of them would accept it (for all were afraid of them, believing that they were testing their loyalty), they betook themselves to Nerva.'

Eutropius is more informative, stating that Nerva, despite being 'an old man, was made emperor through the care taken by Petronius Secundus, the Praetorian Prefect, and Parthenius, the murderer of Domitian'. The numbers involved were small and its leadership focused.[36]

The Prefect and the head chamberlain would have had little opportunity to canvass leading senators in Rome as the court was mostly based in Domitian's Alban villa. Their main contacts would have been members of the emperor's *concilium*, a few of whom were senators with the necessary aristocratic inheritance. Some names stand out, notably the probable City Prefect in command of the Urban Cohorts, and twice consul and a patrician, T. Aurelius Fulvus (father of the emperor Antoninus Pius).

Also needing a mention is Cn. Arrius Antoninus, consul in AD 69 and former governor of the prestigious province of Asia. His daughter was married to Aurelius Fulvus. Enigmatically, he publicly pitied Nerva when he became emperor, and

> 'embraced him and said that he congratulated the senate, people, and provinces, however, in no way Nerva himself, for whom to escape ever-evil *Principes* had been better than, enduring the force of so great a burden, subjections not only to troubles and risks, but also to the assessment of enemies and, equally, of friends, who, since they presume they deserve everything, are bitterer than even enemies themselves, if they do not obtain something.'

Arrius Antoninus was honoured, or possibly placated, with a second consulship from Nerva in March AD 97. Aurelius Fulvus was the father of the emperor Antoninus Pius, whilst Arrius Antoninus was his maternal grandfather. Through his adoption into the imperial family by Hadrian, Nerva became his grandfather. This may account for the absence of their names from the plot against Domitian in the sources used by Dio.[37]

Another man who rejected the purple may have been A. Bucius Lappius Maximus, who had defeated the rebel Saturninus in AD 89 and received consular office from Domitian in AD 86 and 95. He had military experience as governor of Germania Inferior from AD 87–89 and Syria from AD 90–94, and had fought in the Chattan War, so he would have appealed to the armies. He was undoubtedly one of Domitian's close *amici* and was in Rome in AD 96. All were better choices than Nerva, but their rejection of the offers increased the risk of detection.[38]

Nerva had no military experience and possessed a questionable reputation at best. He had been a close advisor to Nero, Vespasian and Domitian, whilst playing a key role in the detection of the Pisonian conspiracy. He was a duplicitous political manipulator who operated in the shadows for his imperial patrons. Pliny the Younger hints at this when he commends him for using his connections to further their interests, saying that Nerva 'even as a private citizen took note of whatever was done in the public interest'. Yet, in his favour, he held a genuine grievance. Domitian had executed the nephew of the former emperor Otho, L. Salvius Otho Cocceianus, for celebrating the birthday of his uncle. He was also the son of Nerva's sister. This, though, was in AD 93, hardly a pressing reason to plot the emperor's death six years later. Although of moderate nobility, Nerva was not married, nor did he have any children or surviving close relatives. Furthermore, his age meant that the long-term question of the succession had merely been put on hold, although his acceptance was no doubt a huge relief to Secundus and Parthenius.[39]

The next decision was to determine where the attack on Domitian should take place and when. There would be no theatrical gestures, no posturing to an imaginary audience. Cold-blooded murder required privacy. There were only a very small number of them, so they had to strike where the emperor would be unguarded. A public arena such as the theatre or an imperial banquet was therefore out of the question. However, the Praetorians were not normally present in his private quarters in his palace, and 'while the conspirators were debating when and how it would be better to murder Domitian in his bath or at dinner, Stephanus offered them his advice and his services'.[40] The implication is that Stephanus approached the plotters, rather than the other way around, which would have added to their anxiety and urgency.

The conspirators waited until the festival of the *Ludi Romani*, from 4–19 September. Domitian would be in Rome to attend the events, which would allow them to present Nerva to the Praetorians straight after the emperor's murder. The emperor was also likely to leave for Pannonia soon after, as he had amassed five legions to cross the Danube and destroy the harvests of the Marcomanni. This campaign also committed the governor of the province, who would not be able to disengage and avenge his emperor with a march on Rome.[41]

Furthermore, the festivities were a public holiday, so most senators would be away on their country estates for the wine harvest or taking their ease away from the blistering heat of the capital. Some senators who had been selected by lot remained in Rome to make a senatorial meeting quorate in the rare eventuality a meeting was called at this time. The Senate, with most of its aristocratic leadership absent, would be faced with a *fait accompli* and merely be asked to ratify Nerva as emperor. However, he was never the Senate's choice, many of whose members owed their career, honours and wealth to Domitian.[42]

Domitian's last day on Earth was 18 September. Parthenius, as his head chamberlain, knew his daily routine. After conducting judicial business in the morning, the emperor liked to retire to his private quarters to relax and take a bath before an afternoon siesta. Stephanus had pretended to injure his arm, and for a week previously had worn bandages. On this day, he concealed a dagger beneath them. During the emperor's absence in the morning, Parthenius had removed the blade to the dagger he knew Domitian kept under his pillow. The handle and scabbard were left in case he checked that they were still there.

Around noon, the emperor approached his bedroom and was met by Parthenius, who told him Stephanus had news of a plot. Stephanus was duly granted an audience. The emperor always heard these reports in isolation, suspecting that court officials might be named. Stephanus followed the emperor into his bedroom. He was a strong, well-built man who could match the physical strength of the emperor. Parthenius then quietly locked the doors, a clear indication that many of the personal servants were not involved in the plot and would attempt to save their master.

Stephanus gave Domitian a document detailing a conspiracy against his life. With the emperor engrossed and distracted, the freedman was able to remove the dagger from beneath his bandages. Also in the room was a small boy who took care of the emperor's shrine to his household gods and goddesses, including Minerva. But Minerva was unable to protect Domitian. The boy raised no alarm, either because he was unaware of the impending attack or because he was struck dumb in shock and horror. He later stood testimony to what happened next. Stephanus stabbed Domitian in the groin. Was this a lowly act derived from bitter hatred or struck in imitation of Brutus, who aimed his attack on Julius Caesar in the same place? There was nothing noble in Stephanus's motivation – he was no liberator. Domitian collapsed to the ground, but the blow had not been fatal. The emperor fought for his life. He called for the boy to get his dagger, but the blade was missing. Instead, he grabbed Stephanus's weapon, lacerating his hands and attempting to gouge his attacker's eyes out. The blows, however, kept coming – seven in total. The shouts, yells and screams of a distraught child told Parthenius that all was not going to plan. His other conspirators had gathered at the door, including Maximus, the Praetorian Clodianus, Satur and the gladiator. Parthenius opened the door, probably claiming it had been locked by the emperor. They had by now been joined by others not involved in the plot. The emperor was dead, but they fell upon Stephanus and he too died under a hail of blows.[43]

Dio infers that Stephanus died after being attacked by servants innocent of the murderous designs of those around them. However, his death suited the freedmen. They could claim that Stephanus acted alone and thereby escape the anger and inevitable retribution of the guard. This would also explain the recruitment of a gladiator. Clodianus would probably have been a member of the cohort on guard, and he could use his position to calm the soldiers as they arrived in the imperial bedroom to see their emperor brutally slaughtered. The two Prefects would then take control of the situation. Nerva was already waiting in the palace for Parthenius to take him with the Prefects to the Praetorian fortress and the ritual acclamation. He would have been presented as a loyal *amicus* of their former leader. A large donative would have temporarily smothered discontent, money saved by Domitian's careful and efficient administration. However, Nerva's courage nearly broke when 'a rumour quickly arose that Domitian lived and would soon be at hand, [and] he was sufficiently terrified so that, pale and unable to speak, he barely held firm. But, bolstered by assurances received from Parthenius, he was turned to festive blandishments.'[44]

A fragment of the *Fasti Ostiensis* shows that Nerva ascended the throne on the same day Domitian was assassinated. The same inscription also notes a *senatus consultum* was issued the following day, indicating that the Senate did not meet until then.[45] Many of those nobles who were on their extensive estates in the wine-growing areas of Campania would have been unable to attend. Nerva was emperor, the hesitant choice of a small group of disaffected freedmen and without the backing of the Praetorian soldiers, armies or even the majority of the Senate. Many senators rejoiced at the overthrow of Domitian. They now had an emperor who would allow them free rein, but Nerva would not have been their choice of successor. His fight for survival began immediately.

The anger of the Praetorians now erupted, and 'although they were barely restrained and only with difficulty by sensible men, eventually they came to an agreement with the nobility.. This 'agreement' was probably a large donative, but they were not satisfied. They demanded the deification of Domitian, which caused problems for his successor as the Senate had just passed a decree of *damnatio memoriae*. This helped to legitimize Nerva's takeover. The treatment of

Domitian's body was controversial, as it was handled like that of a slave, carried out of the palace 'on a common litter by the public undertakers as though he were a pauper', and was claimed by his childhood nurse, Phyllis. She took the corpse to her house outside the city on the Latin Way, cremating it on a pyre she had built in her garden. She took the ashes to the Temple of the Flavians, and there mixed them with those of his niece, Julia. Thus brought together, the remains would not be violated, and he could rest in eternity alongside one of the few people who truly loved him.[46]

Their emperor's murder 'deeply grieved the troops, who at once began to speak of Domitian the God – they would have avenged him had anyone given them a lead', which they did a few months later. An unnamed legion fighting beyond the Danube came close to revolt when it heard of the killing of Domitian. The Praetorian Prefect Norbanus disappears, probably immediately dismissed. His loyalty to Nerva was already suspect due to his ephemeral participation in the assassination of Domitian, making his retention too great a risk. He was replaced by Aelianus, who had been dismissed from Praetorian Prefecture by Domitian. It was no doubt for this reason that Nerva and Parthenius felt they could rely on his allegiance, and his established relationship with the guardsmen would help restore discipline. Their expectations were to prove ill advised.[47]

Another pressing challenge for Nerva and his freedman adherents was detaching themselves from culpability in the murder of their emperor, *amicus* and patron. They also had to damn the rule of Domitian to justify his murder. The pursuit of personal gain or avoidance of justice did not provide firm foundations on which to build a new regime. There was also the lingering threat of the Praetorians, who were not placated but lacked for the time being a leader to harness their anger.[48] In the days and weeks after the ascension of Nerva, all information about the murder was closely controlled and a carefully crafted narrative began to appear, aided and abetted by senators and equestrians keen to earn imperial favour.[49]

Nerva's involvement in the murder of the man who had given him the prestigious honour of a second consulship and invited him to his *concilium* was said by some to be due to Domitian's sudden desire to kill him. Dio reports that Nerva had 'been in peril of his life as a result of being denounced by astrologers who declared that he should be sovereign', and that it was this last circumstance that made it easier for the plotters to persuade him to accept the imperial power. The dubious credibility of this story is further undermined by the claim that Nerva was not executed because 'one of the astrologers who was friendly to the latter declared that the man would die within a few days. And so, Domitian, believing that this would really come to pass, did not wish to be guilty of this additional murder, since Nerva was to die so soon in any case.'

Dio repeats the same story when attempting to absolve Seneca from blame and involvement in the plot with Agrippina and Livilla to murder Gaius. This is stock propaganda regurgitated to sanctify abhorrent actions. The claim that Domitian was about to exile or execute a member of the elite became a badge of honour and a demonstration of their loyalty to the new regime. Pliny the Younger claimed that he too was about to be brought to trial.[50]

Another 'tradition' dressed up as fact by Dio refers to the supposed knowledge of the conspiracy by Domitia, the emperor's wife and daughter of Domitius Corbulo. Dio reports that Domitian hated her and she feared for her life, although Suetonius declares that he was infatuated with her. Dio states that 'I have heard the following account' – the third-century historian allowing the reader to decide its authenticity – that Domitian's wife was passed a list of names of those her husband intended to condemn by a young child who tended his bed chamber. This child, being surprisingly able to read and remarkably politically aware, understood the importance of its contents and stole it to then pass on to the empress, whom he must have trusted implicitly. She immediately passed it on to those named in the list. Not only is this account incredible as it stands, but the same story is repeated virtually word for word in Dio's account of the assassination of the emperor Commodus. The two stories about Domitian are recounted together in Dio's history, suggesting he drew them from a common source. Philostratus even states that Nerva had been exiled, which is clearly untrue. Both are likely to be the result of Nerva's propaganda.[51]

Domitia was allowed to retain the title of Augusta by Nerva and his successors, despite her continuing to publicly declare her relationship to Domitian, in explicit contravention of the *damnatio memoriae* passed by the Senate. Domitia's alleged knowledge of the plot and implied acquiescence in his death helped to propagate the legacy of Domitian the tyrant. Any objections on her part would have led to prosecution and the removal of her illustrious title. She was in her early forties when she was widowed and lived her remaining thirty years mostly on her villa near Gabii, 12 miles east of Rome. She patronized the arts, supporting the historian Josephus, and owned a brick factory nearby. Its bricks were stamped 'from the brickyards of Domitia, wife of Domitian', one of her freedmen referring to her as such in an inscription. When she died in the AD 120s, one of her freedmen erected an elaborate tomb for her. However, lacking her power and influence, he was restricted in composing her epitaph. She was now just 'Domitia Augusta, daughter of Gnaeus Domitius Corbulo'.[52] Hadrian wanted Domitian airbrushed from history as he was the adopted grandson of Nerva. For this reason, Suetonius ignores Nerva's role in the conspiracy; he was secretary to Hadrian, and it was in his reign that he wrote his biographies. History was written by the victors in this battle for survival.[53]

Nerva's political position, which was weak from the moment he accepted the throne, quickly became desperate. In the Senate, a vicious war erupted as the recently empowered members attacked the former supporters of Domitian. Informers were executed, along with any slaves who had provided evidence against their masters. Those previously accused of *maiestas* were released and now sought revenge – 'no little commotion was occasioned by the fact that everybody was accusing everybody else, [and] Fronto, the consul, is said to have remarked that it was bad to have an emperor under whom nobody was permitted to do anything, but worse to have one under whom everybody was permitted to do everything.'[54] Nerva himself had been a committed supporter of the Flavians, including Domitian.[55] Consequently, he suppressed the use of *maiestas* and promised never to put a senator to death. This impunity only spurred on his enemies.

Nerva tried to build bridges with the old aristocracy, knowing his nobility paled against that of the great Republican houses. He honoured Gaius Calpurnius Piso with a *suffect* consulship in March AD 97. Nerva had taken a leading role in uncovering the Pisonian conspiracy against Nero in AD 65. The new emperor hoped the new consul would feel compensated for this nefarious role in the death of his father or grandfather. Another Calpurnii had been executed in AD 69 by a general of Vespasian as his allegiance was considered suspect.[56] However, the Calpurnii were not to be placated. Their old wounds were not to be healed. C. Calpurnius Crassus Frugi Licianus felt entitled to the empire by descent. He was descended from both the Calpurnii and the *triumvir* Marcus Licinius Crassus. He must have been one of many nobles invited to form the new emperor's *concilium* as he had access to the palace. He used this opportunity to tempt 'the minds of the troops with grand promises'. The guard was already disaffected, so he must have thought the risks of discovery were counterbalanced in his favour by the likelihood of success.[57]

However, he and his fellow senators were betrayed. Nerva invited them to sit beside him in the imperial box during a public gladiatorial contest. They were all evidently prestigious nobles, as the invitation was not a surprise. They were still ignorant of their discovery but understood immediately when the emperor 'gave them swords, ostensibly to inspect and see if they were sharp (as was often done), but really to show that he did not care even if he died then and there'.[58] The conspirators would have been surrounded by soldiers and knew any move to attack the emperor would have resulted in a swift death. Calpurnius Crassus was exiled to Tarentum in southern Italy with his wife.[59]

He was to prove a man whose sense of nobility and *auctoritas* overrode any intelligence or prudence. Recalled by Trajan when he ascended the throne, he again conspired, again was betrayed and again exiled, this time to an island.

There he remained, poisoned by his name and burdened by his heritage. When Hadrian became emperor, Calpurnius Crassus attempted to escape but was caught and executed by an imperial procurator. His was a symbolic end of an ancient Republican aristocracy that never came to terms with their political impotence under the Principate. His smashed funerary altar was discovered with his name removed from a public plaque due to *damnatio memoriae*. Even then, his family hid his monument away in a plain family mausoleum so they could continue to pay their respects to their ancestor.[60]

Nerva survived, only to be faced with a revolt of the Praetorians soon after. The Prefect Aelianus harnessed their rage, and a group entered the palace to hunt down Nerva, the other Prefect Petronius Secundus and Parthenius, who they now knew to be the leaders of the plot against Domitian. Nobody came to their aid. They surrounded the emperor and demanded the execution of the men who had given him the throne. There are two accounts of Nerva's failed attempts to protect them. According to a late source,

> 'he was so consternated that he was unable to keep from vomiting or from
> a paroxysm of the bowels, but nevertheless he vehemently objected, saying
> that it was more fitting to die than to befoul the authority of imperium
> as a result of the authors of the power that he was to acquire having
> been betrayed.'[61]

Dio describes a courageous Nerva who 'resisted them stoutly, even to the point of baring his collar bone and presenting them his throat; but he accomplished nothing'.[62] Whichever was true, the injury to his authority was catastrophic.

Aelianus and his soldiers ignored the imperial commands and hunted down their quarry through the palace. The Praetorian Prefect was granted a swift death, as befitted his status. He was dispatched with a single blow. The freedman Parthenius, though, had betrayed his patron, whom he was duty bound to protect. He was held down as his genitals were cut off and forced into his mouth. Then he was garrotted. To add to Nerva's humiliation, he was only able to appease Aelianus and his men 'by means of huge payoffs, who, more insolent than the savage crime, compelled Nerva to give thanks among the people to the soldiers, since they had killed the most base and wicked of all mortals'. Nerva's age and poor health probably saved him. Aelianus merely had to wait for nature to take its cause before using his position to appoint the successor, who would in return secure his future safety.[63]

The sources hint at other plots, and the governor of Syria was rapidly replaced. Nerva sought to reinforce his position by adopting Trajan as his heir. He was a gifted general who owed his career to Domitian and had served him loyally. At the time, Trajan was either governor of Germania Superior or Pannonia, with a huge army that had been acclaimed for a great victory beyond the Danube.[64] Nerva knew his prospects were poor and he also sought vengeance for his humiliation. A diamond ring was sent to Trajan as a symbol of his adoption, along with a letter. Nerva obligated his heir with a quote from Homer's *Iliad*: 'May the Danaans, by thy shafts, requite my tears.' In the poem, the priest of Apollo prayed to the god to avenge the abduction of his daughter by King Agamemnon. The debt would be repaid in full.[65]

Nerva died on the night of 27/28 January AD 98. Aelianus and those Praetorians involved in the humiliation of Nerva were summoned to Trajan's headquarters, and the emperor, 'pretending that he was going to employ them for some purpose … then put them out of the way'. This is a pleasant turn of phrase used by Dio as a euphemism for execution. Historians have understandably questioned the Praetorian Prefect's decision to meet Trajan in his legionary fortress, but what choice did he have? Trajan appointed a new Praetorian Prefect; and when presenting him with a sword as the symbol of office, said: 'Take this, so that if I rule well use it for me, but if badly, against me.' Nerva, along with Trajan, earned the distinction of being one of the few emperors to die a natural death. Trajan died in AD 117 after campaigning against Rome's fearsome enemy in the East, Parthia, whilst Nerva's end was grim and debauched; he became a god by choking to death on his own vomit after an excess of wine when weak from fever.[66]

Conclusions

'It is not Caesar himself that anyone fears, but death, banishment, prison, loss of property, deprival of civic rights. Nor does anyone love Caesar himself, unless he happens to be a man of great worth; but we love riches, a tribunate, a praetorship, a consulship. When we love and hate and fear these things, those who have the disposal of them must necessarily be our masters.'

(Epictetus, *Discourses*, 4.1.60)

The emperor was the ultimate patron and benefactor, commanding the huge resources of the Roman state and also controlling appointments to all its major offices, priesthoods and honours. Nerva, upon ascending the throne, passed an edict that announced he became emperor 'in order that I might confer new *beneficia* and preserve those already granted by my predecessors'. The problem for rulers from Julius Caesar onwards was that there were only about a hundred senatorial or equestrian posts that could be bestowed each year. There were other gifts the emperor could grant but, as Epictetus was aware, magistracies were the most sought-after honour and brought the opportunity to accumulate more wealth.[1] There were many whose ambitions were disappointed.

Most sought-after was the consular office, which ennobled the recipient and their descendants. Even then, they always craved more. If they were appointed to a praetorship, they felt aggrieved if it was not the urban praetorship, or if granted a *suffect* consulship, they resented that they were not made ordinary consuls, giving their name to the year. Many conspirators had high hopes and ambitions for advancement, but were disappointed that they had, in their minds, been thwarted by an unjust emperor. Many of Caesar's assassins felt this way, such as Suplicius Galba or L. Minucius Basilus. In later conspiracies, even men who held consular office expected more. Calpurnius Piso had held the *suffect* consulship early in Claudius's reign, but then his career stalled despite his close association with Nero.[2]

As all senatorial offices were at the disposal of the emperor, it became vitally important to have direct private access to him. This brought great power and influence because patrons became the brokers of imperial patronage, developing their network of *amicitiae* through their *amici* and clients. The aristocracy was totally preoccupied with status, which came from an illustrious name and the ability to brag that 'I am a senator, I'm a personal friend of Caesar, I've been a consul and I own many slaves personally.'[3] This developed a social cohesion centred on the emperor and indirectly extended his control and influence.[4]

The old aristocracy expected to be the recipients of this privileged position, but it was a reciprocal but unequal relationship where the emperor was in a vastly superior position. He was expected to act as though this was a relationship of equals where the reality of the situation was ignored. Consequently, he expected loyalty (or *fides*) in return. Seneca, with obtuse idealism, explained that 'an emperor protected by his own *beneficium* had no need of guards, he keeps arms for decoration'.[5] As a social equal, the emperor was expected to adhere to certain social customs that recognized the status of the senatorial class. He had to kiss the noble on his cheek, as to offer his hand was a demonstration of superiority. An emperor was expected to greet these men privately rather than as part of a group at the morning *salutatio*, and sit them close to him in the evening banquet.

This performance emanated from Augustus's founding of the Principate, where the emperor was presented as the first among equals rather than the absolute monarch. Although a charade, it was set in revered precedence and expectation, and was vitally important to the aristocracy. An emperor who behaved with *civilitas*, as a citizen amongst citizens, was commended as a good emperor by the senatorial writers. However, one who behaved as a monarch or a god was seen as a tyrant.[6] This was highly emotive to Rome's elite. The liberators who murdered Julius Caesar were very effective in portraying him as aiming for monarchy, despite his futile attempts to deny this. Some of his assassins joined the plot for honourable reasons, to restore the Republic. The conspirator Murena was enraged by the arrogance of Augustus when he successfully but illegally intervened to undermine the defence of his client. There was a new political reality which these men were unwilling to accept. Brutus used '*Libertas*' as the password at the Battle of Philippi, and it was the password given by Annius Vinicianus to Chaerea. By AD 41, the word was a rallying call rather than a credible aspiration.

Most conspirators were motivated by personal grievances. After the reign of Augustus, most classes accepted the all-encompassing power of the emperor but were mainly concerned with the emperor's behaviour, their lifestyle, social values and attitudes, etiquette and their relationship with him.[7] Cassius Chaerea was publicly humiliated by Gaius and wanted revenge. Another whose pride was attacked by Gaius was the senator Decimus Valerius Asiaticus, who also suffered public humiliation when Gaius upbraided him for the poor performance of his wife in bed. The poet Lucan hated Nero for the suppression of his work, despite its provocative praise of Caesar's assassins, whilst the tribune Subrius Flavus was disgusted by the emperor's lack of *virtus*. Romans, and especially soldiers, associated this quality with their greatness. *Virtus* characterized the ideal behaviour of a man and was embodied in martial valour and behaviour. However, Nero's appearance on the stage was the antithesis of this quintessential Roman value, justifying the Praetorians' rejection of their military oath to protect him before their own life.

The suppression and punishment of conspirators was also a balancing act for emperors. Conspiracies were often centred around family members and their *amici* and clients. The conspiracy against Julius Caesar was initially restricted to the *amici* of Cassius Longinus. The Spanish senator Aemilius Regulus, who 'hated unjust deeds with the hot temper of a free man', recruited his *amici* to his plot against Gaius. Annius Vinicianus was a close friend of Asiaticus, and he wished to avenge his death. Fear of discovery limited the initial conversations and plans to people the plotters could trust. The main senatorial and equestrian participants in Piso's conspiracy were his *amici* and clients. Seneca was himself condemned by his close friendship with the conspirator. Emperors had to decide where to stop in the punishment of a conspirator's network of friendship and obligation. With the greater threat came greater suppression. Tiberius destroyed all the family, *amici* and clients of Sejanus. Gaius and Claudius followed this model, as did Nero after the 'Vinician' conspiracy.[8]

However, most emperors initially tried to limit the sanctions imposed on family members to those directly involved in plots so as not to create a vendetta that might be passed through the generations. The sons of Camillus Scribonianus, Annius Vinicianus and Caplurnius Piso were allowed to retain the necessary wealth to pursue a senatorial career. Enmities, though, were passed from father to son: they were all later executed for involvement in conspiracies of their own. Furthermore, the suppression of plots led to the creation of martyrs, despite emperors presenting the evidence against them in senatorial trials or publicizing documentation giving the evidence exacted in the investigations or trials held in private by the emperor and his *concilium*. Those convicted, however, were posthumously declared to be innocent victims of tyranny, although most were indeed guilty of the crimes with which they were charged. Dio perceptively comments: '[I]t is not possible, of course, for those on the outside to have certain knowledge of such matters; for whatever measures a ruler takes, either personally or through the Senate, for the punishment of men for alleged plots against himself, are generally looked upon with suspicion as having been done out of spite, no matter how just such measures may be.'[9]

Additional shame and condemnation of the convicted were often inflicted through a senatorial decree of *damnatio memoriae*. The erasure of their names and deeds was meant to remind the viewer of their treason and their punishment. This denial of memory condemned them to the injustice of obscurity for all eternity. This act removed a family member from his social and familial context and denied them the hope of living beyond death. This imperial revenge often served to inflame relatives and *amici* of the convicted, who were outraged by the injustice.[10] The anguish of families and friends are perfectly illustrated in an inscription from *c.* AD 190 for M. Antonius Lupus on the Via Ostiense. He had been charged with *maiestas*, executed and suffered *damnatio memoriae* under the emperor Commodus. His first tomb was destroyed and his name was erased from the inscription. However, Commodus's successor restored his reputation. The words resonate with the emotions of his family:

'To the spirits of the Departed. His *amici* Marcus Valerius Bradua Mauricus, a priest, Antonia Vitellia, and Quintus Fabius Honoratus and Tiberius Annaeus Placidus have completed the second, untouched sepulchre of Marcus Antonius Lupus, pious and faithful augur, patrician, quaestor, associate of Titius, Military Tribune of the 2nd Legion, Prefect, of the highest rank, oppressed by force and whose memory was restored: an undertaking of his wife Claudia Regilla and his daughter Anita Marcellina in order to attest to their piety towards him and celebrate his name in perpetuity.'[11]

The erasure of names and honours but retention of the rest of the inscription stood as a public testament to the shame and dishonour inflicted on these families, whose members often secretly honoured their fallen members as heroes. The elderly jurist Cassius Longinus was exiled to Sardinia for illegally keeping a mask of his ancestor who murdered Julius Caesar, whilst Gaius Silius, the lover of Messalina, kept busts of his father who had suffered *damnatio* in the reign of Tiberius. Exile was also a form of living death. Those exiled and their families lived in the hope of the emperor's death so a successor would permit their return.

Whole aristocratic families were destroyed, partly by their generational conflict with imperial tyranny and partly by their elite status as possible rivals of the emperor. Lucius Junius Silanus, a political rival to the emperor through his grandmother, who was descended from Augustus, was exiled and then executed by a centurion. His father and an uncle had fallen victim to Agrippina, whilst another relative chose suicide rather than relying on Nero's clemency.[12] The Silanii, along with other aristocratic families such as the Aemilii Lepidii and descendants of Pompey the Great and Sulla, were eradicated, victims of their aspirations and imperial suspicions.[13]

Emperors were naturally suspicious of these noble families. They were prepared to offer them the trappings of elite status without bequeathing actual political power. The consular office was their birth rite, along with governorships of Asia or Africa and priesthoods, but not actual positions that could threaten the imperial order. Governorships of imperial provinces with control of the legions were given to 'new men', whose lack of an illustrious lineage meant their careers were reliant on imperial patronage and their loyalty would be ultimately rewarded with consular office. Vespasian owed his rise to the patronage of Gaius, Claudius and Nero, whilst Trajan was a loyal servant of Domitian. This strategy was a direct consequence of the threats posed by the senatorial elite. The military threats of Gaetulicus on the Rhine and Camillus Scribonianus, allied to conspiracies in Rome, alerted emperors to this dual danger. The revolt of Vindex in Gaul and Sulpicius Galba in Spain, combined with the conspiracy of the Praetorian Prefect, Nymphidius Sabinus, in Rome, would remove Nero from the throne.[14]

The Praetorian soldiers remained remarkably loyal to the Julio-Claudians. Although a small number of officers might plot against the emperor, their grievances were personal. It was in the interests of the guard to preserve their status and privileges by preserving the dynasty they served. It was not just the Batavians who sought vengeance on the murderers of Gaius, and the guard seethed with anger against the assassins of Domitian. The Praetorian Prefects, who worked closely with the emperor and possessed vast influence, were also exposed to their suspicions. Few emperors were prepared to risk their safety if they lost trust in the men responsible for their security. Clemens lost the trust of Gaius, as did Nero in Faenius Rufus, whose position was undermined by the whispering campaign of his fellow prefect Tigellinus. The fate of many prefects demonstrates the precarious nature of their positions and lives. Once their relationship with the emperor broke down, it was simply a matter of kill or be killed. Few were retired or promoted to the Senate.[15]

The Praetorians' loyalty to Claudius was not through his tenuous links to Augustus, but as the brother of Germanicus. They also had few alternatives to Claudius after the murder of Gaius, Augustus's great grandson. However, the ascent to the throne of an aristocrat with no direct link to the first emperor served to kindle the aspirations and ambitions of other families with similar or better claims to the throne. Claudius tried to placate these families with a recall of exiles, money gifts and magistracies. This initial attempt at compromise was met with conspiracies and plots. Firstly, Appius Claudius was executed in AD 42, not for his alleged refusal to sleep with Messalina, but for treason. A similar charge had been made against him in AD 32. The Silanii were habitually involved in conspiracies.[16] Appius Claudius's fall led to others taking up the direction of the emerging plan. L. Arruntius Camillus Scibonianus and Annius Vinicianus both had imperial aspirations. Camillus could trace his lineage back to legendary dictator Furius Camillus and Pompey the Great, as well as the dictator Sulla and L. Arruntius, whom Augustus considered capable of imperial power. The only strategies available to emperors were either reward or repression.[17] Rewards and reconciliation had failed, so Claudius unleashed a terror on these families, hidden behind Narcissus and Messalina. It was so effective that there were no further senatorial plots during his reign.

Gaius, Nero, and Domitian were all condemned as tyrants. Their behaviour was used as part-justification for their murders. However, each started their reigns seeking accommodation with the Senate and the aristocracy. They each declared that they would rule in partnership with the Senate and took practical measures to advertise the validity of their intentions. They suppressed the *lex maiestas* passed by Augustus in AD 8 that allowed informers, whether slaves or free, to be rewarded for information leading to a successful prosecution. Claudius, Nero and Domitian executed slaves who had informed on their masters when they took power. However, all of the emperors ultimately rejected this approach as their relationship with the Senate broke down.[18] Gaius abandoned this policy after the detection of the conspiracy involving Aemilius Lepidus, his sisters and Gaetulicus. Claudius instigated a campaign of revenge after the discovery of the conspiracy of Annius Vinicianus and Camillus Scribonianus. Nero only reintroduced *maiestas* after the Pisonian conspiracy, and Domitian only after AD 93 to destroy the Stoic opposition led by Helvidius Priscus the Younger. Each conspiracy resulted in a huge political readjustment by the emperor.[19]

Conspiracies dominated Roman history and political thinking from the mysterious death of Romulus, its first king, through the Republic to the assassination of Julius Caesar. A similar pattern emerges, initiated by these emperors in response to senatorial plots, starting with Augustus. There was little organized opposition to imperial power in the Senate itself. Instead, leadership was provided by disaffected individual nobles, often the supposed 'best' men. Nor were emperors removed due to conflict with the Senate as an institution or for attacking its rights or status.[20] The majority of senators owed their position and status to the emperor's patronage. The Senate was not a united body working to preserve its dwindling status and power. After the conspiracy of Caepio and Murena, there were few demands for a restoration of senatorial government. Even after the murder of Gaius, the initial proposals to restore the Republic were subsumed in intrigue by members of the aristocracy to gather support for their imperial claims. The motivations of most senatorial conspirators were far from idealistic or ideological, but were intrinsically based on personal aspirations. Many nobles were slaves to their ambitions, inherited through a great name and unwillingness to accept the new political reality, or committed through their debts of *amicitiae* to their patron or *amicus*.[21] This wide range of motivations, aspirations and aims meant conspiracies lacked cohesion.

Personalities, behaviours and relationships were vitally important to Rome's elite. Mutual trust was vital to build positive relationships, but, as Epictetus acknowledged, where the emperor held absolute power to reward or punish, all those who met him had to guard their words and anticipate the emperor's response. Claudius's *amici*, Vitellius and Caecina, were caught in an unenviable position when faced with Narcissus's charges against Messalina. Hence their unwillingness to commit and their reluctance to either support the freedman's accusations or defend the empress. The outcome of the power struggle was at that time unknown, and Claudius's reaction was difficult to predict. A free, open and frank discussion between the emperor and his advisors was impossible, leading to flattery and second-guessing the emperor's opinions. This charade meant that all emperors from Tiberius through to Domitian became increasingly isolated, fearful and reactive, leading to incessant plots and conspiracies. Trust was in short supply.[22]

The human condition is ruled by emotion. Love and happiness, though, seem to be rarely present in the lives of most emperors. Instead, the threat of sudden death drove anger and fear. The same was true for courtiers. The rewards of close personal access to the emperor were great, but the risks were greater. The threat of imminent danger also motivated those near to the emperor. The increasingly unpredictable behaviour of Gaius drove the Praetorian Prefects, Claudius and Callistus, into a conspiratorial partnership. They were aware of Gaius's suspicions after the conspirator Betilienus Capito named them as involved in sedition. The ruthless suppression of previous plots added to their sense of insecurity. Furthermore, it was the inevitability of punishment for corruption from Domitian that drew Stephanus and the Praetorian officer Clodianus into a plot. The freedman *cubicularius* Parthenius also felt his position threatened and proved as equally duplicitous as Callistus and Narcissus.

The legal system was an extension of court politics. Prosecution led to inevitable conviction before compliant senators keen to gain imperial favour. It would have been a brave man to vote to acquit any accused on *maiestas* charges. *Delators*, mostly ambitious senators, sought to win the approval of the emperor by charging those who fell from imperial approval. A conviction was also rewarded with a share of their estates, a further incentive to pursue the emperor's enemies.

In the conviction of Annius Vinicainus and Q. Pomponius Secundus, the evidence was provided by the Senate itself. The former had announced his involvement in the successful plot to murder Gaius and then manoeuvred for the throne in opposition to the claims of Claudius. The latter had convened the Senate to restore the Republic and opposed Claudius's coup. The infamous *delator* Suillius Rufus saw rich pickings and attacked Secundus. The future was clear. Secundus joined the conspiracy against Claudius, whilst Annius Vinicianus knew he was next. Suillius Rufus would later prosecute Valerius Asiaticus, who had also reached for the throne upon the death of Gaius and was probably plotting to remove Claudius. He later met his match in Seneca, who was vulnerable after he had fallen from Nero's favour, but the philosopher successfully counter-sued. However, by associating Calpurnius Piso with the charges, Rufus sowed the seeds of his sedition. Public declarations of loyalty were a prerequisite for personal and political survival, and without the public protection of the emperor, an affluent senator or equestrian was exposed and vulnerable. Some, like Pomponius Secundus, decided to act and place their fate in their own hands. His brother, Publius, continued to prosper under Claudius, implying that the emperor recognized Secundus's motivations were entirely personal and not linked to a history of family hostility.[23]

The Republic was dead and the Senate close to an institutional irrelevance. Epictetus dismisses the senator as 'a slave in fine company'. Senators were incapable of instigating policy and instead slavishly looked for an imperial lead, the Senate's *auctoritas* undermined by the senators' desire to gain or retain imperial approval. The old Republican aristocracy accepted imperial power, but some thought themselves more entitled to the throne than its occupant. Others, outside the emperor's inner circle, looked to the succession and gravitated towards potential heirs. The succession was the key issue for both the ruler and the ruled. Many conspiracies had their origins in opposition to the designated heir. The supporters of the legitimate heir contemplated continued or future favours, but those who supported a rival hoped to increase their influence and add to their network of *amici* and clients.[24]

Fate regularly upset the succession plans of Augustus. Many of the great and good flocked to attach themselves to his designated heirs, Lucius and Gaius Caesar. Other nobles allied themselves with their mother, Julia the Elder. Her husband, Tiberius, was on Rhodes. Initially a self-imposed exile, it had become one imposed by Augustus in opposition to his wife, Livia. The emperor's age also fuelled speculation should he die before his two young adopted heirs came of age. The future was fluid and uncertain, presenting opportunities for advancement or power. Julia, the daughter of the emperor, was in an extremely powerful position to manipulate events to her advantage. Her interests were not those of her father or husband, both of whom she had grown to despise. The similarities in the position of Messalina, Claudius's wife, are significant. Both looked to secure their positions through marriage after the deaths of the respective emperors, facing the challenge of retaining imperial power in a man's world. Both chose lovers and future husbands to whom they were attracted in Iullus Antonius and Gaius Silius. Brought up in an environment that suppressed emotions, it is entirely understandable that in a future that empowered them, they chose love over logic. However, both attempted to not only protect their own position, but also that of their children and designated heirs. Threats probably spurred them into action. Julia needed to end her marriage to the dour, dark Tiberius, whilst Messalina did not underestimate the Machiavellian skills of Agrippina the Younger, who championed the claims of her son, the future emperor Nero. He was a direct descendant of Augustus, unlike her son Britannicus.[25]

The succession crisis was reignited with the early deaths of Gaius and Lucius Caesar in AD 2 and 4. Many had previously made impolitic assumptions and alienated Augustus's new heir, Tiberius. Furthermore, although Augustus had adopted him, the aristocracy saw him as a Claudian, just as they later viewed Claudius as an imposter falsely laying claim to a Julian heritage. Julia the Younger became the focus of opposition to Augustus's new plans. Her husband, the noble L. Aemilius Paullus, was exiled for *maiestas*. Another aristocratic family then sought an imperial future. The Junii Silani were again involved, in the figure of Decimus Junius Silanus, whom Julia the Younger had taken as her lover in AD 8. This was a political act, as any association with a member of the imperial house had dynastic implications. Julia had already lost her two elder brothers to political machinations and her mother was exiled to the prison island of Pandateria, with her one surviving brother, Agrippa Postumus, exiled to the island of Planasia. He was an alternative heir to Augustus and there were several attempts to rescue him. The ascendancy of Tiberius resulted in his execution. If Julia had succeeded, their fates would have been reversed.[26]

Emperors were concerned by rivals – potential or real – within the imperial house itself. These men and women were removed by exile and death. Eventually, all the descendants of Augustus and Tiberius were destroyed, followed by the Flavians, who repeated the process with their relatives. As Claudius understood, if you were not on the throne controlling your destiny, you were extremely unlikely to be permitted a natural death. Imperial princesses were in the worst position, being pawns in the dynastic planning of their male relatives or executed as potential assets to rival claimants. Antonia, the daughter of Claudius, was rumoured to be considered as a potential wife of Calpurnius Piso to reinforce his claim to the throne. When she refused to marry Nero after the death of his wife, Poppaea Sabina, she was charged with sedition and executed. Possibly reflecting a widespread view, the philosopher Philo commented that the murder of Tiberius's grandson, Tiberius Gemellus, by Gaius was part of the unalterable law of nature, where the strong devour the weak. This was not seen as murder but as statecraft in removing the threat of civil war. During Gaius's illness, people had already been coalescing around his heir.[27] This threat was real. When Aemilius Lepidus felt his position as Gaius's heir was fatally undermined by the death of Drusilla, he conspired with the emperor's surviving sisters to murder his friend and emperor.

Most of the senatorial sources are equally critical of many of the conspirators as they are of the emperors themselves. They believed that emperors were corrupted by power, but the desire and ambition for absolute power was just as corrosive. Not many conspirators are portrayed in a flattering light. Some act from noble desires such as patriotism, a desire for freedom or genuine revulsion of the tyrannical acts. Yet these were few. Most are instead revealed to be unworthy, their lofty declarations stripped away to reveal self-interest, unadulterated ambition or a vivid hatred motivated by grievances. Seneca dismisses Drusus Libo, who looked to murder Tiberius in AD 16, as a young man who 'was as stupid as he was well born, with higher ambitions than anyone could have been expected to entertain in that epoch, or a man like himself in any epoch at all'. Dio describes him as a man suspected by many of revolutionary designs. Tacitus is equally dismissive of the character of Calpurnius Piso and most of his confederates. He challenges their motivation, ambition and bravery, but marvels at the bravery of those with little to gain from the death of the emperor; women such as Quintilia and Epicharis or soldiers like Cassius Chaerea and Subrius Flavus who embodied true Roman *virtus*.[28]

It seems reasonable to assume that most ordinary senators and equestrians were prepared to cooperate with these emperors so despised by the aristocracy. They owed their status, careers and future honours to them. Their attitudes and views towards those who risked the stability of the realm and threatened civil war are probably reflected by a senator of similar status and heritage, Tacitus. In his work praising his father-in-law, Agricola, he depicts him as an honourable man who was able to preserve his individual freedom and personal integrity whilst serving the state during the tyranny of Domitian. He asserts:

'Let those, whose habit is to admire disobedience, recognize that men can be great even under bad emperors, and that *obsequium* and *modestia*, if allied to industry and energy, can reach that peak of praiseworthiness, which most men attain only by following a perilous course, winning fame, without benefiting the state, by an ostentatious martyrdom.'[29]

There was no need to plot or conspire and thereby threaten the security of all. The Empire would not have survived if most of the elite followed the credo of Piso rather than Tacitus.[30]

Only a very small percentage of senatorial conspiracies grew to be a threat to the life of the emperor. They began in safe and secure discussions amongst friends in the secluded banqueting rooms of the grand townhouses of the elite. Talk was cheap and relatively risk-free when shrouded in the cloak of philosophical discussion. Criticism of the emperor was widespread, to the extent that, according to Epictetus, 'if he punished every person who ever said something bad against him, he would have no one left to rule'.[31] Criticism, however, was markedly different to planning his murder. Many plots stagnated and dissolved like that of Regulus against Gaius, which foundered beyond a nucleus of his *amici* and clients. Firstly, recruitment was difficult. If the leader of the plot was a known opponent of Caesar, many would shy away from any public involvement. Cassius's conspiracy against Julius Caesar was undermined by his own outspoken and public criticism of him, and only developed once Brutus became involved. When the poet Lucan uttered his thunder box recital on the toilet mimicking Nero's poetry, his fellow guests made a rapid exit. The first major hurdle was expanding the plot from this core.

Senators approached their *amici* whom they knew held a grievance against the emperor. Brutus approached his sick friend Ligarius, who bitterly resented his treatment at the hands of Julius Caesar. There was little risk of rejection. Dangers were further reduced by an indirect testing of their attitudes, as Brutus did by chairing a philosophical discussion or dialectic centred on the nature of tyranny. Many conspirators were Stoics or Epicureans or were well versed in their beliefs and traditions. In discussion, two guests were rejected as unsuitable due to being risk averse or lacking the necessary daring. One, Labeo, was considered a potential recruit and questioned later in a more private setting. The Pisonian conspirators are described as 'scattering allusions, therefore, amongst themselves or their *amici* to the crimes of the sovereign'. They enlisted several *equites*, all probably the clients of Piso.[32] Nevertheless, mistakes were made and proved costly. Epicharis approached the naval captain, Volusius Proculus, frustrated by the slow progress of Piso's plot. He was an ideal target, having expressed his resentment at the poor reward he had received for his role in the murder of Agrippina. However, he betrayed her, balancing the risks of success against guaranteed rewards for revealing the plot. Someone also recruited Nerva into the plot; a man with noble ancestry but an ignoble character.

The membership of conspiracies often grew without control or knowledge of the leadership. The exception is that of Domitian's freedmen, which was kept deliberately small for security and probably was formed only a matter of days before the assassination. Several of them had been charged with crimes and corruption and were awaiting an investigation by the emperor. He would not have delayed long before attending to this matter. The plot against Julius

Caesar took shape with the recruitment of Junius Brutus a few weeks before the Ides of March. Details of it, though, had become widespread knowledge. A senator, Popilius Laenas, approached Brutus as he waited for the arrival of Caesar, wishing him luck. Furthermore, a slave had gone to Caesar's house to warn him, and a Stoic philosopher, Artemidorus, who was part of Brutus's household, also tried to warn the dictator.

Senators appear to have imparted knowledge of plots to their *amici*, relying on their established relationship and honesty. Schemes also appear to have been planned within the shared areas of the aristocrats' homes, in front of their slaves and freedmen. This was not an example of naïve trust but a question of ownership and obligation to a master. Slaves were part of the furniture. The conspiracy of Caepio and Murena was betrayed by a man called Castricius, whose name suggests he was of low status. Whilst waiting in the theatre before the murder of Gaius, Bathybius, a Praetorian senator who was sat next to the ex-consul Cluvius Rufus, leaned over and asked him if he had heard any news of the revolution. Rufus, who was not actively involved in the scheme, subtly told him to shut up. Josephus asserts that many in the crowd knew this was the allotted day. The Pisonian conspirator and senator, Scaevinus, was betrayed by his freedman Milichus, who had observed his master's actions and words with baffled incredulity. Plots could only remain active for a short time before discovery.

Soldiers, however, were more circumspect, cautious through experience and guarded via discipline. The tribune Sabinus had for a while considered murdering Gaius, 'but he had not known whom it would be safe to talk to about it and had kept silent' until he was approached by Cassius Chaerea. The latter had been forced to take the risk as he had confided in the Praetorian Prefect Clemens, but his ambiguous and guarded response forced him to act before the plot was revealed.[33] There were only twelve tribunes who reported to the Praetorian Prefects. They probably knew each other well and were aware of their allegiances and grievances. Centurions were probably recruited into conspiracies by their tribunes. It is evident from the assassinations of Gaius, Nero and Domitian that most of the rank and file remained loyal to their emperor and sought revenge on the perpetrators of the crime. Their interests lay in the continuation of the imperial dynasty.

Conspiracies and plots emerged separately and in isolation. Cassius Longinus headed one of several plots against Caesar. Regulus headed one in AD 40/41, at the same time as another that was established by Annius Vinicianus and one centred on Cassius Chaerea. Additionally, Callistus and Claudius made their separate preparations to manage events after the assassination of Gaius. In AD 42, 'Camillus was already making his own plans for an uprising' when he was approached by Annius Vinicianus.[34] It is likely that these coalesced by chance when a member of one conspiracy was approached by someone involved in another.

Most plans would have foundered on the problems of opportunity and the preparations required for surviving the attempt. Julius Caesar had been careless in securing his personal safety, despite being warned that there existed several assassination plots. His successors were not so cavalier, surrounding themselves with German and Praetorian guards. Visits to the Senate were accompanied by an armed escort. Those granted an audience in the palace were searched, and Claudius ordered the rooms searched if he honoured an *amicus* with an imperial visit. Emperors also increasingly avoided appearing in public. Gaius remained in Campania for an extended period after the Plot of the Three Daggers. The opportunities to kill Nero were limited to his vulnerability whilst attempting to quell the fires that destroyed Rome or during a performance on stage. After the destruction of the Palatine, he rarely left his palace in the Servilian Gardens. Piso was pressured to murder him at his villa on the Bay of Naples, as this was one of the few occasions he was without a guard. After the plot of Vinicianus in AD 66, Nero took himself to Greece. Domitian either campaigned on Rome's distant frontiers or withdrew to his Alban villa. Their few public appearances in Rome were during the regular religious festivities that demanded the presence of the emperor. Gaius was murdered during the *Ludi Palatini*, Nero's death was planned during the Circensian Games.

A conspiracy limited to senators and their *amici* had little chance of success. Only those with direct access to the emperor possessed the real opportunity to kill him. These included members of his own family and his *amici Caesari*, who were trusted senators and equestrians and high officials in the imperial bureaucracy.[35] The latter category included the Praetorian Prefects and imperial freedmen. Only when some of these figures formed or joined a conspiracy was the emperor's life in real danger. Their presence added purpose and belief in place of delay and prevarication.

Cassius had little opportunity of approaching Caesar with his personal guards standing close. Junius Brutus had such opportunity, and his involvement brought in others who were implicitly trusted by the dictator, such as Decimus Brutus. Gaius was surrounded by members of his court who either knew of the conspiracy or actively participated in it, and it was the involvement of the Praetorian Prefects and tribunes that transformed the Pisonian conspiracy. The presence of the prefect Faenius Rufus was considered by the conspirators as 'their main strength', so 'they began to show more alacrity in debating the time and place of the assassination'.[36] Before this, Piso's refusal to even consider murdering Nero when he was visiting his villa at Baiae had deprived them of their only realistic chance of executing their plan. For this reason, they had failed to even move their schemes forward.

The civilian conspirators understood that they required military support in one form or another to influence events after the assassination. The murder of Julius Caesar precipitated a civil war, which was an almost inevitable consequence of the removal of the head of state. M. Aemilius Lepidus and Gaius's sisters allied themselves with Cornelius Gaetulicus, who commanded four legions on the Rhine. The emperor also suspected they had an understanding with his prefects. Annius Vinicianus had the tacit support of the Praetorian Prefects in AD 41 but was outmanoeuvred by Callistus and Claudius. In AD 42, Vinicianus understood that the guard was committed to Claudius so he allied with Camillus Scribonianus, who commanded forces in Dalmatia. Piso had the support of one Praetorian Prefect and many tribunes, and the imperial freedmen had also sojourned these commanders' passive acquiescence to their plans in the killing of Domitian. The murder of the emperor would achieve nothing unless the perpetrators had a substantial military force to support their claims in the chaos that would result with the successful conclusion to their treachery.

The Praetorian Prefecture was the highest position in the equestrian *cursus honorum*. It was created by Augustus to be purely responsible for his bodyguard and security. The role was transformed by Sejanus, Tiberius's sole Praetorian Prefect who realized its potential. Unrestricted access to the emperor made him his most influential advisor and the gatekeeper to the information he received. Consequently, they were selected by the emperor for their loyal service, but as equestrians it was believed they lacked the necessary status to become emperors themselves.

Praetorian soldiers were used as the instruments of state security, guarding exiles and political prisoners, torturing suspects, investigating alleged plots and carrying out executions. The Prefects also ran a spy network, where elite guardsmen called *speculatores* dressed as civilians and were used to gather information and hunt down sedition. Epictetus, a source with first-hand experience of the court of Nero, describes a familiar yet feared experience: 'A soldier in civilian dress sits down beside you and begins to criticize the emperor. Then you, encouraged to trust them by the fact that they initiated the conversation, open up on this score too. Next thing you know you are hauled off to prison in chains.'[37] All information was first reported to the tribunes and then the Praetorian Prefects, who decided whether it required imperial attention or action. Conspirators knew that the chance of discovery was vastly reduced if these officers were involved. But for the unbelievable naivety of the senatorial conspirators in AD 65, Nero would have died, with Calpurnius Piso or possibly Seneca declared emperor.

The proximity to power of the Praetorian Prefects politicized their role and that of their subordinates. The close relationship and high level of trust between an emperor and his Praetorian Prefects were crucial. When this broke down, an emperor removed his prefects, sometimes with honorary promotion to the Senate but more often despatched with a sword. Many prefects ended their careers in this way. Consequently, they were often involved in conspiracies, anticipating an emperor's fall or remaining inactive in the face of known treachery, thereby retaining a position of plausible denial if the plot should fail whilst preserving their own life should it succeed.[38]

When plots did form within the Praetorian officer corps, there were daily opportunities to murder the emperor. However, the chances of survival after it were minimal. All soldiers had sworn before the gods to place the emperor's life and that of his family above their own. Furthermore, any successor was unlikely to reward treachery, as this would encourage further threats against their own life. Consequently, Praetorian Prefects and tribunes reached out to senators with the requisite nobility and standing to ascend the throne, who would be indebted and obligated to their military collaborators. In planning the assassination of Gaius, the tribunes Chaerea and Sabinus 'turned to Minucianus (Vinicianus), who was congenial to them in excellence of character and devotion to noble ideals. Gaius, however, viewed him with suspicion because of the death of Lepidus, since Lepidus and Minucianus (Vinicianus) had been very close friends. So he too was in fear of his life.'[39] The Praetorian officers evidently knew Vinicianus from his visits to the palace and that he was under suspicion from their security role, and so would probably accept their offer. It was likely Vinicianus had already formed a plot of which they were aware, but had not informed their superior. Calpunius Piso was also selected for this reason, but he was not the choice of the Praetorian tribunes, who despised him.[40]

Nobility, unmerited prestige and an illustrious name took precedence over courage, charisma, drive and purpose in the leadership of conspiracies. This Roman obsession with status undermined most conspiracies. Both Tacitus and the soldiers who were to strike Nero down knew Piso was an unsuitable choice. Flavus knew his fellow soldiers would not support him as emperor, for 'it was immaterial if a harper was removed, and a tragic actor took his place'.[41] Piso's prevarication and abject lack of leadership eloquently support this judgement. Annius Vinicianus was a serial conspirator; charged with treason in AD 32 during the reign of Tiberius but surviving, he was involved in one, possibly two, plots against Gaius and another against Claudius. Apart from his nobility and importance as an advisor to the emperor, he had no great illustrious career, having only been a member of the Arval Brethren and a *suffect* consul. He added to the chaos in the Senate when Claudius had acted with purpose in seeking the support of the Praetorian Guard by opposing the candidacy of Valerius Asiaticus. When direction and compromise were required for the greater good, Vinicianus proved himself lacking in statesmanship.[42]

Cassius Chaerea, a man of humble origins who had risen from centurion in the Rhine legions, was a man of true nobility and leadership. Josephus describes the secret meeting of Chaerea and his fellow tribune with their superior. The pair, as social custom demanded, ensured 'the proper respects were paid; as on previous occasions, Chaerea and Sabinus deferred to Minucianus' (Vinicianus') pre-eminence, his high nobility, and general excellence of reputation'.[43] These natural leaders were often forced to take secondary roles, even when they were nobles themselves. Cassius won approval for allowing Brutus to take control of the proposals to murder Julius Caesar, even though he knew his friend was making a mistake by opposing the murder of Mark Antony, but his advice was ignored, leading to civil war, defeat and the death of both. Subrius Flavus demonstrated a greater understanding of the realities of the situation than either Piso or the Praetorian Prefect, Faenius Rufus, especially in the desperate hours after the plot's discovery. Chaerea, Sabinus and Flavus paid the ultimate price for deferring to rank.

Tacitus marvelled at the bravery of those in desperate circumstances who came from the lowest rungs of society, whilst despairing of the cowardice and ineptitude of the noble elite. *Virtus*, *dignitas* and *nobilitas* were corrupted by the senators and equestrians involved. Conspiracies were a threat to the established order and an inversion of society. However, the greatest risks appear to have been taken by those who could move freely without drawing attention. A senator visiting a friend would fill the streets with his entourage of freedmen, slaves and guards, and often be approached by his *amici* and clients with requests and petitions. Secrecy was thus difficult to attain. Consequently, messages were passed by those of low rank and never written down in case of arrest. Natalis, Piso's equestrian client, was used to liaise with Seneca and had full knowledge of the plot due to his role.

Women of low status, especially concubines, were ideal conduits to organize and recruit members. Often, they were freedwomen obliged to their patron by the gift of freedom, so were considered loyal and trustworthy. They were also intimate with their clients, able to involve them in delicate conversations with witnesses and, if captured, of such low status and dissolute reputation that any evidence provided by them could be dismissed and disowned. The imperial freedman Narcissus employed two of Claudius's concubines, who probably owed their positions to him, to introduce the allegations of Messalina's supposed treachery. If the conversation went badly, Narcissus would be able to disown them and leave them to their fate.

Claudius had prohibited Praetorians from visiting the homes of senators.[44] However, a concubine could visit officers and men of different ranks in society. Quintilia is described as an actress, freedwoman and mistress to her patron, the consular senator Pomponius, who was involved in the conspiracy against Gaius in AD 41. As she was led away, she trod on the foot of one of her fellow conspirators to reassure them that she would not break and reveal their identity. This person must have been Chaerea. Broken by torture, her beauty and youth destroyed, Quintilia said nothing and was released.[45] Her knowledge of key members of the plot is evident in her role in passing messages between the Praetorian and the senator.

The freedwoman Epicharis probably played a similar role in the Pisonian conspiracy. According to Tacitus, until then she had led a dishonourable life. She was driven, highly intelligent and not one to bow down to status when presented with stupidity. Her intimate relationships with men of much higher status gave her the freedom to speak her mind. Epicharis was a natural leader, and in the face of Piso's obstinacy in failing to agree to attack Nero whilst at his villa, she 'began to animate and upbraid the conspirators'. Dio stresses her importance to the conspirators, for 'she had been included in the conspiracy and all its details had been entrusted to her without reserve'. She was the glue that linked the disparate elements of the plot together, moving unnoticed between its constituent members, carrying in her mind the messages, hopes and opinions of all. She saw the full picture and knew time was not on their side. Frustrated, she seized the initiative by travelling to Campania to suborn a captain in the navy based at Misenum. Betrayed, she was articulate and confident 'when confronted with the informer, and in the absence of corroborating evidence silenced him with ease'.[46] Her arrest had caused panic, and Piso and his advisors were finally forced to act rather than debate. After enduring unimaginable horrors in the palace dungeon, she gave her own life to protect men who had already betrayed their cause. They failed her.

Whilst Seneca sought a good death to reflect the glory of his life, these two women proved themselves the true Stoics. They, not Seneca, lived a life in virtue, having fulfilled their duties to the full.

Conspiracies revealed the very worst and very best of the human condition. Their story is a history of relationships, of hopes, fears, love, greed and unrestrained ambition. There were few heroes and heroines, but all were casualties in one form or another. Contemporaries recognized that they were a perversion of the established order. The conspirators were lauded as tyrannicides fighting for liberty, but also seen as assassins, murderers of a ruler they had sworn an oath to protect. Their success threatened civil war and their failure unleashed a storm of terror, with senatorial informers and *delators* allowed the freedom to sow terror as they sought out the guilty or innocent to win imperial approval or destroy the careers of their rivals. Even those senators who conspired against their emperor were themselves revolutionaries by threatening the Roman order. Furthermore, the prominence of women in the planning and organization of these plots was perceived as an inversion of established society. Romans were conflicted by the contradictory nature of treachery.[47]

Sedition was a major driver of change in Roman social and political structure. Fear was transformative. The threat of sudden death was all-consuming. Few emperors proved to be equal to the demands and solitude of imperial power. Into that illustrious category possibly fall Augustus, Vespasian and Trajan in the first century AD. All, though, were primarily concerned with their survival. The psychological impact is evident in all. Augustus, Gaius, Claudius and Domitian were quick to anger upon the discovery of treason. Augustus celebrated the deaths of Caepio and Murena with sacrifices and festivities as if he had won a great military victory over a foreign foe. This was not only a defensive reaction, but a response to betrayal. Emperors believed that their generosity, the bestowal of offices, wealth, estates and priesthoods, should obligate the recipient to demonstrate loyalty to their ruler. Instead, benevolence was returned with deceit. This undermined the rules of *amicitiae*, the social bonds that formed the basis of Roman society being undermined by self-interest.[48]

The imperial response from Tiberius, Gaius, Claudius, Nero and Domitian was to sow division and conflict amongst the elite.[49] The law of *maiestas* was revived, accusations encouraged by rewarding successful convictions and the evidence provided by slaves against their masters accepted. Furthermore, these emperors channelled *beneficia* through freedmen of low status such as Narcissus, Callistus or Parthenius, humiliating the nobility by the petitioning of these men and having to offer them *gratia* in return. Spies were used to gather information and the Praetorians to engender terror. Mutual fear and suspicions led to hatred; anticipating the fatal blow, either the emperor or conspirator chose to strike first. If politics is war by other means, Rome was consumed in a civil war during much of the first century AD.

Notes

Chapter 1

1. Plutarch, *Life of Caesar* (Penguin Classics, 1982), 56.
2. Goldsworthy, Adrian, *Caesar, The Life of a Colossus* (Weidenfeld & Nicolson, 2006), p.485.
3. Suetonius, *The Twelve Caesars, Julius Caesar* (Penguin Classics, 1986) 78.
4. Cicero, *Letters to Atticus* (Penguin Classics) 14.21.3; Epstein, David F., 'Caesar's Personal Enemies on the Ides of March', *Latomus*, t. 46, Fasc. 3 (Juillet–Septembre 1987), pp.566–70.
5. Goldsworthy, Adrian, *Caesar, The Life of a Colossus*, p.466.
6. Plutarch, *Life of Caesar*, 56.
7. Balsdon, J.P.V.D., 'The Ides of March', *Historia: Zeitschrift für Alte Geschichte*, Bd. 7, H. 1 (Jan 1958), p.88; Lintott, Andrew, 'The Assassination', ch. 6 in *A Companion to Julius Caesar* (Blackwell Publishing, 2009), ed. Miriam Griffin, p.74.
8. Cicero, *Letters to Friends* (Loeb Classical Library, 2001, trans. D.R. Shackleton Bailey), 6.6.10; Cassius Dio (Loeb Classical Library, 1989, trans. E. Cary), 42.6.
9. Cicero, *Philippics* (Loeb Classical Library, 2001, trans. D.R. Shackleton Bailey), 2.26; Balsdon, J.P.V.D., 'The Ides of March', *Historia: Zeitschrift für Alte Geschichte*, Bd. 7, H. 1 (Jan 1958), p.82.
10. Appian, *Civil Wars*, 4.67.
11. Cicero, *Letters to Friends*, 15.16, 18; Clarke, M.L., *The Noblest Roman: Marcus Brutus and His Reputation* (Thames and Hudson, 1981), p.34.
12. Cicero, *Letters to Friends*, 15.19.4.
13. Suetonius, *Julius Caesar*, 77; Holland, Tom, *Rubicon, The Triumph, and Tragedy of the Roman Republic* (Abacus, 2003), p.344.
14. Suetonius, *Julius Caesar*, 76; Cassius Dio, 42.3, 44.1–3; Goldsworthy, Adrian, *Caesar, The Life of a Colossus*, p.486.
15. Plutarch, *Life of Caesar*, 57; Suetonius, *Julius Caesar*, 80.
16. Nicolaus of Damascus, *Life of Augustus* (Attalus), 19.63; Saller, R.P., *Personal Patronage under the Early Empire* (Cambridge University Press, 2010), pp.10–12.
17. Plutarch, *Life of Caesar*, 57.
18. Pliny, *Letters* (Loeb Classical Library, 1989, vol. 1, trans. Betty Radice), 4.15, 5.14; Seneca, *De Providentia* (Loeb Classical Library, 1989, Moral Essays, vol. 1, trans. John W. Basore), 1.5, 16; Saller, R.P., *Personal Patronage under the Early Empire*, p.12; Epstein, David F., 'Caesar's Personal Enemies on the Ides of March', *Latomus*, t. 46, Fasc. 3 (Juillet–Septembre 1987), pp.566–70.
19. Plutarch, *Life of Caesar*, 57; Appian, *Civil War*, 2.137–141.
20. Scott, Anna Elizabeth, *The Influence of the Roman Atrium-House's Architecture and Use of Space in Engendering the Power and Independence of the Materfamilias* (Brigham Young University, 2012), pp.33–34; MacMullen, Ramsey, *Enemies of the Roman Order: Treason, Unrest, and Alienation in the Empire*, p.20.
21. Cicero, *Philippics*, 2.26.

22. Clarke, M.L., *The Noblest Roman Marcus Brutus and His Reputation*, pp.34–35.
23. Plutarch, *Life of Brutus*, 1.1, 8.5; Epstein, David F., 'Caesar's Personal Enemies on the Ides of March,' *Latomus*, t. 46, Fasc. 3 (Juillet–Septembre 1987), pp.566–70.
24. Clarke, M.L., *The Noblest Roman: Marcus Brutus and His Reputation*, pp. 9, 20; MacMullen, Ramsey, *Enemies of the Roman Order: Treason, Unrest, and Alienation in the Empire* (Routledge, 1992), pp.2–3.
25. Cicero, *Letters to Atticus*, 14.1.2.
26. Clarke, M.L., *The Noblest Roman: Marcus Brutus and His Reputation*, p.22.
27. Clarke, M.L., *The Noblest Roman: Marcus Brutus and His Reputation*, p.29.
28. Plutarch, *Life of Brutus*, 5; MacMullen, Ramsey, *Enemies of the Roman Order: Treason, Unrest, and Alienation in the Empire*, pp.4–5.
29. Cicero, *Letters to Atticus*, 13.9; Clarke, M.L., *The Noblest Roman: Marcus Brutus and His Reputation*, p.29.
30. Balsdon, J.P.V.D., 'The Ides of March', *Historia: Zeitschrift für Alte Geschichte*, Bd. 7, H. 1 (Jan 1958), p.92.
31. Plutarch, *Life of Brutus*, 1.1.
32. Cicero, *Letters to Friends*, 3.11.3.
33. Plutarch, *Life of Brutus*, 7; Appian, *Civil Wars*, 2.16.112; Velleius Paterculus, *The Roman History*, 2.56.3; Balsdon, J.P.V.D., 'The Ides of March', *Historia: Zeitschrift für Alte Geschichte*, Bd. 7, H. 1 (Jan 1958), p.93.
34. Appian, *Civil Wars*, 2.16.111; Clarke, M.L., *The Noblest Roman: Marcus Brutus and His Reputation*, p.20.
35. Nicolaus of Damascus, *Life of Augustus* (Attalus), 63; Cassius Dio, 43.47.5.
36. Seneca, *Letters from a Stoic* (Penguin Classics, 2004), LXXXIII; Cicero, *Philippics*, 2.11; Suetonius, *Julius Caesar*, 82.
37. Suetonius, *Galba*, 3.2; Valerius Maximus (Loeb Classical Library, 2000), 6; Epstein, David F., 'Caesar's Personal Enemies on the Ides of March', *Latomus*, t. 46, Fasc. 3 (Juillet–Septembre 1987), pp.566–70; Goldsworthy, Adrian, *Caesar, the Life of a Colossus*, p.502.
38. Appian, *Civil Wars*, 2.1.15; Plutarch, *Brutus*, 15.2–3; *Antony*, 13.2; Cicero, *Philippics*, 2.27, 34; Epstein, David F., 'Caesar's Personal Enemies on the Ides of March', *Latomus*, t. 46, Fasc. 3 (Juillet–Septembre), pp.566–70; Goldsworthy, Adrian, *Caesar, the Life of a Colossus*, p.503; Fuller, Major-General J.F., *Julius Caesar: Man, Soldier, and Tyrant* (Eyre and Spottiswoode, 1965), p.303.
39. Cicero, *Letters to Friends*, 7.30.1–2.
40. Cassius Dio 43.46; Suetonius, *Julius Caesar*, 76.
41. Suetonius, *Julius Caesar*, 75, 80; Nicolaus of Damascus, *Life of Augustus*, 19.59; Balsdon, J.P.V.D., 'The Ides of March', *Historia: Zeitschrift für Alte Geschichte*, Bd. 7, H. 1 (Jan 1958), pp.80–94.
42. Canfora, Luciano, 'The Hetairia of Cassius and the Recruitment of Brutus', in *Julius Caesar: The People's Dictator* (Edinburgh University Press, 2007), p.306.
43. Plutarch, *Brutus*, 7.1.
44. Appian, *Civil Wars*, 2.121.508; 122.511; 123.515; 142.593; Canfora, Luciano, *Julius Caesar: The People's Dictator* (Edinburgh University Press, 2007), p.307.
45. Cicero, *Letters to Atticus*, xiii.52 (Penguin Classics, 353, p.558).
46. Suetonius, *Julius Caesar*, 86.
47. Suetonius, *Julius Caesar*, 76; Cassius Dio 44.9.1; Clarke, M.L., *The Noblest Roman: Marcus Brutus and His Reputation*, p.40; Crettez, Bertrand, and Deloche, Régis, 'An

analytic narrative of Caesar's death: Suicide or not? That is the question', *Rationality and Society* 30:3 (2018), pp.332–49.

48. Suetonius, *Caesar,* 61, 79; Appian, *Civil Wars,* 2.107–108; Nicolaus of Damascus, *Life of Augustus,* 20.67–69; Crettez, Bertrand, and Deloche, Régis, 'An analytic narrative of Caesar's death: Suicide or not? That is the question', *Rationality and Society* 30:3 (2018), pp.332–49.

49. Nicolaus of Damascus, Frag. 130.20.69; Livy, *Epit.* Ii. 6; Velleius Paterculus 2.68.4; Plutarch, *Brutus,* 61.8; Cassius Dio 44.10.1–3; Appian, *Civil Wars,* 2.108; Suetonius, *Julius Caesar,* 60.

50. Appian, *Civil Wars,* 2.109; Suetonius, *Julius Caesar,* 80.

51. Suetonius, *Caesar,* 79; Nicolaus of Damascus, Frag. 130.20.68.

52. Laurence, Ray, 'Rumour and Communication in Roman Politics', *Greece & Rome,* Vol. xli, No. 1 (April 1994), pp. 65, 71.

53. Nicolaus of Damascus, Frag. 130.20.72–73; Appian, *Civil Wars,* 2.109. For Caesar staging the event, see Goldsworthy, Adrian, *Caesar, the Life of a Colossus,* p.504. The gilded chair and kingly regalia worn by Julius Caesar were voted to him by the Senate and he was therefore duty bound to use them; see Valerius Maximus 1.6.13 and Paterson, Jeremy, *The Court and Court Society in Ancient Monarchies* (Cambridge University Press, 2009) p.132.

54. Nicolaus of Damascus, Frag 130.20.75; Appian, *Civil Wars,* 2.110; Cassius Dio 44.11.3; Cicero, *Philippics,* 13.41; Paterson, Jeremy, *The Court and Court Society in Ancient Monarchies,* p.132, for the perceptions of the crowd.

55. Suetonius, *Julius Caesar,* 79.

56. Appian, *Civil Wars,* 2.110; Cicero, *On Divination,* 2.110; Suetonius, *Julius Caesar,* 79.2–80.1; Cassius Dio 44.15.4.

57. Nicolaus of Damascus, Frag. 130.20.79; Cassius Dio 44.8.3–3; Crettez, Bertrand, and Deloche, Régis, 'An analytic narrative of Caesar's death: Suicide or not? That is the question', *Rationality and Society* 30:3 (2018), pp.332–49.

58. Suetonius, *Julius Caesar,* 80; Plutarch, *Brutus,* 10; Appian, *Civil Wars,* 2.111–112; Dio 44.12–14, though, has Brutus taking the lead, but this is dismissed by Clarke, M.L., *The Noblest Roman: Marcus Brutus and His Reputation,* p.37; Canfora, Luciano, *Julius Caesar: The People's Dictator,* p.308.

59. Sedley, David, 'The Ethics of Brutus and Cassius', *The Journal of Roman Studies,* Vol. 87 (1997), pp.41–53.

60. Aristotle, *Politics* (Penguin Classics, 1981, trans. T. Sinclair), 3.5, 4.2; Plato, *Politicus,* 300e–303b; Plato, *Republic* (Penguin Classics, 2007, trans. H.D.P. Lee), 8.564a; Sedley, David, 'The Ethics of Brutus and Cassius', *The Journal of Roman Studies,* Vol. 87 (1997), pp.41–53; Richardson, J.S., *Augustan Rome 44 BC to AD 14: The Restoration of the Republic and the Establishment of the Empire* (Edinburgh University Press, 2012), p.45. For Brutus's loan to the Cretan community, see Goldsworthy, Adrian, *Caesar, the Life of a Colossus,* p.504.

61. Sedley, David, 'The Ethics of Brutus and Cassius', *The Journal of Roman Studies,* Vol. 87 (1997), pp.41–53; MacMullen, Ramsey, *Enemies of the Roman Order: Treason, Unrest, and Alienation in the Empire,* pp.1–2.

62. Cicero, *Philippics,* 2.26; Cicero, *Letters to Atticus,* 13.40.1; Cornelius Nepos, *Life of Atticus,* 18.3 (Attalus, trans. Rev. J.S. Watson); Balsdon, J.P.V.D., 'The Ides of March', *Historia: Zeitschrift für Alte Geschichte,* Bd. 7, H. 1 (Jan 1958), pp.80–94; Clarke, M.L., *The Noblest Roman: Marcus Brutus and His Reputation,* p.10; Crawford, M.H., *Roman Republican Coinage* (Cambridge, 1974), no. 433 1 and 2, p.455.

63. Appian, *Civil Wars*, 2.112.
64. Suetonius, *Julius Caesar*, 80; Cassius Dio 44.12.1–3; Balsdon, J.P.V.D., 'The Ides of March', *Historia: Zeitschrift für Alte Geschichte*, Bd. 7, H. 1 (Jan 1958), p.91.
65. Plutarch, *Life of Brutus*, 7; Canfora, Luciano, *Julius Caesar: The People's Dictator*, p.312.
66. Cicero, *Letters to Friends*, 6.13.1, 6.13.3; Caesar, *De Bello Africo*, 89.2; Plutarch, *Life of Cicero*, 39.6; Plutarch, *Life of Brutus*, 7; Epstein, David F., 'Caesar's Personal Enemies on the Ides of March', *Latomus*, t. 46, Fasc. 3 (Juillet–Septembre 1987), pp.566–70.
67. Plutarch, *Life of Brutus*, 8.
68. Appian, *Civil Wars*, 4.17.135.
69. Plutarch, *The Life of Cato the Younger*, 65, 66, 73; Canfora, Luciano, *Julius Caesar: The People's Dictator*, p.296.
70. Plutarch, *Life of Brutus*, 12.3, 34.4.
71. Canfora, Luciano, *Julius Caesar: The People's Dictator*, p.314; Plutarch, *Life of Brutus*, 8; Sedley, David, 'The Ethics of Brutus and Cassius', *The Journal of Roman Studies*, Vol. 87 (1997), pp.41–53.
72. Cassius Dio 44.14.3–4; Epstein, David F., 'Caesar's Personal Enemies on the Ides of March', *Latomus*, t. 46, Fasc. 3 (Juillet–Septembre 1987), pp.566–70.
73. Plutarch, *Life of Brutus*, 12.4–6; 5.1.2.
74. Cassius Dio 44.16.1; Lintott, Andrew, 'The Assassination', ch. 6 in *A Companion to Julius Caesar*, p.79.
75. Cassius Dio 44.15.1.
76. Plutarch, *Life of Caesar*, 62; *Life of Brutus*, 18.
77. Plutarch, *Life of Caesar*, 62; *Life of Antony*, 12.
78. Suetonius, *Julius Caesar*, 80; Nicolaus of Damascus, 19.59; Eutropius, *Breviarium* (Liverpool University Press, 1993), 6.25, and Orosius 6.17.2 put the number at more than sixty. Appian, *Civil Wars*, 2.111–113, names fifteen. Lintott, Andrew, *The Assassination*, ch. 6 in *A Companion to Julius Caesar*, p.77, suggests the higher numbers reflected those prosecuted later under the Pedian law for conspiring against Caesar, and the lower number those actively involved. Goldsworthy, Adrian, *Caesar, the Life of a Colossus*, p.502, for percentage of senators involved in the conspiracy.
79. Plutarch, *Life of Anthony*, 13; *Life of Brutus*, 18; Clarke, M.L. *The Noblest Roman: Marcus Brutus and His Reputation*, p.39; Cicero, *Letters to Atticus*, 15.11 (7 June 44 BC); Lintott, Andrew, *The Assassination*, ch. 6 in *A Companion to Julius Caesar*, p.80; Fuller, Major-General J.F., *Julius Caesar: Man, Soldier, and Tyrant*, p.303.
80. Suetonius, *Julius Caesar*, 80; Nicolaus of Damascus, Frag. 130.23.81; Velleius Paterculus 2.58; Clarke, M.L., *The Noblest Roman: Marcus Brutus and His Reputation*, p.39; Lintott, Andrew, *The Assassination*, ch. 6 in *A Companion to Julius Caesar*, p.77; Horsfall, Nicolaus, 'The Ides of March: Some New Problems', *Greece & Rome*, Vol. 21, No. 2 (Oct 1974), pp.191–99.
81. Suetonius, *Julius Caesar*, 80; Nicolaus of Damascus, Frag. 130.23.81.
82. Plutarch, *Life of Brutus*, 14; Appian, *Civil Wars*, 2.115 Nicolaus of Damascus, Frag. 130.23.81; Richardson, J.S., *Augustan Rome 44 BC to AD 14: The Restoration of the Republic and the Establishment of the Empire*, p.11; Horsfall, Nicolaus, 'The Ides of March: Some New Problems', *Greece & Rome*, Vol. 21, No. 2 (Oct 1974), pp.191–99.
83. Suetonius, *Julius Caesar*, 81.
84. Plutarch, *Life of Brutus*, 8.
85. Plutarch, *Life of Brutus*, 13.
86. Plutarch, *Life of Caesar*, 63; Suetonius, *Julius Caesar*, 87; Appian, *Civil Wars*, 2.115; Canfora, Luciano, *Julius Caesar: The People's Dictator*, pp.326–27.

87. Suetonius, *Julius Caesar*, 81; Plutarch, *Life of Caesar*, 63–65; Cassius Dio 44.17.1–2; Appian, *Civil Wars*, 2.115–116; Velleius Paterculus 2.57.2–3.

88. Valerius Maximus 18.11.2; Ramsey, John, *At What Hour Did the Murderers Of Julius Caesar Gather On The Ides Of March 44 B.C.?* (www.academia.edu/11118065/), pp.352–63; Plutarch, *Caesar*, 63, says Caesar's comment to Spurinna took place whilst he was on the way to the Senate meeting; however, he was being carried in a litter, which may have been enclosed with curtains. On Spurinna meeting Caesar at the house of Calvinus, see Crettez, Bertrand, and Deloche, Régis, 'An analytic narrative of Caesar's death: Suicide or not? That is the question', *Rationality and Society* 30:3 (2018), pp.332–349.

89. Plutarch, *Life of Brutus*, 10; Cassius Dio 44.16.1; Ramsey, John, *At What Hour Did the Murderers Of Julius Caesar Gather On The Ides Of March 44 B.C.?*, pp.352–63.

90. Nicolaus of Damascus, Frag. 130.26a.98; Cassius Dio 44.16.2; Cicero, *Philippics*, 2.34; *Letters to Friends*, 10.28.1; Horsfall, Nicolaus, 'The Ides of March: Some New Problems', *Greece & Rome*, Vol. 21, No. 2 (Oct 1974), pp.191–99.

91. Appian, *Civil Wars*, 2.115; Plutarch, *Life of Brutus*, 14.

92. Plutarch, *Life of Brutus*, 15.

93. Appian, *Civil Wars*, 2.11; Plutarch, *Life of Brutus*, 15.

94. Plutarch, *Life of Brutus*, 15.

95. Appian, *Civil Wars*, 2.115; Cassius Dio 44.17.3–18.1; Suetonius, *Julius Caesar*, 81.4.

96. Cassius Dio 44.19.3; Suetonius, *Julius Caesar*, 81.4; Nicolaus of Damascus, Frag. 130. 23.82; Crettez, Bertrand, and Deloche, Régis, 'An analytic narrative of Caesar's death: Suicide or not? That is the question', *Rationality and Society* 30:3 (2018), pp.332–49.

97. Nicolaus of Damascus, Frag.130.23.84; Plutarch, *Caesar*, 64; Suetonius, *Julius Caesar*, 81.

98. Plutarch, *Life of Caesar*, 64. Appian, *Civil Wars*, 2.118, 2.116 describes the informant as one of Caesar's 'intimates'.

99. Plutarch, *Life of Brutus*, 16.

100. Plutarch, *Life of Brutus*, 16.

101. Plutarch, *Life of Caesar*, 65, who also records another account that Artemidorus was unable to get near Caesar because of the crowd and it was another person who handed over the written note to Caesar. Casius Dio 44.18.1 mentions an unnamed informant who gave him a note that accurately recorded the details of the plot, but Caesar did not realize the importance of its content.

102. Nicolaus of Damascus, Frag. 130.24.85; Appian, *Civil Wars*, 2.116.

103. Cassius Dio 44.19.1, Appian, *Civil Wars*, 2.116, and Plutarch, *Life of Brutus*, 17, who only mention Trebonius. His presence is confirmed by Cicero, *Philippics*, 2.34. However, Plutarch, *Life of Caesar*, 66 refers to Decimus Brutus. Also, Nicolaus of Damascus, Frag. 130.24.85.

104. Plutarch, *Life of Caesar*, 66; *Life of Brutus*, 17.

105. Suetonius, *Julius Caesar*, 82; Plutarch, *Life of Brutus*, 16; Appian, *Civil Wars*, 2.117.

106. Suetonius, *Julius Caesar*, 82 records a rumour that the second blow, which was supposedly the fatal one, was delivered by Marcus Brutus, to which Caesar said, 'You too, my child.' Caesar did have a liaison with Brutus's mother, but he was only 15 years old when Brutus was born, so it was clearly not true. Plutarch, *Life of Caesar*, 66; Appian, *Civil Wars*, 2.117. According to Nicolaus of Damascus, Frag. 130.24.90, Caesar's body was covered in thirty-five wounds.

107. Plutarch, *Life of Caesar*, 66; *Life of Brutus*, 18; Suetonius, *Julius Caesar*, 82; Syme, Ronald, *The Roman Revolution* (Oxford University Press, 1979), p.100.

108. Cassius Dio 44.22.1–3; Appian, *Civil Wars*, 2.118–119; Nicolaus of Damascus, Frag, 130.26.95; Plutarch, *Life of Caesar*, 67; *Life of Brutus*, 18.

109. Suetonius, *Julius Caesar*, 82.

110. Nicolaus of Damascus, Frag. 130.26.95.

111. Plutarch, *Life of Brutus*, 18; *Life of Caesar*, 67; Cassius Dio 44.22.2; Appian, *Civil Wars*, 2.120–123, 137–141; Nicolaus of Damascus, Frag. 130.26a.98; Richardson, J. S., *Augustan Rome 44 BC to AD 14: The Restoration of the Republic and the Establishment of the Empire*, p.16.

112. Appian, *Civil Wars*, 2.124–126; Cassius Dio 44.34.1–7; Plutarch, *Life of Brutus*, 20; *Life of Mark Antony*, 15; Cicero, *Letters to Atticus*, 14.10.

113. Cicero, *Letters to Friends*, 11.1.2–3; Clarke, M.L., *The Noblest Roman: Marcus Brutus and His Reputation*, p.41; Goldsworthy, Adrian, *Caesar, the Life of a Colossus*, p.510, suggests the funeral was on 18 March.

114. Cassius Dio 44.35; Suetonius, *Julius Caesar*, 83–84.

115. Cicero, *Letters to Atticus*, 14.21.3.

116. Cicero, *Letters to Atticus*, 15.11 (7 June 44 BC).

117. Plutarch, *Life of Brutus*, 44; Richardson, J.S., *Augustan Rome 44 BC to AD 14: The Restoration of the Republic and the Establishment of the Empire*, p.44.

Chapter 2

1. Syme, R., *The Roman Revolution*, p.333, identifies this Murena as the conspirator.

2. Velleius Paterculus, *The Roman History*, 2.91.2.

3. Dio 54.3.4.

4. Horace, *Satires*, 1.5.38; *Odes*, 3.19.11; Syme, R., *The Roman Revolution*, p.334; Sumi, Geoffrey, 'Ceremony and the Emergence of Court Society in the Augustan Principate', *The American Journal of Philology*, Vol. 132, No. 1, Classical Courts and Courtiers (Spring 2011), pp.81–102.

5. CIL 1.2 1.28; Swan, Michael, 'The Consular Fasti of 23 B.C. and the Conspiracy of Varro Murena', *Harvard Studies in Classical Philology*, Vol. 71 (1967), pp.235–47; McDermott, William C., 'Varro Murena', *Transactions and Proceedings of the American Philological Association*, Vol. 72 (1941), pp.255–65. Whilst Stockton, David, 'Primus and Murena', *Historia: Zeitschrift für Alte Geschichte*, Bd. 14, H. 1 (Jan 1965), pp.18–40, and Daley, Lawrence J., 'Augustus and the Murder of Varro Murena ("cos." 23 B.C.)', *Klio* (1 Jan 1984), pp.157–69, believe the nominated consul and conspirator were the same person, Swan, McDermott, and Arkenberg, Jerome S., 'Licinii Murenae Terentii Varrones, and Varrones Murenae: II. The Enigma of Varro Murena', *Historia: Zeitschrift für Alte Geschichte*, Bd. 42, H. 4 (4th Qtr 1993), pp.471–91, convincingly argue they were brothers and formed the basis of the modern consensus. See Richardson, J.S., *Augustan Rome 44 BC to AD 14: The Restoration of the Republic and the Establishment of the Empire* (Edinburgh University Press, 2012), p.104.

6. Velleius Paterculus, *The Roman History*, 2.91.2; Horace, *Odes*, 2.10.1 and 9; Dio 54.3.4; Tacitus, *Annals*, 1.10.3; Suetonius, *Augustus*, 19 and 66.3.

7. Dio 54.3.5; McHugh, John, *Sejanus, Regent of Rome* (Pen & Sword, 2020), pp.2–3; McDermott, William C., 'Varro Murena', *Transactions and Proceedings of the American Philological Association*, Vol. 72 (1941), pp.255–65.

8. Goldsworthy, Adrian, *Augustus: From Revolutionary to Emperor* (Weidenfeld & Nicolson, 2014), pp.278–79; McDermott, William C., 'Varro Murena', *Transactions and Proceedings of the American Philological Association*, Vol. 72 (1941), pp.255–65, citing Dessau (PIR 2.55, number 86); Stockton, David, 'Primus and Murena', *Historia: Zeitschrift für Alte Geschichte*, Bd. 14, H. 1 (Jan, 1965), pp.18–40. However, Arkenberg, Jerome S., 'Licinii

Murenae Terentii Varrones, and Varrones Murenae: II. The Enigma of Varro Murena',
Historia: Zeitschrift für Alte Geschichte, Bd. 42, H. 4 (4th Qtr 1993), pp.471–91, argues that
he was originally a Terentius. Syme, R., *The Roman Revolution*, pp.325–26 n.5, hazards
his full name based on the historical variances as A. Terentius Varro Licinius Murena.

9. CIL 122.1.772; 14.2109; ILS 897; Horace, *Satires*, 1.5.58. For aedileship, see CIL
1.2 2.2.2514, 6.1324; ILS 6075, but may refer to his father. Also, Daley, Lawrence J.,
'Augustus and the Murder of Varro Murena ("cos." 23 B.C.), *Klio* (1 Jan 1984), pp.157–69.

10. Syme, R., *The Roman Revolution*, p.335.

11. Richardson, J.S., *Augustan Rome 44 BC to AD 14: The Restoration of the Republic and the
Establishment of the Empire*, pp.97, 99, 102; Syme, R., *The Roman Revolution*, p.335;
Goldsworthy, Adrian, *Augustus, From Revolutionary to Emperor*, p.276; Crook, J.A.,
Political History, 30 BC to AD 14, in The Cambridge Ancient History (eds A.K. Bowman,
E. Champlin and A. Lintott, 1996), p.84; Stevenson, Tom, 'The Succession Planning
of Augustus', *Antichthon*, Vol. 47: Thematic Issue: Culture, Identity and Politics in the
Ancient Mediterranean World (2013), pp.118–39; Sawiński, Paweł, 'The Succession
of Imperial Power under the Julio-Claudian Dynasty (30 BC–AD 68), Internationaler
Verlag der Wissenschaften (Berlin, 2018), pp.25–27.

12. Richardson, J.S., *Augustan Rome 44 BC to AD 14: The Restoration of the Republic and the
Establishment of the Empire*, p.97; Syme, R., *The Augustan Aristocracy* (Oxford, 1986),
p.383; Fantham, Elaine, *Julia Augusti, The Emperor's Daughter*, p.56; Phillips, Darryl
A., 'The Conspiracy of Egnatius Rufus and the Election of Suffect Consuls under
Augustus', *Historia: Zeitschrift für Alte Geschichte*, Bd. 46, H. 1 (1st Qtr 1997), pp.103–12.

13. Tacitus, *Annals*, 3.56.2; Crook, J.A., *Political History, 30 BC to AD 14*, in The Cambridge
Ancient History (eds A.K. Bowman, E. Champlin and A. Lintott, 1996), p.85; Paterson,
Jeremy, 'Friends in High Places: The Creation of the Court of the Roman Emperor',
in *The Court and Court Society in Ancient Monarchies* (Cambridge University Press,
2009), p.140.

14. *Res Gestae*, 5.2, 15.1; Dio 53.33.5; Suetonius, *Augustus*, 41.2; Richardson, J.S., *Augustan
Rome 44 BC to AD 14: The Restoration of the Republic and the Establishment of the Empire*,
p.103; Crook, J.A., *Political History, 30 BC to AD 14*, in The Cambridge Ancient History,
p.87; Rowland Jr., Robert J., 'The Conspiracy of Varro Murena', *The Classical Journal*,
Vol. 62, No. 8 (May 1967), pp.362–63; Swan, Michael, 'The Consular Fasti of 23 B.C.
and the Conspiracy of Varro Murena', *Harvard Studies in Classical Philology*, Vol. 71
(1967), pp.235–47.

15. Levick, Barbara, *Tiberius, the Politician* (Routledge, 1986), p.21; Atkinson, Kathleen
M.T., 'Constitutional and Legal Aspects of the Trials of Marcus Primus and Varro
Murena', *Historia: Zeitschrift für Alte Geschichte*, Bd. 9, H. 4 (Oct 1960), pp.440–73.

16. Levick, Barbara, 'Primus, Murena, and "Fides": Notes on Cassius Dio Liv. 3', *Greece
& Rome*, Vol. 22, No. 2 (Oct 1975), pp.156–63; Sumi, Geoffrey, 'Ceremony and the
Emergence of Court Society in the Augustan Principate', The American Journal of
Philology, Vol. 132, No. 1, Classical Courts and Courtiers (Spring 2011), pp.81–102.

17. Syme, R., *The Augustan Aristocracy*, pp.274–75; Levick, Barbara, 'Primus, Murena,
and "Fides": Notes on Cassius Dio Liv. 3', *Greece & Rome*, Vol. 22, No. 2 (Oct 1975),
pp.156–63; Flower, Harriet I., *The Art of Forgetting: Disgrace and Oblivion in Roman
Political Culture* (University of North Carolina Press, 2006), p.124.

18. Dio 54.3.2.

19. Sumi, Geoffrey, 'Ceremony and the Emergence of Court Society in the Augustan
Principate', *The American Journal of Philology*, Vol. 132, No. 1, Classical Courts and

Courtiers (Spring 2011), pp.81–102; Levick, Barbara, 'Primus, Murena, and "Fides": Notes on Cassius Dio Liv. 3, *Greece & Rome*, Vol. 22, No. 2 (Oct 1975), pp.156–63.

20. Dio 54.3.3.

21. Levick, Barbara, 'Primus, Murena, and "Fides": Notes on Cassius Dio Liv. 3', *Greece & Rome*, Vol. 22, No. 2 (Oct 1975), pp.156–63; Dio 54.3.3; De La Bédoyère, Guy, *Praetorian: The Rise and Fall of Rome's Imperial Bodyguard* (Yale University Press, 2017), pp.46–47; Daley, Lawrence J., 'Augustus and the Murder of Varro Murena ("cos." 23 B.C.)', *Klio* (1 Jan 1984), pp.157–69; Stockton, David, 'Primus and Murena', *Historia: Zeitschrift für Alte Geschichte*, Bd. 14, H. 1 (Jan 1965), pp.18–40.

22. Dio 54.3.4; Atkinson, Kathleen M.T., 'Constitutional and Legal Aspects of the Trials of Marcus Primus and Varro Murena', *Historia: Zeitschrift für Alte Geschichte*, Bd. 9, H. 4 (Oct 1960), pp.440–73; Wiedemann, T.E.J., 'Tiberius to Nero', *Cambridge Ancient History*, p.198.

23. Velleius Paterculus, *The Roman History*, 2.93.1; Millar, Fergus, *A Study of Cassius Dio* (Oxford, 1999), pp.88–98; Seneca, *De Brevitate Vitae*, 4.5; *De Clementia*, 1.9.6.

24. Dio 54.3.4, 54.3.7.

25. Levick, Barbara, 'Primus, Murena, and "Fides": Notes on Cassius Dio Liv. 3', *Greece & Rome*, Vol. 22, No. 2 (Oct 1975), p.163, n.12.

26. Velleius Paterculus, *The Roman History*, 2.91.2.

27. Lacey, W., 'Augustus and the Senate: 23 B.C.', *Antichthon* 19 (1985), pp.57–67; Holland, Richard, *Augustus: Godfather of Europe* (Sutton Publishing, 2004), p.249; Goldsworthy, Adrian, *Augustus, From Revolutionary to Emperor*, p.282.

28. Tacitus, *Annals*, 1.10; Velleius Paterculus, *The Roman History*, 2.91.2; Macrobius, *Saturnalia*, trans.Robert A. Kaster(Loeb, 2010), 1.11.21.

29. Suetonius, *Augustus*, 56.

30. ILS 2676; Levick, Barbara, 'Primus, Murena, and "Fides": Notes on Cassius Dio Liv. 3', *Greece & Rome*, Vol. 22, No. 2 (Oct 1975), pp.156–63.

31. Suetonius, *Augustus*, 66.

32. Suetonius, *Augustus*, 19.

33. Suetonius, *Tiberius*, 8; Bauman, R.A., 'Tiberius and Murena', *Historia: Zeitschrift für Alte Geschichte*, Bd. 15, H. 4 (Nov 1966), pp.420–32, believes Tiberius's prosecution of Caepio took place in 22 BC, but Levick, Barbara, *Tiberius, the Politician*, p.22, asserts that this was in 23 BC.

34. Dio 54.3.5; Daley, Lawrence J., 'Augustus and the Murder of Varro Murena ("cos." 23 B.C.)', *Klio* (1 Jan 1984), pp.157–69.

35. Dio 54.3.5.

36. Bauman, Richard A., *Crime and Punishment in Ancient Rome* (Routledge, 1996), p.42; Pettinger, Andrew, *The Republic in Danger: Drusus Libo and the Succession of Tiberius* (Oxford University Press, 2012), p.13; Chilton, C.W., 'The Roman Law of Treason under the Early Principate', *The Journal of Roman Studies*, Vol. 45, Parts 1 and 2 (1955), pp.73–81.

37. Dio 54.3.5.

38. Bastomsky, S.J., 'Proculeius and Augustus: A Note on a Friendship turned Sour', *Latomus*, t. 36, Fasc. 1 (Janvier–Mars 1977), pp.129–31.

39. Macrobius, *Saturnalia* (Loeb Vol. 1), 1.11.21; Dio 54.3.7.

40. Dio 54.3.7–8.

41. Atkinson, Kathleen M.T., 'Constitutional and Legal Aspects of the Trials of Marcus Primus and Varro Murena', *Historia: Zeitschrift für Alte Geschichte*, Bd. 9, H. 4 (Oct 1960), pp.440–73.

42. Strabo, *Geography* (Loeb, 1989), 14.670.
43. Strabo, *Geography*, 14.670.
44. Dio 54.3.8; Daley, Lawrence J., 'Augustus and the Murder of Varro Murena ("cos." 23 B.C.)', *Klio* (1 Jan 1984), pp.157–69.
45. Dio 54.3.6; Chilton, C.W., 'The Roman Law of Treason under the Early Principate', *The Journal of Roman Studies*, Vol. 45, Parts 1 and 2 (1955), pp.73–81. Rogers, Robert Samuel, 'Treason in the Early Empire', *The Journal of Roman Studies*, Vol. 49, Parts 1 and 2 (1959), pp.90–94, argues that Roman law was merely a system of directions and guidance on punishments rather than a prescriptive rule book, and so was open to interpretation. However, the use of the death penalty rather than exile was not a matter of interpretation but a subversion of precedent.
46. Dio 54.6.1; Phillips, Darryl A., 'The Conspiracy of Egnatius Rufus and the Election of Suffect Consuls under Augustus', *Historia: Zeitschrift für Alte Geschichte*, Bd. 46, H. 1 (1st Qtr 1997), pp.103–12.
47. Dio 54.3.8; Eck, Werner, *Augustus*, trans. Deborah Lucas Schneider (Blackwell, 1998), p.55; Mason, Steve, 'Of Despots, Diadems and Diadochoi: Josephus and Flavian Politics', in *Writing Politics in Imperial Rome*, ed. W.J. Dominik, J. Garthwaite and P.A. Roche (Brill, 2009), p.344.

Chapter 3

1. Mellor, Ronald, *Tacitus* (Routledge, 1993), pp.82–85.
2. Mason, Steve, Chapter 14, 'Of Despots, Diadems and Diadochoi: Josephus and Flavian Politics', in *Writing Politics in Imperial Rome*, ed. W.J. Dominik, J. Garthwaite and P.A. Roche (Brill, 2009), p.348.
3. Clark, Gillian, 'Roman Women', *Greece and Rome*, Vol. 28, No. 2, Jubilee Year (Oct 1981), p.205.
4. Suetonius, *Augustus*, 64.
5. Clark, Gillian, 'Roman Women', *Greece and Rome*, Vol. 28, No. 2, Jubilee Year (Oct 1981), pp.200–01.
6. Fantham, Elaine, *Julia Augusti, The Emperor's Daughter* (Routledge, 2006), p.56.
7. Suetonius, *Tiberius*, 7.
8. Suetonius, *Tiberius*, 12–13; Dio 55.9.5.
9. Tacitus, *Annals*, 1.53.2; Bauman, Richard A., *Women and Politics in Ancient Rome* (Routledge, 1994), p.111.
10. Tacitus, *Annals*, 1.53.2–4; Fantham, Elaine, *Julia Augusti, The Emperor's Daughter*, p.84; Lacey, W., '2 B.C. and Julia's Adultery', *Antichthon* 14 (1980), pp.127–42.
11. Macrobius, *Saturnalia*, 2.5.9.
12. Fantham, Elaine, *Julia Augusti, The Emperor's Daughter*, p.91.
13. Macrobius, *Saturnalia*, 2.5.5; Seneca, *De Consolatione ad Helvium*, 16.4; Fantham, Elaine, *Julia Augusti, The Emperor's Daughter*, p.91.
14. Macrobius, *Saturnalia*, 2.5.3 and 7.
15. Macrobius, *Saturnalia*, 2.5.6; Bauman, Richard A., *Women and Politics in Ancient Rome*, p.110.
16. Macrobius, *Saturnalia*, 2.5.2; Wallace-Hadrill, Andrew, 'The Imperial Court', *Cambridge Ancient History*, Chapter 7 (Cambridge University Press, 1996), pp.288, 302.
17. Syme, R., *The Augustan Aristocracy*, pp.57, 229.
18. Velleius Paterculus, *The Roman History*, 2.100.5; Dio 55.10.16.
19. Ovid, *Tristia, Ex Ponto*, 4.16.31; Syme, R., 'The Crisis of 2 BC', *The Roman Papers* Vol. III (Clarendon Press, 1981), pp.912–37.

20. Barrett, Anthony A., and Yeardley, J.C., trans. and notes to *Velleius Paterculus, The Roman History*, p.117, n.327; Levick, Barbara, 'The Fall of Julia the Younger', *Latomus*, t. 35, Fasc. 2 (Avril–Juin 1976), pp.301–39.

21. Fantham, Elaine, *Julia Augusti, The Emperor's Daughter*, p.85; Bauman, Richard A., *Women and Politics in Ancient Rome*, p.115.

22. Syme, R., *The Roman Revolution*, p.426; Bauman, Richard A., *Women and Politics in Ancient Rome*, p.105; Crook, J.A., 'Augustus: Power, Authority, Achievement', *Cambridge Ancient History* (Cambridge University Press, 1996), p.142.

23. Bauman, Richard A., *Women and Politics in Ancient Rome*, pp.105–06; Fantham, Elaine, *Julia Augusti, The Emperor's Daughter*, p.42; Syme, R. *The Roman Revolution*, p. 426

24. Fantham, Elaine, *Julia Augusti, The Emperor's Daughter*, p.42; Crook, J.A., 'Augustus: Power, Authority, Achievement', *Cambridge Ancient History* (Cambridge University Press), p.143.

25. Syme, R., *The Roman Revolution*, p.466.

26. Horace, *Odes*, 4.2; Bauman, Richard A., *Women and Politics in Ancient Rome*, p.115.

27. Velleius Paterculus, *The Roman History*, 2.100.4; Barrett, Anthony A., and Yeardley, J.C., trans. and notes to *Velleius Paterculus, The Roman History*, p.117, n.326; Bauman, Richard A., *Women and Politics in Ancient Rome*, p.109.

28. Velleius Paterculus, *The Roman History*, 2.100.5; Dio 55.10.16; Macrobius, *Saturnalia*, 1.2.7. Syme, R., 'The Crisis of 2 BC', *Roman Papers* Vol. III, pp.912–37, suggests Demosthenes was an intellectual moving in high society, whilst Cohen, Sarah T., 'Augustus, Julia and the Development of Exile "Ad Insulam"', *The Classical Quarterly*, New Series, Vol. 58, No. 1 (May 2008), pp.206–17, considers him to be a Greek philosopher. Varner, Eric R., 'Portraits, Plots, and Politics: "Damnatio memoriae" and the Images of Imperial Women', *Memoirs of the American Academy in Rome*, Vol. 46 (2001), pp.41–93, considers he was an actor whose status was used to destroy her reputation, whereas Bauman, Richard A., *Women and Politics in Ancient Rome*, p.115, sees him as a musician and a 'notorious adulterer'.

29. Macrobius, *Saturnalia*, 1.2.7; Levick, Barbara, 'The Fall of Julia the Younger', *Latomus*, t. 35, Fasc. 2 (Avril–Juin 1976), pp.301–39.

30. Velleius Paterculus, *The Roman History*, 2.100.3; Fantham, Elaine, *Julia Augusti, The Emperor's Daughter*, p.82; Syme, R.. 'The Crisis of 2 BC', *The Roman Papers* Vol. III, p.914.

31. Seneca, *De Beneficiis*, in *Moral Essays*, Vol. 3 (Loeb, 1989), 6.32.

32. Dio 55.10.12–13.

33. Pliny, *Natural History*, 21.8–9.

34. Varner, Eric R., 'Portraits, Plots, and Politics: "Damnatio memoriae" and the Images of Imperial Women', *Memoirs of the American Academy in Rome*, Vol. 46 (2001), pp.41–93; Bauman, Richard A., *Crime and Punishment in Ancient Rome* (Routledge, 1996), pp.41–42.

35. Macrobius, *Saturnalia*, 1. 11. 17; Lacey, W., '2 B.C. and Julia's Adultery', *Antichthon*, 14 (1980), pp.127–42.

36. Ovid, *Fasti*, 2.127–32; Fantham, Elaine, *Julia Augusti, The Emperor's Daughter*, p.85; Syme, R., 'The Crisis of 2 BC', *The Roman Papers* Vol. III, p.918.

37. Wiseman, T.P., 'Satyrs in Rome? The Background to Horace's Ars Poetica', *The Journal of Roman Studies* 78 (1988), pp.1–13; Rawson, Piers B., *The Myth of Marsyas in Roman Visual Art* (The University of Manchester, ProQuest Dissertations Publishing, 1986), pp.15–16, 407.

38. On Augustus's uncontrollable anger, see Suetonius, *Augustus*, 65, and Seneca, *De Beneficiis*, 6.32. Also, Fantham, Elaine, *Julia Augusti, The Emperor's Daughter*, p.88.

39. Tacitus, *Annals*, 1.53. Vellius Paterculus, *The Roman History*, 2.100.4, states Iullus Antonius committed suicide, whilst Dio 55.10.15 and Tacitus, *Annals*, 4.44, declare that he was executed, suggesting he was allowed to kill himself having been sentenced to death. Dio 55.10.16 for Gracchus as tribune. For death of son in Massilia, see Tacitus, *Annals*, 4.44. See Rogers, Robert Samuel, 'Treason in the Early Empire', *The Journal of Roman Studies*, Vol. 49, Parts 1 and 2 (1959), pp.90–94, for Antonius's indictment for treason under the *maiestas* laws.

40. Dio 55.10.15.

41. Pliny, *Natural History*, 7.149.

42. Ovid, *Fasti*, 6.595–596, 6.615–161. Wormel, D.E.W., 'Ovid and the "Fasti"', *Hermathena*, No. 127 (Winter 1979), pp.39–50, for date of composition. Fantham, Elaine, *Julia Augusti, The Emperor's Daughter*, p.124.

43. Lacey, W., '2 B.C. and Julia's Adultery', *Antichthon*, 14, pp.127–42; Levick, Barbara, 'The Fall of Julia the Younger', *Latomus*, t. 35, Fasc. 2 (Avril–Juin 1976), pp.301–39; Varner, Eric R., 'Portraits, Plots, and Politics: "Damnatio memoriae" and the Images of Imperial Women', *Memoirs of the American Academy in Rome*, Vol. 46 (2001), pp.41–93.

44. Suetonius, *Augustus*, 65; Cohen, Sarah T., 'Augustus, Julia and the Development of Exile "Ad Insulam"', *The Classical Quarterly*, New Series, Vol. 58, No. 1 (May 2008), pp.206–17; Talbert, Richard J.A., 'The Senate and Senatorial and Equestrian Posts', in *Cambridge Ancient History, From Tiberius to Nero* (Cambridge University Press), p.329.

45. Seneca, *De Beneficia*, 6.32.2.

46. Lacey, W., '2 B.C. and Julia's Adultery', *Antichthon*, 14, pp.127–42.

47. Suetonius, *Augustus*, 65; Dio 55.10.16.

48. Fantham, Elaine, *Julia Augusti, The Emperor's Daughter*, p.89; De La Bédoyère, Guy, *Praetorian: The Rise and Fall of Rome's Imperial Bodyguard* (Yale University Press, 2017), p.62; Crook, J.A., 'Augustus: Power, Authority, Achievement', *Cambridge Ancient History* (Cambridge University Press), p.105; Keppie, Lawrence, 'The Army and Navy', Chapter Eleven, *Cambridge Ancient History* (Cambridge University Press), p.384

49. Suetonius, *Augustus*, 65; Varner, Eric R., 'Portraits, Plots, and Politics: "Damnatio memoriae" and the Images of Imperial Women', *Memoirs of the American Academy in Rome*, Vol. 46 (2001), pp.41–93.

50. Tacitus, *Annals*, 3.24.2.

51. Vellius Paterculus, *The Roman History*, 2.100.5; Fantham, Elaine, *Julia Augusti, The Emperor's Daughter*, p.89.

52. Suetonius, *Tiberius*, 11; Syme, R., *The Roman Revolution*, p.425.

53. Suetonius, *Augustus*, 65.

54. Braginton, Mary V., 'Exile under the Roman Emperors', *The Classical Journal*, Vol. 39, No. 7 (Apr 1944), pp.391–407; Cohen, Sarah T., 'Augustus, Julia and the Development of Exile "Ad Insulam"', *The Classical Quarterly*, New Series, Vol. 58, No. 1 (May 2008), pp.206–17.

55. Suetonius, *Augustus*, 65.

56. Suetonius, *Tiberius*, 23.

57. Suetonius, *Augustus*, 64; Syme, R., *The Roman Revolution*, p.431; Linderski, J., 'Julia in Rhegium', *Zeitschrift für Papyrologie und Epigraphik*, Bd. 72 (1988), pp.181–200.

58. Strabo, *Geography*, 4.259; Fantham, Elaine, *Julia Augusti, The Emperor's Daughter*, p.90.

59. Dio 55.13.1; Linderski, J., 'Julia in Rhegium', *Zeitschrift für Papyrologie und Epigraphik*, Bd. 72 (1988), pp.181–200, suggests Zonoras, in his summary of Dio, misinterpreted Julia's transfer from Pandateria to the mainland for her complete restoration to imperial favour.

60. Dio 55.32.1–2; Birch, R.A., 'The Settlement of 26 June A.D. 4 and Its Aftermath', *The Classical Quarterly*, Vol. 31, No. 2 (1981), pp.443–56; Levick, Barbara, 'The Fall of Julia the Younger', *Latomus*, t. 35, Fasc. 2 (Avril–Juin 1976), pp.301–39; Eck, Werner, *Augustus*, trans. Deborah Lucas Schneider (Blackwell, 1998), p.54.

61. Suetonius, *Augustus*, 65; Tacitus, *Annals*, 1.3, 4.71; Varner, Eric R., 'Portraits, Plots, and Politics: "Damnatio memoriae" and the Images of Imperial Women', *Memoirs of the American Academy in Rome*, Vol. 46 (2001), pp.41–93.

62. Dio 55.26.4–5, 55.27.1–5, 55.31.1; Pliny, *Natural History*, 7.149; Fantham, Elaine, *Julia Augusti, The Emperor's Daughter*, pp.109–10; Syme, R., *The Augustan Aristocracy*, p.122; Pettinger, Andrew, *The Republic in Danger: Drusus Libo and the Succession of Tiberius* (Oxford University Press, 2012), p.85; Levick, Barbara, 'The Fall of Julia the Younger', *Latomus*, t. 35, Fasc. 2 (Avril–Juin 1976), pp.301–39; Bauman, Richard A., *Crime and Punishment in Ancient Rome*, pp.40–41. Rogers, Robert Samuel, 'A Tacitean Pattern in Narrating Treason-Trials', *Transactions and Proceedings of the American Philological Association*, Vol. 83 (1952), pp.279–311, also suggests Cassius Severus was prosecuted in AD 8 for producing libellous writings against noble ladies and gentlemen under the law of *maiestas*. The target of his propaganda may have been supporters of Tiberius and Livia.

63. Suetonius, *Augustus*, 19; Fantham, Elaine, *Julia Augusti, The Emperor's Daughter*, p.144, n.5, argues that they are two separate individuals, whereas Pettinger, Andrew, *The Republic in Danger: Drusus Libo and the Succession of Tiberius*, p.85, considers them the same, as does Levick, Barbara, 'The Fall of Julia the Younger', *Latomus*, t. 35, Fasc. 2 (Avril–Juin 1976), pp.301–39.

64. Suetonius, *Augustus*, 51.1.

65. Birch, R.A., 'The Settlement of 26 June A.D. 4 and Its Aftermath', *The Classical Quarterly*, Vol. 31, No. 2 (1981), pp.443–56.

66. Suetonius, *Claudius*, 26.1; Propertius iv 11.63; Syme, R., *The Augustan Aristocracy*, pp.104, 111, 122; Syme, R., 'The Crisis of 2 BC', *Roman Papers* Vol. III, pp.912–37; Fantham, Elaine, *Julia Augusti, The Emperor's Daughter*, p.109; Shotter, David C.A., 'Agrippina the Elder: A Woman in a Man's World', *Historia: Zeitschrift für Alte Geschichte*, Bd. 49, H. 3 (3rd Qtr 2000), pp.341–57; Pettinger, Andrew, *The Republic in Danger: Drusus Libo and the Succession of Tiberius* (Oxford University Press, 2012), pp.48, 99. Levick, Barbara, 'The Fall of Julia the Younger', *Latomus*, t. 35, Fasc. 2 (Avril–Juin 1976), pp.301–39, identifies marriage links between the Sempronii, the Quinctii Crispini and the Silanii, who constituted a group of supporters of both Julia the Elder and her daughter.

67. Scholiast on Juvenal 6.158; Fantham, Elaine, *Julia Augusti, The Emperor's Daughter*, p.110; Syme, R., *The Augustan Aristocracy*, pp.119–20, 122. Pettinger, Andrew, *The Republic in Danger: Drusus Libo and the Succession of Tiberius*, pp.86, 126, argues that although the Scholiast clearly confuses Herod Agrippa for Agrippa Postumus, he evidently believed Julia the Younger was exiled twice, the first as an informal quarantine and the second a full relegation.

68. Tacitus, *Annals*, 3.24, 4.71; Suetonius, *Augustus*, 65; Allison, J.E., and Cloud, J.D., 'The lex Julia Maiestatis', *Latomus*, t. 21, Fasc. 4 (Octobre–Decembre 1962), pp.711–31.

69. Fantham, Elaine, *Julia Augusti, The Emperor's Daughter*, p.110.

70. Ovid, *Fasti*, 6.595–596; Fantham, Elaine, *Julia Augusti, The Emperor's Daughter*, pp.111–12.

71. Ovid, *Tristia*, 103–110.

72. Ovid, *Tristia*, 3.6.11–16, 4.10.99–101; *Epitome de Caesaribus*, 1.24; Dio 55.27.3; Digest, 47.10.5.11; Ingleheart, Jennifer, 'What the Poet saw: Ovid, the Error and the

Theme of Sight in Tristia 2', *Materiali e discussioni per l'analsi dei testi classici* No. 56 (2006), pp.63–86; Bauman, Richard A., *Women and Politics in Ancient Rome*, pp.121–23; Pettinger, Andrew, *The Republic in Danger: Drusus Libo and the Succession of Tiberius*, p.128; Rutledge, S., *Imperial Inquisitions: Prosecutors and Informants from Tiberius to Nero*, loc. 764.

73. Suetonius, *Augustus*, 19.2; Bauman, Richard A., *Women and Politics in Ancient Rome*, p.119; Pettinger, Andrew, *The Republic in Danger: Drusus Libo and the Succession of Tiberius*, p.139. See Syme, R., *The Roman Revolution*, p.424, for the appointment of Tiberius's partisans and supporters to governorships, consulships and army commands.

74. Tacitus, *Annals*, 2.39; Suetonius, *Augustus*, 19; Suetonius, *Tiberius*, 25; Syme, R., 'Marcus Lepidus, Capax Imperii', *The Journal of Roman Studies*, Vol. 45, Parts 1 and 2 (1955), pp.22–33.

75. Dio 57.16.3.

76. Tacitus, *Annals*, 2.40; Dio 57.16.4; Pettinger, Andrew, *The Republic in Danger: Drusus Libo and the Succession of Tiberius*, pp.139, 211; McHugh, J., *Sejanus, Regent of Rome* (Pen & Sword, 2020), pp.30, 40, 48–49, 57; Shotter, David C.A., 'Agrippina the Elder: A Woman in a Man's World', *Historia: Zeitschrift für Alte Geschichte*, Bd. 49, H. 3 (3rd Qtr 2000), pp.341–57.

77. Tacitus, *Annals*, 1.3 and 7. Also Dio 57.3.6 and Suetonius, *Tiberius*, 22.

78. Tacitus, *Annals*, 1.6.

79. Tacitus, *Annals*, 1.53. Rogers, Robert Samuel, 'The Deaths of Julia and Gracchus, A.D. 14', *Transactions and Proceedings of the American Philological Association*, Vol. 98 (1967), pp.383–90, unconvincingly argues that Julia the Elder, Agrippa Postumus and Gracchus died of natural causes, despite all the sources stating they were executed.

80. Tacitus, Annals, 1.53; Dio 57.18.1ᵃ.

81. Suetonius, *Tiberius*, 25.

82. Ovid, *Tristia*, 3.4.1–4.

83. Mason, Steve, 'Of Despots, Diadems and Diadochoi: Josephus and Flavian Politics', in *Writing Politics in Imperial Rome*, pp.325, 344–48; Stevenson, T., 'The Succession Planning of Augustus', *Antichthon*, 47 (2013), pp.118–39; Wallace-Hadrill, Andrew, 'The Imperial Court', Chapter 7, *Cambridge Ancient History* (Cambridge University Press), pp.288, 304.

84. Syme, R., 'Marcus Lepidus, Capax Imperii', *The Journal of Roman Studies*, Vol. 45, Parts 1 and 2 (1955), pp.22–33.

Chapter 4

1. Wallace-Hadrill, Andrew, 'Civilis Princeps: Between Citizen and King', *The Journal of Roman Studies*, Vol. 72 (1982), pp.32–48; Paterson, Jeremy, 'Friends in High Places: The Creation of the Court of the Roman Emperor', Chapter 4 in *The Court and Court Society in Ancient Monarchies* (Cambridge University Press, 2009), pp.122–25; Saller, R.P., *Personal Patronage Under the Early Empire*, p.74.

2. Suetonius, *Gaius*, 10.

3. Suetonius, *Gaius*, 13.

4. Suetonius, *Gaius*, 15, 24; Dio 59.9.2–3; Winterling, Aloys, *Caligula, A Biography* (University of California Press, 2011), p.2; Burns, Jasper, *Great Women of Imperial Rome: Mothers and Wives of the Caesars* (Routledge, 2007), p.59.

5. McHugh, J.S., *Sejanus, Regent of Rome* (Pen & Sword, 2020), pp.191–207.

6. Dio 59.6.2–4; Suetonius, *Gaius*, 15.

7. Suetonius, *Gaius*, 8.

8. Tacitus, *Annals*, 6.30.2.

9. Tacitus, *Annals*, 4.73; Stewart, Zeph, 'Sejanus, Gaetulicus, and Seneca', *The American Journal of Philology*, Vol. 74, No. 1 (1953), pp.70–85; Syme, R., *The Augustan Aristocracy* (Oxford University Press, 1986), p.427.

10. Tacitus, *Annals*, 6.9; Stewart, Zeph, 'Sejanus, Gaetulicus, and Seneca', *The American Journal of Philology*, Vol. 74, No. 1 (1953), pp.70–85; Syme, R., *The Augustan Aristocracy* (Oxford University Press, 1986), pp.310, 312, tables XXI, XXII.

11. Tacitus, *Annals*, 6.30.

12. Suetonius, *Galba*, 6.

13. Parker, Philip, *The Empire Stops Here, A Journey Along the Frontiers of the Roman World* (Pimlico, 2009), pp.104–09.

14. Fishwick, Duncan, and Shaw, Brent D., 'Ptolemy of Mauretania and the Conspiracy of Gaetulicus', *Historia: Zeitschrift für Alte Geschichte*, Bd. 25, H. 4 (4th Qtr 1976), pp.491–94; McHugh, John S., *Sejanus, Regent of Rome*, pp.149, 231; Syme, R., *The Augustan Aristocracy*, p.68.

15. Syme, R., *The Augustan Aristocracy*, p.239, citing PIR2 C 1390 and 298.

16. Dio 59.13.2; Stewart, Zeph, 'Sejanus, Gaetulicus, and Seneca', *The American Journal of Philology*, Vol. 74, No. 1 (1953), pp.70–85; Barrett, Anthony A., *Caligula, The Corruption of Power* (B.T. Batsford, 1999), p.91; Syme, R., *The Augustan Aristocracy*, tables XXI, XXII, p.194, citing PIR^2 J 835 D and ILS 959.

17. Suetonius, *Gaius*, 52; Wallace-Hadrill, Andrew, 'Civilis Princeps: Between Citizen and King', *The Journal of Roman Studies*, Vol. 72 (1982), pp.32–48.

18. Suetonius, *Gaius*, 54; Dio 59.5.4; Winterling, Aloys, *Caligula, A Biography*, pp.80–81.

19. Suetonius, *Gaius*, 24; Winterling, Aloys, *Caligula, A Biography*, pp.62–63; Varner, Eric R., 'Portraits, Plots, and Politics: "Damnatio memoriae" and the Images of Imperial Women', *Memoirs of the American Academy in Rome*, Vol. 46 (2001), pp.41–93; Sawiński, Paweł, 'The Succession of Imperial Power under the Julio-Claudian Dynasty (30 BC–AD 68)', Peter Lang GmbH, *Internationaler Verlag der Wissenschaften* (Berlin, 2018), p.164.

20. Tacitus, *Annals*, 1.11; Suetonius, *Augustus*, 19; Dio 59.22.6–7; Syme, R., *The Augustan Aristocracy*, pp.104–27 and table IV; Syme, R., 'Marcus Lepidus, Capax Imperii', *The Journal of Roman Studies*, Vol. 45, Parts 1 and 2 (1955), pp.22–33.

21. Dio 49.11.1, 22.6; Suetonius, *Gaius*, 28.

22. Tacitus, *Annals*, 4.60.2, 6.40.3; McHugh, John S., *Sejanus, Regent of Rome*, pp.159–60; Syme, R., *The Augustan Aristocracy*, p.136.

23. Philo, *On the Embassy to Gaius*, 67–71; Barrett, Anthony A., *Caligula, The Corruption of Power*, pp.78–79.

24. Philo, *On the Embassy to Gaius*, 349–52; Crook, J.A., *Concilium Principis* (Cambridge University Press, 1955), pp.39–40.

25. Dio 59.22.6–7; Barrett, Anthony A., *Caligula, The Corruption of Power*, pp.81–82, citing *SEG* 30.1251; Sawiński, Paweł, 'The Succession of Imperial Power under the Julio-Claudian Dynasty (30 BC–AD 68)', Peter Lang GmbH, *Internationaler Verlag der Wissenschaften* (Berlin, 2018), p.164.

26. Suetonius, *Gaius*, 24; Dio 59.11.2–3; Winterling, Aloys, *Caligula, A Biography*, pp.81–84; Burns, Jasper, *Great Women of Imperial Rome: Mothers and Wives of the Caesars* (Routledge, 2006), p.60.

27. Philo, *On the Embassy to Gaius*, 3; Barrett, Anthony A., *Caligula, The Corruption of Power*, p.109; McHugh, John S., *Sejanus, Regent of Rome*, p.229.

28. Winterling, Aloys, *Caligula, A Biography*, pp.86–87; Keppie, Lawrence, 'The Army and the Navy', Chapter 11 in Cambridge Ancient History, Vol. 10, *The Augustan*

Empire (Cambridge University Press, 1996), p.388; Barrett, Anthony A., *Caligula, The Corruption of Power*, p.105; Wiedemann, T.E.J., 'Tiberius to Nero', Chapter 5 in Cambridge Ancient History, p.228.

29. Josephus, *Jewish Antiquities*, 18.256.

30. Tacitus, *Annals*, 6.4.

31. Dio 59.13.1–3.

32. Seneca, *De Beneficia*, 7.31.1; Stewart, Zeph, 'Sejanus, Gaetulicus, and Seneca', *The American Journal of Philology*, Vol. 74, No. 1 (1953), pp.70–85.

33. Dio 59.16.2–7. See also Suetonius, *Gaius*, 30.

34. Dio 59.16.8–10.

35. Winterling, Aloys, *Caligula, A Biography*, pp.96–99.

36. Tacitus, *Annals*, 4.52; Dio 59.19.1–2; Rutledge, Steven H., *Imperial Inquisitions: Prosecutors and Informants from Tiberius to Domitian* (Routledge, 200e, ebook), loc 932–1022.

37. Dio 59.19.6.

38. Dio 59.18.4; Tacitus, *Histories*, 1.48; Syme, R., *The Augustan Aristocracy*, p.298; Rutledge, Steven H., *Imperial Inquisitions: Prosecutors and Informants from Tiberius to Domitian*, loc 8057 n.100.

39. Suetonius, *Gaius*, 25; Winterling, Aloys, *Caligula, A Biography*, p.105.

40. Suetonius, *Gaius*, 33; Wiedemann, T.E.J., 'Tiberius to Nero', Chapter 5 in Cambridge Ancient History, p.226.

41. Suetonius, *Nero*, 5–6; Barrett, Anthony A., *Agrippina: Sex, Power, and Politics in the Early Empire* (Routledge, 1999), p.64.

42. Dio, 59.22.6–9; Suetonius, *Gaius*, 24.3; Syme, R., *The Augustan Aristocracy*, pp.173, 181, citing PIR² A 701 (A 677); Barrett, Anthony A., *Caligula, The Corruption of Power*, p.110.

43. Suetonius, *Gaius*, 24; *Claudius*, 9; Dio 59.22.8; Rutledge, S., *Imperial Inquisitions: Prosecutors and Informants from Tiberius to Domitian*, loc 3910; Bauman, Richard A., *Women and Politics in Ancient Rome* (Routledge, 1994), p.164.

44. Tacitus, *Annals*, 2.6.2, 14.2.2: Philo, *In Flaccum*, 185–191; Josephus, *Jewish Antiquities*, 19.125; Saller, R.P., *Personal Patronage Under the Early Empire*, p.74; Barrett, Anthony A., *Caligula, The Corruption of Power*, p.110; Pagán, Victoria Emma, *Conspiracy Narratives in Roman History* (University of Texas Press, 2004), p.6.

45. Suetonius, *Gaius*, 55.

46. Suetonius, *Gaius*, 43; Dio 59.21.2–3. Phlegon of Tralles, *Book of Marvels* (FGH 2.1179. VII), refers to a sudden sex change that took place here in AD 53: 'There was also an hermaphrodite in Mevania, a town in Italy, in the country house of Agrippina Augusta when Dionysodoros was archon in Athens, and Decimus Junius Silanus Torquatus and Quintus Haterius Antoninus were consuls in Rome.'

47. Dio 59.20.1–3; Suetonius, *Gaius*, 26.

48. Dio 59.20.3; Tacitus, *Annals*, 4.52; Birley, Anthony R., *The Fasti of Roman Britain* (Clarendon Press, 1981), pp.44–49; Rutledge, S., *Imperial Inquisitions from Tiberius to Domitian*, loc 4439 and 5147.

49. Suetonius, *Gaius*, 24.

50. Seneca, *Natural Questions*, IVa Praef. 6 and 15; *Letters*, 31.9; Stewart, Zeph, 'Sejanus, Gaetulicus, and Seneca', *The American Journal of Philology*, Vol. 74, No. 1 (1953), pp.70–85.

51. Seneca, *Epistulae Morales*, 31.

52. Suetonius, *Gaius*, 43; Bingham, Sandra J., *The Praetorian Guard in the Political and Social Life of Julio-Claudian Rome* (PhD Thesis, University of British Columbia, 1977), pp.7, 25.

53. Suetonius, *Galba*, 2.4–5; Wiedemann, T.E.J., 'Tiberius to Nero', Chapter 5 in Cambridge Ancient History, p.227.
54. Dio 59.21.2.
55. Suetonius, *Gaius*, 43.1.
56. Suetonius, *Gaius*, 43.2.
57. Barrett, Anthony A., *Caligula, The Corruption of Power*, p.99; Garzetti, Albino, *From Tiberius to the Antonines, A History of the Roman Empire, AD 14–192* (Routledge, 1974), p.97.
58. Dio 59.22.5.
59. Suetonius, *Galba*, 6; *Vitellius*, 7.
60. Suetonius, *Gaius*, 60.
61. Suetonius, *Gaius*, 44.
62. Suetonius, *Galba*, 6.
63. Winterling, Aloys, *Caligula, A Biography*, p.110.
64. CIL VI 2029, Syme, R., *The Augustan Aristocracy*, table XXI and XXII. His name was erased on an inscription from Vindonissa CIL 13.11513, as cited by Barrett, Anthony A., *Caligula, The Corruption of Power*, p.104.
65. Dio 59.21.4.
66. Dio 59.22.3–4; Winterling, Aloys, *Caligula, A Biography*, p.114.
67. Dio 59.25.1; Suetonius, *Gaius*, 35.1; 14; Fishwick, Duncan, and Shaw, Brent D., Ptolemy of Mauretania and the Conspiracy of Gaetulicus, *Historia: Zeitschrift für Alte Geschichte*, Bd. 25, H. 4 (4th Qtr 1976), pp.491–94.
68. Suetonius, *Gaius*, 24.3, 29; Dio 59.22.6–8; Seneca, *Letters*, 4.7; Orosius 7.5.9; Barrett, Anthony A., *Caligula, The Corruption of Power*, p.106; Winterling, Aloys, *Caligula, A Biography*, pp.107–09; Barrett, Anthony A., *Agrippina: Sex, Power, and Politics in the Early Empire* (Routledge, 1999), p.62; Flaig, Egon, *Plebs und Princeps, Neue Praktiken und semantische Restrukturierungen im frühen Principat* (2021, Academia.edu download), pp.1–17.
69. Suetonius, *Vespasian*, 2.3; Dio 59.23.3; Suetonius, *Gaius*, 48; Barrett, Anthony A., *Agrippina: Sex, Power, and Politics in the Early Empire*, p.66.
70. Dio 59.23.8.
71. Josephus, *Jewish Antiquities*, 19.20, 49, 52; Scholiast on Juv. Sat, 1.55; Dio 59.19.7–8, 59.23.9; 60.8.5; 61.12.1; Tacitus, *Annals*, 14.63.2; Suetonius, *Claudius*, 29.1; Barrett, Anthony A., *Caligula, The Corruption of Power*, pp.108–09, 112; Rogers, Robert Samuel, 'A Group of Domitianic Treason-Trials', *Classical Philology*, Vol. 55, No. 1 (Jan 1960), pp.19–23; Griffen, Miriam T., *Nero, The End of a Dynasty* (Batsford, 1984), p.103; Holmes, Richard, *Nero, The Man Behind the Myth* (Sutton Publishing, 2000), p.20.
72. Suetonius, *Gaius*, 26, 30; Pagán, Victoria Emma, *Conspiracy Narratives in Roman History*, p.18.
73. Dio 59.23.4–7; Suetonius, *Gaius*, 49; *Claudius*, 9; Barrett, Anthony A., *Agrippina: Sex, Power, and Politics in the Early Empire*, p.70.
74. Dio, 59.22.6.
75. Dio 59.26.1; Josephus, *Jewish Antiquities*, 19.64; Winterling, Aloys, *Caligula, A Biography*, p.122; Rutledge, S., *Imperial Inquisitions: Prosecutors and Informants from Tiberius to Domitian*, loc 695.
76. Epictetus, *Discourses*, 4.1.148; Saller, R.P., *Personal Patronage in the Early Empire*, pp.59–61, 66; Wallace-Hadrill, Andrew, 'Civilis Princeps: Between Citizen and King', *The Journal of Roman Studies*, Vol. 72 (1982), pp.32–48.

Chapter 5

1. Dio 59.14.6–7; Suetonius, *Gaius*, 55; Winterling, Aloys, *Caligula, A Biography*, p.103.

2. Suetonius, Gaius, 56.1.

3. Seneca, *De Ira*, 3.18.3.

4. Dio 59.25.5b–7; Tacitus, *Annals*, 15.74.3, 16.17.5; Winterling, Aloys, *Caligula, A Biography*, p.136; Rutledge, S., *Imperial Inquisitions: Prosecutors and Informants from Tiberius to Domitian*, loc. 3910.

5. Suetonius, *Gaius*, 26.3.

6. Dio 59.25.6; Barrett, Anthony A., *Caligula, The Corruption of Power*, pp.156–57.

7. Dio 59.25.8.

8. Suetonius, *Gaius*, 56; Sandison, A.T., 'The Madness of the Emperor Caligula'(Cambridge University Press, 2012), pp.202–09; Winterling, Aloys, *Caligula, A Biography*, p.168.

9. Paterson, Jeremy, Chapter 4, 'Friends in High Places: the Creation of the Court of the Roman Emperor', in *The Court and Court Society in Ancient Monarchies* (Cambridge University Press, 2009), p.136.

10. Dio Chrysostom, *Orations on Kingship*, 6.59.

11. Dio 59.30.2, 59.30.1b; Josephus, *Jewish Antiquities*, 19.15, 19.121–22,19.158–59; Winterling, Aloys, *Caligula, A Biography*, pp.162, 176.

12. Pliny, *Natural History*, 33.134, 36.60. Tacitus, *Annals*, 11.29.1, implies he was involved in the plot. Rutledge, S., *Imperial Inquisitions: Prosecutors and Informants from Tiberius to Domitian*, loc. 716.

13. Josephus, *Jewish Antiquities*, 19.1.10.

14. Dio 59.26.2; Suetonius, *Gaius*, 28; Winterling, Aloys, *Caligula, A Biography*, p.137; Barrett, Anthony A., *Caligula, the Corruption of Power*, p.158.

15. Dio 60.15.5; Winterling, Aloys, *Caligula, A Biography*, p.139.

16. Josephus, *Jewish Antiquities*, 19.12–14; Winterling, Aloys, *Caligula, A Biography*, p.139; Pagán, Victoria Emma, *Conspiracy Narratives in Roman History*, p.19; Rutledge, S., *Imperial Inquisitions: Prosecutors and Informants from Tiberius to Domitian*, loc. 786.

17. He is named as Pomponius in Dio 59.26.4 and Pompedius in Josephus, *Jewish Antiquities*, 19.32–36, and is probably identifiable with Pompeius Pennus in Seneca, *de Beneficia*, 2.12. He is described but not named in Suetonius, *Gaius*, 16.4.

18. Suetonius, *Gaius*, 16.4.

19. Josephus, *Jewish Antiquities*, 19.35.

20. Josephus, *Jewish Antiquities*, 19.37; Wiseman, T.P., *Death of an Emperor: Flavius Josephus*, trans. with introduction and commentary, p.51.

21. Tacitus, *Annals*, 1.32.2.

22. Dio 59.29.1ᵃ.

23. Suetonius, *Gaius*, 56; Dio 59.29.1; Josephus, *Jewish Antiquities*, 19.18.

24. Dio 59.29.2–3; Seneca the Younger, *On the Firmness of the Wise Man*, 18.

25. Josephus, *Jewish Antiquities*, 19.31.

26. Suetonius, *Gaius*, 56.

27. Josephus, *Jewish Antiquities*, 19.21, 28–29, 43. According to Josephus, *Jewish Antiquities*, 19.24–25, Chaerea was also disgusted by Gaius's execution of members of the crowd at the chariot races who demanded a reduction in taxes, but according to Wiseman, T.P., *Death of an Emperor: Flavius Josephus*, p.49, these games were probably the *ludi Romani* in September, four months before his murder. The delay implies that this event was not a key motivation for Chaerea.

28. Josephus, *Jewish Antiquities*, 19.34.

29. Suetonius, *Gaius*, 16.2; Josephus, *Jewish Antiquities*, 19.36; Dio 59.26.2–5; Rutledge, S., *Imperial Inquisitions: Prosecutors and Informants from Tiberius to Domitian*, loc. 3942.

30. Josephus, *Jewish Antiquities*, 19.17–19; Pagán, Victoria Emma, *Conspiracy Narratives in Roman History*, pp.99, 105–06; Wiseman, T.P., *Death of an Emperor: Flavius Josephus*, p.47, notes that both Seneca and Fabius Rusticus came from Corduba, but the latter's historical work has unfortunately been lost.

31. Josephus, *Jewish Antiquities*, 19.20. Wiseman, T.P. *Death of an Emperor: Flavius Josephus*, pp.47–48, notes that whilst Josephus names the conspirator incorrectly as Minucianus, he is evidently identifiable with Vinicianus.

32. Josephus, *Jewish Antiquities*, 19.20; Syme, Ronald, *The Augustan Aristocracy*, p.173.

33. Seneca the Younger, *On the Firmness of the Wise Man*, 18.

34. Josephus, *Jewish Antiquities*, 19.252.

35. Tacitus, *Annals*, 11.1.

36. Josephus, *Jewish Antiquities*, 19.102, mentions that the conspirators wanted to block the departure of Valerius Asiaticus and M. Vinicius from the theatre ahead of Gaius, 'but respect for their dignity made it impossible'. If they had been working together, this problem would not have occurred.

37. Winterling, Aloys, *Caligula, A Biography*, pp.166–71. Barrett, Anthony A., *Caligula, The Corruption of Power*, p.163, points out that January was not the sailing season, and it was extremely dangerous to sail to Egypt during the winter storms.

38. Josephus, *Jewish Antiquities*, 19.27.

39. Josephus, *Jewish Antiquities*, 19.37–45; Bingham, Sandra, *The Praetorian Guard: A History of Rome's Elite Special Forces* (I.B. Taurus, 2015), p.26.

40. Suetonius, *Gaius*, 56; Dio 59.29.1.

41. Josephus, *Jewish Antiquities*, 19.154.

42. Josephus, *Jewish Antiquities*, 19.46–47.

43. Dio 59.29.1, 29.5; Suetonius, *Gaius*, 58.2; Josephus, *Jewish Antiquities*, 19.48; Pagán, Victoria Emma, *Conspiracy Narratives in Roman History*, p.103.

44. Josephus, *Jewish Antiquities*, 19.49.

45. Dio 50.15.1.

46. Josephus, *Jewish Antiquities*, 19.49–51.

47. Wiseman, T.P., *Death of an Emperor: Flavius Josephus*, pp.52–53; Syme, Ronald, *The Augustan Aristocracy*, p.181.

48. Josephus, *Jewish Antiquities*, 19.52–59.

49. Suetonius, *Gaius*, 58.

50. Josephus, *Jewish Antiquities*, 19.60–62.

51. Josephus, *Jewish Antiquities*, 19.62–63

52. Dio 59.29.1–1a.

53. Tacitus, *Annals*, 11.29.2; Winterling, Aloys, *Caligula, A Biography*, pp.165, 171, 176; Rutledge, S., *Imperial Inquisitions: Prosecutors and Informants from Tiberius to Domitian*, loc. 3910; Levick, Barbara, *Claudius*, p.34.

54. Josephus, *Jewish Antiquities*, 19.66–69; Barrett, A., *Agrippina: Sex, Power, and Politics in the Early Empire* (Routledge, 1999), p.70; Levick, Barbara, *Claudius*, p.35; Rutledge, S., *Imperial Inquisitions: Prosecutors and Informants from Tiberius to Domitian*, loc 695.

55. Wardle, David, 'When Did Gaius Die?', *Acta Classica* (http://www.casa-kvsa.org.za/legacy/1991/AC34-14-Wardle.pdf), pp.158–65.

56. Dio 59.29.6; Carandini, Andrea, *The Atlas of Ancient Rome, Biography and Portraits of the City*, Vol. 1 (Princeton University Press, 2017), pp.233–35.

57. Josephus, *Jewish Antiquities*, 19.70–78, 86, 90, 111–112; Winterling, Aloys, *Caligula, A Biography*, p.180; Barrett, Anthony A., *Caligula, the Corruption of Power*, p.163.

58. Josephus, Jewish Antiquities, 19.78–84; Dio 59.29.6.

59. Suetonius, *Gaius*, 58; Barrett, Anthony A., *Caligula, The Corruption of Power*, p.164.

60. Josephus, *Jewish Antiquities*, 19.85–86.

61. Josephus, *Jewish Antiquities*, 19.87–88, and for his complicity in the plot 19.98. See also Suetonius, *Gaius*, 57.4; Woods, David, 'Caligula, Asprenas, and the Bloodied Robe', *Mnemosyne* 71 (2018), pp.873–80.

62. Dio 59.29.5; Josephus, *Jewish Antiquities*, 19.89–99; Paterson, Jeremy, *The Court and Court Society in Ancient Monarchies*, p.148.

63. Josephus, *Jewish Antiquities*, 19.91–92; Wiseman, T.P., *Death of an Emperor: Flavius Josephus*, pp.59–60; Barrett, Anthony A., *Caligula, the Corruption of Power*, p.164; Pagán, Victoria Emma, *Conspiracy Narratives in Roman History*, p.100.

64. Josephus, *Jewish Antiquities*, 19.93.

65. Suetonius, *Gaius*, 57; Josephus, *Jewish Antiquities*, 19.94; Wiseman, T.P., *Death of an Emperor: Flavius Josephus*, p.60; Barrett, Anthony A., *Caligula, the Corruption of Power*, p.163.

66. Suetonius, *Gaius*, 58.

67. Josephus, *Jewish Antiquities*, 96–97.

68. Josephus, *Jewish Antiquities*, 98–101.

69. Josephus, *Jewish Antiquities*, 19.102–104.

70. Suetonius, *Claudius*, 10; Pagán, Victoria Emma, *Conspiracy Narratives in Roman History*, p.99.

71. Suetonius, *Gaius*, 58; Josephus, *Jewish Antiquities*, 19.104; Dio 59.29.6.

72. Josephus, *Jewish Antiquities*, 19.105–109.

73. Suetonius, *Gaius*, 58; Josephus, *Jewish Antiquities*, 19.252.

74. Seneca, *On the Firmness of the Wise Man*, 18.3; Woods, David, 'Caligula, Asprenas, and the Bloodied Robe', *Mnemosyne* 71 (2018), pp.873–80.

75. Suetonius, *Gaius*, 58; Dio 59.29.7–59.30.1; Barrett, Anthony A., *Caligula, the Corruption of Power*, p.165.

76. Josephus, *Jewish Antiquities*, 19.117; Garzetti, Albino, *From Tiberius to the Antonines*, p.103.

77. Josephus, *Jewish Antiquities*, 19.153–154. Barrett, Anthony A., *Caligula, the Corruption of Power*, p.166, speculates that Vinicianus was not involved in the conspiracy, but the evidence to the contrary appears overwhelming.

78. Dio, 59.30.1c; Josephus, *Jewish Antiquities*, 19.119–121.

79. Josephus, *Jewish Antiquities*, 19.122–126; Suetonius, *Gaius*, 58; Woods, David, 'Caligula, Asprenas, and the Bloodied Robe', *Mnemosyne* 71 (2018), pp.873–880; Wiseman, T.P., *Death of an Emperor: Flavius Josephus*, pp.66–67.

80. Josephus, *Jewish Antiquities*, 19.127–144, whose vivid account is probably based on the work of Cluvius Rufus, who was sat in the audience. Barrett, Anthony A., *Agrippina: Sex, Power, and Politics in the Early Empire*, p.80, on the reaction of the crowd in the theatre. Flower, Harriet I., *The Art of Forgetting: Disgrace and Oblivion in Roman Political Culture*, p.149.

81. Josephus, *Jewish Antiquities*, 19.145–147.

82. Josephus, *Jewish Antiquities*, 19.122.

83. Josephus, *Jewish Antiquities*, 19.148. Wiseman, T.P., *Death of an Emperor: Flavius Josephus*, p.69, notes that he is probably the Arruntius Stella who organized Nero's games in AD 55 (Tacitus, *Annals*, 13.22), his son was a consul under the Flavians and a grandson was consul in AD 101.

84. Dio 59.29.2.

85. Suetonius, *Claudius*, 10; Dio 60.1.2–3; Josephus, *Jewish Antiquities*, 19.217–219; Levick, Barbara, *Claudius*, p.35.

86. Suetonius, *Claudius*, 10; Josephus, *Jewish Antiquities*, 19.162–165, 221–226; Dio 60.1.3; Bingham, Sandra, *The Praetorian Guard in the Political and Social Life of Julio-Claudian Rome* (PhD Thesis), p.76, n.33; Barrett, Anthony A., *Agrippina: Sex, Power, and Politics in the Early Empire*, p.72; Barrett, Anthony A., *Caligula, the Corruption of Power*, pp.173–77.

87. Dio 59.30.3; Josephus, *Jewish Wars*, 2.204; Josephus, *Jewish Antiquities*, 19.263.

88. Josephus, *Jewish Antiquities*, 19.185; Syme, R., *The Stemma of the Sentii Saturnini*, Roman Papers, Vol. 2 (Oxford University Press, 1979), pp.605–16; Mason, Steve, 'Of Despots, Diadems and Diadochoi: Josephus and Flavian Politics', Chapter 7 in *Writing Politics in Imperial Rome* (Brill, 2009), p.324.

89. Suetonius, *Gaius*, 60; Josephus, *Jewish Wars*, 2.204; Dio 60.3.5; Barrett, Anthony A., *Agrippina: Sex, Power, and Politics in the Early Empire*, p.71; Barrett, Anthony A., *Caligula, the Corruption of Power*, p.172; Flower, Harriet I., *The Art of Forgetting: Disgrace and Oblivion in Roman Political Culture*, pp.152–53; Rudich, Vasily, *Political Dissidence under Nero: The Price of Dissimulation* (Taylor and Francis Group, 1993), p.88.

90. Josephus, *Jewish Antiquities*, 19.186–189.

91. Josephus, *Jewish Antiquities*, 19.190. Barrett, Anthony A., *Caligula, the Corruption of Power*, p.167, suggests the murder of Caesonia was planned well in advance, but the delay in her execution suggests otherwise. Dio, contradicting Josephus and Suetonius, does imply that she was killed soon after Gaius.

92. Josephus, *Jewish Antiquities*, 19.191–194; Suetonius, *Gaius*, 59; Varner, Eric R., 'Portraits, Plots, and Politics: "Damnatio memoriae" and the Images of Imperial Women', pp.41–93.

93. Josephus, *Jewish Antiquities*, 19.195–199; Suetonius, *Gaius*, 59; Dio 59.29.7.

94. Suetonius, *Claudius*, 10; Dio 60.1.4; Josephus, *Jewish Antiquities*, 19.234–235; Wiseman, T.P., *Death of an Emperor: Flavius Josephus*, p.93; Birley, Anthony R., *The Fasti of Roman Britain*, pp.50–54; Levick, Barbara, *Claudius*, p.31.

95. Suetonius, *Gaius*, 59; Josephus, *Jewish Antiquities*, 19.237; Barrett, Anthony A., *Caligula, the Corruption of Power*, p.167; Flower, Harriet I., *The Art of Forgetting: Disgrace and Oblivion in Roman Political Culture*, p.149.

96. Josephus, *Jewish Wars*, 2.206.

97. Suetonius, *Claudius*, 10; Bingham, Sandra, *The Praetorian Guard in the Political and Social Life of Julio-Claudian Rome*, p.76.

98. Josephus, *Jewish Antiquities*, 19.239–244; Josephus, *Jewish Wars* (Oxford University Press, 2017), 2.207–210.

99. Josephus, *Jewish Antiquities*, 19.227–228, 248–249, 253; Winterling, Aloys, *Caligula, A Biography*, p.183; Garzetti, Albino, *From Tiberius to the Antonines*, p.103; Wiseman, T.P., *Calpurnius Siculus and the Claudian Civil War* (Francis Cairns Publications, 1987), p.89.

100. Dio 60.3.2, 60.15.1–2; Tacitus, *Annals*, 11.1; Josephus, *Jewish Antiquities*, 19.249–252; Plutarch, *Galba*, 3.1, 14.3; Suetonius, *Galba*, 7.1; Levick, Barbara, *Claudius*, p.31; Flaig, Egon, *Plebs und Princeps. Neue Praktiken und semantische Restrukturierungen im frühen Principat*, pp.1–17; Vervaet, Frederik Juliaan, 'Domitius Corbulo and the Senatorial Opposition to the Reign of Nero', *Ancient Society*, Vol. 32 (2002), p.139, notes the passive voice used by Dio in the failed attempt to nominate Vinicianus for the throne. Wiseman, T.P., *Calpurnius Siculus and the Claudian Civil War*, pp.89–92, on the possible claimants. For the claims of Vinicius, see Wiedemann, T.E.J., 'Tiberius to Nero', in A.

Bowman, E. Champlin and A. Lintott (eds), *The Cambridge Ancient History* (Cambridge University Press, 1996), pp.198–255, 230.

101. Josephus, *Jewish Antiquities*, 19.254–258. Rome had four factions of charioteers – known as the Greens, the Reds, the Blues and the Whites – each of which had their fervent supporters, including leading senators and even emperors, including Gaius.

102. Dio 60.1.4; Josephus, *The Jewish War*, 2.211; Josephus, *Jewish Antiquities*, 19.259.

103. Josephus, *Jewish Antiquities*, 19.260–262.

104. Josephus, *Jewish Antiquities*, 19.263–264; Josephus, *The Jewish War*, 2.211–214; Wiseman, T.P., *Death of an Emperor: Flavius Josephus*, p.100, suggests this Aponius was Aponius Saturninus, who fell asleep when Gaius was acting as an auctioneer and, after nodding his way through the bids, woke to find he had bought thirteen gladiators (Suetonius, *Gaius*, 38.4).

105. Dio 60.1.4, 60.3.2; Josephus, *Jewish Antiquities*, 19.267; Barrett, Anthony A., *Caligula, the Corruption of Power*, pp.176–77.

106. Josephus, *Jewish Antiquities*, 19.268–269; Dio 60.3.4–5, 60.4.5; Suetonius, *Claudius*, 11.1; Tacitus, *Histories*, 4.68; Winterling, Aloys, *Caligula, A Biography*, p.175; Barrett, Anthony A., *Caligula, the Corruption of Power*, p.160; Levick, Barbara, *Claudius*, p.38.

107. Josephus, *Jewish Antiquities*, 19.269–272; Dio 60.3.5; Pagán, Victoria Emma, *Conspiracy Narratives in Roman History*, pp.10, 100.

108. Josephus, *Jewish Antiquities*, 19.273.

Chapter 6

1. Seneca, *Apocolocyntosis divi Claudii*, 14; Wiseman, T.P., *Calpurnius Siculus and the Claudian Civil War* (Francis Cairns Publications, 1987), pp. 88, 94. The number of *equites* executed is 300 in Suetonius, *Claudius*, 29. Levick, Barbara, *Claudius* (Routledge, 2001), p.44; Flower, Harriet I., *The Art of Forgetting, Disgrace and Oblivion in Roman Political Culture* (University of North Carolina Press, 2011), p.154.

2. Wiedemann, T.E.J., 'Tiberius to Nero', chapter 5 in *Cambridge Ancient History*, p.229; *Epitome De Caesaribus*, 4.3.

3. Seneca, *Apocolocyntosis*, 10; Suetonius, *Claudius*, 29; Dio 60.8.4–5, 60.14.1–3.

4. RIC 12 (1984), 122; Wiedemann, T.E.J., 'Tiberius to Nero', chapter 5 in *Cambridge Ancient History*, p.232; Bingham, Sandra, *The Praetorian Guard in the Political and Social Life of Julio-Claudian Rome* (PhD thesis, University of British Columbia, 1997), p.77.

5. Suetonius, *Claudius*, 25, 35 also 12.3; Levick, Barbara, *Claudius*, p.51; Wiedemann, T.E.J., 'Tiberius to Nero', chapter 5 in *Cambridge Ancient History*, p.233; Patterson, Jeremy, 'Friends in High Places: the Creation of the Court of the Roman Emperor', in *The Court and Court Society in Ancient Monarchies* (Cambridge University Press, 2009), p.149.

6. Bauman, Richard A., *Women and Politics in Ancient Rome* (Taylor & Francis Group, 1994), p.167; Barrett, Anthony A., *Agrippina: Sex, Power, and Politics in the Early Empire* (Routledge, 1999), p.78.

7. Suetonius, *Claudius*, 11.

8. Barrett, Anthony A., *Agrippina: Sex, Power, and Politics in the Early Empire*, p.73.

9. Bauman, Richard A., *Women and Politics in Ancient Rome*, p.170.

10. Dio 60.8.5–6; Bauman, Richard A., *Women and Politics in Ancient Rome*, p.169.

11. Seneca, *Apocolocyntosis*, 13.

12. Seneca, *Consolatio ad Polybium*, 13.2; Dio 60.8.5 suggests the charge of adultery against Seneca was false, but 61.10.1 implies it was true. Also, Bauman, Richard A., *Women and Politics in Ancient Rome*, p.170; Levick, Barbara, *Claudius*, p.55.

13. Seneca, *Naturales Quaestiones*, 4 prefaces, 15–16.

14. Wilson, Emily, *Seneca, A Life* (Allan Lane, 2015), p.78.

15. Dio 60.14.3–4; Suetonius, *Claudius*, 37; Levick, Barbara, *Claudius*, pp.58–59.

16. Dio 60.15.1.

17. Tacitus, *Annals*, 3.66; Syme, R., *The Augustan Aristocracy*, pp.193–96; Rutledge, S., *Imperial Inquisitions: Prosecutors and Informants from Tiberius to Domitian*, loc. 2029.

18. Tacitus, *Annals*, 6.9.

19. Bauman, Richard A., *Women and Politics in Ancient Rome*, p.170.

20. Wiedemann, T.E.J., 'Tiberius to Nero', chapter 5 in *Cambridge Ancient History*, p.234; Barrett, Anthony A., *Agrippina: Sex, Power, and Politics in the Early Empire*, p.74.

21. Dio 60.15.2; Rutledge, S., *Imperial Inquisitions: Prosecutors and Informants from Tiberius to Domitian*, loc. 4005.

22. Tacitus, *Annals*, 13.43; Josephus, *The Jewish War*, 2.205; Rutledge, S., *Imperial Inquisitions: Prosecutors and Informants from Tiberius to Domitian*, loc. 1002, 5946; Syme, R., 'Domitius Corbulo', *The Journal of Roman Studies*, Vol. 60 (1970), pp.27–39; Vervaet, Frederik Juliaan, 'Domitius Corbulo and the Senatorial Opposition to the Reign of Nero', *Ancient Society*, Vol. 32 (2002), pp.135–93.

23. Dio 60.15.3, 16.4

24. CIL III, 7043 = AE 1993: 435; Tacitus, *Annals*, 2.52.5; Suetonius, *Claudius*, 26; Wiedemann, T.E.J., 'Tiberius to Nero', chapter 5 in *Cambridge Ancient History*, p.234; Levick, Barbara, *Claudius*, pp.58–59; Rutledge, S., *Imperial Inquisitions: Prosecutors and Informants from Tiberius to Domitian*, loc. 3954, 4127; Syme, R., *The Augustan Aristocracy*, pp.138–39, 268, 282, 312; Parat, Josip, 'Reconsidering the Traces of Scribonianus' Rebellion', *Radovi – Zavod za hrvatsku povijest*, Vol. 48 (Zagreb, 2016), pp.191–212; Syme, R., 'Marcus Lepidus, Capax Imperii', *The Journal of Roman Studies*, Vol. 45, Parts 1 and 2 (1955), pp.22–33.

25. Dio 60.15.4; Suetonius, *Claudius*, 36.

26. Dio 60.15.3, 60.15.6.

27. Pliny, *Letters*, 3.16; Dio 60.16.6.

28. Suetonius, *Otho*, 1; Suetonius, *Claudius*, 13; Parat, Josip, 'Reconsidering the Traces of Scribonianus' Rebellion', *Radovi – Zavod za hrvatsku povijest*, Vol. 48 (Zagreb, 2016), pp.191–212.

29. Dio 60.15.3.

30. Suetonius, *Claudius*, 13.

31. Epictetus, *Discourses*, 1.14.15.

32. Philostratus, *Life of Apollonius of Tyana*, 5.35.

33. Seneca, *Letters*, 95.35.

34. Dio 60.15.3; Parat, Josip, 'Reconsidering the Traces of Scribonianus' Rebellion', *Radovi – Zavod za hrvatsku povijest*, Vol. 48 (Zagreb, 2016), pp.191–212.

35. Tacitus, *Histories*, 2.75, names the assassin as Volaginius; Dio 60.15.4, however, says Camillus took his own life. Pliny, *Letters*, 3.16, for the role of his wife.

36. Suetonius, *Otho*, 1.

37. Parat, Josip, 'Reconsidering the Traces of Scribonianus' Rebellion', *Radovi – Zavod za hrvatsku povijest*, Vol. 48 (Zagreb, 2016), pp.191–212; Levick, Barbara, *Claudius*, p.137; https://www.livius.org/articles/legion/legio-viii-augusta/.

38. Suetonius, *Otho*, 1.
39. Pliny, *Letters*, 3.16.
40. Dio 60.16.2.
41. Dio 60.16.3.
42. Pliny, *Letters*, 3.16; PIR² A 1140 names Camillus's wife as Vinicia.
43. Dio 60.16.5–6; Pliny, *Letters*, 3.16.
44. Martial, *Epigrams* (Oxford University Press, 2015), 1.13.
45. Dio 60.16.4–5.
46. Suetonius, *Otho*, 1.
47. Dio 60.15.4–6; Levick, Barbara, *Claudius*, pp.58–59.
48. Dio 60.16.7; Homer, *Iliad*, 24.369, also *Odyssey*, 16.72, 21.133; Seneca, *On Consolation Ad Polybium de Consolatione*, 13.2; Winterling, Aloys, *Caligula*, p.193. Seneca, *Apocolocyntosis*, 8.10, is clear that Claudius alone was responsible for attacks on the Senate, not his wives or freedmen.
49. Dio 60.15.5.
50. Levick, Barbara, *Claudius*, pp.58–59, citing CIL 8.215 for the erasure of his name. Carroll, Maureen, 'Memoria and Damnatio Memoriae. Preserving and Erasing Identities in Roman Funerary Commemoration', in *Living Through the Dead, Burial and Commemoration in the Classical World* (Oxbow, p.87), on the social and political effects of *damnatio memoriae*.
51. Dio 60.16.1–2, 16.8; Levick, Barbara, *Claudius*, pp.58–59.
52. Barry, William D., 'Exposure, Mutilation, and Riot: Violence at the Scalae Gemoniae in Early Imperial Rome', *Greece and Rome* (Second Series), Vol. 55, No. 2 (Oct 2008), pp.222–46.
53. Quintilian 8.5.15; Bauman, Richard A., *Women and Politics in Ancient Rome*, p.171; Levick, Barbara, *Claudius*, pp.58–59; Rogers, Robert Samuel, 'Domitius Afer's Defense of Cloatilla', *Transactions and Proceedings of the American Philological Association*, Vol. 76 (1945), pp.264–70.
54. Dio 60.16.2; McAlindon, D., 'Senatorial Opposition to Claudius and Nero', *The American Journal of Philology*, Vol. 77, No. 2 (1956), pp.113–32.
55. Tacitus, *Annals*, XII, 52.1–3; Levick, Barbara, *Claudius*, p.61; Braginton, Mary V., 'Exile under the Roman Emperors', *The Classical Journal*, Vol. 39, No. 7 (Apr 1944), pp.391–407.
56. Rutledge, S., *Imperial Inquisitions*, loc. 2029.
57. McAlindon, D., 'Senatorial Opposition to Claudius and Nero', *The American Journal of Philology*, Vol. 77, No. 2 (1956), pp.113–32; Rutledge, S., *Imperial Inquisitions*, loc. 164; Rogers, Robert Samuel, 'A Group of Domitianic Treason-Trials', *Classical Philology*, Vol. 55, No. 1 (Jan 1960), pp.19–23; Syme, R., 'Domitius Corbulo', *The Journal of Roman Studies*, Vol. 60 (1970), pp.27–39.
58. Seneca, *Apocolocyntosis*, 13.5; Tacitus, *Annals*, 1.29.2; Dio 60.18.3; Levick, Barbara, *Claudius*, pp.56–57; Barrett, Anthony A., *Agrippina: Sex, Power, and Politics in the Early Empire*, pp.73, 87; Bauman, Richard A., *Women and Politics in Ancient Rome*, p.171.
59. Levick, Barbara, *Claudius*, p.139.
60. Dio 60.27.4; Levick, Barbara, *Claudius*, p.61; Birley, Anthony R., *Fasti of Roman Britain* (Clarendon Press, 1981), p.39; Syme, R., 'M. Vinicius (Cos. 19 B.C.)', *The Classical Quarterly*, Vol. 27. No. ¾ (Jul–Oct 1933), pp.142–48.
61. Seneca, *Dialogues*, 2.18.2.
62. Dio 60.27.4.
63. Tacitus, *Annals*, 11.1.1; Rudich, Vasily, *Political Dissidence under Nero: The Price of Dissimulation* (Taylor and Francis Group, 1993), p.88.

64. Josephus, *Jewish Antiquities*, 19.252; Tacitus, *Annals*, 11.1.2; Dio 59.30.2.

65. Tacitus, *Annals*, 11.1; Winterling, Aloys, *Caligula*, p.175.

66. ILS 212= CIL XIII 1668; Tacitus, *Histories*, 1.59.2, 2.94.2; *Annals*, 11.25; Dio 60.29.4; Rutledge, S., *Imperial Inquisitions*, loc. 2597; Von Stackelberg, Katharine T., 'Performative Space and Garden Transgressions in Tacitus' Death of Messalina', *American Journal of Philology* 130 (2009), pp.595–624; McAlindon, D., 'Claudius and the Senators', *The American Journal of Philology*, Vol. 78, No. 3 (1957), pp.279–86; Joshel, Sandra R., 'Female Desire and the Discourse of Empire: Tacitus's Messalina', *Signs*, Vol. 21, No. 1 (Autumn 1995), pp.50–82.

67. Tacitus, *Annals*, 11.1.

68. Tacitus, *Annals*, 11.4.

69. Tacitus, *Annals*, 11.2.

70. Tacitus, *Annals*, 11.36.5.

71. Tacitus, *Annals*, 11.3.

72. Wiseman, T.P., *Calpurnius Siculus and the Claudian Civil War*, pp.58–60, describes Claudian Rome as in a permanent state of potential war. Also see McAlindon, D., 'Senatorial Opposition to Claudius and Nero', *The American Journal of Philology*, Vol. 77, No. 2 (1956), pp.113–32.

Chapter 7

1. Alston, Richard, *Aspects of Roman History AD 14–117* (Routledge, 1998), p.94; Levick, Barbara, *Claudius*, p.56; L'Hoir, Francesca Santoro, 'Tacitus and Women's Usurpation of Power', *The Classical World*, Vol. 88, No. 1 (Sep–Oct 1994), pp.5–25; Raymond, Nicholas, *Meretrix Augusta, A Literary Examination of Messalina in Tacitus and Juvenal* (MA Thesis, June 1990, McMaster University), pp.1–120; Akinboye, Goke A., 'Women's Ambition, Ambitious Women: The Case of Caesar's Household During the Julio-Claudian Era', *Journal of Management and Social Sciences*, pp.303–15. For examples, see Pliny, *Natural History*, 83.172; Dio 60.18.1; Juvenal, *Satires*, 10.229–345; Tacitus, *Annals*, 11.10–14; Suetonius, *Claudius*, 26, 29, 36. For consideration of the extent of her adultery, see Alston, Richard, *Aspects of Roman History AD 14–117*, p.94.

2. Tacitus, *Annals*, 11.2–3.

3. Suetonius, *Claudius*, 36.

4. Dio 60.18.2; Rutledge, Steven H., *Imperial Inquisitions from Tiberius to Domitian* (Routledge, 2001, Kindle edition), loc. 3559; Bauman, Richard A., *Women and Politics in Ancient Rome* (Taylor & Francis Group, 1994), p.167.

5. Bauman, Richard A., *Women and Politics in Ancient Rome*, pp.105, 167.

6. Dio 60.18.3.

7. Dio 61.31.2.

8. Dio 60.17.8, 61.30.6ᵇ, 61.31.2.

9. Suetonius, *Claudius*, 28; Seneca, *Naturales Quaestiones*, 4 pr.15.

10. Barrett, Anthony A., *Agrippina: Sex, Power, and Politics in the Early Empire*, p.76; Wallace-Hadrill, Andrew, 'The Imperial Court', in *Cambridge Ancient History*, p.297.

11. Dio 60.34.4; Suetonius, *Claudius*, 28; Wallace-Hadrill, Andrew, 'The Imperial Court', in *Cambridge Ancient History*, p.288.

12. Epictetus, *Discourses*, 4.1.45–48; Saller, R.P., *Personal Patronage Under the Early Empire*, p.45; Paterson, Jeremy, 'Friends in High Places: The Creation of the Court of the Roman Emperor', in *The Court and Court Society in Ancient Monarchies* (Cambridge University Press, 2009), p.140.

13. Levick, Barbara, *Claudius*, pp.56–57.
14. Tacitus, *Annals*, 11.36.5; Joshel, Sandra R., 'Female Desire and the Discourse of Empire: Tacitus's Messalina', *Signs*, Vol. 21, No. 1 (Autumn 1995), pp.50–82.
15. Suetonius, *Vitellius*, 2.
16. Tacitus, *Annals*, 11.2; Woods, David, 'The Role of Lucius Vitellius in the Death of Messalina', *Mnemosyne*, Vol. 70, Fasc. 6 (2017), pp.996–1007; Wallace-Hadrill, Andrew, 'The Imperial Court', in *Cambridge Ancient History*, p.301; Joshel, Sandra R., 'Female Desire and the Discourse of Empire: Tacitus's Messalina', *Signs*, Vol. 21, No. 1 (Autumn 1995), pp.50–82.
17. Levick, Barbara, *Claudius*, p.54.
18. Seneca, *Apocolocyntosis*, 1–5; Suetonius, *Claudius*, 2, 31.
19. Dio 60.2.1; Tacitus, *Annals*, 14.22.2; Levick, Barbara, *Claudius*, pp.66, 188; Barrett, Anthony A., *Agrippina: Sex, Power, and Politics in the Early Empire*, p.92.
20. Suetonius, *Nero*, 6.
21. Tacitus, *Annals*, 11.11; Garzetti, Albino, *From Tiberius to the Antonines* (Methuen, 1974), p.116.
22. Tacitus, *Annals*, 11.11–12; Barrett, Anthony A., *Agrippina: Sex, Power, and Politics in the Early Empire*, p.94.
23. Tacitus, *Annals*, 11.11; Barrett, Anthony A., *Agrippina: Sex, Power, and Politics in the Early Empire*, p.96.
24. Bauman, Richard A., *Women and Politics in Ancient World*, pp.175–76.
25. Dio 60.31.2. According to Seneca, *Dialogus*, 11.5.2, Messalina had him killed because she was tired of him as her lover. Also see Bauman, Richard A., *Women and Politics in Ancient Rome*, pp.175–76.
26. Paterson, Jeremy, 'Friends in High Places: The Creation of the Court of the Roman Emperor', in *The Court and Court Society in Ancient Monarchies*, p.137; Rutledge, Steven H., *Imperial Inquisitions from Tiberius to Domitian*, loc. 1022; Bauman, Richard A., *Women and Politics in Ancient Rome*, p.178.
27. Tacitus, *Annals*, 11.5–7; Rutledge, Steven H., *Imperial Inquisitions from Tiberius to Domitian*, loc. 1022.
28. McHugh, John S., *Sejanus, Regent of Rome* (Pen & Sword, 2020), pp.104–06.
29. Barrett, Anthony A., *Agrippina: Sex, Power, and Politics in the Early Empire*, p.91; Syme, R., *The Augustan Aristocracy*, p.379.
30. Tacitus, *Annals*, 11.12.26; Dio 60.31.2.
31. Mellor, Ronald, *Tacitus* (Routledge, 1993), pp.83–85; Keegan, Peter, *Boudica, Cartimandua, Messalina and Agrippina the Younger. Independent Women of Power and the Gendered Rhetoric of Roman History* (2005, www.ancienthistory.com.au/teachers.html), pp.1–43; Holmes, Richard, *Nero, The Man Behind the Myth* (Sutton Publishing, 2000), p.22. The image of Claudius as a fool was propagated by Nero and Seneca after his death; see Wallace-Hadrill, Andrew, 'The Imperial Court', in *Cambridge Ancient History*, p.295.
32. Tacitus, *Annals*, 11.12; Juvenal, *Satires*, 10.330.
33. Tacitus, *Annals*, 11.12; Dio 61.31.3; Bingham, Sandra, *The Praetorian Guard in the Political and Social Life of Julio-Claudian Rome* (PhD thesis, University of British Columbia, 1997), p.85.
34. Tacitus, *Annals*, 11.26; Wiedemann, T.E.J., 'Tiberius to Nero', *Cambridge Ancient History*, p.240.
35. Tacitus, *Annals*, 11.29; Dio 61.31.2; Barrett, Anthony A., *Agrippina: Sex, Power, and Politics in the Early Empire*, p.91.

36. Tacitus, *Annals*, 11.28.
37. Tacitus, *Annals*, 11.26.
38. Tacitus, *Annals*, 11.27; Dio 61.31.5.
39. Seneca, *Octavia* (Loeb, 2018), p–p.257–261.
40. Digest 24.2.9 (Paullus), 24.1.25 (Ulpian); Grubbs, Judith Evans, *Women and the Law in the Roman Empire, a Sourcebook on Marriage, Divorce and Widowhood* (Routledge, 2002), pp.189–90.
41. Tacitus, *Annals*, 11.27. Also Dio 61.31.3.
42. Juvenal, *Satires*, 10.330–345.
43. Von Stackelberg, Kathrine T., 'Performative Space and Garden Transgressions in Tacitus' Death of Messalina', *American Journal of Philology* 130 (2009), pp.595–624.
44. Dio 61.31.4.
45. Tacitus, *Annals*, 11.29.
46. Tacitus, *Annals*, 11.29.
47. Tacitus, *Annals*, 11.30; Dio 61.31.4.
48. Tacitus, *Annals*, 11.30; Suetonius, *Claudius*, 36. Fagan, Garrett G., 'Messalina's Folly', *The Classical Quarterly*, Vol. 52, No. 2 (2002), pp.566–79. Also, Suetonius, *Claudius*, 29, finds it impossible 'to believe that they tricked Claudius into signing the marriage contract between Messalina and her lover Silius by an assurance that the marriage was a mere fiction'. This story should be discounted as it was so preposterous that even the salacious hungry biographer dismisses it.
49. Tacitus, *Annals*, 61.26, 61.30, 61.33. Suetonius, *Claudius*, 37; Barrett, Anthony A., *Agrippina: Sex, Power, and Politics in the Early Empire*, p.92. See Pliny the Elder, *Natural History*, 29.1.8, for Vettius's fame as a doctor. For Plautius and his uncle, see Tacitus, *Agricola*, 14.1, *Annals*, 13.32.3.
50. Tacitus, *Annals*, 11.31.
51. Tacitus, *Annals*, 11.28, 11.33.
52. Tacitus, *Annals*, 11.34; Levick, Barbara, *Claudius*, p.66; Rutledge, Steven H., *Imperial Inquisitions*, loc. 5694.
53. Tacitus, *Annals*, 13.16–17; Wallace-Hadrill, Andrew, *The Imperial Court* in *Cambridge Ancient History*, p.295; Rutledge, Steven H., *Imperial Inquisitions*, loc. 3636.
54. Von Stackelberg, Kathrine T., 'Performative Space and Garden Transgressions in Tacitus' Death of Messalina', *American Journal of Philology* 130 (2009), pp.595–624. Joshel, Sandra R., 'Female Desire and the Discourse of Empire: Tacitus's Messalina', *Signs*, Vol. 21, No. 1 (Autumn 1995), pp.50–82, notes with incredulity the supposed incompetence of the alleged conspirators, as does Fagan, Garrett G., 'Messalina's Folly', *The Classical Quarterly*, Vol. 52, No. 2 (2002), pp.566–79. Also see Levick, Barbara, *Claudius*, pp.66–67, who suggests the marriage ceremony was a charade to prove her commitment to her senatorial allies, including Silius.
55. Ovid, *Heriodes*, 10; Ovid, *Ars Amatoria*, 1.527–64; Von Stackelberg, Kathrine T., 'Performative Space and Garden Transgressions in Tacitus' Death of Messalina', *American Journal of Philology* 130 (2009), pp.595–624.
56. Tacitus, *Annals*, 11.31.4–5.
57. Tacitus, *Annals*, 11.31.6.
58. Tacitus, *Annals*, 11.31 and n.2, p.306; Fagan, Garrett G., 'Messalina's Folly', *The Classical Quarterly*, Vol. 52, No. 2 (2002), pp.566–79; Bauman, Richard A., *Women and Politics in Ancient Rome*, p.177.
59. Tacitus, *Annals*, 11.32.1.

60. Tacitus, *Annals*, 11.32.2.
61. Tacitus, *Annals*, 11.32.
62. Tacitus, *Annals*, 11.32.
63. Tacitus, *Annals*, 11.34.
64. Tacitus, *Annals*, 11.34.
65. Tacitus, *Annals*, 11.35; Joshel, Sandra R., 'Female Desire and the Discourse of Empire: Tacitus's Messalina', *Signs*, Vol. 21, No. 1 (Autumn 1995), pp.50–82.
66. Tacitus, *Annals*, 11.35.
67. Tacitus, *Annals*, 11.35; Suetonius, *Claudius*, 36; Joshel, Sandra R., 'Female Desire and the Discourse of Empire: Tacitus's Messalina', *Signs*, Vol. 21, No. 1 (Autumn 1995), pp.50–82.
68. Tacitus, *Annals*, 11.35; Seneca, *Apocolocyntosis*, 13.
69. Dio 60.22.5; Tacitus, *Annals*, 11.36.1–2; Seneca, *Apocolocyntosis*, 13.
70. Tacitus, *Annals*, 11.36, 13.32.3; Tacitus, *Agricola*, 14.1; Fagan, Garrett G., 'Messalina's Folly', *The Classical Quarterly*, Vol. 52, No. 2 (2002), pp.566–79; Rutledge, Steven H., *Imperial Inquisitions*, loc. 2618.
71. Dio 61.31.5; Tacitus, *Annals*, 13.11. Barrett, Anthony A., *Agrippina: Sex, Power, and Politics in the Early Empire*, p.75.
72. Tacitus, *Annals*, 11.37.
73. Tacitus, *Annals*, 11.37. Juvenal, *Satires*, 14.327–331, refers to 'the riches of Narcissus, to whom Claudius Caesar granted everything and those commands he obeyed when told to kill his wife'. Barrett, Anthony A., *Agrippina: Sex, Power, and Politics in the Early Empire*, p.76.
74. Tacitus, *Annals*, 11.38.
75. Joshel, Sandra R., 'Female Desire and the Discourse of Empire: Tacitus's Messalina', *Signs*, Vol. 21, No. 1 (Autumn 1995), pp.50–82; Raymond, Nicholas, *Meretrix Augusta, A Literary Examination of Messalina in Tacitus and Juvenal* (MA Thesis, June 1990, McMaster University), pp.1–120; L'Hoir, Francesca Santoro, 'Tacitus and Women's Usurpation of Power', *The Classical World*, Vol. 88, No. 1 (Sep–Oct 1994), pp.5–25; Mellor, Ronald, *Tacitus*, p.83; Fagan, Garrett G., 'Messalina's Folly', *The Classical Quarterly*, Vol. 52, No. 2 (2002), pp.566–79.
76. Seneca, *Apocolocyntosis*, 10; Tacitus, *Annals*, 11.38.
77. Suetonius, *Claudius*, 39.
78. Tacitus, *Annals*, 11.38.
79. Suetonius, *Claudius*, 26.
80. Suetonius, *Nero*, 33; Dio 61.34; Barrett, Anthony A., *Agrippina: Sex, Power, and Politics in the Early Empire*, pp.96,140.
81. Barrett, Anthony A., *Agrippina: Sex, Power, and Politics in the Early Empire*, pp.138–40, 155; Wallace-Hadrill, Andrew, 'The Imperial Court', in *Cambridge Ancient History*, p.302.
82. Dio 61.34.6. According to Tacitus, *Annals*, 13.1, he was imprisoned and driven to suicide. Also see Levick, Barbara, *Claudius*, p.69.

Chapter 8

1. Seneca, *De Consolatione ad Polybium*, 13; Tacitus, *Annals*, 12.8; Stewart, Zeph, 'Sejanus, Gaetulicus, and Seneca', *The American Journal of Philology*, Vol. 74, No. 1 (1953), pp.70–85; Wilson, Emily, *Seneca*, pp.78–81, 99–100.
2. Crook, J.A., *Concilium Principis* (Cambridge University Press, 1955), p.45.
3. Dio 62.2; Wiedemann, T.E.J., 'Tiberius to Nero', *Cambridge Ancient History*, p.248.

4. Tacitus, *Annals*, 13.42.
5. Rutledge, Steven H., *Imperial Inquisitions: Prosecutors and Informants from Tiberius to Domitian*, loc. 2691–2701; Rutledge, Steven H., 'Delatores and the Tradition of Violence in Roman Oratory', *The American Journal of Philology*, Vol. 120, No. 4 (Winter 1999), pp.555–573.
6. Wallace-Hadrill, Andrew, 'The Imperial Court', *Cambridge Ancient History*, p.305.
7. Tacitus, *Annals*, 14.7.
8. Suetonius, *Nero*, 34; Wiedemann, T.E.J., 'Tiberius to Nero', *Cambridge Ancient History*, p.247.
9. Tacitus, *Annals*, 14.51.
10. Tacitus, *Annals*, 14.53.
11. Tacitus, *Annals*, 14.57; Suetonius, *Nero*, 35.
12. Tacitus, Annals, 14.57; Rogers, Robert Samuel, 'Heirs and Rivals to Nero', *Transactions and Proceedings of the American Philological Association*, Vol. 86 (1955), pp.190–212; Syme, R., *The Augustan Aristocracy*, p.281.
13. Tacitus, *Annals*, 14.64.
14. Tacitus, *Annals*, 14.65.
15. Rogers, Robert Samuel, 'Heirs and Rivals to Nero', *Transactions and Proceedings of the American Philological Association*, Vol. 86 (1955), pp.190–212; Rutledge, Steven, *Imperial Inquisitions*, loc. 4012.
16. Wilson, Emily, *Seneca, A Life*, pp.184–86.
17. Champlin, Edward, 'The Life and Times of Calpurnius Piso', *Museum Helveticum*, Vol. 46 (1989), pp.101–24.
18. *Laus Pisonis*, in Loeb Classical Library (Harvard University Press, 1934, revised 1935), https://penelope.uchicago.edu/Thayer/E/Roman/Texts/Laus_Pisonis/text*.html, p.295.
19. Dio 59.20.7; Syme, R., *The Augustan Aristocracy*, p.379.
20. Winterling, Aloys, *Caligula, A Biography* (University of California Press, 2011), p.67; Champlin, Edward, 'The Life and Times of Calpurnius Piso', *Museum Helveticum*, Vol. 46 (1989), pp.101–24.
21. Tacitus, *Annals*, 15.48; *Laus Pisonis*, 32, 109, 129, 163–77, 211; Champlin, Edward, 'The Life and Times of Calpurnius Piso', *Museum Helveticum*, Vol. 46 (1989), pp.101–24.
22. Wiedemann, T.E.J., 'Tiberius to Nero', *Cambridge Ancient History*, p.226.
23. Suetonius, *Gaius*, 25.
24. Dio 59.8.8; Winterling, Aloys, *Caligula, A Biography*, pp.66–67.
25. Tacitus, *Annals*, 15.59.
26. Juvenal, *Satires*, 5.109; Tacitus, *Annals*, 15.52, 15.65; Champlin, Edward, 'The Life and Times of Calpurnius Piso', *Museum Helveticum*, Vol. 46 (1989), pp.101–24; Keene, C.H., *Calpurnius Siculus, The Eclogues* (Bristol Classical Press, 2005), p.12.
27. Tacitus, *Annals*, 15.58.
28. Martial, *Epigrams*, 12, 36; Keene, C.H., *Calpurnius Siculus, The Eclogues*, p.12.
29. Martial, *Epigrams*, 8.70; Osgood, Josiah, 'Nero and the Senate', *The Cambridge Companion to the Age of Nero* (Cambridge University Press, 2017), pp.38–39.
30. Suetonius, *Nero*, 12; *Vita Lucani*, livingpoets.dur.ac.uk/w/Suetonius, Vita_Lucani; Osgood, Josiah, 'Nero and the Senate', *The Cambridge Companion to the Age of Nero*, p.42; Wiedemann, T.E.J., 'Tiberius to Nero', *Cambridge Ancient History*, pp.244, 247; Freudenburg, Kirk, 'La corte imperial', *Arqueología e Historia*, n.27 (September 2019), pp.12–17; Griffen, Miriam T., *Nero, The End of a Dynasty* (Batsford, 1984), p.168.
31. Tacitus, *Annals*, 15.49; Martindale, Charles, 'The Politician Lucan', *Greece & Rome*, Vol. 31, No. 1 (Apr 1984), pp. 64–79.

32. Griffen, Miriam T., *Nero, The End of a Dynasty*, p.158.
33. *Vita Lucani*, livingpoets.dur.ac.uk/w/Suetonius, Vita_Lucani.
34. Cowan, Robert, 'Lucan's Thunder-Box: Scatology, Epic, and Satire in Suetonius' "Vita Lucani'", *Harvard Studies in Classical Philology*, Vol. 106 (2011), pp.301–13.
35. *Vita Lucani*, livingpoets.dur.ac.uk/w/Suetonius, Vita_Lucani.
36. Tacitus, *Annals*, 15.38–43; Varner, Eric, *Mutilation and Transformation: Damnatio Memoriae and Roman Imperial Portraiture* (Brill, 2004), p.17.
37. Tacitus, *Annals*, 15.39.
38. Freudenburg, Kirk, 'La corte imperial', *Arqueología e Historia*, n. 27 (September 2019), pp.12–17, citing two lines of Lucan's poem that are preserved by Statius, *Silvae*, 2.7.60–61; Griffen, Miriam T., *Nero, The End of a Dynasty*, p.165.
39. Tacitus, *Annals*, 15.50.
40. Tacitus, *Annals*, 15.67.
41. Tacitus, *Annals*, 15.50.
42. Dio 62.24.1.
43. Tacitus, *Annals*, 15.50.
44. Dio 62.24.1; Tacitus, *Annals*, 12.41.2, 14.49; Bingham, Sandra, *The Praetorian Guard in the Political and Social Life of Julio-Claudian Rome* (PhD thesis, University of British Columbia, 1997), p.87.
45. Eager, Max, *The Pisonian Conspiracy* (MPhil thesis, Oxford University, 2012), www.academia.edu/43203930/The_Pisonian_Conspiracy, pp.69–70; Bingham, Sandra, *The Praetorian Guard in the Political and Social Life of Julio-Claudian Rome*, pp.108, 192, citing CIL 5.7003=ILS 2701.
46. Bingham, Sandra, *The Praetorian Guard in the Political and Social Life of Julio-Claudian Rome*, p.105.
47. Tacitus, *Annals*, 15.60–61.
48. Tacitus, *Annals*, 15.49.
49. Tacitus, *Annals*, 15.52.
50. Tacitus, *Annals*, 13.1, 15.52, 16.7; Dio 61.6.4–5; Syme, R., *The Augustan Aristocracy*, p.192; Rogers, Robert Samuel, 'Heirs and Rivals to Nero', *Transactions and Proceedings of the American Philological Association*, Vol. 86 (1955), pp.190–212.
51. Tacitus, *Annals*, 15.52.
52. Tacitus, *Annals*, 15.48, 15.68–69; Wiedemann, T.E.J., 'Tiberius to Nero', *Cambridge Ancient History*, pp.37, 43; Eager, Max, *The Pisonian Conspiracy* (MPhil thesis, Oxford University, 2012), pp.30–31, citing P.Oxy. 2.250 (26 April–25 May of AD 61), CIG 4957 and CIL XIII, 1668.
53. Tacitus, *Annals*, 15.52, 15.68.
54. Tacitus, *Annals*, 15.52.
55. Tacitus, *Annals*, 15.49, 50, 54–56, 67, 70; Wiedemann, T.E.J., 'Tiberius to Nero', *Cambridge Ancient History*, pp.38, 43; Rudich, Vasily, *Political Dissidence under Nero: The Price of Dissimulation*, p.97.
56. Tacitus, *Annals*, 13.12.
57. Tacitus, *Annals*, 15.50.
58. Tacitus, *Annals*, 15.56, 15.71; Eager, Max, *The Pisonian Conspiracy* (MPhil thesis, Oxford University, 2012), pp.26, 30–31. Tacitus, *Annals*, 15.50, lists them as Cervarius Proculus, Vulcacius Araricus, Julius Augurinus (CIL XIII, 6820), Munatius Gratus and Marcius Festus. For Annius Pollio's links to Domitius Corbulo and the Vinician conspiracy of AD 66, see Syme, R., 'Domitius Corbulo', *The Journal of Roman Studies*, Vol. 60 (1970), pp.27–39.

59. Tacitus, Annals, 11.39, 13.36, 15.49, 15.53; Epictetus, *Discourses*, 1.1.20; Griffen, Miriam T., *Nero, The End of a Dynasty*, p.166.

60. *Vita Lucani*, livingpoets.dur.ac.uk/w/Suetonius, Vita_Lucani.

61. Tacitus, *Annals*, 15.50.

62. Tacitus, *Annals*, 15.51.

63. Tacitus, *Annals*, 15.51.

64. Pagán, Victoria Emma, *Conspiracy Narratives in Roman History* (University of Texas Press, 2004), p.78.

65. Polyaenus, *Stratagems*, www.attalus.org, 8.62; 'Piso and Seneca were accused of a conspiracy against Nero; and Mela, a brother of Seneca, had a mistress whose name was Epicharis. Nero examined her by torture, to discover what she might know of the plot; but she resolutely bore the torture without revealing anything. She was therefore dismissed for the present; but three days afterwards she was ordered to be brought back in a litter. While she was being carried in it, she pulled off her girdle, and strangled herself with it. As soon as the men, who oversaw the litter, had brought it to the place of torture, they set it down, and told Epicharis to come out; but on looking inside the litter, they found only a dead corpse. This circumstance exceedingly irritated the tyrant, who found himself thus outwitted by a prostitute.' The account is very similar to that reported in Tacitus, *Annals*, 15.57, suggesting they both drew on the same source.

66. Tacitus, *Annals*, 15.51.

67. Tacitus, *Annals*, 15.46.

68. Tacitus, *Annals*, 15.51.

69. Tacitus, *Annals*, 15.51.

70. Tacitus, *Annals*, 15.51.

71. Tacitus, *Annals*, 15.53.

72. Tacitus, *Annals*, 15.72; Rudich, Vasily, *Political Dissidence under Nero: The Price of Dissimulation*, pp.87, 100; Woodman, A.J., 'Amateur Dramatics at the Court of Nero, Annals 15.48–74', in *Tacitus and the Tacitean Tradition* (Princeton University Press, 2014), pp.107–08; Holland, Richard, *Nero, The Man Behind the Myth* (Sutton Publishing, 2000), p.188.

73. Tacitus, *Annals*, 15.53; Haynes, Holly, 'The Tyrant Lists: Tacitus' Obituary of Petronius', *The American Journal of Philology*, Vol. 131, No. 1 (Spring 2010), pp.69–99; Woodman, A.J., 'Amateur Dramatics at the Court of Nero, Annals 15.48–74', in *Tacitus and the Tacitean Tradition*, pp.106–07.

74. Eager, Max, *The Pisonian Conspiracy*, p.33; Rudich, Vasily, *Political Dissidence under Nero: The Price of Dissimulation*, p.102; Claridge, Amanda, *Rome, An Archaeological Guide* (Oxford University Press, 2010), p.290.

75. Tacitus, *Annals*, 15.53; Griffen, Miriam T., *Nero, The End of a Dynasty*, p.193, suggests she was uninvolved as she was not arrested after the plot failed.

76. Tacitus, *Annals*, 15.65.

77. Juvenal, *Satires*, 8.211–214; Griffen, Miriam T., *Nero, The End of a Dynasty*, p.174.

78. Tacitus, *Annals*, 15.65.

79. Tacitus, *Annals*, 15.67.

80. Tacitus, *Annals*, 15.60; Wilson, Emily, *Seneca, A Life*, pp.207, 209.

81. Aristotle, *Politics* (Penguin Classics, 1981, trans. T. Sinclair), 3.5, 4.2; Plato, *Politicus*, 300e–303b; Aristotle, *Republic* (Penguin Classics, 2007, trans. H.D.P. Lee), 8.564a.

82. Seneca, *De Ira*, 1.6.3, 1.20.9; *De Benificia*, 1.10.2, 7.20.3; Seneca, *De constantia sapientis*, 18; Seneca, *Letters*, 73.9–10; Griffen, Miriam T., *Nero, The End of a Dynasty*, p.174.

83. Tacitus, *Annals*, 15.54.

84. Tacitus, *Annals*, 15.54; Woodman, A.J., 'Amateur Dramatics at the Court of Nero, Annals 15.48–74' in *Tacitus and the Tacitean Tradition*, pp.109–11, citing Sophocles, *Ajax*, 819–820; Haynes, Holly, 'The Tyrant Lists: Tacitus' Obituary of Petronius', *The American Journal of Philology*, Vol. 131, No. 1 (Spring 2010), pp.69–99.

85. Tacitus, *Annals*, 15.54; Pagán, Victoria Emma, *Conspiracy Narratives in Roman History*, p.84

86. Rudich, Vasily, *Political Dissidence under Nero: The Price of Dissimulation*, p.103.

87. Tacitus, *Annals*, 15.55.

88. Tacitus, *Annals*, 15.56.

89. Plutarch, *Moralia* (English trans. by W.C. Helmbold; Cambridge, MA. Harvard University Press, 1939), 505C.

90. Habaj, Michal, 'Plutarch, Moralia 505C: Some Notes on the Discovery of the Pisonian Conspiracy', *Acta Ant. Hung.*, 56 (2016), pp.341–50.

91. Tacitus, *Annals*, 15.59. See Varner, Eric, *Mutilation and Transformation: Damnatio Memoriae and Roman Imperial Portraiture*, p.17, on the surviving remains of a *domus* found on the Caelian Hill deliberately destroyed during the reign of Nero.

92. Tacitus, *Annals*, 15.57; Dio 62.27.3–4.

93. Epictatus, *Discourses*, 1.26.11; Weaver, P.R.C., 'Epaphroditus, Josephus, and Epictetus', *The Classical Quarterly*, Vol. 44, No. 2 (1994), pp.468–79.

94. Epictetus, *Discourses*, 4.1.148, also 3.7.31, 4.7.19; Saller, R.P., *Personal Patronage in the Early Empire*, pp.66, 76.

95. Epictetus, *Discourses*, 1.1.19–20; Tacitus, *Annals*, 15.60; Eager, Max, *The Pisonian Conspiracy*, p.37.

96. Tacitus, *Annals*, 15.57–59, 15.60; Bingham, Sandra, *The Praetorian Guard in the Political and Social Life of Julio-Claudian Rome*, p.106.

97. Tacitus, *Annals*, 15.60.

98. Tacitus, *Annals*, 15.61.

99. Tacitus, *Annals*, 15.61, 15.64.

100. Tacitus, *Annals*, 15.61.

101. Tacitus, *Annals*, 15.62; Wilson, Emily, *Seneca, A Life*, p.209.

102. Tacitus, *Annals*, 15.62; Dio 62.25.3.

103. Tacitus, *Annals*, 13.20.

104. Tacitus, *Annals*, 15.63; Wilson, Emily, *Seneca, A Life*, p.208.

105. Dio 62.25.1–2

106. Tacitus, *Annals*, 15.63.

107. Seneca, *Letters*, 70.

108. Dio 62.25.2; Plato, *Phaedo*, 116A, 117A–C, 118A.

109. Dio 62.24.4; Tacitus, *Annals*, 15.58; Suetonius, *Nero*, 36.

110. Tacitus, *Annals*, 15.66.

111. Tacitus, *Annals*, 15.67.

112. Tacitus, *Annals*, 15.68, 15.71. The Praetorian tribunes Cornelius Martialis, Statius Domitius and Flavius Nepos were demoted, see Eager, Max, *The Pisonian Conspiracy*, pp.69–70; Griffen, Miriam T., *Nero, The End of a Dynasty*, pp.173–74.

113. Rudich, Vasily, *Political Dissidence under Nero: The Price of Dissimulation*, p.122.

114. Tacitus, *Annals*, 15.69.

115. Tacitus, *Annals*, 15.71, 15.73; Philostratus, *Life of Apollonius*, 7.16; Braginton, Mary V., 'Exile under the Roman Emperors', *The Classical Journal*, Vol. 39, No. 7 (Apr 1944), pp.391–407.

116. *Vita Lucani,* livingpoets.dur.ac.uk/w/Suetonius, Vita_Lucani; Tacitus, *Annals,* 15.70–71; Rudich, Vasily, *Political Dissidence under Nero: The Price of Dissimulation,* p.94.

117. Tacitus, *Annals,* 15.72; Eager, Max, *The Pisonian Conspiracy,* p.45.

118. Eager, Max, *The Pisonian Conspiracy,* p.46; Rudich, Vasily, *Political Dissidence under Nero: The Price of Dissimulation,* p.128; Berriman, Andrew, and Todd, Malcolm, 'A Very Roman Coup: The Hidden War of Imperial Succession, AD 96–8', *Historia: Zeitschrift für Alte Geschichte,* Bd. 50, H. 3 (3rd Qtr 2001), pp.312–31; Southern, Pat, *Domitian, Tragic Tyrant* (Routledge, 2009), p.40; Mellor, Ronald, *Tacitus* (Routledge, 1993), p.629; Collins, Andrew W., 'The Palace Revolution: The Assassination of Domitian and Accession of Nerva', *Phoenix,* Vol. 63, No. 1/2 (Spring–Summer 2009), pp.73–106.

119. Suetonius, *Nero,* 56; Wiedemann, T.E.J., 'Tiberius to Nero', *Cambridge Ancient History,* p.252.

120. Tacitus, *Annals,* 16.6; Suetonius, *Nero,* 35.3; Dio 63.28.1; Griffen, Miriam T., *Nero, The End of a Dynasty,* p.168; Wilson, Emily, *Seneca, A Life,* p.213.

121. Tacitus, *Annals,* 16.7.4, 16.7.9; Suetonius, *Nero,* 37; Dio 62.27.1; Rutledge, Steven, *Imperial Inquisitions,* loc. 3714; Rogers, Robert Samuel, 'A Tacitean Pattern in Narrating Treason-Trials', *Transactions and Proceedings of the American Philological Association,* Vol. 83, pp.279–311.

122. Juvenal, *Satires,* 3.116–118.

123. Tacitus, *Annals,* 16.33.4; Dio 62.26.1–2; Rutledge, Steven, *Imperial Inquisitions,* loc. 973, 1127.

124. Tacitus, *Annals,* 16.30–33; Rutledge, Steven, *Imperial Inquisitions,* loc. 2886.

125. Tacitus, *Histories,* 4.10; Rutledge, Steven, *Imperial Inquisitions,* loc. 2886–98.

126. Tacitus, *Annals,* 16.30–33; Dio 62.26.2.

127. CIL VI, 2044; Suetonius, *Nero,* 36, who calls the conspiracy the 'Viniciana'; Dio 62.7.1; Griffen, Miriam T., *Nero, The End of a Dynasty,* p.178; Wiedemann, T.E.J., 'Tiberius to Nero', *Cambridge Ancient History,* p.254; Rutledge, Steven, *Imperial Inquisitions,* loc. 4115, 4138; Vervaet, Frederik Juliaan, 'Domitius Corbulo and the Senatorial Opposition to the Reign of Nero', *Ancient Society,* Vol. 32 (2002), pp.161, 163.

128. Dio 62.23.5, 63.17.5–6; Syme, R., 'Domitius Corbulo', *The Journal of Roman Studies,* Vol. 60 (1970), pp.27–39; Rudich, Vasily, *Political Dissidence under Nero: The Price of Dissimulation,* p.194; Mellor, Ronald, *Tacitus,* p.560.

129. Suetonius, *Nero,* 37; Dio 62.27.1; Rutledge, Steven, *Imperial Inquisitions,* loc. 4127; Vervaet, Frederik Juliaan, 'Domitius Corbulo and the Senatorial Opposition to the Reign of Nero', *Ancient Society,* Vol. 32 (2002), p.158; Syme, R., 'Domitius Corbulo', *The Journal of Roman Studies,* Vol. 60 (1970), pp.27–39.

130. Tacitus, *Histories,* 4.41.2; Vervaet, Frederik Juliaan, 'Domitius Corbulo and the Senatorial Opposition to the Reign of Nero', *Ancient Society,* Vol. 32 (2002), p.166; Rudich, Vasily, *Political Dissidence under Nero: The Price of Dissimulation,* p.194.

131. Suetonius, *Nero,* 36; Paterson, Jeremy, 'Friends in High Places: The Creation of the Court of the Roman Emperor, Chapter 4 in *The Court and Court Society in Ancient Monarchies* (Cambridge University Press, 2009), p.137; Garzetti, Albino, *From Tiberius to the Antonines* (Methuen, 1974), pp.167–68; Rudich, Vasily, *Political Dissidence under Nero: The Price of Dissimulation,* p.123.

132. Pagán, Victoria Emma, *Conspiracy Narratives in Roman History,* pp.88–89; Mellor, Ronald, *Tacitus,* p.79.

133. Paterson, Jeremy, *The Court and Court Society in Ancient Monarchies,* p.138; McAlindon, D., 'Senatorial Opposition to Claudius and Nero', *The American Journal of Philology,* Vol. 77, No. 2 (1956), pp.113–32; Mellor, Ronald, *Tacitus,* p.110.

134. Tacitus, *Annals*, 13.42.1–8, condemns Seneca for his hypocrisy. Woodman, A.J., 'Amateur Dramatics at the Court of Nero, Annals 15.48–74', in *Tacitus and the Tacitean Tradition*, p.127; Rutledge, Steven H., 'Delatores and the Tradition of Violence in Roman Oratory', *The American Journal of Philology*, Vol. 120, No. 4 (Winter 1999), pp.555–73.

Chapter 9

1. Southern, Pat, *Domitian, Tragic Tyrant* (Routledge, 1997), pp.2, 9, 109. For Nerva's early relationship with Domitian, see Suetonius, *Domitian*, 1.1, and Murison, Charles Leslie, 'M. Cocceius Nerva and the Flavians', *Transactions of the American Philological Association*, Vol. 133, No. 1 (Spring 2003), pp.147–57.

2. Suetonius, *Domitian*, 10; Dio of Prusa, *Orations*, 13.1; Dio 67.1.2; Southern, Pat, *Domitian, Tragic Tyrant*, pp.43, 60.

3. Dio 67.13.3–4, 67.16.1; Pleket, H.W., 'Domitian, the Senate, and the Provinces', *Mnemosyne*, Fourth Series, Vol. 14, Fasc. 4 (1961), pp.296–315; Syme, R., *Antonius Saturninus*, Roman Papers, Vol. III (Oxford University Press, 1984), pp.1070–85; Rutledge, S., *Imperial Inquisitions*, loc. 4191.

4. See Suetonius, *Domitian*, 8.1, and Dio 67.1.4 for Domitian's initial attempts to restrict the role of *delators*. Szoke, Martin, 'Condemning Domitian or Un-damning Themselves? Tacitus and Pliny on the Domitianic "Reign of Terror"', *Illinois Classical Studies*, Vol. 44, No. 2 (Fall 2019), University of Illinois, pp.430–52; Johansson, Britta Signe, *Damning Domitian: A Historiographical Study of Three Aspects of His Reign* (Thesis for degree, University of Queensland, November 2013), p.9; Rutledge, S., *Imperial Inquisitions*, loc. 764; Jones, Brian W., *The Emperor Domitian* (Routledge, 1993), p.160. For the role of slaves as informers, see Pliny the Younger, *Panegyrics*, 42.3–4; Tacitus, *Histories*, 1.31.1, and Dio 68.1.2–3.

5. Suetonius, *Domitian*, 17.

6. Dio 67.1.3; Historia Augusta, *Alexander Severus*, 65.5; Saller, R.P., *Personal Patronage under the Early Empire*, pp.41–77; Southern, Pat, *Domitian, Tragic Tyrant*, p.122; Jones, Brian W., *The Emperor Domitian*, pp.161, 172, 177; McAlindon, D., 'Senatorial Opposition to Claudius and Nero', *The American Journal of Philology*, Vol. 77, No. 2 (1956), pp.113–32.

7. Rutledge, S., *Imperial Inquisitions*, loc. 9675; Jones, Brian W., *The Emperor Domitian*, p.61.

8. Suetonius, *Domitian*, 21.

9. Southern, Pat, *Domitian, Tragic Tyrant*, p.122; Jones, Brian W., The *Emperor Domitian*, pp.197–98.

10. Dio 67.1.2, 67.16.1; Suetonius, *Domitian*, 4, 15.

11. Saller, R.P., *Personal Patronage under the Early Empire*, pp.21 and 69-70

12. Pliny the Younger, *Letters*, 2.11, 2.12, 3.9, 4.9, 5.20, 4.5, 4.13, 7.6, 7.10; Suetonius, *Domitian*, 8; Pleket, H.W., 'Domitian, the Senate and the Provinces', *Mnemosyne*, Fourth Series, Vol. 14, Fasc. 4 (1961), pp.296–315, citing SEG XVII 755; Waters, K.H., 'The Character of Domitian', *Phoenix*, Vol. 18, No. 1 (Spring 1964), pp.49–77; Fraser, Trudie, E., 'Domitia Longina: An Underestimated Augusta (c. 53–126/8)', *Ancient Society*, Vol. 45 (2015), p.96.

13. Suetonius, *Domitian*, 8.4; Dio 67.3.4; Jones, Brian W., *The Emperor Domitian*, pp.101–02; Syme, R., *Antonius Saturninus*, Syme Roman Papers, Vol. III (Oxford University Press, 1984), pp.1070–85.

14. Suetonius, *Domitian*, 3, 9; Dio of Prusa, *Orations*, 6.59; Southern, Pat, *Domitian, Tragic Tyrant*, pp.123–25; Patterson, Jeremy, 'Friends in High Places: The Creation of the

Court of the Roman Emperor', in *The Court and Court Society in Ancient Monarchies* (Cambridge University Press, 2009), pp.121–56.

15. Suetonius, *Domitian*, 15. Southern, Pat, *Domitian, Tragic Tyrant*, p.115, dates Glabrio's exile to AD 95, contradicting the assumption of Gallivan, Paul, 'Who was Acilius?', *Historia: Zeitschrift für Alte Geschichte*, Bd. 27, H. 4 (4th Qtr 1978), pp.621–25, who dates it to the year of his consulship in AD 91, with his execution in AD 95. However, the sources imply his death rapidly followed his banishment.

16. Dio 67.14.2–3.

17. Jones, Brian W., *The Emperor Domitian*, p.48; Braginton, Mary V., 'Exile under the Roman Emperors', *The Classical Journal*, Vol. 39, No. 7 (Apr 1944), pp.391–407.

18. Suetonius, *Domitian*, 17; Southern, Pat, *Domitian, Tragic Tyrant*, p.115

19. Eusebius, *The History of the Church* (Penguin Classics, 1983), 4.17; Crook, J.A., *Concilium Principis* (Cambridge University Press, 1955), p.45.

20. Dio 67.14.3; Suetonius, *Domitian*, 10; Juvenal, *Satires*, 4.97.

21. Juvenal, *Satires*, 4.94–102.

22. Suetonius, *Domitian*, 10; Philostratus, *Life of Apollonius*, 7.8, 7.33, 8.7; Rutledge, S., *Imperial Inquisitions*, loc. 3244.

23. Suetonius, *Nero*, 37; Dio 62.27.1.

24. Philostratus, *Life of Apollonius*, 7.8, 7.33, 8.7, 8.10; Jones, Brian W., *The Emperor Domitian*, pp.183–84.

25. Dio 67.14.4; Jones, Brian W., *The Emperor Domitian*, p.60. Philostratus, *Life of Apollonius*, 7.32, describes Aelianus giving preferential treatment to the seer which may have warranted his dismissal.

26. Suetonius, *Domitian*, 9.

27. Dio 76.14.4–5. Also see Suetonius, *Domitian*, 14; Syme, R., *Domitian: The Last Years* (Chiron, 1983), pp.121–46.

28. Suetonius, *Nero*, 49; Martial, *Epigrams*, 5.6.2, 4.45, 8.63, 8.68; Weaver, P.R.C., 'Epaphroditus, Josephus, and Epictetus', *The Classical Quarterly*, Vol. 44, No. 2 (1994), pp.468–79; Dobbin, Robert, *Epictetus, Discourses and Selected Writings* (Penguin Classics, 2008), p.X; Jones, Brian W., *The Emperor Domitian*, p.61.

29. Frontinus, *De aquaeductu*, 2.68 and 2.69 mentions the *horti Epaphroditiani* in his work on aqueducts. Epictetus, *Discourses*, 1.19.1; Weaver, P.R.C., 'Epaphroditus, Josephus, and Epictetus', *The Classical Quarterly*, Vol. 44, No. 2 (1994), pp.468–79.

30. Paul, *Letter to the Philippians*, 2:25, 4:18.

31. ILS 1679; Suetonius, *Domitian*, 7.2, 15.1; Jones, Brian W., *The Emperor Domitian*, pp.65, 177; Collins, Andrew W., 'The Palace Revolution: The Assassination of Domitian and Accession of Nerva', *Phoenix*, Vol. 63, No. 1/2 (Spring–Summer 2009), pp.73–106; Pleket, H.W., 'Domitian, the Senate, and the Provinces', *Mnemosyne*, Fourth Series, Vol. 14, Fasc. 4 (1961), pp.296–315. Saller, R.P., *Personal Patronage under the Early Empire*, p.30 citing *Digest*. 1.16.6.3 on the expectation of gifts at the discretion of the magistrate.

32. Suetonius, *Domitian*, 17, states that Stephanus was charged with theft, whilst Philostratus, *Life of Apollonius*, 8.23–25, says he wanted to avenge the death of Clemens and all other victims of the tyrant.

33. Suetonius, *Domitian*, 17; Dio 67.15.1–2.

34. Dio 67.15.1; Eutropius 8.1; Suetonius, *Domitian*, 16.2; Epitome de Caesaribus 11.11–12.

35. Dio 67.15.5; Eutropius 8.1; Epitome de Caesaribus 11.11–12.

36. Dio 67.15.4–5; Eutropius 8.1.

37. Historia Augusta, *Antoninus Pius*, 1.4; Epitome de Caesaribus 12.3.
38. Jones, Brian W., *The Emperor Domitian*, p.59; Grainger, John D., *Nerva and the Roman Succession Crisis, 96–99 AD* (Routledge, 2003), p.20; Collins, Andrew W., 'The Palace Revolution: The Assassination of Domitian and Accession of Nerva', *Phoenix*, Vol. 63, No. 1/2 (Spring–Summer 2009), pp.73–106.
39. Pliny the Younger, *Letters*, 7.33.9; Collins, Andrew W., 'The Palace Revolution: The Assassination of Domitian and Accession of Nerva', *Phoenix*, Vol. 63, No. 1/2 (Spring–Summer 2009), pp.73–106, notes his father, the emperor Otho's elder brother, was married to a Cocceia, probably a sister of Nerva. Although a patrician, whose grandfather and great grandfather were consular senators, he is described by Eutropius 8.1 as being of moderate nobility. For the date of Otho's trial, see Rogers, Robert Samuel, 'A Group of Domitianic Treason-Trials', *Classical Philology*, Vol. 55, No. 1 (Jan 1960), pp.19–23, and Roche, P.A., 'The Execution of L. Salvius Otho Cocceianus', *The Classical Quarterly*, New Series, Vol. 53, No. 1 (May 2003), pp.319–22.
40. Suetonius, *Domitian*, 17; Bingham, Sandra, *The Praetorian Guard: A History of Rome's Elite Special Forces* (I.B. Tauris, 2013), p.85.
41. Grainger, John D., *Nerva and the Roman Succession Crisis, 96–99 AD*, pp.25, 35.
42. Collins, Andrew W., 'The Palace Revolution: The Assassination of Domitian and Accession of Nerva', *Phoenix*, Vol. 63, No. 1/2 (Spring–Summer 2009), pp.73–106; Berriman, Andrew, and Todd, Malcolm, 'A Very Roman Coup: The Hidden War of Imperial Succession, AD 96–8', *Historia: Zeitschrift für Alte Geschichte*, Bd. 50, H. 3 (3rd Qtr 2001), pp.312–31; Talbert, Richard J.A., *The Senate of Imperial Rome* (Princeton, 1984), pp.211–13.
43. Dio 67.17.1–2; Suetonius, *Domitian*, 17.
44. Epitome de Caesaribus 12.2; Jones, Brian W., *The Emperor Domitian*, p.195; Collins, Andrew W., 'The Palace Revolution: The Assassination of Domitian and Accession of Nerva', *Phoenix*, Vol. 63, No. 1/2 (Spring–Summer 2009), pp.73–106; Grainger, John D., *Nerva and the Roman Succession Crisis, 96–99 AD*, p.3; Syme, R., *Tacitus* (Oxford University Press, 1958), p.629.
45. *Fasti Ostiensis* xiiid; Collins, Andrew W., 'The Palace Revolution: The Assassination of Domitian and Accession of Nerva', *Phoenix*, Vol. 63, No. 1/2 (Spring–Summer 2009), pp.73–106.
46. Suetonius, *Domitian*, 17; Dio 67.18.2; Aurelius Victor, *De Caesaribus*, 11; Kłodziński, Karol, and Sawiński, Pawel, 'Domitian's Damnatio: A Critical Case Analysis', *Palamedes* 13 (2019/2020), p.232.
47. Suetonius, *Domitian*, 23; Philostratus, *Lives of the Sophists*, 1.7.1.
48. Suetonius, *Domitian*, 23.
49. Szoke, Martin, 'Condemning Domitian or Un-damning Themselves? Tacitus and Pliny on the Domitianic "Reign of Terror"', *Illinois Classical Studies*, Vol. 44, No. 2 (Fall 2019), pp.430–52; Johansson, Britta Signe, *Damning Domitian: A Historiographical Study of Three Aspects of His Reign*, pp.9–12; Waters, K.H., 'The Character of Domitian', *Phoenix*, Vol. 18, No. 1 (Spring 1964), pp.49–77.
50. Dio 67.15.6. For the story about Seneca, see Dio 59.19.8. Pliny the Younger, *Letters*, 3.11.3–4, 7.27.14. Szoke, Martin, 'Condemning Domitian or Un-damning Themselves? Tacitus and Pliny on the Domitianic "Reign of Terror"', *Illinois Classical Studies*, Vol. 44, No. 2 (Fall 2019), pp.430–52.
51. Dio 67.15.2–4; Suetonius, *Domitian*, 22. For revolts and mutinies in the army on the death of Domitian, see Philostratus, *Life of Apollonius*, 7.8, and Pliny, *Panegyrics*, 5.7, 6.2.

Also see Murison, Charles Leslie, 'M. Cocceius Nerva and the Flavians', *Transactions of the American Philological Association (1974–2014)*, Vol, 133, No. 1 (Spring 2003), pp.147–57; Bennett, Julian, *Trajan Optimus Princeps* (Routledge, 2001), p.35; Syme, R., 'Princesses and Others in Tacitus', *Greece and Rome*, Vol. 28, No. 1, Jubilee Year (Apr 1981), pp.40–52; Waters, K.H., 'The Character of Domitian', *Phoenix*, Vol. 18, No. 1 (Spring 1964), pp.49–77.

52. CIL XV 7293 for brick stamp and CIL XV 553 for the inscription of her freedman. Burns, Jasper, *Domitia Longina, the Survivor* (Routledge, 2007), p.100; Fraser, Trudie E., 'Domitia Longina: An Underestimated Augusta, (c. 53–126/8)', *Ancient Society*, Vol. 45 (2015), pp.205–66.

53. Jones, Brian W., *The Emperor Domitian*, p.194.

54. Dio 68.1.3; Szoke, Martin, 'Condemning Domitian or Un-damning Themselves? Tacitus and Pliny on the Domitianic "Reign of Terror"', *Illinois Classical Studies*, Vol. 44, No. 2 (Fall 2019), pp.430–52.

55. Jones, Brian W., *The Emperor Domitian*, p.195.

56. Grainger, John D., *Nerva and the Roman Succession Crisis, 96–99 AD*, p.42; McAlindon, D., 'Senatorial Opposition to Claudius and Nero', *The American Journal of Philology*, Vol. 77, No. 2 (1956), pp.113–32.

57. Epitome de Caesaribus 12.6; Grainger, John D., *Nerva and the Roman Succession Crisis, 96–99 AD*, pp.69–70; McAlindon, D., 'Senatorial Opposition to Claudius and Nero', *The American Journal of Philology*, Vol. 77, No. 2 (1956), pp.113–32.

58. Dio 68.3.2.

59. Epitome de Caesaribus 12.6.

60. Dio 68.16.2; Historia Augusta, *Hadrian*, 5.6; Carroll, Maureen, *Living Through the Dead, Burial and Commemoration in the Classical World*, ed. Maureen Carroll and Jane Rempel (Oxbow Books, 2011), p.73; McAlindon, D., 'Senatorial Opposition to Claudius and Nero', *The American Journal of Philology*, Vol. 77, No. 2 (1956), pp.113–32.

61. Epitome de Caesaribus 12.7.

62. Dio 68.2.4.

63. Epitome de Caesaribus 12.8; Dio 68.3.3–4; Pliny the Younger, *Panegyric*, 6.1; Grainger, John D.', *Nerva and the Roman Succession Crisis, 96–99 AD*, p.95.

64. Bennett, Julian, *Trajan, Optimus Princeps*, pp.45-46; Szoke, Martin, 'Condemning Domitian or Un-damning Themselves? Tacitus and Pliny on the Domitianic "Reign of Terror"', *Illinois Classical Studies*, Vol. 44, No. 2, (Fall 2019), pp.430–52.

65. Dio 68.3.4; Homer, *Iliad*, 1.43. Kienast, D., 'Nerva und das Kaisertum Trajans,' *Historia* 17 (1968), pp.51–71, suggests Trajan was behind the Praetorian mutiny, but the evidence is tenuous at best.

66. Dio 68.5.4, 68.16.1²; Bennett, Julian, *Trajan, Optimus Princeps*, pp.40, 49. Berriman, Andrew, and Todd, Malcolm, 'A Very Roman Coup: The Hidden War of Imperial Succession, AD 96–8', *Historia: Zeitschrift für Alte Geschichte*, Bd. 50, H. 3 (3rd Qtr 2001), pp.312–31, suggests Aelianus travelled to Trajan's headquarters on the Rhine, suggesting that he was in league with him but was executed as their association was a political embarrassment.

Conclusion

1. Pliny the Younger, *Letters*, 10.58.7–10; Saller, R.P., *Personal Patronage Under the Early Empire*, p.41; Millar, Fergus, *The Emperor in the Roman World* (Duckworth, 1977), p.144.

2. Suetonius, *Galba*, 3, 35. Nicolaus of Damascus, *Life of Augustus* (Attalus), 63; Dio 43.47.5; Paterson, Jeremy, 'Friends in High Places', in *The Court and Court Society in*

Ancient Monarchies (Cambridge University Press, 2009), p.133; Saller, R.P., *Personal Patronage Under the Early Empire*, p.50.

3. Epictetus, *Discourses*, 4.1.6.

4. Saller, R.P., *Personal Patronage Under the Early Empire*, p.78.

5. Seneca, *De Clementia*, 1.13.5; Paterson, Jeremy, 'Friends in High Places', in *The Court and Court Society in Ancient Monarchies*, p.143. See also Pliny, *Panegyrics*, 2.4.

6. Wallace-Hadrill, Andrew, 'Civilis Princeps: Between Citizen and King', *The Journal of Roman Studies*, Vol. 72 (1982), pp.32–48.

7. Paterson, Jeremy, 'Friends in High Places', in *The Court and Court Society in Ancient Monarchies*, p.122.

8. Josephus, *Jewish Antiquities*, 19.17–19; Pagán, Victoria Emma, *Conspiracy Narratives in Roman History*, pp.99, 105–06.

9. Dio 54.15.2–3; Paterson, Jeremy, 'Friends in High Places', in *The Court and Court Society in Ancient Monarchies*, p.137; Rutledge, S., *Imperial Inquisitions: Prosecutors and Informants from Tiberius to Domitian*, loc. 164.

10. Pliny the Younger, *Letters*, 3.5.4; Omissi, Adrastos, 'Damnatio Memoriae or Creatio Memoriae? Memory Sanctions as Creative Processes in the Fourth Century AD', *The Cambridge Classical Journal*, Vol. 62 (2006), pp.170–99; Carroll, Maureen, *Living Through the Dead*, pp.73, 83.

11. Varhelyi, Zsuzsanna, *The Religion of Senators in the Roman Empire: Power and Beyond* (Cambridge University Press, 2010), pp.199–200, citing CIL VI 1348.

12. Syme, R., *The Augustan Aristocracy*, p.192; McAlindon, D., 'Senatorial Opposition to Claudius and Nero', *The American Journal of Philology*, Vol. 77, No. 2 (1956), pp.113–32.

13. Syme, R., *The Augustan Aristocracy*, pp.255–69.

14. Królczyk, K., 'Rebellion of Caius Iulius Vindex Against Emperor Nero', Vestnik of Saint Petersburg University, *History*, Vol. 63, issue 3 (2018), pp.858–71.

15. Bingham, Sandra, *The Praetorian Guard: A History of Rome's Elite Special Forces*, pp.38–39, 85.

16. Dio 60 14.4; Tacitus, *Annals*, 6.9; McAlindon, D., 'Senatorial Opposition to Claudius and Nero', *The American Journal of Philology*, Vol. 77, No. 2 (1956), pp.113–32.

17. Paterson, Jeremy, 'Friends in High Places', in *The Court and Court Society in Ancient Monarchies*, p.137.

18. Dio 55.27.3; Digest 47.10.5.11; Rutledge, S., *Imperial Inquisitions*, loc. 786, 3127.

19. Rutledge, S., *Imperial Inquisitions*, loc. 164; Pagán, Victoria Emma, *Conspiracy Narratives in Roman History*, p.88.

20. Winterling, Aloys, *Politics and Society in Imperial Rome* (Wiley-Blackwell, 2009), p.32, who interprets some conspiracies as a form of institutional conflict due to the paradoxical position of a constitution that recognized Republican institutions at the same time as sanctioning the absolute monarchical power of an emperor.

21. McAlindon, D., 'Senatorial Opposition to Claudius and Nero', *The American Journal of Philology*, Vol. 77, No. 2 (1956), pp.113–32.

22. Paterson, Jeremy, 'Friends in High Places', in *The Court and Court Society in Ancient Monarchies*, pp.133–37; Winterling, Aloys, *Politics and Society in Imperial Rome*, p.93.

23. Tacitus, *Annals*, 13.43.3; Rutledge, S., *Imperial Inquisitions*, loc. 828, 2700.

24. Epictetus, *Discourses*, 4.39; Paterson, Jeremy, 'Friends in High Places', in *The Court and Court Society in Ancient Monarchies*, pp.139–40; Rutledge, S., *Imperial Inquisitions*, loc. 2040.

25. Rutledge, S., *Imperial Inquisitions*, loc. 3559.

26. Syme, R., *The Augustan Aristocracy*, p.122.
27. Philo, *Embassy to Gaius*, 68; Barrett, Anthony A., *Caligula, the Corruption of Power*, p.76; Winterling, Aloys, *Caligula, A Biography*, pp.65–66.
28. Seneca, *Moral Letters to Lucilius*, 70.10; Tacitus, *Annals*, 15.48; Mellor, Ronald, *Tacitus*, pp.77, 110; Marsh, Frank Burr, 'Tacitus and Aristocratic Tradition', *Classical Philology*, Vol. 21, No. 4 (Oct 1926), pp.289–310; Paterson, Jeremy, 'Friends in High Places', in *The Court and Court Society in Ancient Monarchies*, p.138; Syme, R., *Tacitus*, p.574.
29. Tacitus, *Agricola*, 42.
30. Paterson, Jeremy, 'Friends in High Places', in *The Court and Court Society in Ancient Monarchies*, p.138.
31. Epictetus, *Discourses*, 3.8.
32. Tacitus, *Annals*, 15.50.
33. Josephus, *Jewish Antiquities*, 19.46–48.
34. Dio 60.15.2.
35. Saller, R.P., *Personal Patronage Under the Early Empire*, p.59.
36. Tacitus, *Annals*, 15.50.
37. Epictetus, *Discourses*, 4.13.5.
38. Bingham, Sandra, *The Praetorian Guard in the Political and Social Life of Julio-Claudian Rome*, pp.72–73.
39. Josephus, *Jewish Antiquities*, 19.49. Due probably to a copyist's error, the conspirator Vinicianus is named as Minucianus in the original manuscript.
40. Tacitus, *Annals*, 15.47, 65.
41. Tacitus, *Annals*, 15.65.
42. Bingham, Sandra, *The Praetorian Guard in the Political and Social Life of Julio-Claudian Rome*, pp.76–78.
43. Josephus, *Jewish Antiquities*, 19.52–53.
44. Suetonius, *Claudius*, 25, 35, also 12.3.
45. Josephus, *Jewish Antiquities*, 19.32–35; Suetonius, *Gaius*, 16.4; Rutledge, S., *Imperial Inquisitions*, loc. 3942.
46. Tacitus, *Annals*, 15.51, 15.57; Dio 62.27.3.
47. Pagán, Victoria Emma, *Conspiracy Narratives in Roman History*, pp.6,16; Paterson, Jeremy, 'Friends in High Places', in *The Court and Court Society in Ancient Monarchies*, p.140.
48. Mellor, Ronald, *Tacitus*, p.105; Saller, R.P., *Personal Patronage Under the Early Empire*, pp.15, 71.
49. Saller, R.P., *Personal Patronage Under the Early Empire*, p.78.

Bibliography

Abbreviations
AE - *L'Annee Epigraphique* (Paris, 1888)
CIL - *Corpus Inscriptionum Latinarum* (Berlin, 1867)
ILS - Dessau, H., *Inscriptiones Latinae Selectae* (Berlin, 1892–1916)
PIR - *Prosopographia Imperii Romani* (Berlin and Leipzig, 1933)

Ancient sources
Appian, *The Civil Wars* (Penguin, 1996)
Aristotle, *Politics*, trans. T. Sinclair (Penguin Classics, 1981)
Aurelius Victor, *De Caesaribus*, trans. H.W. Bird (Liverpool University Press, 1994)
Caesar, *De Bello Africo*, trans. and notes Thomas De Quincey (CreateSpace Independent Publishing Platform, Illustrated edition, 8 Jan. 2014)
Calpurnius Siculus, *The Eclogues*, trans. and commentary C.H. Keene (Bristol Classical Press, 2005)
Cassius Dio, *Roman History*, trans. E. Cary (Loeb Classical Library, 1989)
Cicero, *Letters to Atticus* (Penguin Classics)
Cicero, *Letters to Friends*, trans. D.R. Shackleton Bailey (Loeb Classical Library, 2001)
Cicero, *On Divination*, trans. W.A. Falconer (Loeb Classical Library, 1989)
Cicero, *Philippics*, trans. D.R. Shackleton Bailey (Loeb Classical Library, 2001)
Cornelius Nepos, *Life of Atticus*, trans. Rev J.S. Watson (Attalus)
Dio Chrysostom (Dio of Prusa), *Orations on Kingship*, in *Discourses* 1–11, trans. J.W. Cohoon (Loeb, 1932)
Epictetus, *Discourses*, trans. W.A. Oldfather (Loeb, 1989)
Epitome de Caesaribus, https://web.archive.org/web/20220311020340/http://www.roman-emperors.org/epitome.htm
Eusebius, *The History of the Church*, trans. G.A. Williamson (Penguin, 1989)
Eutropius, *Breviarium*, trans. and commentary H.W. Bird (Liverpool University Press, 1993)
Frontinus, 'De aquaeductu', in *The Complete Works of Frontinus* (Delphi Classics, 2015)
Historia Augusta, *Alexander Severus*, vol. 2, trans. David Magie (Loeb, 1989)
Historia Augusta, *Antoninus Pius*, vol. 1, trans David Magie (Loeb, 1989)
Historia Augusta, *Hadrian*, vol. 1, trans. David Magie (Loeb, 1989)
Homer, *Iliad*, trans. Martin Hammond (Penguin, 1987)
Horace, *The Complete Odes and Satires of Horace*, Lockert Library of Poetry in Translation, trans. Sydney Alexander (Princeton University Press, 1999)
Josephus, *Jewish Antiquities* (Wordsworth Classics of World Literature, 2006)
Josephus, *The Jewish Wars*, trans. Martin Hammond (Oxford University Press, 2017)
Justinian, *Digest of Justinian* (University of Pennsylvania Press, 2008)
Juvenal, *Satires*, in *Juvenal and Persius*, trans. Susanna Morton Braund (Loeb, 2004)
Laus Pisonis, in Loeb Classical Library (Harvard University Press, 1934, revised 1935)
Macrobius, *Saturnalia*, trans. Robert A. Kaster (Loeb, 2010)

Martial, *Epigrams*, trans. Gideon Nisbet (Oxford University Press, 2015)

Nicolaus of Damascus, *Life of Augustus* (Attalus)

Orosius, *Seven Books of History Against the Pagans* (Liverpool University Press, 2010)

Ovid, *Heriodes*, trans. Harold Isbell (Penguin, 1990)

Ovid, *Fasti*, in *Metamorphoses*, trans. Frank Justus Miller (Loeb, 1989)

Ovid, *Tristia, Ex Ponto*, trans. A.L. Wheeler (Loeb, 1989)

Paul, *Letter to the Philippians*, trans. Gordon D. Fee (Eerdmans, 1995)

Philo, *In Flaccum*, in *Philo*, vol. 1, trans. F.H. Colson and G.H. Whitaker (Loeb, 1989)

Philo, *On the Embassy to Gaius*, in *Philo*, vol. 1, trans. F.H. Colson and G.H. Whitaker (Loeb, 1989)

Philostratus, *Life of Apollonius of Tyana* (Legare Street Press, 2022)

Philostratus, *Lives of the Sophists*, in *Philostratus, Lives of the Sophists and Eunapius, Lives of the Philosophers* (Loeb, 1813)

Phlegon of Tralles, *Book of Marvels*, trans. William Hansen (Liverpool University Press, 1997)

Plato, *Phaedo*, trans. David Gallop (Oxford University Press, 2009)

Plato, *Politicus* (Routledge and Kegan Paul, 1952)

Plato, *Republic*, trans. H.D.P. Lee (Penguin Classics, 2007)

Pliny the Elder, *Natural History*, trans. John Bostock (independently published, 2021)

Pliny the Younger, *Letters*, vol. 1, trans. Betty Radice (Loeb Classical Library 1989)

Pliny the Younger, *Panegyricus*, vol. 1, trans. Betty Radice (Loeb Classical Library 1989)

Plutarch, *Life of Antony* (Penguin Classics, 1982)

Plutarch, *Life of Brutus* (Penguin Classics, 1982)

Plutarch, *Life of Caesar* (Penguin Classics, 1982)

Plutarch, *Life of Galba*, in *Lives*, vol. XI (Loeb, 1989)

Plutarch, *Moralia*, trans. W.C. Helmbold (Harvard University Press, 1939)

Polyaenus, *Stratagems* (www.attalus.org)

Quintilian, *Complete Works of Quintilian* (Delphi Classics, 2015)

Res Gestae Divi Augusti, ed. and commentary P.A. Brunt and J.M. Moore (Oxford University Press, 1967)

Seneca, *Apocolocyntosis divi Claudii*, in *Petronius: The Satyricon* and *Seneca: The Apocolocyntosis* (Penguin, 1977)

Seneca, *De Beneficiis*, in *Moral Essays*, vol. 3, trans. John W. Basore (Loeb, 1989)

Seneca, *De Brevitate Vitae*, in *Moral Essays*, vol. 2, trans. John W. Basore (Loeb, 1932)

Seneca, *De Clementia*, in *Moral Essays*, vol. 1, trans. John W. Basore (Loeb, 1989)

Seneca, *De Consolatione ad Helvium*, vol. 2, trans. John W. Basore (Loeb, 1932)

Seneca, *De Consolatio ad Polybium*, in *Moral Essays*, vol. 2, trans. John W. Basore (Loeb, 1932)

Seneca, *De Constantia Sapientis*, in *Moral Essays*, vol. 1, trans. John W. Basore (Loeb, 1989)

Seneca, *De Ira*, in *Moral Essays*, vol. 1, trans. John W. Basore (Loeb, 1989)

Seneca, *De Providentia*, in *Moral Essays*, vol. 1, trans. John W. Basore (Loeb Classical Library, 1989)

Seneca, *Dialogues*, in *Dialogues and Letters*, trans. C. Costa (Penguin, 1997)

Seneca, *Epistulae Morales*, trans. Richard M. Gummere (Loeb, 1989)

Seneca, *Letters from a Stoic* (Penguin Classics, 2004)

Seneca, *Moral Letters to Lucilius* (CreateSpace Independent Publishing Platform, 2018)

Seneca, *Natural Questions*, trans. Thomas H. Corcoran (Loeb, 1989)

Seneca, *Octavia*, in *Tragedies*, vol. 2, *Oedipus, Agamemnon, Thyestes, Hercules on Oeta, Octavia* (Loeb, 2018)

Strabo, *Geography*, trans. Horace Leonard Jones (Loeb, 1989)

Suetonius, *The Twelve Caesars* (Penguin Classics, 1986)

Tacitus, *Agricola*, in *Agricola and Germania*, trans. H. Mattingly (Penguin, 2010)

Tacitus, *Annals*, trans. John Jackson (Loeb Classical Library, 1989)

Tacitus, *Histories*, trans. Clifford H. Moore (Loeb, 1989)

Valerius Maximus, *Memorable Deeds and Sayings* (Hackett Publishing Company, 2004)

Velleius Paterculus, *The Roman History*, trans. and notes J.C. Yardley and Anthony A. Barrett, (Hackett Publishing Company, Inc., 2001)

Vita Lucani (livingpoets.dur.ac.uk/w/Suetonius, Vita_Lucani; website now defunct)

Modern

Akinboye, Goke A., 'Women's Ambition, Ambitious Women: The Case of Caesar's Household During the Julio-Claudian Era', *Journal of Management and Social Sciences* (2017).

Allison, J.E., and Cloud, J.D., 'The lex Julia Maiestatis', *Latomus*, t. 21, Fasc. 4 (Octobre–Decembre 1962)

Alston, Richard, *Aspects of Roman History AD 14–117* (Routledge, 1998)

Arkenberg, Jerome S., 'Licinii Murenae Terentii Varrones, and Varrones Murenae: II. The Enigma of Varro Murena', *Historia: Zeitschrift für Alte Geschichte*, Bd. 42, H. 4 (4th Qtr 1993)

Atkinson, Kathleen M.T., 'Constitutional and Legal Aspects of the Trials of Marcus Primus and Varro Murena', *Historia: Zeitschrift für Alte Geschichte*, Bd. 9, H. 4 (Oct 1960)

Balsdon, J.P.V.D., 'The Ides of March', *Historia: Zeitschrift für Alte Geschichte*, Bd. 7, H. 1 (Jan 1958)

Barrett, Anthony A., *Agrippina: Sex, Power, and Politics in the Early Empire* (Routledge, 1999)

Barrett, Anthony A., *Caligula, The Corruption of Power* (B.T. Batsford, 1999)

Barrett, Anthony A., and Yeardley, J.C., trans. and notes to *Velleius Paterculus, The Roman History* (Hackett Publishing Company, Inc., 2001)

Barry, William D., 'Exposure, Mutilation, and Riot: Violence at the Scalae Gemoniae in Early Imperial Rome', *Greece, and Rome* (Second Series), Vol. 55, No. 2 (Oct 2008)

Bastomsky, S.J., 'Proculeius and Augustus: A Note on a Friendship turned Sour', *Latomus*, t. 36, Fasc. 1 (Janvier–Mars 1977)

Bauman, R.A., *Crime and Punishment in Ancient Rome* (Routledge, 1996)

Bauman, R.A., 'Tiberius and Murena', *Historia: Zeitschrift für Alte Geschichte*, Bd. 15, H. 4 (Nov 1966)

Bauman, R.A., *Women and Politics in Ancient Rome* (Routledge, 1994)

Bennett, Julian, *Trajan Optimus Princeps* (Routledge, 2001)

Berriman, Andrew, and Todd, Malcolm, 'A Very Roman Coup: The Hidden War of Imperial Succession, AD 96–8', *Historia: Zeitschrift für Alte Geschichte*, Bd. 50, H. 3 (3rd Qtr 2001)

Bertrand Crettez, Bertrand, and Deloche, Régis, 'An analytic narrative of Caesar's death: Suicide or not? That is the question', *Rationality and Society* (2018)

Bingham, Sandra J., *The Praetorian Guard: A History of Rome's Elite Special Forces* (I.B. Tauris, (2015)

Bingham, Sandra J., *The Praetorian Guard in the Political and Social Life of Julio-Claudian Rome* (PhD Thesis, University of British Columbia, 1977)

Birch, R.A., 'The Settlement of 26 June A.D. 4 and Its Aftermath', *The Classical Quarterly*, Vol. 31, No. 2 (1981)

Birley, Anthony R., *The Fasti of Roman Britain* (Clarendon Press, 1981)

Braginton, Mary V., 'Exile under the Roman Emperors', *The Classical Journal*, Vol. 39, No. 7 (Apr 1944)

Burns, Jasper, *Domitia Longina, the Survivor* (Routledge, 2007)

Burns, Jasper, *Great Women of Imperial Rome: Mothers and Wives of the Caesars* (Routledge, 2006)

Canfora, Luciano, *The Hetairia of Cassius and the Recruitment of Brutus in Julius Caesar, The People's Dictator* (Edinburgh University Press, 2007)

Carandini, Andrea, *The Atlas of Ancient Rome, Biography and Portraits of the City*, Vol. 1 (Princeton University Press, 2017)

Carroll, Maureen, 'Memoria and Damnatio Memoriae. Preserving and Erasing Identities in Roman Funerary Commemoration', in *Living Through the Dead, Burial and Commemoration in the Classical World* (Oxbow Books, 2011)

Champlin, Edward, *The Life and Times of Calpurnius Piso* (Museum Helveticum, Vol. 46, (1989)

Chilton, C.W., 'The Roman Law of Treason under the Early Principate', *The Journal of Roman Studies*, Vol. 45, Parts 1 and 2 (1955)

Claridge, Amanda, *Rome, An Archaeological Guide* (Oxford University Press, 2010)

Clark, Gillian, 'Roman Women', *Greece and Rome*, Vol. 28, No. 2, Jubilee Year (Oct 1981)

Clarke, M.L., *The Noblest Roman: Marcus Brutus and His Reputation* (Thames and Hudson, 1981)

Cohen, Sarah T., 'Augustus, Julia and the Development of Exile "Ad Insulam"', *The Classical Quarterly*, New Series, Vol. 58, No. 1 (May 2008)

Collins, Andrew W., 'The Palace Revolution: The Assassination of Domitian and Accession of Nerva', *Phoenix*, Vol. 63, No. 1/2 (Spring–Summer/printemps–été 2009)

Cowan, Robert, 'Lucan's Thunder-Box: Scatology, Epic, and Satire in Suetonius' "Vita Lucani"', *Harvard Studies in Classical Philology*, Vol. 106 (2011)

Crawford, M.H., *Roman Republican Coinage* (Cambridge, 1974)

Crook, J.A., 'Augustus: Power, Authority, Achievement', in *The Cambridge Ancient History* (eds Bowman, A.K., Champlin, E., and Lintott, A, 1996)

Crook, J.A., *Concilium Principis* (Cambridge University Press, 1955)

Crook, J.A., 'Political History, 30 BC to AD 14', in *The Cambridge Ancient History* (eds Bowman, A.K., Champlin, E., and Lintott, A., 1996)

Daley, Lawrence J., 'Augustus and the Murder of Varro Murena ("cos" 23 B.C.)', *Klio* (1 Jan 1984)

De La Bédoyère, Guy, *Praetorian: The Rise and Fall of Rome's Imperial Bodyguard* (Yale University Press, 2017)

Dobbin, Robert, *Epictetus, Discourses and Selected Writings* (Penguin Classics, 2008)

Eager, Max, *The Pisonian Conspiracy* (MPhil thesis, 2012, Oxford University, www.academia.edu/43203930/The_Pisonian_Conspiracy)

Eck, Werner, *Augustus*, trans. Deborah Lucas Schneider (Blackwell, 1998)

Epstein, David F., 'Caesar's Personal Enemies on the Ides of March', *Latomus*, t. 46, Fasc. 3 (Juillet–Septembre 1987)

Fagan, Garrett G., 'Messalina's Folly', *The Classical Quarterly*, Vol. 52, No. 2 (2002)

Fantham, Elaine, *Julia Augusti, The Emperor's Daughter* (Routledge, 2006)

Fishwick, Duncan, and Shaw, Brent D., 'Ptolemy of Mauretania, and the Conspiracy of Gaetulicus', *Historia: Zeitschrift für Alte Geschichte*, Bd. 25, H. 4 (4th Qtr 1976)

Flaig, Egon, *Plebs und Princeps, Neue Praktiken und semantische Restrukturierungen im frühen Principat* (2021, Academia.edu download)

Flower, Harriet I., *The Art of Forgetting: Disgrace and Oblivion in Roman Political Culture* (University of North Carolina Press, 2006)

Fraser, Trudie E., 'Domitia Longina: An Underestimated Augusta, (c. 53–126/8)', *Ancient Society*, Vol. 45 (2015)

Freudenburg, Kirk, 'La corte imperial', *Arqueología e Historia*, n. 27 (September 2019)

Fuller, Major-General J.F., *Julius Caesar: Man, Soldier, and Tyrant* (Eyre and Spottiswoode 1965)

Gallivan, Paul, 'Who was Acilius?', *Historia: Zeitschrift für Alte Geschichte*, Bd. 27, H. 4 (4th Qtr 1978)

Garzetti, Albino, *From Tiberius to the Antonines, A History of the Roman Empire, AD 14–192* (Routledge, 1974)

Goldsworthy, Adrian, *Augustus, From Revolutionary to Emperor* (Weidenfeld & Nicolson, 2014)

Goldsworthy, Adrian, *Caesar, The Life of a Colossus* (Weidenfeld & Nicolson, 2006)

Grainger, John D., *Nerva and the Roman Succession Crisis, 96–99 AD* (Routledge, 2002)

Griffen, Miriam T., *Nero, The End of a Dynasty* (B.T. Batsford, 1984)

Grubbs, Judith Evans, *Women and the Law in the Roman Empire, a Sourcebook on Marriage, Divorce and Widowhood* (Routledge, 2002)

Habaj, Michal, 'Plutarch, Moralia 505C: Some Notes on the Discovery of the Pisonian Conspiracy', *Acta Ant. Hung.*, 56 (2016)

Haynes, Holly, 'The Tyrant Lists: Tacitus' Obituary of Petronius', *The American Journal of Philology*, Vol. 131, No. 1 (Spring 2010)

Holland, Richard, *Augustus: Godfather of Europe* (Sutton Publishing, 2004)

Holland, Tom, *Rubicon: The Triumph and Tragedy of the Roman Republic* (Abacus, 2003)

Holmes, Richard, *Nero, The Man Behind the Myth* (Sutton Publishing, 2000)

Horsfall, Nicolaus, 'The Ides of March: Some New Problems', *Greece & Rome*, Vol. 21, No. 2 (Oct 1974)

Ingleheart, Jennifer, 'What the Poet saw: Ovid, the Error and the Theme of Sight in Tristia 2', *Materiali e discussioni per l'analsi dei testi classici*, No. 56 (2006)

Johansson, Britta Signe, *Damning Domitian: A Historiographical Study of Three Aspects of His Reign* (Thesis for degree, University of Queensland, November 2013)

Jones, Brian W., *The Emperor Domitian* (Routledge, 1993)

Joshel, Sandra R., 'Female Desire and the Discourse of Empire: Tacitus's Messalina', *Signs*, Vol. 21, No. 1 (Autumn 1995)

Keegan, Peter, *Boudica, Cartimandua, Messalina and Agrippina the Younger. Independent Women of Power and the Gendered Rhetoric of Roman History* (www.ancienthistory.com. au/teachers.html, 2005)

Keene, C.H., *Calpurnius Siculus, The Eclogues* (Bristol Classical Press, 2005)

Keppie, Lawrence, 'The Army and Navy' (Chapter Eleven), in *The Augustan Empire, 43 BC–69 AD*, Cambridge Ancient History, vol. 10, ed. Alan K. Bowman, Edward Champlin and Andrew Lintott (Cambridge University Press, 1996)

Kienast, D., 'Nerva und das Kaisertum Trajans', *Historia* 17 (1968)

Kłodziński, Karol, and Sawiński, Pawel, 'Domitian's Damnatio: A Critical Case Analysis', *Palamedes* 13 (2019/2020)

Królczyk K., 'Rebellion of Caius Iulius Vindex Against Emperor Nero', Vestnik of Saint Petersburg University, *History*, Vol. 63, issue 3 (2018)

Lacey, W., 'Augustus and the Senate: 23 B.C.', *Antichthon*, 19 (1985)

Lacey, W., '2 B.C. and Julia's Adultery', *Antichthon*, 14 (1980)

Laurence, Ray, 'Rumour and Communication in Roman Politics', *Greece & Rome*, Vol. 41, No. 1 (April 1994)

Levick, Barbara, *Claudius* (Routledge, 1990)

Levick, Barbara, 'Corbulo's Daughter', *Greece and Rome*, Vol. 49, No. 2 (2002)

Levick, Barbara, 'Primus, Murena, and "Fides": Notes on Cassius Dio Liv. 3', *Greece & Rome*, Vol. 22, No. 2 (Oct 1975)

Levick, Barbara, 'The Fall of Julia the Younger', *Latomus*, t. 35, Fasc. 2 (Avril–Juin 1976)

Levick, Barbara, *Tiberius, the Politician* (Routledge, 1986)

L'Hoir, Francesca Santoro, 'Tacitus and Women's Usurpation of Power', *The Classical World*, Vol. 88, No. 1 (Sep–Oct 1994)

Linderski, J., 'Julia in Rhegium', *Zeitschrift für Papyrologie und Epigraphik*, Bd. 72 (1988)

Lintott, Andrew, 'The Assassination', Chapter 6, in *A Companion to Julius Caesar*, ed. Miriam Griffin (Blackwell Publishing, 2009)

MacMullen, Ramsey, *Enemies of the Roman Order: Treason, Unrest, and Alienation in the Empire* (Routledge, 1992)

Marsh, Frank Burr, 'Tacitus and Aristocratic Tradition', *Classical Philology*, Vol. 21, No. 4 (Oct 1926)

Martindale, Charles, 'The Politician Lucan', *Greece & Rome*, Vol. 31, No. 1 (Apr 1984)

Mason, Steve, 'Of Despots, Diadems and Diadochoi: Josephus and Flavian Politics', in *Writing Politics in Imperial Rome*, ed. W.J. Dominik, J. Garthwaite and P.A. Roche (Brill, 2009)

McAlindon, D., 'Senatorial Opposition to Claudius and Nero', *The American Journal of Philology*, Vol. 77, No. 2 (1956)

McDermott, William C., 'Varro Murena', *Transactions and Proceedings of the American Philological Association*, Vol. 72 (1941)

McHugh, John, *Sejanus, Regent of Rome* (Pen & Sword, 2020)

Mellor, Ronald, *Tacitus* (Routledge, 1993)

Millar, Fergus, *The Emperor in the Roman World* (Duckworth, 1977)

Millar, Fergus, *A Study of Cassius Dio* (Oxford, 1999)

Murison, Charles Leslie, 'M. Cocceius Nerva and the Flavians', *Transactions of the American Philological Association*, Vol. 133, No. 1 (Spring 2003)

Omissi, Adrastos, 'Damnatio Memoriae or Creatio Memoriae? Memory Sanctions as Creative Processes in the Fourth Century AD', *The Cambridge Classical Journal*, Vol. 62 (2006)

Osgood, Josiah, 'Nero and the Senate', in *The Cambridge Companion to the Age of Nero* (Cambridge University Press, 2017)

Pagán, Victoria Emma, *Conspiracy Narratives in Roman History* (University of Texas Press, 2004)

Parat, Josip, 'Reconsidering the Traces of Scribonianus' Rebellion', *Radovi – Zavod za hrvatsku povijest*, Vol. 48 (Zagreb, 2016)

Parker, Philip, *The Empire Stops Here, A Journey Along the Frontiers of the Roman World* (Pimlico, 2009)

Paterson, Jeremy, 'Friends in High Places: The Creation of the Court of the Roman Emperor', in *The Court and Court Society in Ancient Monarchies*, ed. A.J.S. Spawforth (Cambridge University Press 2009)

Pettinger, Andrew, *The Republic in Danger: Drusus Libo and the Succession of Tiberius* (Oxford University Press, 2012)

Phillips, Darryl A., 'The Conspiracy of Egnatius Rufus and the Election of Suffect Consuls under Augustus', *Historia: Zeitschrift für Alte Geschichte*, Bd. 46, H. 1 (1st Qtr 1997)

Pleket, H.W., 'Domitian, the Senate, and the Provinces', *Mnemosyne*, Fourth Series, Vol. 14, Fasc. 4 (1961)

Ramsey, John, *At What Hour Did the Murderers Of Julius Caesar Gather On The Ides Of March 44 BC?* (www.academia.edu/11118065/)

Rawson, Piers B., *The Myth of Marsyas in Roman Visual Art* (ProQuest Dissertations Publishing, 1986)

Raymond, Nicholas, *Meretrix Augusta, A Literary Examination of Messalina in Tacitus and Juvenal* (MA Thesis, McMaster University, June 1990)

Richardson, J.S., *Augustan Rome 44 BC to AD 14: The Restoration of the Republic and the Establishment of the Empire* (Edinburgh University Press, 2012)

Roche, P.A., 'The Execution of L. Salvius Otho Cocceianus', *The Classical Quarterly*, New Series, Vol. 53, No. 1 (May 2003)

Rogers, Robert Samuel, 'A Group of Domitianic Treason-Trials', *Classical Philology*, Vol. 55, No. 1 (Jan 1960)

Rogers, Robert Samuel, 'A Tacitean Pattern in Narrating Treason-Trials', *Transactions and Proceedings of the American Philological Association*, Vol. 83 (1952)

Rogers, Robert Samuel, 'Domitius Afer's Defense of Cloatilla', *Transactions and Proceedings of the American Philological Association*, Vol. 76 (1945)

Rogers, Robert Samuel, 'Heirs and Rivals to Nero', *Transactions and Proceedings of the American Philological Association*, Vol. 86 (1955)

Rogers, Robert Samuel, 'The Deaths of Julia and Gracchus, A.D. 14', *Transactions and Proceedings of the American Philological Association*, Vol. 98 (1967)

Rogers, Robert Samuel, 'Treason in the Early Empire', *The Journal of Roman Studies*, Vol. 49, Parts 1 and 2 (1959)

Rowland, Jr, Robert J., 'The Conspiracy of Varro Murena', *The Classical Journal*, Vol. 62, No. 8 (May 1967)

Rudich, Vasily, *Political Dissidence under Nero: The Price of Dissimulation* (Taylor and Francis Group, 1993)

Rutledge, Steven H., 'Delatores and the Tradition of Violence in Roman Oratory', *The American Journal of Philology*, Vol. 120, No. 4 (Winter 1999)

Rutledge, Steven H., *Imperial Inquisitions: Prosecutors and Informants from Tiberius to Nero* (Routledge, 2001, Kindle edition)

Saller, R.P., *Personal Patronage under the Early Empire* (Cambridge University Press, 2010)

Sandison, A.T., 'The Madness of the Emperor Caligula' (Cambridge University Press, 2012)

Sawiński, Paweł, 'The Succession of Imperial Power under the Julio-Claudian Dynasty (30 BC–AD 68)', *Internationaler Verlag der Wissenschaften* (Berlin, 2018)

Scott, Anna Elizabeth, *The Influence of the Roman Atrium-House's Architecture and Use of Space in Engendering the Power and Independence of the Materfamilias* (Brigham Young University, 2012)

Sedley, David, 'The Ethics of Brutus and Cassius', *The Journal of Roman Studies*, Vol. 87 (1997)

Shotter, David C.A., 'Agrippina the Elder: A Woman in a Man's World', *Historia: Zeitschrift für Alte Geschichte*, Bd. 49, H. 3 (3rd Qtr 2000)

Southern, Pat, *Domitian Tragic Tyrant* (Routledge, 2009)

Stevenson, Tom, 'The Succession Planning of Augustus', *Antichthon*, Vol. 47, Thematic Issue: Culture, Identity and Politics in the Ancient Mediterranean World (2013)

Stewart, Zeph, 'Sejanus, Gaetulicus, and Seneca', *The American Journal of Philology*, Vol. 74, No. 1 (1953)

Stockton, David, 'Primus and Murena', *Historia: Zeitschrift für Alte Geschichte*, Bd. 14, H. 1 (Jan 1965)

Sumi, Geoffrey, 'Ceremony and the Emergence of Court Society in the Augustan Principate', *The American Journal of Philology*, Vol. 132, No. 1, Classical Courts and Courtiers (Spring 2011)

Swan, Michael, 'The Consular Fasti of 23 B.C. and the Conspiracy of Varro Murena', *Harvard Studies in Classical Philology*, Vol. 71 (1967)

Swan, McDermott, and Arkenberg, Jerome S., 'Licinii Murenae Terentii Varrones, and Varrones Murenae: II. The Enigma of Varro Murena', *Historia: Zeitschrift für Alte Geschichte*, Bd. 42, H. 4 (4th Qtr 1993)

Syme, Ronald, *Antonius Saturninus*, Roman Papers, Vol. III (Oxford University Press, 1984)

Syme, Ronald, *Domitian: The Last Years* (Chiron, 1983)

Syme, Ronald, 'Domitius Corbulo', *The Journal of Roman Studies*, Vol. 60 (1970

Syme, Ronald, 'Marcus Lepidus, Capax Imperii', *The Journal of Roman Studies*, Vol. 45, Parts 1 and 2 (1955)

Syme, Ronald, 'M. Vinicius (Cos. 19 B.C.)', *The Classical Quarterly*, Vol. 27. No. ¾ (July–Oct 1933)

Syme, Ronald, 'Princesses and Others in Tacitus', *Greece and Rome*, Vol. 28, No. 1, (April 1981)

Syme, Ronald, *Tacitus* (Oxford University Press 1958)

Syme, Ronald, *The Augustan Aristocracy* (Clarendon Press-Oxford, 1986)

Syme, Ronald, *The Crisis of 2 BC*, Roman Papers, Vol. III (Clarendon Press, 1981)

Syme, Ronald, *The Roman Revolution* (Oxford University Press, 1979)

Syme, Ronald, *The Stemma of the Sentii Saturnini*, Roman Papers, Vol. II (Oxford University Press, 1979)

Szoke, Martin, 'Condemning Domitian or Un-damning Themselves? Tacitus and Pliny on the Domitianic "Reign of Terror"', *Illinois Classical Studies*, Vol. 44, No. 2, (Fall 2019, University of Illinois)

Talbert, Richard J.A., 'The Senate and Senatorial and Equestrian Posts', in *The Augustan Empire, 43 BC–69 AD*, Cambridge Ancient History, Vol. 10, ed. Alan K. Bowman, Edward Champlin and Andrew Lintott (Cambridge University Press, 1996)

Varhelyi, Zsuzsanna, *The Religion of Senators in the Roman Empire: Power and Beyond* (Cambridge University Press, 2010)

Varner, Eric R., 'Portraits, Plots, and Politics: "Damnatio memoriae" and the Images of Imperial Women', *Memoirs of the American Academy in Rome*, Vol. 46 (2001)

Vervaet, Frederik Juliaan, 'Domitius Corbulo and the Senatorial Opposition to the Reign of Nero', *Ancient Society*, Vol. 32 (2002)

Von Stackelberg, Katharine T., 'Performative Space and Garden Transgressions in Tacitus' Death of Messalina', *American Journal of Philology*, 130 (2009)

Wallace-Hadrill, Andrew, 'Civilis Princeps: Between Citizen and King', *The Journal of Roman Studies*, Vol. 72 (1982

Wallace-Hadrill, Andrew, 'The Imperial Court', Chapter 7, in A. Bowman, E. Champlin and A. Lintott (eds), *The Cambridge Ancient History*, Vol. X (Cambridge University Press, 1996)

Waters, K.H., 'The Character of Domitian', *Phoenix*, Vol. 18, No. 1 (Spring 1964)

Wardle, David, 'When Did Gaius Die?', *Acta Classica* (http://www.casa-kvsa.org.za/legacy/1991/AC34-14-Wardle.pdf)

Weaver, P.R.C., 'Epaphroditus, Josephus, and Epictetus', *The Classical Quarterly*, Vol. 44, No. 2 (1994)

Wiedemann, T.E.J., 'Satyrs in Rome? The Background to Horace's Ars Poetica', *The Journal of Roman Studies*, 78 (1988)

Wiedemann, T.E.J., 'Tiberius to Nero', Chapter 5, in A. Bowman, E. Champlin and A. Lintott (eds) *The Cambridge Ancient History*, Vol. X (Cambridge University Press, 1996)

Wilson, Emily, *Seneca, A Life* (Allan Lane, 2015)

Winterling, Aloys, *Caligula, A Biography* (University of California Press, 2011)

Winterling, Aloys, *Politics and Society in Imperial Rome* (Wiley-Blackwell, 2009)

Wiseman, T.P., *Death of an Emperor: Flavius Josephus*, trans. with introduction and commentary (University of Exeter Press, 1991)

Wiseman, T.P., *Calpurnius Siculus and the Claudian Civil War* (Francis Cairns Publications, 1987)

Woodman, A.J., 'Amateur Dramatics at the Court of Nero, Annals 15.48–74', in *Tacitus and the Tacitean Tradition*, ed. Torrey James Luce (Princeton University Press, 2014)

Woods, David, 'Caligula, Asprenas, and the Bloodied Robe', *Mnemosyne*, 71 (2018)
Woods, David, 'The Role of Lucius Vitellius in the Death of Messalina', *Mnemosyne*, Vol. 70, Fasc. 6 (2017)
Wormel, D.E.W., 'Ovid and the "Fasti"', *Hermathena*, No. 127 (Winter 1979)

Index

Dear Reader,

We hope you have enjoyed this book, but why not share your views on social media? You can also follow our pages to see more about our other products: facebook.com/penandswordbooks or follow us on X @penswordbooks

You can also view our products at www.pen-and-sword.co.uk (UK and ROW) or www.penandswordbooks.com (North America).

To keep up to date with our latest releases and online catalogues, please sign up to our newsletter at: www.pen-and-sword.co.uk/newsletter

If you would like a printed catalogue with our latest books, then please email: enquiries@pen-and-sword.co.uk or telephone: 01226 734555 (UK and ROW) or email: uspen-and-sword@casematepublishers.com or telephone: (610) 853-9131 (North America).

We respect your privacy and we will only use personal information to send you information about our products.

Thank you!